Designing the Perfect
Résumé

by Pat Criscito, CPS

**President and Founder
ProType, Ltd.
Colorado Springs**

A unique "idea" book filled with
hundreds of sample resumes created
using WordPerfect® software

BARRON'S

WordPerfect®
WordPerfect is a registered trademark of WordPerfect Corporation

© Copyright 1995 by Pat Criscito
ProType, Ltd.
Post Office Box 49552
Colorado Springs, Colorado 80949
(719) 592-1999

All inquiries should be addressed to:
Barron's Educational Series, Inc.
250 Wireless Boulevard
Hauppauge, New York 11788

Library of Congress Catalog Card No. 95-5699

International Standard Book No. 0-8120-9329-1

Library of Congress Cataloging-in-Publication Data

Criscito, Pat. 1953–
    Designing the perfect résumé / by Pat Criscito
        p. cm.
    Includes index
    ISBN 0-8120-9329-1
    1. Résumés (Employment) I. Title
HF5383.C74 1995
808.06665—dc20   95-5699
                                            CIP

PRINTED IN THE UNITED STATES OF AMERICA
678 100 987654

ACKNOWLEDGMENTS

To Mike for his support and unending patience with my hectic schedule, and to my mother and father for their lifetime of encouragement. Without all of you, I wouldn't be where I am today. I love you.

This book wouldn't be possible without Dana Pipkins, my right hand since 1989. She was always there when I needed her help. Thank you, Dana.

And thank you to my clients, without whose resumes you would have nothing to see!

CONTENTS

Page

1	The Perfect Resume?	1
2	Action Verbs	3
3	Stand-out Names	5
4	Address Positions	31
5	Headings to Define Your Sections	59
6	Those Difficult Dates	77
7	Geographic Location	99
8	Paragraph Style	107
9	Functional Versus Chronological	117
10	Personal Information and References	133
11	Fonts and Bullets	141
12	Graphic Lines	175
13	Graphic Design Elements	189
14	Creative Resumes	203
15	Long Resumes and Curriculum Vitae	215
16	When is 11″ x 17″ Paper Appropriate?	247
17	Foreign Languages	261
18	Letterheads, Cover Letters, and Paper Colors	271
19	Index of Job Titles	283

1 THE PERFECT RESUME?

The *perfect* resume fits the personality of its owner. That means there are as many "perfect resumes" as there are kinds of people! Well, you won't find millions of resumes in *this* book, but you should find at least one that is a good match for your personality.

The intent of this book is to help you express yourself visually. The choice of overall style, fonts, graphics, and even paper color says something about a person. You will be able to garner some ideas from this book to use either in your personal resume or, if you are a professional resume designer or consultant, in your work with other people's resumes.

Remember, a resume is just a way to get your foot in the door. It is a marketing tool. The *perfect resume* will get interviews for you by making a strong impression. It doesn't have to be all-inclusive. It should be "clean" and easy to read, and that usually means sentences that are short, sweet, and to the point. Busy executives have little time for anything else.

Even though content is important, many times well-qualified people aren't considered for positions because of a poorly designed resume, and just the opposite can be true. Even if your qualifications aren't the greatest, a well-designed resume improves your chances of getting an interview.

I feel strongly that a resume should reflect the personality of the person it represents, so I respect my clients' wishes when it comes to the actual content of their resumes. They usually come to me with words already on paper, which I then polish. This means that, even though I design, edit, and/or write more than a thousand resumes every year for clients all over the world, no two are exactly alike. Therefore, you have a wealth of information in this book from which to choose, more than in any other resume book on the market today. If you find wording that works for you, please feel free to use it as a foundation for your own words. The index at the end of this book will help you find specific job titles which might describe your experience, if not in a whole resume, then at least in a line or two under someone's past experience.

Regarding anonymity and fake addresses, all of these resumes are authentic. They were used by real people to get real jobs. However, to avoid invading the privacy of over two hundred people, all of the personal information has been changed. Many times words were taken from within the resume itself to create a name, so please don't think that everyone in this book worked for his or her father's company!

2 ACTION VERBS

A

accelerated
accomplished
accounted for
achieved
acquired
acted
adapted
added
adjusted
administered
advanced
advised
aided
altered
analyzed
answered
applied
appraised
approved
arbitrated
arranged
articulated
assembled
assessed
assigned
assisted
attained
attended
audited

B

balanced
bid
blended
budgeted
built

C

calculated
calibrated
carved
categorized
chaired
charted
chose
clarified
classified
coached
collaborated
collated
collected
combined
communicated
compiled
completed
composed
compounded
computed
conceived
conducted
confirmed
conserved
considered
consolidated
constructed
consulted
contacted
contributed
controlled
convinced
coordinated
copied
corresponded
counseled
created
criticized

D

decided
defined
delegated
delineated
delivered
demonstrated
designated
designed
detected
determined
developed
devised
diagnosed
differentiated
directed
disbursed
discovered
dispensed
disproved
distinguished
distributed
drew up

E

edited
effected
elaborated
eliminated
enabled
encouraged
established
estimated
evaluated
examined
executed
exhibited
expanded
expedited
explained
extended
extracted

F

facilitated
filed
fixed
followed
forecast
formulated
found
founded
framed
functioned as
furnished

G

gained
gathered
generated
governed
greeted
guaranteed
guided

H

halted
handled
headed
helped
hired

I

identified
illustrated
implemented
improved
increased
influenced
informed
initiated
inspected
installed
instituted
instructed
integrated
interacted
interpreted
interviewed
invented
invested
investigated
isolated
itemized

J

joined
judged
justified

L

launched
lectured
led
lessened
litigated
limited

located
logged

M

maintained
managed
manipulated
manufactured
marketed
mastered
measured
mediated
memorized
met
moderated
modified
molded
monitored
motivated

N

named
narrated
navigated
negotiated
neutralized
nominated
normalized
notified
nurtured

O

observed
obtained
offered
operated
orchestrated
ordered
organized
originated
outlined
overhauled
oversaw

P

participated
perceived
performed
persuaded
pinpointed
planned
predicted
prepared
prescribed
presented
printed
processed
produced
proficient in
programmed
projected
promoted
proposed
protected
proved
provided
purchased

Q

qualified
quantified
quoted

R

realized
rearranged
received
recommended
recorded
recruited
reduced
referred
regulated
reinforced
related
rendered
reorganized
repaired

replaced
replicated
reported
represented
reproduced
researched
resolved
responded
restored
restructured
retrieved
revamped
reversed
reviewed
revised
revitalized

S

scheduled
screened
sculptured
searched
selected
served
set up
shortened
signed
simplified
sketched
smoothed
sold
solved
spearheaded
speculated
sponsored
streamlined
strengthened
structured
studied
succeeded
suggested
summarized
supervised
supplied
supported
surveyed
synthesized

T

tabulated
tallied
tasted
taught
tempered
tested
testified
traced
tracked
trained
translated
trimmed
troubleshot
tutored

U

uncovered
underlined
underscored
undertook
underwrote
unearthed
unified
united
updated
upgraded
used
utilized

V

validated
vaulted
verified
volunteered

W

won
worked
wrote

3 STAND-OUT NAMES

Let's start at the top. You want people to remember your name. To accomplish that, there is really only one rule to remember: *Your name should be easy to read and it should stand out above the rest of the text.* That can be done by using. . .

A Larger Font in Upper/Lower Case

The Same Only Darker

ALL CAPS

SMALL CAPS

Or

A Headline Font

On the samples in this section, you will also notice the use of graphic elements and lines to help define the name and separate it from the rest of the text. Even scanned clip art letters or a signature can be used to enhance a resume, but the latter only works when you have great handwriting. Your name, however, should not distract the reader from the message. Make it part of the overall design of your resume but separate it from the body text with lines or spacing.

The most important thing is to make sure the style of your name reflects your personality. If you are flamboyant and are looking for a job in advertising, then you have a license to be creative. Go for it! If, on the other hand, you work in a conservative industry or you feel uncomfortable with your name printed large, then it is important to tone it down.

Robert Alexander Trader

EDUCATION

American Graduate School of International Management
May 1995
Thunderbird Campus, Glendale, Arizona
Master of International Management
Concentration: International Marketing and European Studies
Honors: Thunderbird Scholarship Recipient
- **Institut de Gestion Sociale**, Paris, France — Summer 1994
  Studied Business French and International Business.
- **Paul Löbe Institute**, Berlin, Germany — Summer 1994
  Attended seminars concerning German reunification.

Northwestern University, Evanston, Illinois
June 1993
Bachelor of Arts in History
Concentration: European and American History
Honors: Graduated with honors. Selected for honors history thesis.
- **University of Sussex**, Falmer, England — 1991 – 1992
  Studied British History and Law.
- **University of Paris, La Sorbonne**, Paris, France — Summer 1991
  Studied intensive French and Parisian History.

EXPERIENCE

Greater Cleveland Growth Association, Cleveland, Ohio
Fall 1995
International Department
Marketing Intern
Designed and implemented program budget. Researched and updated international trade directory database. Assisted staff with organization of international business seminars.

United States Department of Commerce, Cleveland, Ohio
Summer 1995
International Trade Administration
International Trade Intern
Assisted International Trade Specialists in providing export counseling and marketing support to U.S. companies. Organized and made clients aware of export promotion activities. Assessed industry competitiveness. Developed marketing opportunities according to industry, country, and target market.

American Graduate School of International Management
1994 – 1995
Graduate Research Assistant
Researched and edited a textbook on international political and economic relations. Proctored and graded exams.

Cristal Lalique, Paris, France
Summers 1991, 1992
Bilingual Sales Representative
Handled international sales and deliveries of crystal from Paris headquarters. Conducted floor sales in French and English. Arranged for export of product, by surface and air, including duty and taxes.

Clark Oil and Chemical, Cleveland, Ohio
Fall 1991
Computer Operator
Transferred company files to new IBM system. Assisted Plant Controller in developing a coherent invoice and chemical records program accessible to all company personnel.

OTHER SKILLS

Language: Highly proficient in French
Computer: Lotus 1-2-3, dBASE, BASIC, WordPerfect, Microsoft Word, Excel

INTERESTS

Counselor – Camp Highlands: Responsible for six 15-year-olds for eight weeks
Travel: Extensive travel – Europe, Australia, and New Zealand
Sports: Skiing, tennis, basketball

ADDRESS   12345 Gates Fence Boulevard, Pepperville, Ohio 44124   (216) 555-1234

6

Todd M. Winkel

OBJECTIVE	A marketing or finance position leading to a career in international management

EDUCATION

MASTER OF INTERNATIONAL MANAGEMENT GPA 3.80 May 1995
American Graduate School of International Management
Thunderbird Campus, Glendale, Arizona
Graduated *with distinction*

BACHELOR OF ARTS GPA 3.32 Dec. 1993
University of Northern Iowa, Cedar Falls, Iowa
- Major: Finance
- Minor: German
- International Business Certificate

FOREIGN STUDY

EUROPEAN BUSINESS SCHOOL (EBS) Feb. – May 1995
Oestrich-Winkel, Germany
- Studied a curriculum of business classes conducted in German

INTENSIVE GERMAN LANGUAGE PROGRAM Feb. – May 1990
Klagenfurt Universität, Klagenfurt, Austria
- Sponsored by the University of Northern Iowa

EXPERIENCE

INTERNSHIP – JOHN DEERE EXPORT June – Aug. 1995
Deere & Company, Mannheim, Germany
- Responsible for warranty claim authorization
- Proposed parts sales budget for 1995
- Analyzed parts supply problems in Hungary
- Evaluated transportation costs to dealers in Hungary

RESEARCH ASSISTANT – CAREER SERVICE CENTER Feb. 1994 – May 1995
American Graduate School of International Management
- Handled student inquiries regarding career planning
- Researched and prepared information for staff
- Coordinated group sessions for recruiters
- Assisted staff in administering marketing surveys and mailings

LOAN PROCESSING CLERK Summer 1993
First Bank, Davenport, Iowa
- Recorded new loans and applications
- Responded to customer loan inquiries
- Obtained credit information
- Prepared loan and credit reports

SALESPERSON Summer 1992
Michael J's, Cedar Falls, Iowa
- Involved in sales, cash transactions, and closing of store
- Coordinated fashion shows

SKILLS

Fluent in German • Lotus 1-2-3 and WordPerfect

ACTIVITIES
- Active Red Cross Volunteer (8/90 – 5/92)
- Alumnus of Sigma Alpha Epsilon Fraternity
- University of Northern Iowa Men's Track Team
- Active Member of German Club

ADDRESS Stuebenstrasse 80 #123, D-6800 Mannheim, Germany (319) 555-1234

Karen Diane Sales

OBJECTIVE
A position in international production management

SKILLS
- Six years work experience in an industrial environment
- Advanced degree in international management
- Strong technical and engineering background
- Working knowledge of French

EXPERIENCE

AMERICAN GRADUATE SCHOOL OF INTERNATIONAL
MANAGEMENT, Glendale, Arizona   1993 – 1994
Teaching Assistant
- Instructed students in SPSSX statistical software for use in
  paired comparison projects
- Administered group projects for International Marketing Research class
- Analyzed data for university market research surveys

AMOCO PERFORMANCE PRODUCTS, Marietta, Ohio   1991 – 1992
Associate Editor
- Developed and wrote articles and designed layout of
  newsletter for plastics plant of 300 employees

CORNING GLASS WORKS, Zircoa Specialty Ceramics, Solon, Ohio 1984 – 1990
Quality Control Technician
- Performed all phases of quality assurance testing, including
  wet chemical analysis, x-ray diffraction, microstructural analysis,
  photomicrography, and thermal expansion testing
- Instituted Statistical Process Control in all areas of responsibility

Purchasing Assistant
- Coordinated all plant orders with outside vendors
- Negotiated purchase of supplies for plant
- Handled raw material orders through corporate headquarters

Production Supervisor
- Managed day-to-day operations of 15-20 union operators in
  batching, pressing, and firing departments
- Supervised operation of six hydraulic presses of up to 75 tons,
  eight kilns running from 2750° to 3200° F on 1-8 day schedules

EDUCATION

MASTER OF INTERNATIONAL MANAGEMENT   1994
American Graduate School of International Management
Thunderbird Campus, Glendale, Arizona

BACHELOR OF ARTS IN MANAGEMENT, *cum laude*   1992
Marietta College, Marietta, Ohio

ASSOCIATE OF APPLIED SCIENCE   1990
In Architectural and Construction Engineering Technology
Cuyahoga Community College, Cleveland, Ohio

**HONORS &
ACTIVITIES**
Member, Phi Beta Kappa National Honor Society
Member, Tau Alpha Pi, National Engineering Technology Honor Society
Charitable work includes St. Jude's Children's Hospital, Meals on Wheels (elderly)

12345 Bellevue Drive ❖ North Olmsted, Ohio 44070 ❖ (216) 555-1234

Camilla Portfolios

OBJECTIVE   A career in **international marketing management** utilizing cross-cultural communication skills

QUALIFICATIONS
- Five years of international marketing experience
- Managed Northern and Southern European banking markets
- Able to conduct business in French, German, Swedish, and English
- Firsthand experience living and working in France, Germany, and Sweden

EDUCATION

THE AMERICAN GRADUATE SCHOOL OF INTERNATIONAL MANAGEMENT
Thunderbird Campus, Glendale, Arizona
Master of International Management   GPA 3.6   Dec. 1994
Emphasis: International Marketing Management and Cross-cultural Communication
- Market Research Director for Sterling Winthrop InterAd Team
  - Created comprehensive marketing, advertising, and sales promotion plan for launch of
    Andrews Antacid in Costa Rica
  - Conducted primary market research in Costa Rica
- Assisted in creating winning InterAd strategic marketing plan for *Allergan* product launch in Mexico
- Wrote management training manuals on business practices in Spain and Chile

VILLANOVA UNIVERSITY, Villanova, Pennsylvania
Bachelor of Arts Economics and Modern Languages   *cum laude*   May 1985

NEW YORK UNIVERSITY, LA SORBONNE
INSTITUT D'ETUDES SCIENCES POLITIQUES DE PARIS, Paris, France   Spring 1984
French Literature and Language and International Relations

EXPERIENCE

IBJ SCHRODER BANK AND TRUST COMPANY, New York, New York
Assistant Vice President. Relationship Manager for portfolio of 75 European accounts with   1992 – 1993
annual revenue of 500K
- Successfully marketed variety of credit and correspondent banking products
- Designed strategic marketing plan for new target market of recently internationalized banks,
  implementing plan with quarterly sales trips to Europe
- Evaluated existing revenue structure and created new pricing strategy for products in key
  target market. Exceeded revenue target by 25% in 1990
Assistant Treasurer. Relationship Manager for portfolio of 40 Scandinavian   1989 – 1992
and French accounts with annual revenue of 225K
- Successfully marketed variety of credit and correspondent banking products
- Analyzed credit condition of clients and presented proposals to senior management
- Exceeded revenue target by 20% in 1988 and 40% in 1989

IRVING TRUST COMPANY, New York, New York
Marketing Representative/Europe Division   1985 – 1989
- Completed Account Officer Development Program, emphasizing Corporate Credit Analysis,
  Financial Accounting, Corporate Finance, International Banking and Selling Techniques
- Designed and executed marketing programs to initiate new businesses

BOEHRINGER INGELHEIM, Ridgefield, Connecticut
Research Assistant   Summers 1983
- Analyzed data and prepared reports on experimental prescription drug products   1984, 1985
  pending FDA approval

HONORS & ACTIVITIES   Phi Kappa Phi National Honor Society ▣ Sigma Phi Iota ▣ Research Associate – World Business Department ▣ Vice President – Marketing Club ▣ Publicity Director – Women in International Trade ▣ Member – Admissions Review Board

LANGUAGES   Bilingual in **English** and **Swedish** ▣ Highly proficient in **French** ▣ Proficient in **German**

Address ▣   123 Peaceable Street   ▣   Ridgefield, Connecticut 06877   ▣   (203) 555-1234

KIMBERLY STAR

CAREER GOAL A Marketing Management position

EXPERIENCE

L'OREAL
(Health/Beauty Products)
Merchandiser – part-time while attending graduate school

Current

SPRINGS INDUSTRIES, GRABER PRODUCTS
(Manufacturer of Window Treatments)

June 1988
to Jan. 1992

International Marketing Specialist (1990 – 1992)
- Managed regional territories and developed products for Asia, Australia, France, Canada, and Latin America
- Expedited export arrangements and maintained current information on export tariffs, licenses, and restrictions
- *Accomplishments:*
  - Increased sales in Asia by 15% and Latin America by 31%
  - Researched, planned, and implemented the company's first international direct retail program (Canada)

Sales/Service Representative (1988 – 1990)
- Sold, serviced, and trained distributor/fabricator and retail accounts in Arizona and southern Nevada
- *Accomplishments:*
  - Exceeded sales goals each year
  - Promoted to International Marketing Specialist

STAR OF INDIA
(International clothing wholesaler/retailer)

Oct. 1986
to June 1988

Store Manager
- Accountable for overall performance of store operations, hiring, and supervision of employees
- *Accomplishments:*
  - Sales ranking #1 in Arizona
  - Store produced highest percentage of goods sold, best average ticket sales, and highest dollar production
  - Devised new inventory system implemented in all stores

EDUCATION

MASTER OF INTERNATIONAL MANAGEMENT
American Graduate School of International Management
Thunderbird Campus, Glendale, Arizona
- International Marketing
- Graduate Teaching Assistant, Marketing Research Projects

May 1993

BACHELOR OF SCIENCE *magna cum laude*
University of Nebraska, Omaha
- Public Relations/Journalism

Aug. 1986

KANSAI GAIDAI UNIVERSITY OF FOREIGN STUDIES
Japan
- Independent Study, Asian Studies

May 1986

LANGUAGES Spanish

Current Address • *1234 W. Glendale Avenue* • *Phoenix, Arizona 85051* • *(602) 555-1234*
Permanent Address • *123 610th Street, S.W.* • *Humboldt, Iowa 50548* • *(515) 555-1234*

MICHELLE M. LAUDE

EDUCATION

MASTER OF INTERNATIONAL MANAGEMENT — May 1995
American Graduate School of International Management
Thunderbird Campus, Glendale, Arizona
Emphasis: International Marketing
Professor's Assistant, International Advertising Workshop
- Advised two teams of students on the marketing/advertising of Smirnoff vodka in Japan and Tabasco sauce in Italy

BACHELOR OF ARTS *cum laude* — Dec. 1991
University of West Florida, Pensacola, Florida
Major: International Studies • Minor: History

OVERSEAS EDUCATION
University of Klagenfurt, Austria — 1991, 1992
University of Tampere, Finland — 1990 – 1991

EXPERIENCE

CONSULTANT — 1994 – 1995
Thunderbird Corporate Sponsored Projects, Glendale, Arizona
- **Art Deco, Inc.:** Designed market entry plan for NEVO board games in Europe and Japan – *Account Executive* for a nine-member team
- **Coleman Powermate, Inc.:** Created market entry strategy for power generators in Europe

SALES REPRESENTATIVE — Summer 1994
Abbigliamento F. Varriale, Tarvisio, Italy
- Marketed Italian apparel to retailers in Hungary, Yugoslavia, and Germany
- Conducted business in Italian, German, and English
- Outstanding performance led to an offer of permanent employment

INTERNATIONAL TRAVEL CONSULTANT — Fall 1993
Egan Tour Service, Phoenix, Arizona
- Coordinated reception of foreign visitors to the United States
- Conducted tours of the Southwest United States in German and Italian

MARKET RESEARCH ASSISTANT — Spring 1993
O'Neil Associates, Tempe, Arizona
- Designed public opinion surveys for government agencies
- Recruited and interviewed focus groups and analyzed findings

ACCOUNTING ASSOCIATE — Fall 1991
American Armed Forces Exchange Service, Garmisch, Germany
- Balanced daily deposits for six independent shops and main exchange store
- Utilized in-store computer software to maintain records

LANGUAGES

Fluent in **Italian** and **German** • Knowledge of **Finnish**

CITIZENSHIP

Dual: United States/Italian

HONORS & ACTIVITIES

- Associated Students Legislative Council Representative
- Treasurer of German Club
- Scholarship recipient to University of Klagenfurt, Austria
- Dean's List, University of Tampere, Finland
- Scholarship recipient to University of Tampere, Finland

ADDRESS 1234 East Palm Street, Chandler, Arizona 85213 (602) 555-1234

KENNETH L. DAVIS

3725 Quiet Circle East ▸ Colorado Springs, Colorado 80917-2009 ▸ (719) 573-0365

OBJECTIVE

A challenging position in Logistics Management, Inventory Management, or a related field

QUALIFICATIONS

- ▸ Nineteen years of logistical management experience
- ▸ Three years of college – currently pursuing B.S. in Business Administration
- ▸ Computer literate with experience in WordPerfect, Quattro Pro, and MAPCON

EXPERIENCE

ANTARCTIC SUPPORT ASSOCIATES, Englewood, Colorado (10/93 – 10/94)
Senior Materialsperson for McMurdo Power and Water Plants, Antarctica
- ▸ One-year contract to manage and account for supplies, parts, and equipment needed to maintain the operation of the power and water plants
- ▸ Coordinated the requisitioning of parts and equipment through MAPCON Power "1000"
- ▸ Conducted aisle audits to ensure proper accounting and receipt of items issued from stock
- ▸ Performed any other duties required by plant or logistics supervisor

U.S. ARMY (5/93 – 9/93 and 7/91 – 1/92)
Material Handler – Civilian
- ▸ Received supplies and equipment and moved items by forklift, handcart, conveyor, etc.

ANTARCTIC SUPPORT ASSOCIATES, Englewood, Colorado (10/92 – 4/93)
Materialsperson for Palmer Station on the Peninsula, Antarctica
- ▸ Interfaced with laboratory supervisor to ensure timely requisition, receipt, and distribution of science cargo for various science groups
- ▸ Automated Palmer Station's parts and supply inventory into MAPCON
- ▸ Hazardous cargo packing/shipping for transport on commercial and DOD systems

UNIVERSITY OF SOUTHERN COLORADO, Peterson AFB, Colorado (9/89 – 7/91)
Administrative Clerk
- ▸ Counseled veterans regarding their education benefits part-time while attending the University

U.S. ARMY (6/66 – 9/89)
Supply/Accounting Sergeant
- ▸ Twenty-four years of active duty military service, including fifteen years of logistical experience and nine years of aviation maintenance experience
- ▸ Instrumental in managing three separate property book accounting teams for three different Army divisions made up of 27 combat units/companies each
- ▸ Maintained document files and property records for equipment totaling $800 million to $2.5 billion
- ▸ Supervised the Retail Supply operation for 52 units, including requisition, warehousing, and issue procedures for Army equipment and repair parts
- ▸ Managed a multinational work force of 30 Korean nationals and 31 military personnel
- ▸ Identified areas requiring change and specifically revised logistical practices and procedures which streamlined property storage, distribution, and accountability
- ▸ Conducted cyclic inventories and logistic operation inspections
- ▸ Managed all capital and organizational equipment requisitioning
- ▸ Coordinated retrograde procedures for unserviceable equipment
- ▸ Assistant logistics manager for brigade-level supply operations, maintaining authorized levels of organizational equipment and repair parts
- ▸ Honors included:
  - Army Meritorious Service Medal for successfully coordinating the deployment and fielding of two Patriot Missile Batteries to Germany, controlling and establishing accountable property records for equipment shipped totaling $1.3 billion
  - Five Army Commendation Medals for superior performance in logistical management
  - Army Bronze Star Medal (Vietnam) for supervision of an efficient and effective maintenance program on twelve U-21 fixed wing aircraft with no loss of aircraft or crew and limited down time

12

Mark A. Hill

OBJECTIVE

A career in Management utilizing my educational background and experience

EDUCATION

Master of International Management   Jan. 1995
American Graduate School of International Management, Glendale, Arizona
Selected Courses:
- Cross-cultural Communications for International Managers
- Multinational Business Management
- International Marketing Management
- International Marketing Research
- International Finance and Trade
- Cost and Managerial Accounting

Winterim program in Costa Rica   Jan. 1994

Bachelor of Arts   May 1993
Iowa State University, Ames, Iowa
   Major: Political Science
   Second Major: International Studies specializing in Great Britain

Semester at University of Stirling, Scotland   Fall 1990

EXPERIENCE

Office Assistant: Student Services/Financial Aid   June 1994
American Graduate School of International Management, Glendale, Arizona   Aug. 1994
- Notified banks of graduates using dBASE III Plus and First Choice
- Filed, sorted, and gathered information

Office Manager   Sep. 1993
Pirro Research, Ames, Iowa   Dec. 1993
- Managed Ames branch of Pirro Research
- Developed computer telecommunication system
- Assisted in market research
- Scheduled personnel and assisted with payroll

Office Assistant: ISU Police & Traffic Control   Jan. 1992
Iowa State University, Ames, Iowa   Sep. 1993
- Operated mainframe system at ISU
- Handled customers and resolved complaints
- Filed, sorted, and gathered information
- Worked as security for Rolling Stones concert

LANGUAGE

Proficiency in Spanish

COMPUTERS

Telecommunications experience in mainframes and PC's
Lotus 1-2-3, dBASE III Plus, Harvard Graphics, First Choice, WordPerfect

ACTIVITIES

Active in the Church of Scotland	Intramural Volleyball
Tenshinkan Karate Club in Scotland	Jogging, Swimming, Golf
Tae Kwon Do, Hapkido	Political Science Club
"Hello Dolly!" Musical	ISU Karate Club

ADDRESS

123 College Lane, Marshalltown, Iowa 50158, (515) 123-1234

MARIA SALVATORE

SELECTED WORK EXPERIENCE

Retail System Administrator
Salvatore Ferragamo   New York, New York

> *Developed new position as operational liaison to retail stores.*
> *Train cashiers and shipping staff in all Ferragamo stores on new computerized system.*
> *Supervise staff in maintenance of large, dynamic database.*
> *Communicate frequently with computer programmers in Italy to recommend improvements and adjustments.*
> *Responsible for flow of information to accounting department, merchandise buyers, and company executives.*
> *Travel often to U.S. stores and headquarters in Italy.*

1991 – Present

Assistant to Director of Administration
The Americas Society   New York, New York

> *Commended in writing by president of Society as outstanding employee in 1989.*
> *Assisted in all areas of personnel management, including administering benefits and interviewing prospective employees.*
> *Supervised Spanish-speaking maintenance staff.*
> *Purchased all supplies for organization.*
> *Coordinated high-level special events with caterers and internal program directors.*

1989 – 1991

Customs Liaison
Esprit de Corp   San Francisco, California

> *Served as a link between U.S. Customs, brokers, and production staff to ensure smooth importation of all goods and samples manufactured overseas.*
> *Made seasonal presentations of Esprit's entire line to U.S. Customs officials.*
> *Regularly persuaded Customs to reconsider tariffs on high-duty items by using knowledge of import laws and garment/fabric construction.*
> *Taught Italian to employees twice weekly through company-sponsored program.*

1987 – 1988

EDUCATION

Master of International Management
American Graduate School of International Management (AGSIM)
Thunderbird Campus   Glendale, Arizona   GPA 3.34

May 1987

Bachelor of Arts in Political Science
Bachelor of Arts in Italian Language
University of Arizona   Tucson, Arizona   GPA 3.15

May 1985

LANGUAGES & COMPUTERS

Fluent in Italian	*Highly proficient in Spanish*
Working knowledge of German	*Advanced knowledge of Lotus 1-2-3*
Working knowledge of French	*Knowledge of word processing software*

OTHER EXPERIENCE

> *Designed original artwork used for displays in Ferragamo's Fifth Avenue show windows* — 1992
> *Executive Board, AGSIM Alumni Chapter, New York* — 1990 – Present
> *Passed Foreign Service Officer examination, including oral and written portions, and State Department security clearance* — 1990
> *Variety of retail sales positions* — 1982 – 1990
> *Studied and traveled extensively throughout Italy and Mexico* — 1984 – 1986
> *Summer internship with Outdoor Advertising Association of America* — 1984

ADDRESS

123 East 99th Street #123, New York, New York 10017   (212) 555-1234

James M. DeAmericas

QUALIFICATIONS
- Seven years management experience – domestic and international
- Three years import/export experience in South America and Africa
- Three years financial analysis experience
- Degrees in Biology, Physiology, and International Management
- Highly proficient in Spanish

EXPERIENCE

AMERICAN GRADUATE SCHOOL OF INTERNATIONAL MANAGEMENT, Glendale, AZ
Treasurer of the Associated Students Legislative Council (2 terms)
- Responsible for pro-bono budget of $400,000 annually

Teaching Assistant for Finance, World Business, and Language Departments (1993 – 1994)
- Negotiated computer contracts for school newspapers
- Researched and provided input for decision on food service management group selection
- Produced Arizona trade newsletter for World Business Department

PIASA PARTNERS INVESTMENT GROUP, West Palm Beach, FL & New York, NY
Investment and Financial Analyst (1991 – 1994)
- Assisted in acquiring and restructuring small manufacturing companies
- Purchased real estate – Licensed real estate salesperson in Florida
- Analyzed pre-purchase financing, negotiated contracts, and finalized deals

VIKING FARMS INC., West Palm Beach, FL & New York, NY
President (1989 – 1993)
- Recruited, hired, trained, motivated operations staff
- Automated company finances, prepared financial statements
- Imported products from South America and Europe; supervised domestic and international operations
- Formed and competed on various professional teams with 86% winning percentage

OXRIDGE POLO AND HUNT CLUB, Darien, CT
Operations and Polo Manager (1988 – 1989)
- Manager and Chief Instructor
- Marketed and acquired sponsorship for international and domestic events
- Inaugurated and managed food service and catering operations
- Coach and consultant to University of Connecticut Polo Teams
- Increased club membership 127% during tenure

J. COPPERFIELD LTD., Vernon & Avon, CT
Restaurant Manager (1985 – 1988)
- Managed two units, each grossing $2.2 million annually
- Supervised payroll, cost control of total operations staff of 120
- Researched and implemented point-of-sale computerized management system

EDUCATION

MASTER OF INTERNATIONAL MANAGEMENT (MIM) – Thunderbird (May 1994)
American Graduate School of International Management, Glendale, AZ
- Concentration in International Finance and Risk Management with additional course work in International Marketing
- Degree conferred with honors – GPA 3.7

BACHELOR OF SCIENCE (2) (May 1986)
University of Connecticut, Storrs, CT
- Majors in Biology and Animal Physiology – top 10% of class

LANGUAGES
English and Spanish

HONORS
Undergraduate: Beta Gamma Sigma, National All-Star Polo 2 years
Thunderbird: Citibank Scholarship; General Motors Scholarship; Paul & Pauline Wilson Assistantship; Delegate to Canadian Business Council, 1992 York University; Student Chair of World Business Investment Scholarship Fund

ACTIVITIES & INTERESTS
Royal Academy of Arts, Global Conservation Corporation, American Cancer Society
Golf, tennis, polo, reading, and travel

CURRENT ADDRESS: 12345 North 59th Avenue #123, Glendale, AZ 85306, (602) 555-1234, FAX (602) 123-1234
PERMANENT ADDRESS: 1234 Runbrook Drive, West Palm Beach, FL 33414, (407) 555-1234, FAX (407) 123-1234

15

Elizabeth M. Columbia

OBJECTIVE
A position in international trade or finance leading to a career in International Management

PROFILE
- Earned advanced business degree
- Able to conduct business in three languages
- Eligible to work in the United States and Colombia

EDUCATION

MASTER OF INTERNATIONAL MANAGEMENT   December 1994
American Graduate School of International Management   GPA 3.7
Thunderbird Campus, Glendale, Arizona
Courses include:
- Export-Import Management
- Advanced Managerial Finance
- International Finance and Trade
- Entrepreneurship

BACHELOR OF ARTS   June 1990
Northwestern University, Evanston, Illinois   GPA 3.7
Major: Political Science
Minor: Economics
Courses include:
- International Relations
- Comparative Political Systems
- Foreign Policies
- Politics of the Global Economy

WORK EXPERIENCE

MARKETING COORDINATOR   1991 – 1993
A. M. Kinney Associates, Inc., Architects and Engineers, Evanston, Illinois
- Developed and administered execution of two annual marketing plans
- Supervised design of new marketing materials and logo
- Prepared proposals and sales packages for clients
- Coordinated marketing effort through cross-functional marketing team
- Contributed to company's first year of profit in three years

SECRETARY OF PHYSICAL THERAPY   1990 – 1991
Evanston Hospital, Evanston, Illinois
- Greeted patients and handled scheduling and complaints
- Coordinated scheduling among four rehabilitation therapy departments
- Assisted with billing and monthly reports

ACTIVITIES
Health Volunteer, Amigos de las Americas, Summer of 1990 in Brazil and Summer of 1982 in Mexico; Teaching Assistant for Management Science course; Tutor of English as a Second Language, Literacy Volunteers of Chicago; Tutor, Howard Area Community Center; Resident Assistant, high school youth group

LANGUAGES
Fluent in **Spanish** • Proficient in **Portuguese**

COMPUTERS
Lotus 1-2-3, Microsoft Excel, WordPerfect, Microsoft Word, dBASE III Plus, Filemaker Plus, Microsoft File, LINDO, QSB+, At Risk; Familiar with both DOS and Macintosh computers

---

School Address: 12345 North 59th Avenue #123 • Glendale, Arizona 85306 • (602) 555-1234
Permanent Address: 1234 Wilmette Avenue • Wilmette, Illinois 60091 • (708) 555-1234

Georgia Secretary

EXPERIENCE   **FEDERAL AERONAUTICAL CENTER**, Oklahoma City, Oklahoma   May 1991 to Present

Office Automation Assistant (12/90 to Present)
- Assist supervisor and subordinates in expediting the work of the office
- Utilize personal computer to compose and prepare correspondence
- Locate and assemble information for correspondence, reports, and briefings
- Effectively organize the flow of the clerical process
- Use tact, diplomacy, and sensitivity in coordinating information with FAA/Air Traffic employees, contractors, students, and outside agencies

Aircraft Registration Clerk (3/87 to 12/90)
- Investigated aircraft records, cross-referenced files, and made CRT inquiries to gather information on individual aircraft
- Composed statements and prepared transcripts of civil aircraft records for use in federal and state courts of record
- Analyzed work of conveyance examiners to ensure accuracy and completeness before inputting data on registrations
- Developed knowledge of the related domestic and international organizations

Secretary (1/85 to 3/87)
- Reviewed and analyzed all incoming and outgoing correspondence for conformity with proper format and distribution
- Researched and evaluated procurement needs
- Initiated and typed requests for training

OKLAHOMA CITY UNIVERSITY, Oklahoma City, Oklahoma   Oct. 1988 to May 1991

Billing Clerk / Assistant Credit Manager
- Interacted with local and international students to assist in resolving billing and credit problems
- Composed business letters
- Extended credit to students and handled credit loans
- Organized files of international students to maintain follow-up

SPECIAL SKILLS   Computers: MS-DOS, Network, WordPerfect 5.1 • Bookkeeping

EDUCATION   **OKLAHOMA CITY COMMUNITY COLLEGE**   1988 to Present
Have completed 92 credits toward a bachelor's degree

COURSES COMPLETED (Partial List)
Through FAA, Oklahoma City Community College, and Oklahoma State University-Technical Branch
- Business Law
- American Business
- Business Communications
- Business Administration
- Management Conflict
- Technical Report Writing
- Principles of Public Relations
- Introduction to Transactional Analysis
- Criminal Justice Investigations
- MS-DOS

McALESTER HIGH SCHOOL, McAlester, Oklahoma   May 1969

REFERENCES   **John Doe**, 123 E. Car Lane, Mustang, OK 73064   (405) 555-1234
Jane Doe, 1234 E. Longing Lane, Mustang, OK 73064   (405) 555-1234
Pat Smith, S.W. of Oklahoma City, Mustang, OK 73064   (405) 555-1234

123 East Carson Lane • Mustang, Oklahoma 73064 • (405) 555-1234

BERNADETTE D'EVES

EXPERIENCE

NISSAN NORTH AMERICA, Torrance, California   July 1991 – Present
Product and Market Strategy Analyst
- Explore and analyze needs and trends of American consumers to aid long-term corporate and product development
- Develop product concepts based on analysis of market viability and regulatory requirements, and coordinate with Nissan entities as lead analyst of electric vehicle program
- Coordinate and implement innovative primary research with aid of outside consultants
- Work as team member with product planners in vehicle development
- Determine future implications for Nissan in changing political and regulatory environment
- Act as voice of U.S. market for Japanese colleagues

SAATCHI & SAATCHI DFS/PACIFIC [Advertising], Torrance, California   Oct. 1986 – Nov. 1989
Assistant Account Executive (10/88 – 11/89)
- Coordinated development and production of broadcast, print, and collateral national and regional advertising for Toyota Motor Sales
- Handled business-to-business advertising for Toyota Industrial Equipment
- Maintained working production budgets and coordinated print and broadcast media allocations
- Supervised Account Coordinator
- Acted as Account Executive on $4 million campaign

Print Traffic Assistant (11/87 – 9/88)
- Scheduled and coordinated the creation and production of print materials for accounts such as Toyota, Yamaha, MGM/UA, Physician's Formula Cosmetics
- Monitored project costs

Broadcast Traffic Forwarder (10/86 – 10/87)
- Coordinated broadcast allocations for airing on radio and television networks and spot stations throughout the country
- Restructured position which improved operations and increased job responsibilities

DAILEY AND ASSOCIATES [Advertising], Los Angeles, California   Dec. 1985 – June 1986
Business Coordinator
- Monitored cost control of estimates and invoices
- Assisted Account Management group

LE PHARE JEAN D'EVE, S.A., La Chaux-de-Fonds, Switzerland   June 1986 – Sep. 1986
Marketing Intern
- Researched history of international Swiss watch company and proposed advertising, public relations, and promotional ideas for company's centennial celebration
- Conducted business entirely in French

LOS ANGELES OLYMPIC ORGANIZING COMMITTEE   May 1983 – Aug. 1984
Customer Service Supervisor
- Supervised customer service staff at USC Olympic Village
- Arranged transportation for visiting athletes and delegates
- Wrote and implemented procedures plan for customer service operations

Assistant to Vice President of Transportation
- Completed a variety of short-term projects, including a Los Angeles traffic study

EDUCATION

MASTER OF INTERNATIONAL MANAGEMENT   Jan. 1991
American Graduate School of International Management (Thunderbird), Glendale, AZ
Marketing Director for Taco John's International, Inc. – InterAd Group Project

BACHELOR OF ARTS, ENGLISH   Dec. 1985
University of California, Los Angeles (UCLA)
University of Paris, Sorbonne   Fall Semester 1984

LANGUAGES

ENGLISH (Native), **SPANISH** (Proficient), **FRENCH** (Proficient)
Computers: **Canvas, Lotus 1-2-3, Microsoft Word, Excel, DeltaGraph, WordPerfect**

ADDRESS

1234 South Redford Drive, Apt. 1, Los Angeles, California 90035   (310) 555-1234

LEWIS H. DURANGO

OBJECTIVE	To obtain a career-oriented, entry-level position	

EDUCATION

BACHELOR OF ARTS — May 1995
Fort Lewis College, Durango, Colorado
Major: Political Science
Concentration: Business Administration

WORK EXPERIENCE

BARBACK AND BOUNCER — 1994 – 1995
Shooters Tequila Bar, Durango, Colorado
Provided security for a 200-person capacity night club, including compliance with federal regulations. Assisted bartenders with drink preparation and distribution of bar supplies.

DISC JOCKEY — 1993 – 1994
KDUR Radio Station, Durango, Colorado
Involved in all aspects of a federally licensed and regulated radio station. Sole on-air personality for three-hour music and information program. Chose format, completed all Federal Communication Commission (FCC) documentation, and maintained music library.

MANUFACTURING STATION WORKER — Summer 1992
Rubbermaid, Incorporated, Greenville, Texas
Worked thirty-person third shift in Just-In-Time workshop producing molded plastic piecewear. Operated molding machines and assisted supply room manager.

COURIER — 1990 – 1992
First National Bank of Trenton, Texas
Delivered documents, daily transactions, and large sums of cash to branch offices and vendors.

BOY SCOUTS OF AMERICA

* Nine years involvement in all aspects of program
* Member of the National *Eagle Scout* Association
* Member of the Order of the Arrow
* Attended Philmont Scout Ranch, 1984
* Attended National Jamboree, Fort A. P. Hill, 1981
* Selected to attend Council-Wide Youth Leadership Training

COMPUTER SKILLS

WordPerfect, Lotus 1-2-3, First Choice, MS-DOS, and GW BASIC

ADDRESS

123 East 100th Street, Durango, Colorado 81301 — (303) 555-1234

MAARIT JUTTA FINLAND

Current:
1234 W. Greenway Road #123
Glendale, Arizona 85306
(602) 555-1234

Permanent:
Loukonlahdentie 12 D
33950 Pirkkala, Finland
Fax: 555-1234

OBJECTIVE *A career in international finance / trade*

EDUCATION

MASTER OF INTERNATIONAL MANAGEMENT Aug. 1995
American Graduate School of International Management
Thunderbird Campus, *Glendale, Arizona*
GPA 3.57

BACHELOR OF SCIENCE IN BUSINESS ADMINISTRATION June 1994
University of Denver, *Denver, Colorado*
Major: Finance/Marketing
GPA in major 3.81 – Listed twice on National Dean's List

COMMERCIAL COLLEGE GRADUATE, UNDERGRADUATE LEVEL May 1991
Kuopio Commercial College (Kuopion Kauppaoppilaitos), *Kuopio, Finland*
Major: Accounting
Among top 5% of graduates

ROTARY CLUB EXCHANGE STUDENT Aug. 1987 – May 1988
Northern State College, *Aberdeen, South Dakota*

EXPERIENCE

MARKETING INTERN Jan. 1994 – June 1994
World Trade Center Association, *Denver, Colorado* (Part-Time)
- *Assisted in organizing and implementing a South American Mining Conference, World Trade Day, and Import/Export Workshop Series*
- *Provided customer service and worked as an office assistant*

INSURANCE LIAISON July 1991 – Mar. 1992
Verdandi Life Insurance Company (Henkivakuutus Osakeyhtiö Verdandi), *Finland*
- *Provided consultation to sales personnel as a liaison between the field and headquarters*
- *Processed insurance and loan applications and claims*
- *Calculated quotations for clients and performed accounting for insurance premiums*
- *Researched markets and reported to home office*
- *Planned and organized conventions*
- *Assisted in hiring and trained new employees*
- *Served and supported current clients*
- *Assisted in developing and implementing a marketing plan*

BANK CLEARANCE DEPARTMENT RESEARCHER June 1990 – Aug. 1990
Post Bank (Postipankki), *Finland* Feb. 1989 – July 1989
- *Researched accounts and resolved problems*
- *Handled client complaints and provided customer service*
- *Monitored error accounts*

LANGUAGE SKILLS *Native in **Finnish** • Proficient in **Swedish** • Knowledge of **German***

SCHOLARSHIPS
- *Foundation for Economic Education Scholarship – Thunderbird*
- *Finnish Government Scholarship – Thunderbird, University of Denver*
- *Finnish Chamber of Commerce Scholarship – University of Denver*
- *Wihuri Aarnio Oy Scholarship – University of Denver*

INTERESTS *Toastmasters International, Finlandia Foundation, Phi Beta Delta - International Honor Society, Marketing Club*

20

PAULA A. SALVATORE

EXPERIENCE

INTERNATIONAL BUSINESS DEVELOPMENT

MARKETING CONSULTANT & BUSINESS DEVELOPMENT INTERN
Tenneco, International Marketing & Sourcing, Inc.
September 1994 – April 1995: Compiled an extensive report on the North American Free Trade Agreement (NAFTA) for Tenneco and its subsidiaries, including an analysis of opportunities for and effects on Tenneco. Attended the Institutional Investor Conference in New York and others on NAFTA. Worked on all phases of project to market refurbished used farm and construction equipment to Third World markets. Responsible for maquiladora manufacturing facility selection in Mexico. Compiled extensive report on applicable import regulations. Developed business plan and assisted in establishment of international agency network.

ENTREPRENEURIAL MARKETING

FOUNDER AND DIRECTOR, Access Australia, Inc., Phoenix, Arizona
September 1991 – Present: Developed nationwide artwear clothing business from idea stage to $20,000 in monthly sales in two years. Responsible for personnel and financial management, corporate prospectus and stock issue, marketing (including national participation in trade shows, establishment of national sales force, development of marketing strategy), strategic planning, product development, and production management. Products represented and sold in over 40 states and overseas.
January 1991 – September 1991: Assessed export potential and conducted market analysis of the American market for four Australian wine companies.

GEOLOGICAL

GEOLOGIST, Tarcoola Gold, Ltd., Tarcoola, Australia
April 1990 – January 1991: Assisted in all phases of organizing the business, a gold exploration company. Assessed viability of projects, researched investments, and liaisoned with government environmental departments to ensure compliance. Responsible for all phases of a $2 million tailings project. Wrote all exploration reports.

GEOLOGIST, South Australian Department of Mines & Energy, Oil and Gas Division, Sydney, Australia
March 1989 – December 1989: Solely responsible for organizing a computer database of all petroleum-related information in South Australia and the statistical analysis of petroleum information supplied to the public and to the Department. Contract with the Department was extended.

GEOLOGICAL ASSISTANT, RPI Texas, Inc., Dallas, Texas
May 1988 – December 1988: Advanced to Production Data Coordinator. Responsible for all production-related information extracted for each well. Trained and scheduled personnel.

STUDENT ASSISTANT, University of Texas, Geology Department, Austin, Texas
September 1986 – May 1987: Student Assistant to Dr. Amos Salvador. Responsible for compilation and organization of information for current projects.

COMMUNITY SERVICE

Former Vice Chairman of Austin-Adelaide Sister City Committee. Former Member Adelaide, Australia, City Council "Austin/Adelaide Sister City" Committee. Duties included organizing visits of dignitaries, corresponding with Mayor's office, managing exchanges between sister-cities, and professional/business liaison.

Founder of the South Australian Crohns and Colitis Association (SACCA), a nonprofit educational and support organization. Duties included public speaking and organization of support groups and educational meetings, presiding over committee meetings, and leading the association.

EDUCATION

MASTER OF INTERNATIONAL MANAGEMENT (MIM)   August 1995
American Graduate School of International Management (Thunderbird), Glendale, Arizona
Emphasis in International Marketing and Trade in Australasia and Latin America
• Teaching Assistant to Professor Garvin for International Marketing Management, Spring 1995. Assisted in developing and grading tests and related course work.
• Assisted in organization of NAFTA Conference

BACHELOR OF ARTS, GEOLOGY   **Minor: Business**   1987
University of Texas, Austin, Texas

ACTIVITIES

Formerly active in volunteer work for the National Foundation for Ileitis and Colitis – Certificate of Merit, 1988; Licensed Real Estate Salesperson by Texas Real Estate Commission; Extensive international and national travel; Participated in various sports; Trained aerobics instructor; Vice President of Aerobics Club at Thunderbird

Member: American Association of Petroleum Geologists (AAPG), Geological Society of Australia (GSA), Thunderbird: Environmental Club, Nonprofit Club, Outdoor Club, Toastmasters.

PUBLISHED ARTICLES

Free-lance writer for Dun & Bradstreet's "Jobson's Mining Yearbook". Contracted to write article on an overview of the Australian Gold Mining Industry. Published June 1991.

ADDRESS

1234 Ivy Lane, Houston, Texas 77070, (713) 555-1234

21

LORI LYN DONALD

PROFESSIONAL EXPERIENCE	**HONEYWELL IAC**, Phoenix, Arizona	Sep. 1992 – Present

System Wiring Factory
Associate Manufacturing Specialist (Jan. 1994 – Present)
* Purchase, receive, and track material
* Ensure material quality, delivery, and pricing and resolve non-conformance issues

RSIC, Southwest Region
Factory Systems Coordinator (Contractor) (Sep. 1992 – Jan. 1994)
* Liaison between project managers and factory
* Scheduled system expansion orders
* Coordinated orders among subfactories and expedited emergency orders

Honeywell Classes: L.E.T., Product Overview, TDC 3000 Overview, ISO 9000
Auditor Training, Tour Guide Training, Quality College II

HUMBERTO VALENCIA, Ph.D., Phoenix, Arizona   Mar. 1992 – June 1992
Market Research Consultant
* Researched Hispanic markets and prepared client presentations

FOREIGN TRADE BANK, Paris, France   Mar. 1988 – June 1989
Assistant to the Vice President of International Finance
* Handled the syndication of loans for foreign companies – worked
   primarily with English, Spanish, and Portuguese speaking clients

THE AMERICAN COLLEGE IN PARIS, France   Sep. 1985 – June 1987
Office of Alumni, Development and Communications
* Organized fund-raising activities and prepared alumni newsletters
* Produced brochures and pamphlets promoting the college

EDUCATION

MASTER OF INTERNATIONAL MANAGEMENT (MIM)   May 1991
American Graduate School of International Management (Thunderbird)
Glendale, Arizona
Major Emphasis: International Marketing
Related Courses:
* International Marketing Management, International Consumer Marketing,
   International Marketing Research
* Consumer Marketing Workshop – Design, implementation, and analysis
   of research and market entry strategy for Texas Instruments, leading to a
   marketing plan for U.S. Hispanics

BACHELOR OF ARTS (BA)   June 1988
The American College in Paris, France
Major: French with concentration in French Literature

CERTIFICAT PRATIQUE DE LANGUE FRANÇAISE (CPLF)   June 1988
Université de Paris – Sorbonne Paris IV   (1er Degré)

FOREIGN STUDY: 2ND B.U.P.   Sep. 1982 – June 1983
Universidad Laboral de Cáceres, Cáceres, Spain

COMPUTER   Wordstar, WordPerfect, Lotus 1-2-3, Harvard Graphics, SPSS PC, HMS, SYNC,
TIMS, Excel, Microsoft Word, Windows, QEDIT, PowerPoint

LANGUAGES   French (Fluent) * Spanish (Fluent) * Portuguese (Working Knowledge)

JILL M. DeSALES

EDUCATION

MASTER OF INTERNATIONAL MANAGEMENT — Dec. 1994
American Graduate School of International Management — GPA 3.7
Thunderbird Campus, Glendale, Arizona
- Specialized course work: Financial Statement Analysis, Intermediate Accounting, Multinational Corporate Finance, International Banking, International Securities Investment, Business Policy and Decision-Making

Nahual, Instituto de Español, Antigua, Guatemala — 1994
Eurocentros Language Institute, Barcelona, Spain — 1989
Goethe Institut, Göttingen, West Germany — 1989, 1986

BACHELOR OF ARTS, ECONOMICS AND GERMAN — Dec. 1988
College of St. Thomas, St. Paul, Minnesota
- Concentration in Mathematics

EXPERIENCE

FINANCIAL ANALYST INTERN, Latin America/Middle East/Africa Group — 1994
NCR International, Inc., World Headquarters, Dayton, Ohio
- Prepared and analyzed profit and loss statements for the major proposals from the seven country areas
- Prepared executive guidelines for major proposals and for all pricing activities for local country marketing groups
- Performed financial analysis for the group on the effect of transfer pricing for the new PC-relaunch program

MARKET ANALYST — 1993
Edina Realty, Edina, Minnesota
- Provided home profile and marketing information to real estate agents
- Maintained client base

SALES CONSULTANT — 1992 – 1993
Dayton Hudson Department Stores Corp., Minneapolis, Minnesota
- Supervised staff of 40
- Participated in buying, management, and sales seminars
- Top commissioned sales consultant

COLLECTIONS AGENT — 1991
Norwest Bank, Minneapolis, Minnesota
- Handled international bank draft and currency transactions
- Issued payments on Norwest bonds and coupons
- Monitored client federal tax payments

TRUST OPERATIONS ADMINISTRATOR — 1990 – 1991
Norwest Bank, Minneapolis, Minnesota
- Researched and resolved trust account problems for portfolio managers
- Valued Norwest Bond Funds for month-end evaluations
- Developed an efficient and money-saving billing system for the proxy department

LANGUAGES

Highly proficient in **German** • Highly proficient in **Spanish**

HONORS & ACTIVITIES

- Elected to the Executive Council, Associated Student Legislative Council
- Participant in Toastmasters International
- Active member of the Career Services Student Committee
- Coordinator of the Bizarre Bazaar, Student Fund-raising Event
- Recipient of academic excellence grant
- Dean's Honor List
- Bush Foundation Economics Research Assistant
- Four-year recipient of the Mayo Foundation Scholarship
- Member of Economics and Foreign Language Honor Societies

ADDRESS

1234 E. Doublebar Ranch Rd., Scottsdale, Arizona 85258 — (602) 555-1234

Natalie J. England

EXPERIENCE

THE LONDON INSTITUTE, London, England
Development Training
Human Resource Development Assistant   **1995**
- Formulated training seminars for retail organizations
- Attended conferences on European-wide education qualifications
- Promoted the Institute's resource services throughout London

IBM CORPORATION, Washington, D.C.
Atlantic Area Workstation Marketing
Atlantic Confidential Disclosure Coordinator   **1992 – 1994**
- Supported 24 Atlantic area branches with confidential customer disclosures and bids
- Coordinated procedures through the branches, area, and headquarters

Loaner Equipment Branch Office Interface   **1992 – 1993**
- Evaluated equipment requests for possible marketing opportunities
- Controlled all loanable assets for the Atlantic region in excess of one million dollars
- Administrative Coordinator for PS/2 Workstation Forums in conjunction with Microsoft Corporation

IBM CORPORATION COOPERATIVE EDUCATION PROGRAM, Atlanta, Georgia
Marketing Education Headquarters
Marketing Education Support Assistant   **1992**
- Assisted sales school instructors in administrative capacity
- Participated in sales school classes and lectures
- Organized sales school manuals and other materials

THE EUROPEAN BANK FOR LATIN AMERICA, Brussels, Belgium
Intern   **1992**
- Analyzed economic indicators and trend patterns
- Prepared action reports for bank evaluations
- Assisted in financial statement preparation

IBM CORPORATION, Arlington, Virginia
Marketing Sales Assistant   **1991**
- Assisted copier marketing representatives in daily activities
- Conducted demonstrations for customers
- Made cold calls on customers to promote the IBM copier program

EDUCATION

AMERICAN GRADUATE SCHOOL OF INTERNATIONAL MANAGEMENT   **1995**
THUNDERBIRD, Glendale, Arizona
Master of International Management

INTERAD: Advanced International Marketing and Advertising Workshop
Creative Director, Team Kellogg
- Selected as a member of team to develop marketing plan for Kellogg's Corn Flakes in India
- Developed creative aspects of advertising campaign including print and television ads
- Responsible for design of team introductory book
- Coordinated production of 40-minute multimedia presentation for an audience of 300

THE AMERICAN UNIVERSITY, Washington, D.C.
Bachelor of Arts in International Studies   **1989 – 1993**
- Concentrations in European Studies and International Relations
- Minors in Business Administration and Economics

AWARDS
& HONORS
- Board of Directors, Arizona Women in International Trade, 1995
- Most Active Campus Club Award recipient, Thunderbird, 1995
- Recipient of $5,000 American University Scholarship, 1992, 1993

Current Address • P.O. Box 1234 • 12345 North 59th Avenue • Glendale, Arizona 85306 • (602) 555-1234
Permanent Address • 12 Bridle Lane • Marietta, Georgia 30068 • (404) 555-1234

24

KAREN J. LEVITOW

OBJECTIVE

Seeking a United States Air Force commission in an effort to gain more responsibility, which will allow me to serve my country with dedication, integrity, and professionalism

ACHIEVEMENTS

- Staff Sergeant select
- Accepted into Operation Bootstrap Program   8/93 – 2/94
- Spearheaded National Children's Dental Health Month   1992
  for the Air Force Academy
- Certified Dental Assistant   1990 – Present

AWARDS

- John Levitow and Military Citizen Awards at Airman   1993
  Leadership School
- Selected Airman of the Quarter for USAF Academy Hospital   Spring 1992
- Awarded Air Force Commendation Medal   1991
- Awarded Good Conduct Medal   1991
- Selected Airman of the Year for 831 Air Division and Medical
  Group, George AFB, California   1990
- Nominated for the Twelve Outstanding Airmen of 12th Air Force   1990
- Nominated for Tactical Air Command's Dental Airman of the Year   1990
- Selected Senior Airman Below the Zone   1990
- Selected Airman of the Month for the 831 Medical Group, George
  AFB, California   4/89, 6/90

EXPERIENCE

UNITED STATES AIR FORCE   1988 – Present
Dental Assistant Specialist

- Assist dental officer in treatment of patients
- Developed instruction program for Red Cross volunteers and
  trained six students every semester in periodontics
- Developed a sterilization program for dental burs, which
  increased efficiency and improved patient care standards
- Assign duties to subordinates and evaluate their work standards
  and directives
- Maintain dental health records, filing system, and publications
- Expose and process dental x-ray films
- Perform dental charge of quarters, as assigned

EDUCATION

B.S., BUSINESS ADMINISTRATION   May 1994
Regis University, Denver, Colorado

- Emphasis in Management and Communication
- Expected completion February 1994

AIRMAN LEADERSHIP SCHOOL   1993
United States Air Force Academy, Colorado

ASSOCIATE IN APPLIED SCIENCE   1992
Community College of the Air Force

123 East Elm Drive   ❖   USAF Academy, Colorado 80840   ❖   (719) 555-1234

MARIA S. SANTOS

PROFESSIONAL EXPERIENCE

1995

LANGUAGE INSTRUCTOR
American Graduate School of International Management, Thunderbird Campus, Glendale, Arizona
- Taught intensive conversational Portuguese classes to graduate students
- Placed in top 2% of all instructors after student evaluation

1995

LANGUAGE INSTRUCTOR
Berlitz School of Languages, Phoenix, Arizona
- Taught private classes in business and advanced English using the Berlitz method
- Evaluated students in their Portuguese language fluency

1992

BILINGUAL TEACHER'S ASSISTANT
Gault Elementary School, Santa Cruz, California
- Assisted teacher in bilingual classroom
- Translated in Portuguese and Spanish as a liaison between parents and school

1990 – 1991

TRANSLATOR & ABSTRACTOR (Free-lance)
ABC-CLIO Information Services, Santa Barbara, California
- Translated and abstracted articles from publications on history and art history in Portuguese, French, Spanish, and English
- Typed all abstracts according to specific guidelines

1988 – 1990

LABORATORY SUPERVISOR & PURCHASING AGENT
Twyford Plant Laboratories, Inc., Santa Paula, California
- Media Preparation Department – Produced nutrient substrates for plant biotechnology
- Built and updated information on suppliers and items used in lab
- Maintained inventory of supplies and equipment
- Prepared weekly report on production and personnel requirements
- Responsible for safety training and policy enforcement

1988

INFORMATION SPECIALIST
West Tuality, Forest Grove, Oregon
- Answered public inquiries regarding child care providers with the assistance of a computer
- Assisted center director in creating and implementing marketing strategies for services offered

1987 – 1988

TRANSLATOR
Berlitz School of Languages, Portland, Oregon
- Free-lance translations of business papers

LANGUAGE SKILLS

Portuguese (Native Speaker) • **English** (Fluent)
French (Highly Proficient) • **Spanish** (Highly Proficient)
German (Knowledge) • **Japanese** (Knowledge)

EDUCATION

INTERNATIONAL TRADE AND BANKING COURSE (1988)
Portland Community College, Portland, Oregon

CERTIFICATE OF PRACTICAL AND COMMERCIAL FRENCH (1984)
French Institute, Glasgow, Scotland

BACHELOR OF SCIENCE WITH HONORS IN HORTICULTURE (1984)
University of Strathclyde, Glasgow, Scotland

JEFFREY ALAN PESTER

1234 N. Magnol
Chicago, Illinois 60613
Phone (312) 555-1234

SUMMARY OF QUALIFICATIONS

- Highly proficient in trading strategy development and execution
- Significant trading experience in futures and options markets
- Additional experience in equity, credit, and spot FX markets
- Skilled in technical and psychological aspects of trading and portfolio management
- Excellent mathematical, analytical, and communication abilities
- Former Member – Chicago Mercantile Exchange

PROFESSIONAL EXPERIENCE

MINAKWA INTERMARKET, Chicago, Illinois   3/94 – Present
- Trading consultant and strategist concentrating on futures and options trading

GELDERMANN, INC., Chicago, Illinois   3/93 – 2/94
- Market strategist specializing in trading strategy development for institutional clients, including banks, hedge funds, and proprietary traders

MINAKWA INTERMARKET, Chicago, Illinois   1/92 – 2/93
- Developer of proprietary trading systems and strategies

AKITA CAPITAL ADVISORS, Denver, Colorado   11/86 – 5/89
- Principal of investment advisory firm, specializing in futures and options trading and risk management consulting

WM. BLAIR & CO., Denver, Colorado   10/85 – 11/86
- Institutional broker engaged in futures, options, and equity trading

BOETTCHER & CO., Denver, Colorado   3/85 – 9/85
- Institutional broker engaged in futures, options, and equity trading

CONTIFINANCIAL, INC., Chicago, Illinois   10/82 – 11/84
- Manager of S&P 500 futures institutional trading desk responsible for generating, recommending, and executing various trading strategies for clients, including equity block desks, arbitrageurs, and investment advisors

PUBLISHED ARTICLES

"Understanding Program Trading," *Denver Business Magazine*, February 1987
"S&P 500 Update," *ContiFinancial Weekly Briefing*, October 1982 – October 1984

EDUCATION

AMERICAN GRADUATE SCHOOL OF INTERNATIONAL MANAGEMENT Attended 1/90 – 5/91
"THUNDERBIRD," Glendale, Arizona
- President, International Finance Club
- Corporate Fundraiser, Thunderbird Hot Air Balloon Classic

COLORADO STATE UNIVERSITY, Fort Collins, Colorado   Graduated 5/82
Bachelor of Science: Business Administration
- Major: Finance – Minor: Economics
- Phi Kappa Phi Academic Honors Recipient

Margaret R. Canon

PROFILE:
- Work experience in market analysis, penetration, and development
- Knowledge of media placement and promotion
- Hands-on experience with direct marketing campaign planning and implementation
- Strong interpersonal and organization skills

EXPERIENCE:

Consumer Direct Access, Inc.   1993 – Present
Assistant Marketing Manager, San Francisco, CA
- Coordinated and implemented follow-up promotional mailings for The National Consumer Guide, which included ordering lists, writing all merge/purge instructions, and taking responsibility for meeting the mail date
- Assisted with the preparation of promotional plans and budgets
- Analyzed demographic information regarding the subscriber base
- Managed conversion process of subscriber file to Neodata Services
- Developed billings/renewals series and requalification efforts for CATALYST™
- Negotiated with copywriters, designers, and printers to obtain best possible prices for all marketing projects
- Directed the creative development of all promotional materials from conception through production
- Promoted after one year from Consumer Marketing Coordinator

CNN International Sales, Ltd.   1992
Research Assistant, London, England
- Compiled European market research to develop target markets, including demographics, communication, and industrial base statistics
- Developed and updated a global distribution database to track market penetration
- Administered the 1992 Worldwide Hotel Viewing Survey
- Evaluated competitors' retail incentives

HOME Magazine, Knapp Communications Corporation   1989 – 1991
Circulation Assistant, Los Angeles, CA
- Provided ongoing and special project support to circulation staff of seven for a magazine with a circulation of 925,000
- Acted as primary liaison with list management company and fulfillment bureau
- Implemented and coordinated cross promotions of space ads and inserts

Magnavox Advanced Products and Systems Company   1987 – 1988
Intern – Export and Sales Administration Department, Torrance, CA
- Supervised and coordinated training of administrative personnel
- Responded to foreign and domestic correspondence relating to product sales

EDUCATION:

MASTER OF INTERNATIONAL MANAGEMENT   1992
American Graduate School of International Management
Thunderbird Campus, Glendale, Arizona

BACHELOR OF SCIENCE, Business Administration   *magna cum laude*   1988
California State University, Dominguez Hills
Concentration: International Business and Marketing

LANGUAGES: Working knowledge of **German** • Fluent in **Tagalog**
COMPUTERS: WordPerfect, LOTUS 1-2-3, Harvard Graphics, MS Word, PowerPoint, Excel

Current Address • 1234 Laguna Beach, Apt. 50, Los Angeles, California 94010 • (415) 555-1234
Permanent Address • 123 E. Denny Drive, Carson, California 90746 • (310) 555-1234

Susan J. Peace

1234 1st Street, N.W.   •   Washington, D.C. 20012   •   (202) 555-1234

EXPERIENCE	**UNITED STATES PEACE CORPS**	**1990 – 1993**

Hospital Administrator
Makeni Government Hospital, Makeni, Sierra Leone, West Africa
- Supervised buying and distribution of drugs for hospital dispensary
- Organized and balanced monthly budgets
- Obtained and distributed building materials for construction of new maternity building in conjunction with Plan International
- Requested and administered project funds through written proposals to Peace Corps Partnership and the United States Embassy for construction of a birthing house for Mabonkani village
- Acquired materials and supervised construction of birthing house

Water and Sanitation Technician
Meals for Millions, Freedom from Hunger Foundation
Binkolo, Sierra Leone, West Africa
- Developed improved water and sanitation sources utilizing appropriate technology and local materials in conjunction with the Ministry of Health, Primary Health Care
- Coordinated workshops to instruct villagers on the necessity of clean water and sanitation
- Assisted in the construction of latrines and native wells in five villages
- Coordinated a vaccination campaign with UNICEF for women and children in 12 surrounding villages

S & S CATERING COMPANY, Denver, Colorado   **Summers 1987, 1988**
Owner   **1983 – 1985**
- Owned and operated a successful catering company
- Managed all aspects of the business including finances, budgeting, inventory control, and personnel administration

EDUCATION   **AMERICAN GRADUATE SCHOOL OF INTERNATIONAL MANAGEMENT**   **May 1995**
Glendale, Arizona
Master of International Management
Course Work Concentration: International Marketing Management, Multinational Business Management, Technology Transfer, and Direct Foreign Investment

PITZER COLLEGE, Claremont, California   **1985 – 1989**
Bachelor of Arts in Anthropology and Asian Studies

LONDON UNIVERSITY SCHOOL OF ORIENTAL AND AFRICAN STUDIES   **Fall 1988**
Semester Abroad, London, England

THE EXPERIMENT IN INTERNATIONAL LIVING SCHOOL FOR   **Fall 1986**
INTERNATIONAL TRAINING, Semester in Nepal

SKILLS   Proficient in French, Krio   •   Lotus 1-2-3, WordPerfect, BASIC

ACTIVITIES   President Africa Club, Organizer and Coordinator of Sunset Concert Series, Women's Rugby Club, Outdoor Club

29

Carola Hoechst

OBJECTIVE	A career in international marketing management utilizing my international experience and language skills	
EDUCATION	**MASTER OF INTERNATIONAL MANAGEMENT**, May 1995 **American Graduate School of International Management** Thunderbird Campus, Glendale, Arizona Course Work Concentration: • International Business-to-Business Marketing • International Marketing Management • Multinational Business Management • International Finance and Trade	**USA**
	SEMESTER ABROAD, Summer 1994 **Universidad Autónoma de Guadalajara**, Guadalajara Semester in Mexico to study language and culture	**Mexico**
	BACHELOR OF INTERNATIONAL BUSINESS, August 1992 **United States International University**, San Diego, California	**USA**
	INTENSIVE ENGLISH LANGUAGE PROGRAM, Fall 1989 **E.F. Language College**, San Diego, California	**USA**
EXPERIENCE	**TECHNÍCON INSTRUMENTS CORPORATION**, Tarrytown, New York **Communications Department/Diagnostic Systems Division** Intern, Mar. 1993 – Aug. 1993 • Communicated new product features to advertising agencies and customers • Conducted market analysis on the effectiveness of promotional pieces • Provided administrative support	**USA**
	HOECHST AG, Frankfurt **Sales and Market Department/Pharmaceutical for Africa and Latin America** Intern, Oct. 1992 – Mar. 1993 • Obtained official export documents for tender quotes from German authorities and the Ethiopian Embassy • Assisted in the management of tender quotes for UNICEF	**Germany**
	BANK COMPANIE NORD, Kiel **Credit, Investments, Customer Service** Intern, Summer 1989 • Work/study program in various bank departments	**Germany**
LANGUAGES	• **German** – native • **English** – fluent • **Spanish** – proficient	
ADDRESSES	**Present:** P.O. Box 1234, Glendale, Arizona 85306, (602) 555-1234 **Permanent:** Wiesenweg 12, 1234 Felde, FRG, 49-555-1234	**USA** **Germany**

4 ADDRESS POSITIONS

People must be able to locate you, but the address and phone number are some of the least important marketing details on a resume. Some managers spend only a few seconds perusing a resume and might get through the first third of it, if you are lucky. The reader's eyes should be drawn immediately to the things that will motivate him or her to read all the way to the bottom.

However, you don't want to make the reader work too hard when it is time to make that critical call for an interview! You should make the address section part of the overall design of the resume so it doesn't detract from the text, much as you did with your name, but keep it in an easy-to-find location. That can be done by placing the address(es) either at the top or the bottom of the resume.

Two addresses, a current and permanent, are often needed when a person is still in school. Presenting them at the top sometimes creates design problems and requires a bit of imagination (pages 32, 35, 38, 42, 46). Placing two addresses at the bottom is easier.

An address at the top of the resume should be made part of the design so that the reader's eyes easily skip over it to begin reading the text. Graphic lines are particularly useful in this case (pages 38 and 39), and so is the judicious use of italics (pages 35, 42).

Matching lines at the bottom of a resume sometimes help to create a sense of balance so the resume is not top heavy (pages 51–55). The address can be centered under the line(s) (page 51), made to follow the same format as the text of the resume (pages 52 and 53), justified right and left (page 55), or tab aligned (page 57).

Leslie Neal Sonata

Dirección: Edificio San Remo • Calle Coronel Carlos Guerrero y Bosemediano • Quito, Ecuador • Teléfono: 123-456
Permanent Address: 1234 Sonata Street • New Orleans, Louisiana 70115 • (504) 555-1234

OBJECTIVE	A challenging position that will utilize my highly developed interpersonal and analytical skills and will allow me to grow into positions of broader responsibility

SUMMARY OF QUALIFICATIONS

- Master of International Management Degree with emphasis in marketing
- Excellent sales and marketing skills, with seven years experience in highly competitive markets
- Skilled in planning and organization; outstanding persuasive abilities
- Effective team player experienced in developing successful marketing/network teams
- Resourceful, creative, and articulate; results-oriented individual with high standards of job performance
- Proficient in Spanish

PROFESSIONAL EXPERIENCE

UNDERWRITER   Apr. 1992 – Oct. 1992
National Union Fire Insurance Company, New York, New York
(Subsidiary of American International Group, Inc.)
- Researched and analyzed documentation on companies to assess solvency and risk factors
- Reviewed financial reports, litigation history, and insurance history
- Exclusively handled accounts of $25 million and above

FINANCIAL COUNSELOR   June 1991 – Apr. 1992
Integrated Resources Investment Center, Smithtown, New York
- Introduced financial services to customers in seven branch banks
- Conducted consultations and sold financial products
- Broadened client base through development of interbank referral network
- Educated bank personnel in financial services and built effective marketing teams

ACCOUNT EXECUTIVE   Sep. 1988 – June 1991
Merrill Lynch Pierce Fenner & Smith, Inc., Melville, New York
- Established and developed client base through cold-calling
- Conducted seminars and coordinated direct mail marketing
- Provided investment advice and services to clients
- Hired as youngest broker in branch

ACCOUNT EXECUTIVE   Sep. 1987 – Sep. 1988
Douglas Bremen & Co., Cold Spring Harbor, New York
- Served as account executive for this small brokerage firm while completing studies for Series 7 Securities License

ACCOUNT EXECUTIVE   Dec. 1985 – Aug. 1987
Dreyfus Service Corporation, Garden City, New York
- Provided information and assistance to clients regarding mutual fund activities
- Responsible for sales and servicing of IRA, Keogh, money markets, and other new bank products in the Specialty Sales Division
- Selected to participate in marketing task force for life insurance product

EDUCATION

MASTER OF INTERNATIONAL MANAGEMENT   Dec. 1994
American Graduate School of International Management
Thunderbird Campus, Glendale, Arizona
Emphasis: Marketing

BACHELOR OF ARTS: PSYCHOLOGY   1985
University of Florida at Gainesville
Minor: Business

INTERNATIONAL STUDIES
Guadalajara, Mexico   Summer 1994
Antigua, Guatemala   Winter 1993–1994
Quito, Ecuador   Mar. – June 1993
University of Innsbruck, Austria   Summer 1983

ANITA NORWEGIAN

Caleruega 12 → 28033 Madrid, Spain → (91) 555-1234

EDUCATION

MASTER OF INTERNATIONAL MANAGEMENT   5/95
American Graduate School of International Management
Thunderbird Campus, Glendale, Arizona
Emphasis: International Marketing and Trade
Courses included: Business-to-Business Marketing, International
Business Policy, Export/Import Management, International Marketing
Management, International Marketing Research, International Consumer Marketing, Intermediate Accounting

BACHELOR OF BUSINESS ADMINISTRATION   12/93
The University of Oklahoma, Norman, Oklahoma
Major in Finance, Minor in Economics
Courses included: Capital Budgeting, Investments, Commercial
Banking, Insurance, International Finance and Trade,
Production/Operation Management

EXPERIENCE

GREATER PHOENIX ECONOMIC COUNCIL, Phoenix, Arizona   2/95 – 5/95
International Investment Specialist – Europe
→ Developed an industrial profile of Canada that will be used by
   GPEC to target corporations (in key industries) interested in direct
   investment opportunities in the greater Phoenix area

L.K. KARLSEN, Bøstad, Norway   6/93 – 8/93
Department Store Intern   6/92 – 8/92
→ Sold and ordered technical products
→ Calculated prices and discounts
→ Displayed point-of-purchase setups

BILBØRSEN DATABANK, Oslo, Norway   6/90 – 8/90
Broker
→ Matched buyers and sellers in the used-car market

TRADE MARKETING, Oslo, Norway   6/90 – 8/90
Freelancer-Sales
→ Telemarketing of promotional products

LANGUAGES

Fluent in **Norwegian** and **English**
Highly proficient in **Swedish** and **Danish**

COMPUTER

Lotus 1-2-3, Quattro Pro 2, WordPerfect, dBASE III, Harvard Graphics

ACTIVITIES

→ Active member in Export/Import Club, Women Leadership Club, and
   Toastmasters International
→ Member of the Student Advisory Council in the CBA Leadership Program
→ Chairperson of Investment in the OU Finance Club
→ ANSA Representative at University of Oklahoma

HONORS

→ College of Business Administration Leadership Program
→ Financial Management Association National Honor Society
→ Golden Key National Honor Society

33

Erminio "Shorty" Super

1234 West Desert Cove ▸ Phoenix, Arizona 85029 ▸ Home: (602) 555-1234 ▸ Work: (602) 555-1234

EXPERIENCE

CITY OF PHOENIX, ARIZONA   1968 – Present

Equipment Maintenance Superintendent (1982 – Present)
- Direct the operation of automotive shops for the repair and maintenance of 5,000+ pieces of automotive, construction, and special duty equipment.
- Supervise more than 300 employees.
- Establish work policies, schedules, repair and maintenance work standards.
- Supervise the presentations of monthly and annual maintenance cost reports, and prepare budget estimates for maintenance operations.
- Investigate personnel problems and submit reports and recommendations.
- Assisted in the design of an employee attitude survey.
- Coordinator for the Public Works Department Partnership Program (quality circle program).
- Served on the Supervisory Development Advisory Council to formulate criteria for the Phoenix Supervisor Academy.
- Member of Total Quality Management Task Force and Apprenticeship Program Committee (Chairman since 1982)

Equipment Shop Supervisor (1981 – 1982)
- Directed the maintenance performed on equipment management fleet at the satellite shops, police substations, landfills, and water treatment plants.
- Managed project for rebuilding landfill equipment, saving an average of $60,000 per vehicle.

Equipment Shop Foreman (1972 – 1981)
- Set priorities, planned, assigned, and coordinated all the work for the heavy duty, welding, tire, and battery shops.
- Played a role in setting a nationwide trend toward using mechanical lifting devices in refuse collection. Assisted in designing some of the first vehicles used for this purpose.
- Supervised building trucks from the ground up, reconditioning them in order to save the expense of purchasing new vehicles.
- Member of the Organization Development Steering Committee, which acted as a change agent in the assembly, marketing, and support of city-wide improvements.

Heavy Equipment Mechanic, Auto Mechanic, and Mechanic's Helper (1969 – 1972)

EDUCATION

PHOENIX COLLEGE, Phoenix, Arizona   1972 – 1977
Associate of Arts Degree in Public Administration (82 hours)

TRAINING PROGRAMS

Equipment Maintenance/Management Conference (3 days)	1990
Advanced Public Works Supervision for the 1990's (2 days)	1989
Business Writing Skills (1 day)	1989
Strategies of Effective Writing (1 day)	1989
Introduction to Microcomputers	1985, 1988
Introduction to Lotus 1-2-3	1988
Assertive Management, ASU	1987
Partnership Leader Training	1985
Preventive Maintenance for Fleet Operations (1.4 CEU's)	1985
Improving Management Skills for New Managers	1985
Supervisor as Counselor	1980
National Safety Council Key Man Development Program	1979
Arc and Gas Welding Certificate (16 weeks)	1968
U.S. Army Light/Heavy Truck and Full Track Mechanics (24 weeks)	1956, 1957

PROFESSIONAL MEMBERSHIPS

- American Society for Public Administration	1982 – Present
- Rocky Mountain Maintenance Association	1983 – Present
- Phoenix Sister Cities Commission (Hermosillo Committee Chairman)	1988 – Present
- ASPTEA – Administrative, Supervisory, Professional, and Technical Employees Association of the City of Phoenix, Arizona	1989 – Present
- Institute for Equipment Services	1983 – Present
- Arizona Fleet Maintenance Council	1986 – Present
- Maricopa Technical Community College (Chairman)	1982 – 1990

C. David Market

Current:
1234 W. Eugie Avenue, #1234
Glendale, Arizona 85304
Phone: (602) 555-1234
Fax: (602) 555-1234

Permanent:
123 Racquette River Dr., Box 123
Tupper Lake, New York 12986
Phone: (518) 555-1234
Fax: (518) 555-1234

EXPERIENCE

THUNDERBIRD, Glendale, Arizona
Department of Modern Languages – Arabic Program
Graduate Assistant

June 1994 through Dec. 1994

- Performed feasibility study of the Arab Gulf via primary research and data analysis to establish an international institute for technology transfer
- Developed teaching curriculum for an interactive computer program used in Arabic language classes

TEXAS INSTRUMENTS, Dallas, Texas
Educational Products Division
Marketing Research Consultant

Feb. 1994 through May 1994

- Determined market potential and formulated entry strategies for a new product line in the U.S. Hispanic market
- Designed and implemented qualitative and quantitative research methods to assess: 1) barriers to market entry, 2) channels of distribution, 3) product modifications, 4) product positioning, 5) key purchasers and influencers of purchase

XEROX CORPORATION, Rochester, New York
United States Marketing Group, Major Markets Contract Pricing Administration
Marketing Intern

Jan. 1993 through May 1993

- Generated reports needed for feasibility analyses and strategic pricing
- Created pricing matrices to reflect changes in major government contracts
- Expedited the authorization process for revisions to government contracts

CAMIL G. MAROUN, JR. INSURANCE AGENCY, Tupper Lake, New York
General Insurance Agency, Personal and Commercial Lines
General Office Assistant

Summers 1989–1993

- Generated new accounts and recommended appropriate coverages for clients
- Originated and designed procedural manuals for quotations and policy endorsements
- Prepared accounting data for monthly batch

EDUCATION

MASTER OF INTERNATIONAL MANAGEMENT
American Graduate School of International Management
Glendale, Arizona

Dec. 1994

- International Consumer Marketing Workshop
- Marketing to U.S. Hispanics Seminar
- Advanced Commercial Spanish
- International Insurance
- Co-Chair, Middle East Club

BACHELOR OF SCIENCE IN MANAGEMENT
St. John Fisher College, Rochester, New York

May 1993

Concentration: International Business   **Minor:** Spanish
- Business Manager for the Spanish Club   • Spanish Tutor

FOREIGN STUDY
Universidad de Salamanca, Salamanca, Spain
American Institute for Foreign Studies (AIFS)

Sep. 1991 through May 1992

LANGUAGES & SKILLS

English (native) • **Spanish** (fluent) • **Arabic** (proficient)
Computer: Harvard Graphics, Lotus 1-2-3, Macintosh, SPSSpc, WordPerfect

SCHOLARSHIPS & HONORS

R. K. Thomas Assistantship (1994) • Arabic Scholarship (1994) • Presidential Scholarship (1992–1994) • Dean's List (1992–1994) • Alpha Mu Gamma (National Collegiate Foreign Language Honor Society) (1992–Present) • Admissions Scholarship (1989–1991) • Thunderbird Honor Student

ADAM L. WASHINGTON

12345 N. 59th Avenue #123 • Glendale, Arizona 85306 • Phone/Fax: (602) 555-1234

SKILLS

QUANTITATIVE

EXPERIENCE
- Research and analysis of U.S. economic data and the federal budget for U.S. Senator
- Financial analysis and forecasting for commercial real estate properties
- Market research of commercial real estate markets
- Computer: designed spreadsheet models and constructed databases

EDUCATION
- Graduate level: Finance, Accounting, Statistics, Marketing Research, Economics

QUALITATIVE

EXPERIENCE
- Drafted U.S. Senator's positions on especially sensitive issues, including Political Action Committees, campaign finance reform, and congressional perquisites
- Responded in writing daily to political constituents on a range of important issues
- Designed marketing strategies for a nonprofit health association, an information company (with proprietary computer databases), and a real estate development company
- Project presentation experience
- Computer: utilized word-processing and database programs

EDUCATION
- Graduate: management, marketing, team-based work, project presentation, public speaking
- Undergraduate: liberal arts, political science, literature, extensive writing courses

INTERNATIONAL

EDUCATION
- Master of International Management: May, 1995
- International Studies concentration: Western European Integration, Eastern Europe, Russia
- World Business concentration: International Marketing and Finance
- Countertrade and Offset Management: Certificate of Competency

LANGUAGES
- French: U.S. State Department Level 3
- English: Native speaker with exceptional writing abilities

EXPERIENCE
- Atlantic Treaty Association Conference, U.S. Delegate, Paris   1992
- American Council of Young Political Leaders, Reception Host for Australian Delegation   1993
- Friends of Costa Rica (Earthquake Relief Effort), Fund-raising Committee Member   1993
- Institute for Comparative Political and Economic Systems, Alumni Board Member   1994 – 1995

EMPLOYMENT HISTORY

1993 – 1994	Market Analyst/Admin. Asst.	Carey Winston Company	Washington, DC
1993	Membership Director	National Assn. of Nonsmokers	Washington, DC
1991 – 1992	Legislative Assistant	U.S. Senator William S. Cohen	Washington, DC
1992	Staff Assistant (concurrently)	GAC Oversight Subcommittee	Washington, DC
1990	Administrative Assistant	Brick Landing Plantation	Ocean Isle Beach, NC

ACADEMIC DEGREES & HONORS

MASTER OF INTERNATIONAL MANAGEMENT – May, 1995   GPA: 3.9
American Graduate School of International Management, Thunderbird Campus, Glendale, AZ
Thunderbird Scholar, American Graduate School of International Management, 1994

BACHELOR OF ARTS, GOVERNMENT – 1990
University of Virginia, Charlottesville, VA

INSTITUTE FOR COMPARATIVE POLITICAL AND ECONOMIC SYSTEMS, Graduate – 1988
Georgetown University, Washington, DC
Trustee Merit Scholar, University of Southern California, 1987 – 1988
Cum Laude Society, admitted to the fellowship in recognition of meritorious attainments, 1987

CARROLL W. HALLMARK

123 Cliff Falls Court, Colorado Springs, CO 80919
Home: (719) 555-1234 • Office: (719) 555-1234

SUMMARY	*Consistent progression in 22-year career spanning general operations as well as marketing and sales. Responsibilities have included the full product range from personal workstations to mainframes in all lines of business by managing high levels of direct and indirect channels of distribution.*

EXPERIENCE

1993 – Present

R&D SYSTEMS

Vice President, Support and Services, *Denver, Colorado*
- *Responsible for all services within the company (approximately 70 people):*
  - *Hot-line support*
  - *Training*
  - *Systems implementation*
  - *Software integration (custom modifications)*
- *Improved level of service while increasing revenue per person.*
- *Increased service revenue as a percentage of total revenue from 21% to 27% in one year.*
- *Introduced new implementation process that greatly improved customer expectations and satisfaction.*

1970 – 1993

UNISYS CORPORATION

President, Value Added Marketing, United States Information Systems Division
Blue Bell, Pennsylvania (1990 – 1993)
- *Full P&L responsibility for all aspects of U.S. indirect channels of distribution, including field sales, customer support, finance, marketing programs, and channel programs on a $200 million revenue base.*
- *Improved profitability by $20 million over two years:*
  - *8 point improvement in gross margin*
  - *47% reduction in SG&A*
  - *Reduced accounts receivable greater than 90 days from 32% to 12%*
- *Aligned Value Added Marketing recruiting and promotional activities with U.S. line of business strategy.*
- *Developed plan to move Value Added Marketing field sales and technical support under the control of the geographic group vice president.*

Vice President, Third Party Marketing, Commercial Systems Division
Blue Bell, Pennsylvania (1989 – 1990)
- *Developed and executed a plan to promote third-party solutions into the commercial line of business:*
  - *Selected/recruited 100 third-party sales managers.*
  - *Developed compensation plans, quota assignments, and training programs.*
  - *Reviewed third-party sales manager performance twice quarterly.*
- *Program adopted by other line of business division in the U.S.*
- *Exceeded order and revenue goals.*
- *Achieved Unisys "CLUB" 1989.*

Regional Vice President, Southern Industrial and Commercial Region
Atlanta, Georgia (1987 – 1988)
- *Created the Southern Industrial and Commercial Region with full P&L responsibility.*
  - *Selected all sales, support, and administrative personnel (535 persons) to form a vertical line of business organization.*
  - *Responsible for sales of full product line in an eleven-state area with $125 million revenue objective.*
- *Achieved order, revenue, and profit productivity that has not since been exceeded in commercial accounts in that area.*
- *Received largest single order within division—$20 million from Home Shopping Network.*

37

CARLOS J. CARIBBEAN

OFFICE ADDRESS	123 Rivera Manuel Ave., Suite 1234, San Juan, PR 00918	Telephone: (809) 555-1234
HOME ADDRESS	P. O. Box 12345, Hato Rey, PR 00912	Telephone: (809) 555-1234

OBJECTIVE

A Challenging Position in **International Operations** leading to Senior Management Opportunities

SKILLS

- **ASSERTIVENESS** – Earned six promotions and four merit nominations in less than four years at Pepsi-Cola. Reached record sales and market shares within months.
- **FOCUS** – Consistent ability to identify and exploit major growth opportunities and effectively address the "real" issues – proven in both highly developed and underdeveloped markets.
- **LEADERSHIP** – Commitment, integrity, and dedication have allowed me to motivate and work effectively through bottlers, peers, and subordinates. Co-instructed a Dale Carnegie course on self-confidence, public speaking, and interpersonal skills at the age of 19.
- **SELF-STARTER** – Four years of entrepreneurial experience. Require minimal supervision. Have been able to materialize and implement key projects long delayed in the planning process. Self-financed 100% of graduate and 50% of undergraduate education.
- **LANGUAGES** – Fluent in English and Spanish. Working knowledge of Portuguese.
- **COMPUTERS** – Lotus 1-2-3, Excel, DW4, WordPerfect, Harvard Graphics, On Target, Windows, DOS

EXPERIENCE

PEPSI-COLA CARIBBEAN, San Juan, Puerto Rico .... Jan. 1989 – Present
- P&L and market share responsibilities – primary link between company and bottlers
- Brand and Key Account Management, Market Development, Strategic Planning
- Also accountable for Packaging Innovation, Distribution, Merchandising, and Promotions

Operations → District Manager PUERTO RICO .... **Oct. 1991 – Present**
- Manage four subordinates, a $9,000,000 budget, and 35% of regional volume
- Gained brand leadership for Pepsi-Cola in less than a year on the job
  (our main competitor had uninterruptedly been the #1 brand for over seven years)
- Reversed declining sales trends (−15% → +23%) amid a heavily taxed soft drink industry
- Instrumental in creating and implementing a three-year leadership plan with Bacardi

Operations Manager HISPANIOLA DISTRICT .... **Jan. – Sep. 1991**
- Managed four countries, a $1,400,000 budget, and 26% of regional volume
- Reversed volume drops in Dominican Republic (−25% → +27%), Haiti (−20% → +26%), and Jamaica (−44% → −2%) amid worsening economic and political conditions
- Launched Sprite in the Dominican Republic, capturing 50% share of segment within six months
- Pioneered a Street Vendor Cooler project in Haiti, creating a new trade channel

Country → Operations Manager N.E. CARIBBEAN .... **Jan. – Dec. 1990**
- Managed 14 territories, a $400,000 budget, and 12% of regional volume
- Achieved record growth in Bahamas (+24%) and USVI (+18%) with profits 10% above budget

Account Services Representative → Cold Drink Manager .... **Jan. – Dec. 1989**
- Instrumental in gaining exclusivity-conversions in key fountain accounts in Puerto Rico

SELF-EMPLOYED, Austin, Texas .... July 1983 – Aug. 1987
- Introduced CONTI designer apparel and test marketed Latin American products
- Founded the 1st Ticket Brokerage Agency in Central Texas (Showtime Tickets, Inc.)

EDUCATION

MASTER OF INTERNATIONAL MANAGEMENT .... Dec. 1988
American Graduate School of International Management, Glendale, Arizona
- Emphasis on Investments and Multinational Operations
- Worked as a Marketing Intern for Pepsi-Cola Caribbean (June–August 1988)
- First scholar to take majority of graduate courses at the most advanced level

BACHELOR OF BUSINESS ADMINISTRATION .... May 1985
University of Texas, Austin, Texas   **Major:** Business/Electrical Engineering

SEMINARS & WORKSHOPS (Sponsored by Pepsi-Cola) .... 1989 – 1992
Customer Service, Key Account Management, High-Performance Organizations, Train the Trainer, Project Management, Pricing & Packaging, International Merchandising, Communications Skills

MARTA FINNISH

1234 Greenhaven Place
Alexandria, Virginia 22310

(703) 555-1234
(703) 555-1234

EXPERIENCE

EXPORT MANAGER
Jan. 1995 – Present

Parallel Systems Services, Inc., *Alexandria, Virginia*
- *Planned, implemented, and managed a consumer goods export project to Romania*
- *Coordinated export financial and logistical details, including freight forwarding, customs clearances, distribution, and collections, and otherwise ensured that goals and objectives of the project were accomplished within prescribed six-month time limitation*
- *Hired, motivated, and supervised local sales staff*
- *Initiated contacts and negotiated contracts with suppliers and buyers*
- *Conducted market analysis through personal contact with buyers and on-site exploration in Romania for three months*

CONFERENCE LIAISON
Sep. 1994

World Economic Development Congress, *Washington, DC*
- *Assisted in implementing a high-profile international conference with duties in public relations and logistics*

MARKETING INTERN
Jan. 1993 – June 1993
(Part-Time)

World Trade Center Association, *Denver, Colorado*
- *Assisted in organizing and implementing a South American Mining Conference, World Trade Day, and Import/Export Workshop Series*
- *Provided customer service and worked as an office assistant*

INSURANCE LIAISON
July 1990 – Mar. 1991

Verdandi Life Insurance Company *(Henkivakuutus Osakeyhtiö Verdandi), Finland*
- *Provided consultation to sales personnel as a liaison between the field and headquarters*
- *Processed insurance and loan applications and claims*
- *Calculated quotations for clients and performed accounting for insurance premiums*
- *Researched markets and reported to home office*
- *Planned and organized conventions*
- *Assisted in hiring and training new employees*
- *Served and supported current clients*
- *Assisted in developing and implementing a marketing plan*

BANK CLEARANCE DEPARTMENT RESEARCHER
June 1989 – Aug. 1989
Feb. 1988 – July 1988

Post Bank (Postipankki), *Finland*
- *Researched accounts, resolved problems, and monitored error accounts*
- *Handled client complaints and provided customer service*

EDUCATION

MASTER OF INTERNATIONAL MANAGEMENT
Aug. 1994

American Graduate School of International Management
Thunderbird Campus, *Glendale, Arizona*   GPA 3.57
Semester abroad at Helsinki School of Economics MBA Program
Scholarships: Foundation for Economic Education, Finnish Government

BACHELOR OF SCIENCE IN BUSINESS ADMINISTRATION
June 1993

University of Denver, *Denver, Colorado*
Major: Finance/Marketing   GPA in major 3.81
Listed twice on National Dean's List, inducted into Phi Beta Delta International Honor Society
Scholarships: Finnish Chamber of Commerce, Wihuri Aarnio, Finnish Government

COMMERCIAL COLLEGE GRADUATE, UNDERGRADUATE LEVEL
May 1990

Kuopio Commercial College (Kuopion Kauppaoppilaitos), *Finland*
Major: Accounting—among top 5% of graduates

ROTARY CLUB EXCHANGE STUDENT
Aug. 1986 – May 1987

Northern State College, *Aberdeen, South Dakota*

LANGUAGE SKILLS   *Native in* **Finnish** • *Proficient in* **Swedish** • *Knowledge of* **German**

Lisa L. Price
12345 Leaning Oak
Oklahoma City, Oklahoma 73120
Telephone: (405) 555-1234

STRENGTHS:

Financial Sales / Staff and Project Management
- History of rapid promotions
- Outstanding accomplishment in financial sales and marketing
- Skilled staff trainer and motivator

EXPERIENCE:

Bank of Oklahoma, Oklahoma City, Oklahoma, April 1994 – November 1994
Branch Manager
- Train and motivate staff in cross-selling techniques
- Manage all aspects of branch operations and activities
- Establish branch staffing and budget needs
- Promote bank products and services

Bank of America, Ft. Worth, Texas / Phoenix, Arizona, October 1990 – March 1994
Branch Manager / Customer Service Manager / Personal Banker
- Formulate/implement marketing and sales plans
- Promote bank products, sales, and services to area businesses
- Originate and package real estate and consumer loan applications

Homestead Savings and Loan, San Francisco, California, July 1989 – August 1990
Branch Manager / Customer Service Manager / District Sales Trainer
- Managed customer service personnel and operations staff of 12
- Formulated and implemented sales and marketing training material for district branches
- Oversaw resolution of customer problems at the district level

American Home Savings and Loan, Edmond, Oklahoma, July 1986 – July 1989
Account Executive / Personal Banker
- Number One in Sales, 1988 and first two quarters of 1989
- Trained sales staff on telemarketing solicitation, face-to-face presentations, and closing techniques
- Guided investment decisions, representing annuities, certificates of deposit, money market accounts, and loans

EDUCATION:

B.A., Oral Communication (Public Relations and Advertising), 1987
Central State University, Edmond, Oklahoma

Continuing Education
- Mortgage, Consumer, and Small-Business Lending Training
- Merchant Services
- Internal and External Selling Techniques
- Managing Change
- Financial Services
- Human Resources Guidelines

JEFFREY K. ENGLEWOOD

1234 Hollow Drive, Colorado Springs, Colorado 80920

(719) 555-1234

OBJECTIVE   To develop and implement marketing strategies that will promote products and/or services and enhance the growth of a business such as yours

QUALIFICATIONS
- Highly creative, self-motivated individual
- Team player with exceptional interpersonal skills
- Sixteen years of managerial and marketing experience
- Area representative with the Christian Booksellers Association
- B.A. degree in business administration with an emphasis in both management and marketing

EXPERIENCE

VICE PRESIDENT AND GENERAL MANAGER *(1982 – Present)*
The Lord's Vineyard, Inc., *Colorado Springs, Colorado*
- Responsible for consistent growth from start-up to $2.3 million, including management, inventory control, accounting, marketing, and customer service functions
- Hired, scheduled hours worked, and organized job descriptions for twenty store personnel
- Managed a diverse staff and succeeded in motivating employees to excellence
- Developed cash management, forecasting, and budgeting systems
- Supervised computer and information systems and assisted in developing computer programs
- Designed and managed inventory tracking systems and sales/shipping procedures
- Analyzed the market using various research methods to better determine customer desires
- Informed sales personnel of customer buying habits, buying motives, and likes and dislikes regarding products and services through weekly staff meetings
- Developed and facilitated strategic product promotions and in-store sales events
- Scripted and produced radio and television commercials with successful results
- Discovered customer wants that could only be satisfied by new or improved products and then provided product development ideas for the CBA industry

ADVERTISING & PROMOTION MANAGER *(1986 – 1989)*
Mustardseed Bible Bookstores, *Englewood, Colorado*
- Entered into a partnership with two other individuals and purchased a chain of five bookstores in the Denver metropolitan area
- Directed the advertising, promotion, and product marketing strategies of these five retail stores in Denver, in addition to three store locations in Colorado Springs under *The Lord's Vineyard*
- Achieved a 50% increase in sales by the end of the three years
- Assisted in purchasing inventory and managing the inventory tracking systems
- Sold interest in the business in order to concentrate on the Colorado Springs stores

GENERAL MANAGER *(1979 – 1982)*
Living Word Christian Supply, *Albuquerque, New Mexico*
- Part owner responsible for managing, inventory control, and marketing of the business
- Doubled sales in three years
- Managed six employees and was directly involved in purchasing, sales, marketing of the store and its products, and customer service
- Sold business and moved to Colorado to start The Lord's Vineyard, Inc.

RETAIL SALES MANAGER *(1978 – 1979)*
National Pen Corporation, *San Diego, California*
- Responsible for product development and the implementation of distribution strategies
- Determined through market research which products to sell
- Designed products from start to finish and determined methods of distribution
- Learned the necessity of increased efficiency in reducing the costs of distribution
- Test marketed the products in the San Diego area and was about ready to head the hiring of a national sales force when I received a call to move to Albuquerque to become involved with the Living Word Christian Supply

41

Dawn S. Banker

Current Address: *12345 N. 59th Avenue #123, Glendale, Arizona 85306*   *(602) 555-1234*
Permanent Address: *123 Old Toll Road, Madison, Connecticut 06443*   *(203) 555-1234*

OBJECTIVE

To obtain a position in **banking** or **finance** utilizing my international experience. Major areas of interest are: Trade Finance, Capital Markets, Corporate Finance, and Treasury Risk Management

QUALIFICATIONS

✦ Extensive exposure to equity, equity derivative products, money market instruments, fixed income products, and security borrowing and lending
✦ Understanding of firm finance, trade finance, and hedging strategies
✦ Advanced degree in international business focusing on international securities markets
✦ Hold current German work permit with three years of in-country experience

EXPERIENCE

SALOMON BROTHERS AG, Frankfurt, Germany   Mar. 92 – Present
Finance Desk Assistant
✦ Prepared treasury reports relating to balance sheet management and reports used for profit and loss calculation
✦ Assisted with daily operations, including overnight trades, security borrowing and lending, and fixed income agreements

Supervisor Management Accounting
✦ Supervised group in the production and analysis of product-driven profit and loss and acted as liaison between the department and dealers
✦ Improved work efficiency by developing, testing, and implementing new systems for securities trade maintenance, profit and loss calculation, position reconciliation, and cost of financing

BASF AG, Ludwigshafen, Germany   Sep. 91 – Feb. 92
Intern to Director of Biotechnology
✦ Launched a market research study to determine the marketability of a specific by-product as an aid in cancer research
✦ Researched, documented, and presented findings for joint-venture opportunities

EDUCATION

MASTER OF INTERNATIONAL MANAGEMENT   Aug. 95
American Graduate School of International Management
Thunderbird Campus, Glendale, Arizona
✦ Emphasis: International Finance
✦ Area Studies: Asia

BACHELOR OF ARTS IN INTERNATIONAL TRADE   Aug. 91
University of Connecticut, Storrs, Connecticut
✦ Emphasis: International Economics, German
✦ Study Abroad
   - **University Mannheim**, Mannheim, Germany   Apr. 91 – Jul. 91
   - **Goethe Institute**, Mannheim, Germany   Feb. 91 – Mar. 91

ASSOCIATE OF SCIENCE IN ENVIRONMENTAL SCIENCE   May 87
Middlesex Community College, Middletown, Connecticut
✦ Emphasis: Chemistry
✦ Received full academic scholarship

SKILLS

Language: Highly proficient in **German** (Level 3)
Computers: Lotus 1-2-3, Excel, Microsoft Word, Paradox, PASCAL, BASIC

ACTIVITIES

✦ Connecticut Small Business Development Center: Export Research Team
✦ Mannheim Program for Bilingual Careers
✦ Member of Kappa Kappa Gamma National Sorority

DAVID ALAN CHINA

1234 Cortese Circle, San Jose, California 95127   (408) 555-1234

OBJECTIVE   A career in international business management

AREAS OF EXPERTISE

- Equipment Leasing Experience
- Contract Analysis
- Outside Sales & Promotional Programs
- Trade Shows
- Government Procurement Sales

- Multicultural Exposure
- Mandarin Chinese Language
- Problem Resolution
- Computer Proficiency
- Technical Product Experience

EXPERIENCE

HITACHI DATA SYSTEMS, Santa Clara, California   1991 – Present
Lease Administrator – Remarketing Analyst
- Developed the operational procedures for the newly created End of Lease Group within Hitachi Data Systems Credit Corporation (HDSCC)
- Resolve lease administration issues between HDSCC's investors and end users
- Structure renewal and buyout transactions for existing customers whose lease schedules are coming to term
- Support HDS sales personnel by structuring new lease schedules for end-user accounts using off-lease equipment or equipment purchased in the brokerage community

Mainframe Computer Broker   1990 – 1991
- Provided trade-in pricing for used computers and storage products to an HDS sales force of over 200 people
- Generated a weekly market forecast report with current pricing information on both used HDS and non-HDS products
- Remarketed end-of-lease and trade-in equipment to brokers throughout the U.S. and Canada

TAIPEI LANGUAGE INSTITUTE, Shilin, Taiwan   1988 & 1989
English Teacher
- Instructed group and individual classes
- Organized and marketed special group language programs to Taipei's business community

JAMES ASSOCIATES, Denver, Colorado   1985 – 1987
Marketing Coordinator and Sales Representative
- Marketed food service equipment to distributors, chain store accounts, food service companies, architects, and consultants
- Coordinated and implemented promotional programs targeting distributor sales teams
- Developed end-user demand through periodic sales calls on hotels, universities, and other large food service accounts
- Organized and operated national and regional trade show exhibits
- Developed and administered an equipment leasing program
- Established a sales program with U.S. government procurement agencies for refrigeration equipment

EDUCATION

MASTER OF INTERNATIONAL MANAGEMENT   December 1989
American Graduate School of International Management
Thunderbird Campus, Glendale, Arizona
Emphasis on World Business, Cultural Studies, and Chinese Language

INTENSIVE CHINESE LANGUAGE AND CULTURAL PROGRAM   1988 & 1989
Taipei Language Institute, Shilin, Taiwan

BACHELOR OF ARTS   1984
Fort Lewis College, Durango, Colorado
Double Major: Economics and Business Administration

LANGUAGE   Proficient in Mandarin Chinese

COMPUTERS   Excel, Lotus, LINDO, SPSS, QSB, @RISK, word processing software

43

Dorothy W. Valley

1234 Calle del Riviera, N.W. • Albuquerque, New Mexico 87104 • (505) 555-1234

EXPERIENCE

VICE PRESIDENT & CORPORATE SECRETARY   1975 – Present
S.B.E., Inc. (Fixed Base Airport Operations), Albuquerque, New Mexico
- Responsible for long-term risk management and strategic planning
- Political liaison, marketing, and public relations

CORPORATE SECRETARY   1985 – Present
Sun Valley Aviation, Inc. (Fixed-Base Airport Operations), Hailey, Idaho
- Coordinate corporate correspondence and strategic planning

BOARD OF DIRECTORS   1989 – Present
S.B.S. Engineering (Aerospace Engineering Corp.), Albuquerque, New Mexico
- Provide leadership
- Long-term strategic planning

GENERAL MANAGER   1990 – Present
Black Ranch (Cattle Company), Albuquerque, New Mexico
- Manage assets of the ranch and provide long-term planning
- Oversee purchase and sales of cattle

MANAGING PARTNER   1985 – 1992
Dos Hermanos Partnership (Commercial Development), Albuquerque, New Mexico
- Assist in management of commercial properties

EDUCATION

GREAT BOOKS STUDIES, University of Albuquerque, New Mexico
- Two years of advanced study of the Humanities

BACHELOR OF UNIVERSITY STUDIES, University of New Mexico, Albuquerque
- Emphasis on Art History and History, 1986

TEXAS WOMEN'S UNIVERSITY, Denton, Texas
- Emphasis on Interior Design and Liberal Arts

SPECIAL HONORS

Trustee, Institute of American Indian Arts, Santa Fe, New Mexico, 1984 – 1986
Official Observer, Ninth Inter-American Indian Congress, Santa Fe, New Mexico, 1985
Albuquerque City Council "Decade of Service Award" Recipient (one of four), 1972
Junior Leagues of America, Regional Conference Delegate, Honolulu, Hawaii, 1969
United Cerebral Palsy National Convention, Keynote Speaker, Washington, D.C., 1968

COMMUNITY INVOLVEMENT

New Mexico Symphony Guild (President, 1969), 1963 – Present
Senator Pete Domenici Senate Campaign Finance Co-Chairman, 1989 – 1990
Santa Fe Opera Board of Directors, 1975 – 1979, 1988 – 1990
New Mexico Symphony Board, 1964 – 1974, 1988 – 1990
Presbyterian Hospital Foundation Board, 1986 – 1988
NCAA National Women's Golf Championship Association Director, 1987
New Mexico Governor's Inaugural Co-Chairman, 1987
Gary Carruthers for Governor, New Mexico Finance Co-Chairman, 1986
Chaparral Girl Scout Board, 1975 – 1976
Albuquerque Junior League (Secretary, Board of Directors, Chairman), 1964 – 1975
Albuquerque United Fund Budget Committee, 1970 – 1974
University of New Mexico Friends of Art Board, 1969 – 1974
New Mexico Opera Guild Board, 1969 – 1974
Albuquerque Opera Guild Board (President, 1970), 1968 – 1974
University of New Mexico Alumni Board, 1969 – 1973
Albuquerque Arts Council, 1969 – 1972
Albuquerque March of Dimes Fund Drive Chairman, 1972
New Mexico Cerebral Palsy Association (State Women's Chairman, 1968), 1963 – 1970

KIMBERLY A. COLLECTOR

12 Bridgewater Court
Marlton, New Jersey 08053
(609) 555-1234

OBJECTIVE   A management position utilizing my experience, interests, and abilities

QUALIFICATIONS
- Opened and managed two commercial bank branch offices
- Demonstrated managerial competence as evidenced by rapid promotions
- Experienced in training and development
- Excellent communication skills

EXPERIENCE   **SENIOR COLLECTOR**   11/94 – 5/95
First Interstate Bank of Arizona, Phoenix, Arizona
- Managed individual portfolio of delinquent accounts
- Negotiated and implemented repayment plans with customers and outside agencies
- Prepared, summarized, and recommended accounts for senior management and legal review
- Exceeded established departmental and individual delinquency goals

BANK OFFICER/BRANCH MANAGER   2/89 – 10/90
Jefferson Bank of New Jersey, Mt. Laurel, New Jersey
- Opened and managed $38 million branch
- Functioned as liaison between bank president and all other internal departments
- Designed and marketed branch's business development activities
- Administered all personnel decisions, including hiring and firing
- Developed and implemented training program for branch employees
- Performed all phases of consumer loan requests and participated in commercial loan analysis
- Maintained all internal policies, security procedures, and audit controls

BRANCH MANAGER/ASSISTANT BRANCH MANAGER   2/88 – 2/89
Chemical Bank of New Jersey, N.A., Marlton, New Jersey
- Managed daily operation of branch office
- Performed outside sales efforts and planned marketing strategies
- Directed all inside sales promotions
- Conducted cross-training for branch employees
- Approved consumer loan requests
- Supervised staff and produced monthly management reports

MANAGEMENT TRAINEE   5/86 – 2/88
Chemical Bank of New Jersey, N.A., Oaklyn, New Jersey
- Performed all assistant management duties, including joint sales calls
- Troubleshooter for various branch locations and departments

BANK TELLER   1984 – 1986
United Jersey Bank, Cinnaminson, New Jersey

EDUCATION   **B.A. BUSINESS ADMINISTRATION**   1989
Rutgers University, Camden, New Jersey
- Course work concentrations in Management and Business Law
- Group leader, marketing project – developed, authored, and presented strategic marketing decisions for a national corporation

INTERESTS   Horseback riding, reading, traveling

45

Current Address
Jl. Bukit Tamanang
Jakarta Selatan, Indonesia 12345
Phone 555-1234

Stewart J. Baroid

Permanent Address
1234 East Fifth Street
Duluth, Minnesota 55812, U.S.A.
Phone (218) 555-1234

EDUCATION	<u>**Master of International Management**</u> GPA 3.5/4.0	*12/94*
	American Graduate School of International Management (Thunderbird)	*Glendale, Arizona*

<u>**Bachelor of Science, Economics**</u>   *6/87*
University of Utah   *Salt Lake City, Utah*

TRAINING & SEMINARS

- International Trade Conference, University of Wisconsin, 2/18/93, Superior, WI
- International Marketing Seminar, Minnesota World Trade Association, 11/10/92, Minneapolis, MN
- 1992 ASEAN Ambassadors' Tour, U.S.-ASEAN Council, 10/23/92, Minneapolis, MN
- A Briefing on Indonesia, American Indonesian Chamber of Commerce, 9/22/92, Washington, DC
- Various Technical Training Programs, NL Baroid, 1983–1986, U.S.A. & Indonesia
- Certificate, Management Development Program in Export Trade Development, 5/81, University of Utah

EXPERIENCE

Part-Time Assistant   *12/91 – 12/94, Duluth, Minnesota*
- Set up software system and database for an import-export business. Assist in maintaining accounting, financial, and inventory records.

<u>**Pacific Consultants International**</u> – Japan's second largest private civil engineering consulting firm; a leader among top international design firms.

Consultant   *8/91; Jakarta, Indonesia*
- Determined office and computer needs for 250 new employees. Scheduled the data processing of five million national survey samples. Analyzed work flow and productivity of 40 employees.

Project Analyst   *9/86 – 5/89; Jakarta, Indonesia*
- Conducted financial and economic feasibility analyses of business development proposals and infrastructure projects financed by the Japan International Cooperation Agency and the World Bank ($1.3 billion).
- Integrated the work of many multinational consultants using spreadsheet models and macros, which increased efficiency, accuracy, and clarity.
- Assisted in project management and improved relations with World Bank and Indonesian government.

<u>**P.T. Baroid Indonesia**</u> – Joint venture of NL Baroid, a division of NL Industries, Inc. – a Fortune 500 petroleum services, chemical and equipment company; a leader in the petroleum services industry.

Sales and Service Engineer   *6/83 – 8/86; Jakarta, Indonesia*
- Promoted and sold specialty chemicals, fluids, and services to multinational oil and gas companies throughout Indonesia.
- Directed, supervised, and coordinated fluid formulation and usage. Tested and maintained fluid to minimize clients' operating costs, maximize oil and gas production, and ensure safety.
- Developed and presented a training seminar for a major client.
- Revised Standard Operating Procedures for Baroid's laboratory, resulting in reduced costs and improved operations.
- Performed in top 10% of more than 50 senior colleagues.
- Finished at top of initial three-month training program in Houston, Texas.

COMPUTERS   Experienced with IBM PCs and Lotus 1-2-3, SuperCalc, WordStar, and WordPerfect

LANGUAGES   **Indonesian** – highly proficient   ◆   **Malay** – proficient   ◆   **Spanish** – strong foundation

MEMBERSHIPS   Minnesota World Trade Association   ◆   American Indonesian Chamber of Commerce

VOLUNTEER EXPERIENCE

<u>**American Field Service**</u>, *Group Leader*   *6/76; 7/77 – 8/77, Central Java & Kalimantan, Indonesia*
- Supervised and led a group of fellow international high school students in public meetings, cultural activities, and community projects. Was spokesman, interpreter, and liaison for all public activities.

PETER B. OSAKA

12345 Cavalry Drive
Fairfax, Virginia 22030
(703) 555-1234

JAPANESE-SPEAKING PRODUCT MANAGER with broad experience in planning and product management at Ford Motor Company and Inter-Tel, Inc., a software intensive telecommunications company. Highly experienced in Japan-U.S. new business coordination. Lived in Japan five years; reads, writes, speaks fluent Japanese. International M.B.A. Highly computer literate, familiar with voice/data communications, networking, UNIX, C.

EXPERIENCE	**INTER-TEL, INC., Product Manager, Asian Region**	
	Corporate Headquarters, Chandler, Arizona	1989 – Present
	Inter-Tel, Japan, Tokyo, Japan	May – Oct. 1989

- Responsible for start-up, sales, and support of $2,000,000 Japanese key telephone project for Teleway Japan and Canon
- Established Inter-Tel office in Tokyo, Japan
- Interfaced with Japanese customers and Inter-Tel's C and 68000 assembly language programmers for host computer download
- Investigated new markets for Inter-Tel IBM PC-based, 600 port ISDN PABX, key telephone systems, and voice mail
- Interfaced with management and engineering on international telecommunication market trends, system revisions, system approvals
- Trained by Inter-Tel in telecom sales, PABX/PC market trends, peripheral device sales, ISDN concepts

	FORD MOTOR COMPANY, Product Engineer	
	Plastic Products Division (PPD), Dearborn, Michigan	1985 – 1987
	PPD Far East Office, Hiroshima, Japan	1984 – 1985

- Worked directly with PPD top management on advanced planning, purchasing, sourcing, and engineering for first Mazda project
- Coordinated establishment of PPD tech office in Hiroshima
- Identified communication problems; saved engineering and tooling costs of $500,000
- Returned to U.S. in October 1985 to follow PPD JIT program supplying instrument panels and consoles to Mazda's Flat Rock, Michigan assembly plant
- Trained by Ford in Total Quality Control, JIT, SPC, CAD

JAPAN LIFE PLAN ASSOCIATION, Tokyo, Japan, Salesman   1983

- Marketed English tape systems to Japanese businesspeople. All sales and transactions in Japanese

TEIJIN INC., Osaka, Japan, Translator/Language Coordinator   1980 – 1983

- Translated technical material from Japanese to English. Major translations in electronic product development

EDUCATION	**MASTER OF INTERNATIONAL MANAGEMENT**	1988
	American Graduate School of International Management	
	Thunderbird Campus, Glendale, Arizona	

- Concentration in technical product marketing
- Major research papers on business computer systems, networking, and computer hardware/software

BACHELOR OF FINE ARTS   1980
Parson's School of Design, New York City, New York

- Concentration in product design

HENRY LAURENS, III

1 Rivers Avenue
Laurens, South Carolina 29123
Telephone: (803) 555-1234

OBJECTIVE   A training or technician's position within the aerospace industry

EXPERIENCE

UNITED STATES AIR FORCE   1982 – Present

F-15 Maintenance Instructor   1988 – Present
- Developed lesson plans and taught classes in Cross-Country Piloting, Supervisory Management, Forms Documentation (CAMS), Phase III & IV F-15A&E (APG, Pneudraulics, Engines), Engine Run, and related systems
- Achieved 7-level with five years of experience on the F-15 aircraft, including A,B,D, and E models

Crew Chief   1984 – 1992
- Launched and recovered F-15 aircraft, including towing, jacking, ground handling, engine runs, and preflight, thruflight and postflight inspections
- Diagnosed and solved maintenance problems of pneudraulic, electrical, powerplant, auxiliary power unit, environmental systems, oxygen, fuel, and related aircraft systems
- Determined requirements for parts, clearances, tolerances, fuel leaks, corrosion, tire wear, skin damage, cracks, and performance of aircraft systems
- Troubleshot, repaired, serviced, and modified tactical aircraft, components, systems, and related equipment (including aircraft structures, landing gear, flight surfaces and controls, anti-icing, ventilation and heating systems)
- Served as flight chief on many occasions, coordinating and adjusting daily maintenance plans to meet operational commitments
- Trained and supervised subordinates in all aspects of aircraft maintenance
- Commended for maintaining aircraft at a mission capable rate of 89 percent, 6 percent above the TAC standard
- Selected as instructor to teach in-shelter hot pit operation and external fuel tank installation
- Performed flight line duties on F-4E, F-4G, and T-37 aircraft for 2½ years

EDUCATION

FAA AIRFRAME & POWER PLANT LICENSE   March 1992
Embry-Riddle Aeronautical University, Luke AFB, Arizona

ASSOCIATE DEGREE IN AIRCRAFT MAINTENANCE TECHNOLOGY   Nearing
Community College of the Air Force – 50 credit hours   Completion

TECHNICAL TRAINING

F-15E Engine Run Certification/Trim Pad (68 hours)	1991
Pneudraulic System Technician (F-15) Course (76 hours)	1989
Phase III (ENG) Maintenance Qualification Training (136 hours)	1989
Jet Engine Technician (F-15) Course (73 hours)	1989
Dedicated Crew Chief Program (40 hours)	1988
NCO Leadership School (Management Training)	1987
Tactical Aircraft Maintenance Specialist Course (93 hours)	1987
Aircraft Maintenance Technician (F/RF-4 Supervisor) Familiarization (36 hours)	1984
Phase III (F-4 Phantom II) Qualification Program (120 hours)	1984
Aircraft Maintenance Specialist Course (150 hours)	1982

HONORS & AWARDS
- Honorable Discharge from the U.S. Air Force
- Two Air Force Good Conduct Medals
- Suggestion Award – Prevented Possible Damage to Equipment/Personnel
- Training Management Division NCO of the Quarter
- Commendation from the Northern European Command for Outstanding Maintenance Support at Karup Airbase, Denmark

Emma C. Jacobson

1234 N. 99th Avenue #1234
Peoria, Arizona 85345
(602) 555-1234

Dynamic, results-oriented problem solver offers highly refined leadership skills; management, marketing, credit and collections expertise; and a commitment to accuracy and effectiveness for a progressive, quality-driven organization.

SUMMARY OF QUALIFICATIONS

- *More than 18 years of office and property management experience*
- *Background in marketing, sales, credit, collections, and supervision*
- *Effective communicator; demonstrated ability to interact well with all levels of personnel*
- *Self-starter; goal-oriented problem solver with strong organizational skills*

PROFESSIONAL EXPERIENCE

5/90 – 1/95　　**AMERICAN EXPRESS – TRS**, *Phoenix, Arizona*
CREDIT ANALYST
Evaluated credit limits, collected 30/60 day monies and return checks. Position involved constant customer interfacing. Operated computerized bank card system. Member of Pacing Team to improve customer relations and implement cost-reduction strategies.

10/88 – 2/90　　**REPUBLIC MANAGEMENT**, *Tempe, Arizona*
BUSINESS MANAGER (128 Units)
Supervised maintenance and office staff, inspected property, scheduled vendors, collected rents, and handled delinquencies, accounts payable, accounts receivable, end-of-month and owner reports. Heavy use of public relations, marketing, and leasing skills.

8/86 – 6/88　　**JACOBSON'S DEPARTMENT STORE**, *Tampa, Florida*
OFFICE MANAGER
Balanced cash and special accounts, operated computer, and ordered supplies. Scheduled personnel and supervised 10-12 employees.

7/83 – 7/86　　**HAVATAMPA ELI WITT CREDIT UNION**, *Tampa, Florida*
MANAGER
Overall responsibility for bookkeeping, including cash and journal, general ledger, trial balance, and financial statements. Interviewed, hired, and trained new employees. Managed collections.

8/82 – 7/83　　**PINECREST MANOR APARTMENTS**, *Ft. Lauderdale, Florida*
ASSISTANT MANAGER / BOOKKEEPER / LEASING AGENT
(Florida Real Estate License)
Assisted in the management of 323-unit apartment complex and supervised 15 people.

Nyja N. Marques

1234 Friars Road, Apt. #12, San Diego, California 92108   (619) 555-1234

QUALIFICATIONS	• Experienced in freight movement and export processes • Demonstrate strong and recognized marketing foundation • Experienced problem solver, meeting customer satisfaction • Formal (professional) and informal (conversational) Spanish	

EDUCATION

MASTER OF INTERNATIONAL MANAGEMENT   May 1994
American Graduate School of International Management
Thunderbird Campus, Glendale, Arizona
• Thunderbird Scholarship, Fall 1992, Spring 1993 and 1994   *GPA 3.88*
• *Courses: Export/Import Management, Cross-Cultural Communications, Regional Business Environment – Latin America*

BACHELOR OF SCIENCE, BUSINESS ADMINISTRATION   *cum laude*   May 1992
Georgetown University, Washington, D.C.
• Double Major: Marketing and International Management
• Shandwick PLC Marketing Scholar Award, May 1992   *GPA 3.65*
• *Courses: International Marketing Management, Marketing Research, Consumer Behavior, Channels of Distribution*

EXPERIENCE

IBM, International Purchasing Office & Distribution Center, Boulder, Colorado   1993
Export Assistant/Intern
• Reduced European and Canadian problem export shipments by 87% and 93%, respectively, decreasing audit exposure and increasing customer satisfaction
• Actively participated in new freight forwarder selection from negotiation to contract implementation
• Coordinated one-week training program for 20 freight forwarders and export coordinators, developing training manuals, preparing facilities, and scheduling sessions, facilitating a successful contract change
• Calculated measurements of freight movement process used for management review and decision making

CIPRA, Central American Scholarship Program, Washington, D.C.   1991–1992
Intern
• Analyzed financial reports (mostly in Spanish) of eight foreign branches and assessed budgetary conflicts
• Researched feasibility of expansion into Nicaragua
• Helping to secure a USAID grant
• Coordinated travel of over 400 foreign nationals traveling from the United States to over 10 Latin American and Caribbean countries
• Produced report of donations received by ten overseas branches in FY91, classifying items and making proper currency conversions

GEORGETOWN UNIVERSITY, Athletic Department, Washington, D.C.   1988–1992
Team Manager
• Supported media relations and produced press releases
• Developed system to organize and maintain files of prospective athletes
• Supervised game staff and calculated statistics for departmental records

LANGUAGE   **Spanish:** Proficient • **German:** Working Knowledge

COMPUTERS   Highly proficient in WordPerfect, Lotus 1-2-3, Harvard Graphics, FoxPro

50

DEBRA LYNN VECTOR

EXPERIENCE

INTERNATIONAL CORPORATE MARKETING CONSULTANT　　　　　2/95 – 5/95
DowBrands, Consumer Marketing Workshop, Thunderbird Campus
- Developed comprehensive market entry strategy for consumer goods products in Mexico
- Analyzed competition, conducted consumer surveys, formulated all aspects of marketing mix

INTERNATIONAL MARKETING INTERN·　　　　　2/95 – 5/95
SmartPractice, Phoenix, Arizona
- Evaluated five European countries for export market potential in the dental supply industry
- Assisted in development and launch of a direct mail catalog for U.K. dental professionals
- Surveyed dental professionals and patients regarding product acceptability

FINANCIAL ANALYST　　　　　2/92 – 5/94
General Dynamics, Rancho Cucamonga, California
- Forecasted expenditures and developed annual overhead budgets valued at $25 million
- Prepared and presented comprehensive monthly financial performance summaries

ASSISTANT SALES MANAGER　　　　　8/90 – 2/92
The Oak Trunk, Crestline, California
- Implemented national promotional strategy and assisted in control of $200K inventory
- Managed point-of-sale merchandising systems
- Supervised 20 support personnel and conducted new employee training
- Contracted with sales representatives to feature selected merchandise

SALES REPRESENTATIVE　　　　　5/89 – 8/89
Vector Marketing Services, Riverside, California
- Designed, implemented, and evaluated a hands-on regional sales campaign for CUTCO, a U.S. manufacturer of consumer cutlery products
- Generated additional sales revenue of $9,000 for a 3-month period
- Developed public relations skills through in-home product demonstrations and follow-up customer service to a network of 600 customers

EDUCATION

MASTER OF INTERNATIONAL MANAGEMENT　　　GPA: 3.7　　　　　5/95
Thunderbird, American Graduate School of International Management, Glendale, Arizona
Emphasis: International Consumer Marketing
- Researched and presented a marketing plan for ugosito fruit juice in Venezuela
- Conducted comparative market research of leading brands within the frozen pizza market
- Opened distribution channel and completed documentation to export Indian jewelry to Finland

BACHELOR OF SCIENCE　　　GPA: 3.6　　　　　3/93
California State University, San Bernardino
Major: International Business　　　　　Minor: French

FOREIGN STUDY
Institute of French Studies for Foreign Students, Aix-Marseilles, France　　　8/89 – 5/90
American Field Service, one-year exchange program to Finland　　　8/86 – 5/87

SKILLS

French: Highly Proficient　•　**Finnish:** Working Knowledge　•　**Spanish:** Knowledge

ACTIVITIES
- External Marketing Committee, Thunderbird
- Assistant Director, Intramural Sports, Thunderbird
- NCAA III Intercollegiate Women's Volleyball, California State University

AWARDS
- Scholarship Recipient, Thunderbird, 1994
- Scholarship Recognition Awards, California State University, 1991 and 1992
- Scholarship Key Award, Alpha Kappa Psi, 1991

Current Address　•　123 N.E. 152nd Circle, Vancouver, Washington 98686　•　(206) 555-1234
Permanent Address　•　P. O. Box 1234, Crest Butte, California 92325　•　(714) 555-1234

MELINDA M. BOWEN

EDUCATION	**American Graduate School of International Management** **Thunderbird Campus**, Glendale, Arizona Master of International Management: Concentration in Finance – GPA 3.7 Thunderbird Scholarship Recipient Teaching Assistant for Finance	May 1995
	University Autónoma de Guadalajara, Mexico Thunderbird exchange program – Completed courses in business, politics, culture, and environment in Mexico and lived with a Mexican family	Summer 1994
	Colgate University, Hamilton, New York B.A. in International Relations	May 1990
	American College of Switzerland, Leysin, Switzerland	Fall 1986
EXPERIENCE	**CALLAN ASSOCIATES INC.**, New York, New York **Marketing Assistant, Manager Services Division** • Responsible for primary client management for 80+ international and domestic money managers, assisted senior consultants with account servicing and prospecting activities • Coordinated and produced quantitative analyses and portfolio evaluations for international and domestic prospects and clients • Developed customized marketing exhibits and sales presentations for in-house consultants and client money managers	8/92 – 12/93
	PRUDENTIAL-BACHE SECURITIES, New York, New York **Associate Marketing Coordinator, Financial Services Division** • Marketed Managed Assets Consulting Services to Prudential-Bache account executives, conducted MACS training seminars in three western regions, increasing sales by 85% after promotional program • Created regional newsletters and wrote bimonthly articles for national Prudential-Bache's sales publication, addressing MACS program developments and highlights	3/91 – 6/92
	PRUDENTIAL-BACHE SECURITIES, New York, New York **Marketing Assistant, Joint Marketing and Sales Department** • Developed and maintained professional relationships with Prudential representatives and Prudential-Bache account executives in 17 states • Helped to establish new business opportunities between intra-company sales units	6/90 – 2/91
LANGUAGES	Proficient in **Spanish**	
LICENSES	Series 7 and 63 – Brokerage and New York State	
COMPUTERS	MS-DOS, Lotus Freelance, Harvard Graphics, Lotus 1-2-3, WordPerfect 5.1	
ACTIVITIES & INTERESTS	• Student Development Committee, Toastmasters, Latin American Club • Head coach for women's ice hockey team in New York City • Class alumni coordinator for Colgate's annual fund-raising campaigns • Colgate's Varsity Lacrosse and Club Ice Hockey teams • Golf, tennis, jogging, watercoloring, reading, and traveling	
ADDRESS	123 Prince Avenue, Princeton, New Jersey 08540	(609) 555-1234

CAROLYN R. MONITOR

OBJECTIVE

A challenging position in marketing management that would utilize my organizational, human relations, and linguistic/cultural skills to successfully meet corporate objectives

EXPERIENCE

Export

ASSISTANT EXPORT COORDINATOR   1993 – Present
IBM Corporation, Boulder, Colorado
International Purchasing Office & Distribution Center (IPODC)
- Developed procedures for export processes based on corporate audit recommendations
- Implemented measurements and controls to safeguard key processes against audit exposures
- Designed training manuals for IPODC export coordinators, supplier country coordinators, and export agents
- Monitored and authorized the movement of "immediate dispatch" freight
- Created and distributed a survey to measure the quality of our suppliers, which ensured excellent service to our international clients
- Participated in IBM classes sponsored by the World Trade Institute

Import/Export

EXPORT INTERN   1990
Business & Industry Center, Fredonia, New York
- Worked closely with government agencies to provide local businesses with import and export information, education, and marketing assistance
- Conducted import/export product research
- Utilized research findings to assist businesses in locating the best foreign market for their products

Sales/Marketing

MARKETING AND SALES REPRESENTATIVE   1988
Concepts, Amherst, New York
- Developed innovative methods to sell a diversified portfolio of products
- Built awareness of this portfolio through personal sales and telemarketing

Management

FRONT END MANAGER   1985 – 1987
Bells Supermarket, Cheektowaga, New York
- Acted as a liaison with the general public and the corporation
- Supervised the daily performance of approximately 10 employees

INTERNATIONAL EXPERIENCE

TRAINING DIRECTOR   1989
L'Amanguier, Paris, France
- Directed and supervised a restaurant staff of 5
- Mastered the French language through daily business transactions

EDUCATION

MASTER OF INTERNATIONAL MANAGEMENT   Dec. 1993
American Graduate School of International Management
Thunderbird Campus, Glendale, Arizona
Tripartite Focus: International Marketing, European Studies, and French/German Languages

BACHELOR OF SCIENCE   *cum laude*   May 1991
State University of New York at Fredonia
Major: Business Administration with concentration in International Business
Minors: Economics and French

COMPUTERS

Lotus 1-2-3, dBASE, BASIC, WordPerfect, Script/GML, Bookmaster, Xedit, MDQMS

ADDRESS   123 Cornice Avenue, New York, New York 14226   (716) 555-1234

KURT R. JAMES

OBJECTIVE   To enter a lifelong career that is challenging and fulfilling

EXPERIENCE   **BERLITZ SCHOOL OF LANGUAGES**, Osaka, Japan
English Instructor
January 1987 – Present
- Taught company classes
- Assisted in product development

TARGET MARKETING CO-OP, San Francisco, California
Sales and Customer Service Representative
March 1986 – October 1986
- Acquired new accounts for this direct mail company
- Serviced house accounts
- Designed and laid out advertisements

JAMES BROTHERS, Boulder, Colorado
Owner and Manager
1981 – 1986
- Construction subcontractor
- Responsible for accounting, contract negotiation, advertising, and supervision of labor

TENNIS & SWIMMING INSTRUCTOR, Boulder, Colorado
Pre-1981

EDUCATION   **AMERICAN GRADUATE SCHOOL OF INTERNATIONAL MANAGEMENT**
Thunderbird Campus, Glendale, Arizona
Master of International Management
May 1992

INSTITUTE FOR INTERNATIONAL STUDIES AND TRAINING, Fujinomya, Japan
Intensive study of Japanese language and business practices
Summer 1991

UNIVERSITY OF COLORADO, Boulder, Colorado
Bachelor of Arts in International Relations
1979–1984

UNIVERSITY OF VERA CRUZ, Mexico
Study Abroad Program
1982

JONES REAL ESTATE COLLEGE, Fort Collins, Colorado
Real Estate Sales License

LANGUAGES   Fluent in *English* • Proficient in *Japanese* • Knowledge of *Spanish*

ACHIEVEMENTS
- Bicycle tour of Europe (3,000 miles solo)
- Representative to Model United Nations, New York – Finance Committee
- Winner of the prestigious annual "Little Johnny" Award from the *Denver Post* as outstanding junior tennis player in Colorado

INTERESTS   Triathlon, running (1983 Denver Marathon), basketball, cooking

1234 Caribbean • Glendale, Arizona 85306 • (602) 555-1234

CHRISTOPHER J. DOLIBOIS

OBJECTIVE

An internship in a multinational corporation that will allow me to improve and build my understanding of international marketing and sales

EDUCATION

MASTER OF INTERNATIONAL MANAGEMENT   *May 1995*
American Graduate School of International Management
Thunderbird Campus, Glendale, Arizona
Emphasis on Marketing in Europe

BACHELOR OF SCIENCE IN BUSINESS ADMINISTRATION   *August 1993*
Miami University, Oxford, Ohio
Major Area of Concentration: Business Economics
Minor: International Marketing

SPECIALIZED COURSES

SEMESTER ABROAD   *Spring 1992*
John E. Dolibois Center in Luxembourg
❖ AIESEC – Luxembourg
❖ Economic survey and field studies of modern Europe

EXPERIENCE

LANDSCAPING BUSINESS   *1994*
Owner
❖ Hired, trained, and supervised employees

MIAMI UNIVERSITY, INTERNATIONAL PROGRAMS   *Summer 1993*
Assistant to the Director
❖ Assisted foreign students
❖ General office duties

J. K. HEIDRICH, Cincinnati, Ohio   *Summer 1992*
General Maintenance
❖ Coordinated ground management of estate

CITY OF CINCINNATI, Cincinnati, Ohio   *Summers 1990 – 1991*
Municipal Facility Worker
❖ Planned events and meetings for conventions

LANGUAGE

Working knowledge of French

COMPUTERS

Experience on Apple and IBM personal computers
Knowledge of WordPerfect, Lotus 1-2-3, Microsoft Word

ACTIVITIES

French Club, Campus Ambassadors
Intramural Basketball and Softball

INTERESTS

Travel in Europe, 20th Century History, Baseball

Current Address:
P.O. Box 1234
Glendale, Arizona 85306
(602) 555-1234

Permanent Address:
1234 Michigan Avenue
Cincinnati, Ohio 45208
(513) 555-1234

PATRICK H. BRINKER

OBJECTIVE   A career in sales/marketing utilizing my communication skills and leadership qualities

EDUCATION

MASTER OF INTERNATIONAL MANAGEMENT   Dec. 1994
American Graduate School of International Management
Thunderbird Campus, Glendale, Arizona
- Summer semester in Mexico (1993) at *Universidad Autonoma de Guadalajara*
- Summer semester in France (1994) at *Eurocentres*
- Winter semester in Costa Rica and Nicaragua (1993/1994)

BACHELOR OF BUSINESS ADMINISTRATION   GPA 3.4   1989 – 1992
University of Miami, Coral Gables, Florida
- Triple major in Marketing, Management, and Entrepreneurship
- Dean's List 3 semesters

EXPERIENCE

COMMERZBANK AG, Germany   Spring 1994
Intern – Full-Time Paid
- Import and export department
- Branch office Düsseldorf

GEDANKO FINE ARTS BV   1990 – 1994
Salesman
- Initiated and set up contacts for art dealership while in Miami and Mexico and worked part-time in an art gallery in Paris (Summer 1994)
- Facilitated the buying and selling of paintings

DUTCH ARMY   1988 – 1989
Reserve Officer
- Served in NATO, stationed in Germany
- Supervised personnel and organized maneuvers
- Received various awards

AERAMPHIC BV   1987 – 1988
Salesman
- Sold and promoted pharmaceutical products in The Netherlands and the United Kingdom
- Increased sales by 18% in the U.K.
- Assisted in packaging and processing medical products

LANGUAGES   Fluent in Dutch, English, and German • Proficient in Spanish and French

CITIZENSHIP & TRAVEL   Citizen of The Netherlands; EC Passport
Lived in The Netherlands, Spain, Indonesia, Brazil, United Kingdom, Germany, the United States, Mexico, and France and further traveled to many other countries

PROFESSIONAL MEMBERSHIPS   American Marketing Association, Executive Vice President
University of Miami Chapter – Award of Excellence

HONORS   Selected for a Rotary Scholarship to study one year abroad towards an MBA

SPECIAL SKILLS & SPORTS   Private Pilot working toward Instruments License – Rescue Scuba Diver – Sky Diver
Soccer, Tennis, Squash, Golf, Rugby, and Triathlon

ADDRESSES

Present:	P.O. Box 123, Glendale, Arizona 85306	(602) 555-1234
U.S. Residence:	1234 Bricker Avenue #123, Miami, Florida 33129	(305) 555-1234
Permanent:	Hilversumseweg 1, 1234 Larsen, The Netherlands	31-555-1234

56

MARIA E. McLANE

OBJECTIVE	A growth-oriented position in Marketing leading to a career in Product Management

QUALIFICATIONS

- Advanced Degree in International Management
- Demonstrated Entrepreneurial Leadership Capabilities
- Supervised and Managed Large Group in Complex, Stressful Projects
- Mastered Technical Detail of Industrial Equipment and Products

INTERNSHIPS

INTERNATIONAL TRADE SPECIALIST   Sept. – Dec. 1994
U.S. Department of Commerce
International Trade Administration, Phoenix, Arizona

- Directly consulted clients in developing marketing research for exporting ventures
- Coordinated marketing plan for overseas trade show in Hong Kong and Singapore for potential joint ventures and partnerships
- Resourced foreign market research information for clients interested in exporting

CORPORATE CONSULTANT   Sept. – Dec. 1994
Corporate Consulting Program
Ausco Hydraulic Brakes, Benton Harbor, Michigan

- Developed and implemented market research for feasibility of product distribution in Mexico
- Directed analysis for optimum market-entry strategy
- Presented marketing plan and consulted client with strategy implementation

EXPERIENCE

PURCHASING AGENT   1992 – 1993
Victory Wholesale Grocers, Boca Raton, Florida

- Managed purchasing in six-state area
- Designed and implemented Investment Buying Programs
- Negotiated contracts generating $300,000 profit

DRY GROCERY BUYER/MERCHANDISER   1991 – 1992
McLane Suneast Grocery Wholesale, Poinciana, Florida

- Maintained 98% service level for 2,500 item inventory
- Designed and implemented Forward Buying Program that generated $250,000 profit
- Merchandised new product lines in trade shows

EDUCATION

MASTER OF INTERNATIONAL MANAGEMENT   Dec. 1994
American Graduate School of International Management
Thunderbird Campus, Glendale, Arizona

SUMMER FOREIGN STUDIES PROGRAM – SPAIN   Summer 1991
Towson State University, Maryland
Madrid Campus, Spain

BACHELOR OF BUSINESS ADMINISTRATION   May 1991
MINOR IN SPANISH
Stetson University, Deland, Florida

LANGUAGES   **Spanish:**   Bilingual fluency

ADDRESSES

Current:	Permanent:
12345 N. 59th Ave. #123	1234 Shady Lake Lane
Glendale, Arizona 85306	Lakeland, Florida 33813
(602) 555-1234	(813) 555-1234

WILLIAM J. TIMONIUM, JR.

QUALIFICATIONS
- Advanced degree in international management
- Specialization in finance
- Five years military office and supervisory experience

EDUCATION

MASTER OF INTERNATIONAL MANAGEMENT   Aug. 1995
American Graduate School of International Management
Thunderbird Campus, Glendale, Arizona
Relevant Course Work:

- International Finance & Trade
- Money, Banking & Financial Markets
- Financial Statement Analysis
- International Banking
- International Securities Investment
- Advanced Corporate Finance
  - Conducted corporate capital structure budgeting and cash flow analyses
- Multinational Corporate Finance
- Advanced Financial Accounting
- International Marketing Management
- International Marketing Research
  - Planned and designed international market research studies
- International Consumer Marketing
- Business-to-Business Marketing
- Advanced Business Russian Language
- Doing Business In Eastern Europe and Russia
- Negotiation and Countertrade
- GPA 3.7

BOSTON UNIVERSITY, Berlin, Germany   1989 – 1991
- Graduate studies in International Relations (21 hours)

BACHELOR OF ARTS   1987
University of Maryland, College Park Campus
- Major: Political Science with Specialization in International Economics
- Minor: Psychology and Russian

Self-financed 100% of undergraduate and 75% of graduate education

EXPERIENCE

HERITAGE FOUNDATION, Washington, D.C.   1992 – 1994
Intern, Foreign Policy Department, Office of Russian Studies
- Research current economic and political trends in Russia
- Translate Russian publications to aid in research
- Prepare and arrange seminars and presentations

U.S. ARMY FIELD STATION, Berlin, Germany   1987 – 1992
Russian/English Interpreter, Intelligence Analyst
- Supervised an office of 15 translators and interpreters
- Quality controller in National Security Agency Foreign Office
- Received Top Secret/Codeword Security Clearance
- Produced, edited, and analyzed final product intelligence reports
- Operated a multimillion dollar transcription computer system
- Worked closely with European NATO intelligence agencies

LANGUAGE SKILLS
Highly proficient in **Russian**
Working knowledge of **German**

ACTIVITIES & HONORS
Alpha Tau Omega Fraternity – Treasurer
Russian Club Member – Thunderbird
Teaching Assistant – International Finance & Trade
Association of the Army Award for Academic Excellence
Lacrosse Half Scholarship – undergraduate

ADDRESS   123 Burning Fence Road, Baltimore, Maryland 21093   (410) 555-1234

5 HEADINGS TO DEFINE YOUR SECTIONS

Headings are one of the major design elements of a resume. How you choose to divide sections determines the readability of the resume. Graphic lines and/or white space help define groups of like information and draw the reader's eyes down the page.

Since people read from the top to the bottom and from left to right, begin your resume with the most important information. Then work your way down.

So, which section goes first? Should it be education or experience? Start with the section that contains your strongest qualifications for the job you would like to have. If you have had little experience in your prospective field, but have a degree that qualifies you for a starting position in the industry, then by all means list your education first. Most people eventually move their education below their experience as they get further from their school days.

There are two basic positions for your headings. One is centered (pages 62–66) with or without lines, and the other is left justified (pages 67–76). Which style you choose depends on your personality. There is no right or wrong way. Some of your options include:

- All caps (page 61, 73)
- Small caps (pages 63, 72)
- Upper/lower case (pages 62, 64, 67, 75, 76)
- All lower case (page 74)
- Very large fonts (page 69)
- Underlines (pages 66, 70)
- Reverse boxes (page 68)
- Special headline fonts (pages 65, 71)

The same idea goes for information within each section. For instance, if you went to an Ivy League school, you can list the school before the degree. Look at the difference in emphasis between these two methods:

HARVARD, Cambridge, Massachusetts
Master of Business Administration

MASTER OF BUSINESS ADMINISTRATION
Little Known College, Backwoods, Idaho

59

The same principle applies to your experience. If your job title is more impressive than where you worked, then list it first.

ASSISTANT EXPORT COORDINATOR
IBM Corporation, Boulder, Colorado

IBM CORPORATION, Boulder, Colorado
Assistant Export Coordinator

Avoid the use of underlining since it cuts into the descenders in lower case letters. For example, notice the "p" in:

<u>**Assistant Export Coordinator**</u>

It is acceptable to use underlining when the letters are all capitalized since there are no descenders:

<u>**ASSISTANT EXPORT COORDINATOR**</u>

Italics, **bold**, ALL CAPITALS, and FIRST LETTER LARGER are all good ways to make certain information stand out within the text. You will notice the bolding of foreign languages on a few of these resumes, since the ability to speak those languages was very important to the person's objective. However, it can be overdone very easily. To make them more effective, use these type treatments sparingly.

BRUCE TECHNICAL SALES

1234 W. Aster Drive
Peoria, Arizona 85381
(602) 555-1234

PROFESSIONAL OBJECTIVE:

A career in sales/marketing that will provide a variety of customer relation settings and challenges. My goal is to progress to a management position in a corporation with $25 million or more in sales.

WORK EXPERIENCE:

Technical Sales Representative, Spencer Fluid Power, Phoenix, Arizona
Sold and serviced hydraulic motors, pumps, and valves as components. In addition, designed systems and power units. Developed new accounts for a new branch office in the Southwest. Responsible for customers in New Mexico and Arizona. (April 1992 – Present)

Technical Sales Representative, R.D. Playman Company, Phoenix, Arizona
(May 1991 – April 1992)

Sales Representative, Chas. D. Jones Co., Phoenix, Arizona
Sold and serviced electronic controls, recorders, and sensors to industrial/commercial customers throughout Arizona. Developed monthly plans to increase sales and deepen market penetration. Asset responsibilities included demonstration equipment and company car. (September 1990 – March 1991)

Territory Manager, Air-Draulics Co., Phoenix, Arizona
Service and sales to over 200 user, O.E.M., and resale accounts were my primary tasks. Was also responsible for utility company and municipal accounts. Sold pumps, cylinders, valves, and hose as components in addition to involvement with design of systems/power units. Developed weekly and annual plans to increase sales, improve service, and deepen customer relations. Asset responsibilities included company car, expense account, and selling samples. (August 1985 – September 1990)

District Sales Manager, Gates Rubber Co., Denver, Colorado
Responsible for a sales territory tracking at $1.5 million annually. Securing orders and being awarded advance product approval on specifications were the primary tasks. This position required overnight travel across Arizona and to El Paso, Texas. Other responsibilities included trouble shooting existing applications for the end user, making joint sales calls with distributor sales people on major end users, designing and recommending new belt drives for industrial accounts, and scheduling deliveries of product on a contract basis. (April 1984 – August 1985)

Account Executive, Air Couriers International, Phoenix, Arizona
Developed new accounts and serviced existing customers in the electronic and industrial markets. The service consisted primarily of 5-15 hour package delivery nationwide. (July 1983 – April 1984)

District Sales Manager, Rognlien, Nix, and Pickrel, Inc., Los Angeles, California
Responsibilities included servicing over 100 accounts in southern Nevada and all of Arizona; training distributor sales force on product lines and their hands-on applications; and formulating plans for continued market penetration on a quarterly basis. Won quota buster trips to Hawaii two years in a row by selling safety equipment, industrial hose, O-rings, hydraulic fittings, adhesives, and other heavy-duty supplies to distributors, jobbers, and original equipment manufacturers. Worked with national and regional sales managers on a steady basis to develop key accounts throughout my territory. (January 1979 – January 1983)

EDUCATION:

- B.A. Degree, Business Management, University of Northern Iowa, Cedar Falls, Iowa, December 1978
- Final semester attended Arizona State University, Tempe, Arizona
- Dale Carnegie Sales Course Graduate, October 1981

Mark E. Hinckley

1234 West Crocus Drive • Phoenix, Arizona 85023 • (602) 555-1234

Overview

Enthusiastic and highly motivated self-starter with a proven record of success developing new markets while building and motivating results-oriented teams.

Prepared for a challenging opportunity where individual performance is recognized and making a significant contribution to the organization's marketing efforts is rewarded.

Strengths

Diversified management, training, technical, and sales background
Good listener, keen observer, and effective communicator
Skilled at setting priorities and achieving difficult objectives
People-oriented and sensitive to customer's needs
Well organized, personable, and results-oriented

Career Chronology

HINCKLEY & SCHMITT   1989 – Present
Route Salesman . . . Servicing over 600 customers with a variety of purified drinking water and related products. Responsibilities include customer service, accounts receivable, establishing new business and residential accounts.
- Currently ranked within the top 10% of the southwest zone in establishing new customer accounts. Earned Route Salesman of the Month three times and won three company trips.
- Achieved Hinckley & Schmitt's top pay bonus 45 out of 48 weeks.

BOYD'S COFFEE SERVICE   1988 – 1989
Service Representative . . . Serviced accounts with coffee and related products, introducing new products, maintaining and repairing a variety of equipment.
- Traveled the state servicing accounts while creating and selling new accounts and new products, resulting in significant growth in the company's bottom line.
- Drew on technical and analytical skills. Was able to diagnose and repair equipment failures rapidly, thereby maintaining customer relations.

PHOENIX GAZETTE   1982 – 1988
District Sales Manager . . . Experience managing five different districts, training over 100 new carriers, developing new districts, implementing new sales and service procedures, consistently reaching 100% of sales goal, motivating and supervising a sales force of 20–25 adult and youth carriers.
- Developed and implemented an incentive program for increasing subscriptions, expanding circulation, and improving customer service.
- Planned all direct sales and marketing programs for a district territory with over 1,300 subscriber accounts.

UNITED STATES AIR FORCE   1977 – 1981
Captain and Combat Crew Commander for the 66th Strategic Missile Squadron. Supervised over 100 people in day-to-day operations. Responsible for the $75 million Launch Control Facility.
- Position required qualifications in communication, crypto, computer operations, emergency life support, logistics, and command leadership and management skills.
- Selected to train and guide new officers and earned four highly qualified ratings in recognition for service.

Education

MASTER OF PUBLIC ADMINISTRATION DEGREE, University of South Dakota, 1981
BACHELOR OF SOCIAL SCIENCE DEGREE, Northern Arizona University, 1976

ROBERT H. LAARS

123 Whittaker Drive • Stratham, New Hampshire 03885 • (603) 555-1234

EMPLOYMENT HISTORY

CONTROLLER, Teledyne Laars, Rochester, New Hampshire . . . . 1989 to Present
Teledyne Laars is a $15MM division of Teledyne, Inc., a $3 billion conglomerate. Teledyne Laars/Rochester manufactures hot water boilers for domestic and hydronic heating for commercial and residential applications.

- Report to General Manager – dotted line to corporate office in Los Angeles.
- Responsible for financial and administrative operations, including cash management, financial analysis, financial statements, quarterly reviews, audit packs, tax packs, internal controls, profit plans, and financial presentations.

Accomplishments – Start Up:
- Member of the Executive Committee, which was responsible for the successful start-up operation of a new facility in Rochester, New Hampshire.
- Over the past 32 months, individually responsible for sourcing and implementing the following: office layout and furnishings; telephone system; security system; office equipment; conducting wage and benefit surveys, reviewing, recommending, and implementing same; recruiting and hiring office personnel; transferring machinery, equipment, and inventory from California and Oakville, Ontario.

Major Projects:
- Implemented procedures for financial controls, data processing, inventory control, and quality control.
- Conducted nine-month search, review, and recommendations for network computer system, successfully implemented in January 1991. Ongoing implementation of MRP.
- Implemented computer system supports: sales order entry, inventory control, AP, AR, GL, and financial statements. Network supports Harvard Graphics, WordPerfect, CAD System, and Lotus 1-2-3.

CONTROLLER, Teledyne Laars, Oakville, Ontario, Canada . . . . 1986 to 1989
Teledyne Laars/Oakville manufactured three product lines: swimming pool heaters, commercial and residential boilers.

- Responsible for all financial and administration functions of this company.
- In early 1989, a decision was made to move manufacturing operations to New Hampshire.

Accomplishments:
- Reduced accounting overtime by streamlining systems and procedures.
- Implemented cost-reduction program to reduce inventory and manufacturing, administrative, and marketing overhead.
- Improved financial visibility and awareness to management team through effective financial presentations and report writing.

CONTROLLER, B.D. Wait Co., Oakville, Ontario, Canada . . . . 1980 to 1986
B.D. Wait Co. was a $22 million, privately owned leading manufacturer of gas products, including gas barbecues, heaters, camping equipment, industrial heating equipment, and drum-type humidifiers.

- Responsible for all financial activity of the company, plus treasury duties, including bank negotiations for long-term debt, current line of credit, and international currency transactions.

Accomplishments:
- Researched, recommended, and implemented a Honeywell minicomputer system over a two-year period.
- Took the company from a completely manual system to computerized MRP, sales order entry, AP, AR, GL, and financial statements.
- Financial statement preparation was improved from manual quarterly statements prepared one month after the quarter to monthly statements prepared ten days after month end.
- Year-end audit was finalized six weeks after year end, compared to previous four months after year end.

EDUCATION

BACHELOR OF ARTS IN BUSINESS ADMINISTRATION AND ACCOUNTING (1978)
York University, Atkinson College, Toronto, Ontario, Canada

CONTINUING MANAGEMENT COURSES
Motivation, time management, credit management, total quality management (TQM), and Lotus 1-2-3

Joseph D. Mechanic

| 12345 North 11th Avenue | Phoenix, Arizona 85027 | (602) 555-1234 |

. . . . *Experience* . . . .

SENIOR REFRIGERATION SHOP MECHANIC   April 1980 – Present
St. Joseph's Hospital & Medical Center
Responsible for maintenance and repair of all equipment associated with air conditioning, heating, and refrigeration. Responsible for ordering shop stock and repair parts. Involved in primary start-up of new air handling equipment.

FIELD REPRESENTATIVE   September 1979 – April 1980
Ramada Energy Systems
Ramada Energy Systems was involved in the research and development of a solar collector made of a clear plastic materials. My responsibilities included the construction of mounting devices and related equipment for testing of the panels. Monitored the systems being tested and made modifications to the systems.

MAINTENANCE MECHANIC, CONSTRUCTION TECHNICIAN   June 1979 – September 1979
Universal Propulsion Corporation, Division of Talley Industries
Constructed new buildings and installed new machinery. Remodeled buildings to suit the needs of the growing company, including layout and construction of electrical power lines, pneumatic lines, and water lines. Maintained buildings, including carpentry, roofing, and painting. Constructed small building for experimental work. Installed and performed primary checkout of two-million-volt x-ray unit. Performed preventive maintenance on air compressors, A/C, hydraulic pumps, leak detector, and x-ray unit. Experienced in the use of hand tools, carpentry tools, A/C gauges, meters, power tools, ditch witch, jack hammer, forklift, and paint sprayer, among others.

REFRIGERATION SHOP MECHANIC   April 1978 – May 1979
St. Joseph's Hospital & Medical Center
Maintained and repaired hospital heating, A/C and refrigeration equipment. Performed trouble shooting and repairs to ice machines, refrigerators, air conditioners, freezers, exhaust fans, air handlers, pneumatic and electric thermostats, water towers, and booster pumps. Preventively maintained thermal systems equipment, water treatment, wash down coils, and water towers.

ROUTE DRIVER, SALES REPRESENTATIVE   September 1975 – July 1977
Wometeo Coca-Cola Bottling Company of Northern Arizona
Started as route driver, which included delivery of sold product and stocking of space provided. Was promoted to sales representative, which included selling products, writing invoices, laying out truck loads, promoting product discounts, securing space for product, selling product and coolers, performing maintenance and making minor repairs to venders and coolers, and collection of money.

SEAMAN ABOARD USS HENRY CLAY & USS DULUTH   September 1972 – September 1975
United States Navy
Aboard the USS Henry Clay: helmsman, prepared the ship for going to sea, lookout until submerged, maintained steady course of ship while underway, assisted in galley. On the USS Duluth: Changed rating from seaman to fireman, performed preventative maintenance and repairs on boiler, evaporator, and supporting systems.

. . . . *Training* . . . .

1990	Staefa Building Controls – one week
1985	Honeywell Building Controls, Level Two Seminar – one week
1984	Honeywell Building Controls, Level One Seminar – one week
1/80 – 8/82	Maricopa Community College, successfully completed courses pertaining to solar energy and air conditioning and other courses required for an A.S. Degree
8/77 – 4/78	Universal Technical Institute – Extensive training in diagnosis, repair, installation, and maintenance of air conditioning units, heat pumps, gas furnaces, and refrigeration equipment and their controls
9/72 – 9/75	U.S. Navy Training – Basic Submarine (4 months), Basic Electrical (6 weeks), Demolition (2 weeks), Fire Fighting (2 weeks), Piping and Welding (3 weeks), Evaporator (6 weeks)

Christopher J. Tulane

1234 N. Tenth Street • Apartment 123 • Burbank, California 91501 • (818) 555-1234

QUALIFICATIONS

- Experience in managing business operations
- Proven ability to articulate and sell ideas

- Powerfully positive attitude and dynamic enthusiasm
- Knowledge of Asian markets and cultures

EDUCATION

American Graduate School of International Management, Thunderbird, Glendale, Arizona
   Master of International Management   Dec. 1994
      Course work included Consolidation of Financial Statements, Analysis of Financial Statements, Investments and Portfolio Management, Southeast Asia and China Regional Business, Political and Cultural Studies

University of International Business and Economics (UIBE), Beijing, China
   Intensive Chinese Language, Socio-Political, and Business Environment Studies   Summer 1994

Tulane University, New Orleans, Louisiana
   Chinese Language and Cultural/Historical Studies   Sep. 1992 – May 1993

Xavier University of Louisiana, New Orleans, Louisiana
   Bachelor of Science, Economics   May 1992
   Minor in Chemistry

EXPERIENCE

Food and Beverage Supervisor
   Windsor Court Hotel, New Orleans, Louisiana   Feb. 1988 – May 1993
- Assisted in managing and training staff
- Conceived and implemented theme programs and sales promotions
- Coordinated and designed direct mail packages with promotional efforts
- Managed all hotel departments as Management Intern
- Financed entire undergraduate education

Sales Representative
   Martha Ann Samuel Realtors, New Orleans, Louisiana   Dec. 1989 – Dec. 1992
- Created and actuated new, effective marketing plan for Lakefront condominiums
- Sold over $1 million in condominiums and unique historic properties

LANGUAGES & SKILLS

Highly proficient in Mandarin Chinese, Knowledge of Spanish
Literacy in Lotus 1-2-3, dBASE III PLUS, WordPerfect, and MS Word

HONORS AND ACTIVITIES

- Gail Roessel Memorial Scholarship Designate – Selected by faculty and professors as recipient of endowment grant for overseas study – Summer 1994
- Ombudsman, Associated Students Legislative Council (ASLC) – Confronted problems and issues facing students and faculty – Conceived and implemented proposals to satisfy needs and address pressing concerns – Spring 1994
- Teacher's Assistant – Beijing Summer Program – Summer 1994
- Scholarship Committee of Thunderbird – Spring 1994
- Vice President Thunderbird Chapter of Toastmasters International – Spring 1994
- Southeast Asia Club – International Finance Association – Rugby Club – Cycling Club – Sky Diving

65

MARY JANE PRICE

12345 East Becker Lane
Phoenix, Arizona 85032
(602) 555-1234

SUMMARY

Certified Public Accountant with over five years of auditing experience with Price Waterhouse, in addition to six years of experience as controller for several interrelated small real estate investment companies. Honors graduate with exceptional mathematical talents. Strengths include perseverance, a very positive attitude, and good interpersonal skills.

EXPERIENCE

PRICE WATERHOUSE, Staff & Senior Auditor   December 1980 – October 1983, July 1990 – Present

EXTENSIVE TRAINING PROGRAM

Working as part of an efficient audit team gave me experience working under the pressure of deadlines and an invaluable knowledge of a wide variety of accounting systems. Industry experience includes Insurance, Retail, Manufacturing, Banking, and Health Care. PC skills include Lotus and WordPerfect.

SUPERVISORY SKILLS

Assignments supervising up to five staff. Experience in delegation, training, communication, and review. Responsible for planning engagements and evaluating staff.

SAC REAL ESTATE INVESTMENT COMPANY, Controller   October 1983 – June 1990

IBM PC EXPERIENCE

Responsible for all aspects of accounting, including cash management, monthly reports, general ledger (BPI Accounting program on IBM PC), financial statements, and consolidated statements. Developed great organizational and problem solving skills.

SELF-STARTER

Special projects included financial analysis of land sales, financing, construction spending, property taxes, insurance, and preparation of financial data as needed for marketing purposes.

MANAGEMENT CAPABILITIES

Assisted in interactions with lenders, attorneys, lessees, and subcontractors. Responsible for tax planning and coordination of work with tax specialists and external auditors.

EDUCATION

BACHELOR OF SCIENCE
Magna Cum Laude
Business Administration
Major: Accounting
Arizona State University
December 1980

4.0 Accounting GPA
3.78 Overall GPA

HONORS
Beta Alpha Psi
Beta Gamma Sigma
Phi Kappa Phi
Arizona Board of Regents'
Academic Scholarship

Minor
Music: Classical Piano

Thomas H. Cable
1234 North 23nd Lane, Phoenix, Arizona 85035, (602) 555-1234

Objective
To continue my career in Cable Communications Plant Operations Management

Work Experience

TECHNICAL/PLANT OPERATIONS MANAGER — *6/86 – Present*
Republic Cable, *Glendale, Arizona*
Responsible for 58 people. Contractor/In-House Construction, Engineering/Design, Blue Stake Facilities Locating, Warehouse and Inventory Control, Installation MDU/SDU, Quality Assurance and Field Audits, Fleet Control, all Technical Operations. Previous Technical Supervisor, Chief Technician. System size: 48,000 subscribers, 1,100 miles of plant.

INSTALLER TECH, TECH III, TECH II — *6/86 – 8/82*
Storer Cable Communications, *Glendale, Arizona*
Lead Technician and Field Supervisor.

SELF-EMPLOYED CABLE CONTRACTOR — *8/81 – 7/82*
Metro Boston Area
CATV installation/splicing – insured.

TRAINING/FOREMAN — *9/79 – 8/81*
Links Inc., *Norwood, Massachusetts*
Cable television installation. Aerial/UG, SMATV, MATV, pre/post wire.

RF TECHNICIAN — *2/77 – 7/79*
GTE Sylvania, *Burlington, Massachusetts*
Technician, MATV/SMATV/MDS systems for large hotels and apartment complexes. Tower work, System Design, Service. CATV construction/splicing.

BENCH TECHNICIAN — *1/77 – 7/77*
Nieco Microwave, *Burlington, Massachusetts*
Bench Technician – Tuning, alignment and calibration of bandpass filters for government aircraft radar systems.

SELF-EMPLOYED — *6/76 – 1/77*
Tower Service & Antenna Installation

MANAGER, ASSISTANT MANAGER, SALESMAN — *5/74 – 6/76*
Tandy Corporation/Radio Shack

Education
- **Don Bosco Technical High School**, *Boston, Massachusetts: Drafting, Basic Electronics, Electricity, Design, College Prep*
- **Greenfield Community College**, *Quincy, Massachusetts: Audio-Visual Communications*
- **Quincy Junior College**, *Quincy, Massachusetts: Advanced CATV Technology*
- **GTE Cable Construction Training**, *Cleveland, Ohio*
- **Other**: *14 assorted seminars and special courses, including Hughes AML, General Instrument Addressable Control Systems, SA and Sylvania Broadband Design, Magnavox Training, Computer Classes, Certified SCTE/BCT Broadband Design*

Special Skills
Motivation, perseverance, trouble shooting, confidence, diplomatic "King Solomon," well versed and exposed to all facets of cable communication operations.

Career Interests
Return to school for Business Administration. To be a major player in the rise of cable communications to maturity as a well-respected, truly professional industry!

Interests
Sports, reading trade magazines, mastering my own personal computer, personal achievements. Instrumental in organizing SCTE Cactus Chapter, Phoenix, Arizona, past Board of Directors, present Secretary. SCTE National Member 4 years.

67

R. BOSWORTH REPORTER

QUALIFICATIONS

- Master of International Management degree (May 1993)
- Four years of journalism experience (3 at editor level)
- Work and academic background in energy and the environment
- Experienced with government at local and federal level
- Travel throughout U.S., Asia, and Europe

INTERNATIONAL WORK EXPERIENCE

9/90 – 11/93   **Reporter, Deputy Editor, Editor (January 1990–November 1991),** *South China Morning Post,* Hong Kong
- Editor of business features and general supplements department for Hong Kong's major English language daily
- Managed a multinational staff of 12 and an annual discretionary budget of US$150,000
- Section titles included the weekly *Property Post* and *Technology Post**, the monthly *Motoring Post**, and weekly business pages on banking, personal finance, media, management, shipping and transport, and China trade
  * Developed and launched during my tenure as editor

8/90 – 9/90   **Business Sub-Editor,** *Hong Kong Standard,* Hong Kong
- Edited and prepared daily business section for publication

10/89 – 7/90   **Deputy Editor,** *Petroleum News S.E.A. Ltd.,* Hong Kong
- Edited weekly newsletter, *Energy Asia,* and a monthly magazine, *Petroleum News*

DOMESTIC WORK EXPERIENCE

1986 – 1988   **Manager, Land Services Division,** *Z-Axis Exploration Co.,* San Francisco, California
- Managed environmental field logistics for geophysical exploration teams and conducted geophysical field work
- Assisted in project design to ensure conformance with applicable laws
- Researched and reported on local geological and environmental conditions

1985 – 1986   **Research Analyst,** *Local Agency Formation Commission,* Marin County, California
- Researched and wrote for publication feasibility studies for county government, including policy, budget, planning analyses
- Prepared other written and oral presentations for Governing Board

1983 – 1985   **Partner,** *Dewey-Clokey Associates,* Marin County, California
- Started and ran a landscaping and carpentry business

1979 – 1980   **Advertising Manager (Disc Jockey),** *WRMC-FM,* Middlebury, Vermont
- Sold advertising air time, marketed and produced specialty radio shows and program magazine, wrote ad copy and articles

Summer 1979   **Research Assistant,** *American Gas Association,* Washington, D.C.
- Researched and synthesized information from U.S. Congress and Agencies for Congressional Relations Department

EDUCATION & LANGUAGES

May 1995   *Master of International Management,* American Graduate School of International Management (Thunderbird) Glendale, Arizona

1983   *Bachelor of Arts,* Middlebury College, Middlebury, Vermont
- Major in Environmental Science with minor in Geography and Economics
- Senior research in community development in native areas of the circumpolar north

1978   St. Albans School, Washington, D.C.

Languages: Proficient in French, Mandarin, Cantonese, Spanish, Phi Sigma Iota (foreign language honor society)

Present Address • P.O. Box 1234 • 12345 North 59th Avenue • Glendale, Arizona 85306 • (602) 555-1234
Permanent Address • 12345 Chestnut Street • San Francisco, California 94133 • (415) 555-1234

Peter Grant Osaka

1234 Foxglove Drive ♦ Nashville, Tennessee 37215 ♦ (615) 555-1234

Education

Master of International Management
American Graduate School of International Management (AGSIM)
Thunderbird Campus
Specialized in Japanese language, financial analysis, and accounting

May 1995
Glendale, Arizona
GPA 3.88/4.0

♦ Environmental Club, President 1994 – established and maintained successful campus-wide recycling program (glass, plastics, aluminum, and newspaper). Chairman of Earth Day 1994 – responsible for $1500 budget.
♦ Japan Club
♦ Captain of Ultimate Frisbee Team
♦ Continuing Student Grants – 3 semesters

Bachelor of Arts – Asian Studies   **High Honors**
University of Florida

December 1991
Gainesville, Florida
GPA 3.56/4.0; 3.83 in major

♦ Phi Beta Kappa Honor Society; Dean's List
♦ National Merit Finalist and Scholarship Recipient
♦ Golden Key National Honor Society; Alpha Lambda Delta Honor Society
♦ Japan Club; Friends of Japan
♦ Pi Lambda Phi Fraternity
♦ Karate Club; Ultimate Frisbee Team

Kansai Foreign Language University
Concentrated in Japanese language and business studies

September 1990 – June 1991
Hirakata City, Osaka, Japan

Experience

Environmental Coordinator
Glendale, Arizona

AGSIM
Spring 1995

Proposed and created a funded student government committee to oversee and maintain all campus environmental policies and practices. Maintained, expanded, and promoted current recycling programs. Responsible for creating new campus-wide environmental policies.

Teaching Assistantships
Intermediate Accounting
Introduction to Finance

AGSIM
Spring 1995
Spring 1994

Responsible for teaching weekly review sessions for class of 60. Graded homework and served as proctor.

Export Office Internship
Nashville, Tennessee

State of Tennessee
January 1992 – May 1992

Assisted in assembling an International Trade Directory. Assisted public with inquiries regarding trade.

Tutor/English
Osaka, Japan

Self-employed
October 1990 – May 1991

Assisted Japanese students of English with pronunciation and grammar.

Sales Representative
Independent Dealer, Minnesota; based in Nashville, Tennessee

Southwestern Company
May 1989 – August 1989

Admitted to the 200 Unit Club for earning over $700 in one week. Received the Southwestern Gold Award for working over 75 hours per week. Responsible for selling educational handbooks door to door and performing small business duties.

Languages and Travel

♦ **Japanese** (U.S. State Department proficiency level 4) – Studied for 7 years and extensive travel and education in Japan. Foreign Exchange Program in Japan. Lived with Japanese family for one year.
♦ **French** (U.S. State Department proficiency level 2) – Studied 5 years and travel experience.
♦ Work and travel overseas in **Eastern Asia, Europe, Middle East**, and **Nepal**
♦ **Computers:** Lotus 1-2-3, WordPerfect, Excel, MS Word, dBASE, BASIC, Macintosh

69

THOMAS W. EISENBERG

OBJECTIVE: To utilize my experience, sales skills, and enthusiasm in an entrepreneurial environment of an international firm

QUALIFICATIONS:
- Proven ability to develop new business and maintain profitable client relationships
- Exceptional research, negotiating, and problem solving skills
- Well-developed skills for marketing and sales
- Able to work independently and as a cooperative team member

EDUCATION:

Master of International Management
American Graduate School of International Management
Thunderbird Campus, Glendale, Arizona
Aug. 1995

Bachelor of Science, Marketing
Arizona State University, Tempe, Arizona
Self-financed 50% of education through employment
May 1989

EXPERIENCE:

Commercial Real Estate Broker
Eisenberg Company, Phoenix, Arizona
Sep. 1991 to Aug. 1994
- Implemented marketing programs for shopping centers with an aggregate value of over $50 million
- Officiated as liaison between shopping center owners and prospective tenants
- Consulted and advised developers, financial institutions, and retail tenants in all aspects relevant to the shopping center industry
- Performed extensive client prospecting
- Represented a prominent national retail tenant and spearheaded the economic negotiations and site selection within the state of Arizona
- Performed pro-forma analysis of potential shopping center developments
- Conducted numerous oral presentations
- Negotiated financial and legal aspects of contractual agreements

Leasing Representative/Project Manager
W. M. Grace Development Company, Phoenix, Arizona
July 1989 to Aug. 1991
- Oversaw the leasing of 15 shopping centers
- Commanded the leasing and management of a multimillion dollar shopping center in Wyoming
- Performed extensive client prospecting
- Identified as top-producing leasing representative

Executive Assistant
Grubb & Ellis Commercial Brokerage, Phoenix, Arizona
Dec. 1987 to June 1989
- Researched properties
- Updated prospective client lists
- Developed marketing packages for existing and future listings
- Formulated data for presentations

LANGUAGES: **English:** Native • **Croatian:** Highly Proficient • **German:** Knowledgeable

INTERESTS & ACTIVITIES: Golf, biathlons, travel, skiing, world affairs
Pi Kappa Alpha Alumni Advisor • Croatian-American Club • German Club

1234 North 60th Avenue • Phoenix, Arizona 85013 U.S.A. • (602) 555-1234

DONNIE SALES

1234 West El Camino, #123 North End > Phoenix, Arizona 85051 > (602) 555-1234

OBJECTIVE

A challenging sales/marketing position with an organization that offers growth based on dedication and proven ability. The ideal position would offer long-term commitment conducive to professional growth and achievement.

QUALIFICATIONS

> Proven results-oriented sales leader
> Skilled in timely project management and attention to detail
> Strong communication skills with international experience
> Articulate, creative, and innovative

EXPERIENCE

SOUTHWEST REGIONAL SALES REPRESENTATIVE   1991 – Present
Med Val Finger Splints, Tucson, Arizona
> Increased monthly sales volume by 35%

SALES/MARKETING REPRESENTATIVE   1992 – 1993
Browning-Ferris Industries, Phoenix, Arizona
> Sold construction sweeping equipment and portable j-jons for on-site use to large construction companies in the Arizona District
> Monthly volume of $12,000
> Prepared financial statements, invoices, and cost-effective closeouts
> Sales Representative of the Month for February and March 1993

MARKETING/SALES REPRESENTATIVE   1992
Eric Bergman's, Phoenix, Arizona
> Sold dry wall for this independent contractor in the Phoenix metro area
> Received numerous commendations for outstanding salesperson with lowest selling cost and highest profit margin of all positions

MANAGER   1991
The Cave, Las Vegas, Nevada
> Responsible for inventory control, hiring and supervision of personnel, daily sales statements, and monthly profit and loss statements
> Ensured that start-up and equipment costs were kept in line

PROFESSIONAL ICE HOCKEY PLAYER   1987 – 1991
> Played three months with Phoenix Road Runners, then moved to Europe
> Played my remaining career in France, Spain, and Germany

SALES REPRESENTATIVE   Summers
Med Val Finger Splints, Tucson, Arizona   1985 – 1989
> Developed and distributed a unique medical product throughout U.S. and North America to large hospitals

EDUCATION

BACHELOR OF ARTS   1988
Oswego State University, Oswego, New York
> Major in Communications/Marketing
> Full scholarship (for athletics)

HONORS & AWARDS

> Received full scholarship to play hockey
> Named to second All-American Team in the NCAA finals
> Played on the first All-American Team in the ECAC
> Won the NCAA National Championship for Division II
> Captain of National Championship Team

PERSONAL

> Highly proficient in **German**
> Willing to travel and relocate

PAUL CENEX

OBJECTIVE	A career promoting international economic development	

EDUCATION

MASTER OF INTERNATIONAL MANAGEMENT — May 1995
American Graduate School of International Management
Thunderbird Campus, Glendale, Arizona
- Extensive simulated computer trading of agricultural and financial futures
- Specialization in International Market Research, Agricultural and Food Marketing

BACHELOR OF ARTS IN ECONOMICS — Dec. 1993
Colorado State University, Fort Collins, Colorado
- Certificate of Latin American Studies
- Completed a summer of study in Guadalajara, Mexico

EXPERIENCE

INTERNATIONAL MARKETING INTERN — Sep. 1994 – Jan. 1995
Foreign Agricultural Service, U.S. Department of Agriculture
Washington, D.C.
- Published articles in the international agribusiness journal *AgExporter*
- Promoted the export of U.S. agricultural products by advising exporters and through direct trade assistance
- Edited intergovernmental publications aimed at increasing the effectiveness of market promotions abroad
- Evaluated funds spent

INTERN — 1992
International Center for Agricultural and Resource Development
Fort Collins, Colorado
- Planned and led field trips to agribusiness firms throughout Colorado for foreign postgraduate students

RESIDENT ASSISTANT — 1994, 1995
American Graduate School of International Management
Glendale, Arizona
- Received financial aid for managing 50 on-campus housing units

---

LANGUAGE — Proficient in **Spanish**

COMPUTERS — Adept in WordPerfect, TSP, Lotus 1-2-3, Harvard Graphics, PS&D, MS-DOS

LEADERSHIP — President, International Career Opportunities (ICO) Latin America

SCHOLARSHIP — Cenex Cooperative Studies Scholarship, January 1991

APTITUDE — Passed the U.S. Department of State's Foreign Service Exam
FSI Language Aptitude Score of 49

TRAVEL EXPERIENCE — Lived and studied in The Gambia, West Africa, and in Latin America
Traveled in Europe

Current Address • Post Office Box 12345, Glendale, Arizona 85306 • (602) 555-1234
Permanent Address • 12345 Baywatch Road, Fort Collins, Colorado 80524 • (303) 555-1234

ALEXANDER U. TOSCHI

Address:
12345 Leadington Street
Van Nuys, California 91405

Phone:
(818) 555-1234
(602) 555-1234

OBJECTIVE

A position utilizing my marketing and management experience

EXPERIENCE

1994
PRIVATE LABEL ADVANTAGE, *Encino, California*
General Manager
- *Marketed a private label program to the natural foods industry*
- *Coordinated the manufacturing, purchasing, distribution, and sales of 30 products*
- *Managed all facets of our business, including packaging, warehousing, and inventory control*
- *Created a unique partnership with 40 individual retail stores through proactive customer service and customized selling*

1993
OLD WORLD RESTAURANT, *Los Angeles, California*
Manager
- *Exercised language and cross-cultural skills managing a multicultural staff*

1993
SPORTMART, *Los Angeles, California*
Department Manager
- *Supervised 20 sales personnel*
- *Analyzed statistical reports to ensure proper ordering and merchandise display*

1992
SIGNER, EGLI & PARTNER INTERNATIONAL A.G., *San Diego, California*
Account Executive
- *Promoted regional sporting events*
- *Solicited title sponsors*

1990
TELEDYNE LAARS, *Los Angeles, California*
Corporate Consultant
- *Conducted business intelligence to measure feasibility of new product in the U.S.*
- *Recommended future company direction and strategy to corporate management*

1988
BENNIGAN'S RESTAURANT, *Saddle Brook, New Jersey*
Management Trainee
- *Completed Manager-in-Training Program*
- *Trained in all aspects of restaurant management: staffing, personnel training, budgeting, and inventory control*

1982 – 1986
KILROY'S WONDER MARKET, *Glen Rock, New Jersey*
Assistant Manager
- *Trained and supervised personnel*
- *Reviewed advertising to determine proper ordering and merchandise placement*

EDUCATION

1992
MASTER OF INTERNATIONAL MANAGEMENT
American Graduate School of International Management – Thunderbird, *Glendale, Arizona*
- *Concentration – Marketing with an emphasis on International Marketing*
- *International Industrial Marketing Workshop – Account Executive for a corporate consulting team*
- *Currency Futures Trading Project through computer simulation*

1987
BACHELOR OF ARTS IN COMMUNICATION
William Paterson College, *Wayne, New Jersey*
- *Concentration – Interpersonal Communications with an emphasis on Public Speaking*
- *Minor in Business Administration*
- *Extracurricular Activities – Varsity Football, Student Council, Debate Team*

QUALIFICATIONS

*Highly proficient in **Spanish***
Computer literate in Lotus 1-2-3, WordPerfect, MS Word, Excel, Windows, QuickBooks

MARCELA BOLIVIAN

12345 N. 59th Avenue, #123
Glendale, Arizona 85306
(602) 555-1234

education

1994 – 1995

AMERICAN GRADUATE SCHOOL OF INTERNATIONAL MANAGEMENT (THUNDERBIRD)   **PHOENIX, AZ**

Candidate for Master of International Management degree, December 1995. International Management curriculum with emphasis on marketing. Selected by faculty to tutor foreign language students. Organized Thunderbird International Symposium with Latin American and Andean Clubs. Member of Marketing and Import/Export Clubs.

1987 – 1991

UNIVERSITY OF COLORADO   **BOULDER, CO**

Awarded Bachelor of Arts degree in Business Spanish for the Professions, an interdisciplinary program in business and the Spanish language and culture. Concentration in business development in Latin America. Awarded Regent Academic Scholarship and University Research Opportunities Scholarship. Published paper on sports injuries in children. Wrote senior thesis on the Spanish language and its problems in the U.S. after serving 10 months as volunteer Assistant Probation Officer for Hispanic offenders. Elected president and treasurer of Spanish Club. Overseas study in Madrid, Spain.

experience

1993 – 1994

CIBA-GEIGY PHARMACEUTICALS   **BOGOTA, COLOMBIA**

Product Manager, Cardiovascular Line

Responsible for enhancing profitability, sales, and market share of cardiovascular products through the development and implementation of strategic and tactical marketing plans, encompassing all traditional brand management activities.

- Devised marketing strategy for product launch of new Ace-Inhibitor in Colombia.
- Developed advertising campaign for national product launch.
- Led focus groups and conducted interviews with physicians, pharmacists, and distributors.
- Conducted all prelaunch financial analyses and feasibility studies.
- Developed and expanded market share by an average of 13% for three cardiovascular products.
- Presented market share analysis and recommendations to International Product Management.
- Designed and supervised physician and prescription market research program.
- Trained 80 sales representatives on the cardiovascular system and its corresponding product line.

1992 – 1993

Assistant to Marketing Manager

- Implemented Resource Allocation Model for optimal utilization of funds in the Marketing Division at all levels.
- Monitored and presented monthly spending and cost applications per product.
- Acted as liaison between product managers and advertising agency.

1991 – 1992

BANCO POPULAR   **BOGOTA, COLOMBIA**

International Development Manager

- Evaluated branch viabilities in Miami and the Cayman Islands.
- Prepared and presented official applications for first branch office in the U.S. to the Central Banking Authority of Colombia as well as the Federal Reserve of the United States.
- Designed and recommended office structure and job descriptions for new office in Miami; handled all administrative procedures.
- Negotiated investment terms and analyzed legal documentation for a personal money transfer system from the United States to Colombia.
- Aided in the creation of a five-year business plan. Developed financial model to generate and control monthly income statements, balance sheets, and cash flows for the distinct international divisions in 60 regional offices.

personal

U.S./Colombian/Bolivian citizenships
Fluent in **Spanish** • Fluent in **English** • Knowledge of **French**
Enjoy traveling, triathlons, tennis, and hospital volunteer work

Mary Ann Whitman
12345 North 71st Avenue
Glendale, Arizona 85308
(602) 555-1234

Objective

To provide elementary students with a stimulating learning environment oriented to many learning styles. It is very important to enhance this environment with encouragement, kindness, and feelings of success.

Certificates

- Arizona Elementary Certificate K-8
- Oregon Basic Elementary Certificate K-8

Experience

SUBSTITUTE TEACHER . . . . 9/94 – 6/95
Deer Valley and **Peoria Unified School Districts**, Phoenix, Arizona
Long-term assignments at Village Meadows School and Greenbrier School.

TEACHER, KINDERGARTEN . . . . 9/92 – 6/94
Ainsworth Elementary School, 1245 Vista Verde, Portland, Oregon 97201
Successfully provided full curriculum, including language arts (i.e., phonics, *Success in Reading* program, journal writing, literature-based and language-experience-based reading program using a whole language approach, drama), *Math Their Way* program, science, health, social studies, music, art, and italic printing. Many lessons planned using ITIP formula. Successfully worked with special education children mainstreamed into the kindergarten class. Utilized parent helpers when appropriate to provide lower student/adult ratio.

SUBSTITUTE TEACHER . . . . 2/92 – 6/94
Portland Public Schools, 123 N. Dixie, Portland, Oregon 97282
Substituted at grade levels K-8. During this period, became familiar with many styles of teaching and many programs.

STUDENT TEACHING, FIRST GRADE . . . . 9/91 – 12/91
Whitman Elementary School, 1234 S.E. Flavour, Portland, Oregon
A successful and delightful experience with first grade—a great opportunity for growth.

Education

B.S. ELEMENTARY EDUCATION, Portland State University, 1991

Staff Development and Continuing Education

- Spanish foreign language experience
- Higher level thinking skills
- Early childhood education seminars
- *Math Their Way* classes
- Art projects for elementary children
- Multicultural education – African American history
- Nellie Edge seminars, whole language (musical)
- Valerie Welk seminar, whole language (enrichment)

Other Experience with Children

- FIELD EXPERIENCE with Portland State University classes, providing a variety of experiences with children in grades K-4. Worked with *Writing to Read* programs and prepared many art/social studies projects.
- Camp Fire leader with second grade Bluebird group
- Child care co-op volunteer, N.E. YMCA, Portland, Oregon
- Team Manager, Wilshire Little League, girls minor softball team

Margaret Erin Obirin

Qualifications
- Masters degree in International Management with emphasis on International Insurance
- Proven leadership and communication skills
- Three years experience in the insurance industry
- Computer literacy with multiple operating systems and applications

Professional Experience

Chubb Group of Insurance Companies, *International Underwriter*, 2/92 – Present
- Solicit and service international accounts
- Demonstrate Chubb global expertise in the marketplace
- Analyze and strengthen current global insurance programs
- Educate clients on the complexities and necessity of international insurance
- Prospect current domestic clients with probable international exposures
- Specialized training includes nine intensive weeks in Warren, New Jersey, at the Chubb Commercial Lines School of Insurance

SAFECO Insurance Company, *Underwriter*, 5/88 – 8/90
- Managed a field of 30 independent insurance agencies
- Analyzed applications, claims, and other data to select insurance risks
- Communicated underwriting accept or reject decisions to the independent agency force in the field

Special projects included:
- Selected as department coordinator to work with the home office to launch an automated computer decision system
- Planned and organized a full-day seminar for company Vice Presidents and local branch staff
- Conducted informational seminars for the independent agency field and newly appointed SAFECO agents
- Analyzed agency loss ratio data and provided recommendations to increase agency growth and profitability
- Trained new underwriters

Tektronix, Inc., *Summer Employment*, 1984 – 1987
- Increased responsibilities from an hourly Technical Typist to a salaried Technical Writer. Final project was the documentation set for a major software product
- Organized large amounts of information and presented it in a concise format
- Worked closely with the marketing and engineering departments
- Participated on the product launch team

Education

Master of International Management, 1991 (GPA 3.7)
American Graduate School of International Management,
Thunderbird Campus, Glendale, Arizona
- Focus on Insurance/Risk Management and Finance
- Participated in International Insurance and Risk Management Conference
- Recipient – Hugh M. Blake International Insurance Scholarship
- Recipient – Mavis Voris Partial Assistantship

Bachelor of Arts, International Studies, 1988 (GPA 3.33)
University of Oregon, Eugene, Oregon

Foreign Study, 1987
Obirin College, Tokyo, Japan
An intensive semester study of Japanese business, society, and language. Program included seminars with various Japanese companies.

Languages

Proficient in **Japanese** • Knowledge of **French**

12345 Goshen Avenue #12 • San Francisco, California 90049 • (310) 555-1234

6 | THOSE DIFFICULT DATES

Where should you place your dates? It all depends on how much importance you want to give them. If you have gaps in your employment history that you would rather explain in an interview, then the dates should be less obvious (pages 91, 92, 93, and 95). You can even leave them off altogether and list totals instead (page 89).

Another reason to de-emphasize dates is your age. If you would rather not give your age away, then make the reader work to figure it out. Tuck dates against the text with parentheses (pages 91, 93, and 95) or bury them somewhere else in the resume (page 92).

Accuracy and *honesty* are the most important considerations when it comes to dates. Don't lie! I had a client who chose to fudge on his dates. He was invited for an interview and then lost the job when previous employers were contacted and the dates didn't match. It wasn't worth it. Honesty is always the best policy.

There are many ways to make room for the dates. One is to establish a clear column of dates to the right of a resume, which keeps the text from looking cluttered and makes the dates easy to find. Putting them on the left, on the other hand, gives them a great deal of importance. Since people read from left to right, information on the left of the page is read first and carries greater weight. Make sure you really want your dates to be that important before placing them in the left-hand column.

You may use months with years or years only. Some people feel more comfortable with a full accounting of their time and prefer the month/year method. However, making room for all those words becomes a problem if you choose to spell out the month, as in:

January 1989 to February 1993

Abbreviations or numbers for months makes designing your resume a little easier:

Jan. 1989 – Feb. 1993

or

Jan 1989 – Feb 1993

or

1/89 – 2/93

It is possible to stack the dates (as on pages 79, 96, and 97) in order to make more room. For example:

Jan. 1989	or	January 1989
– Feb. 1993		to February 1993

Dot leaders can help draw the eye to the dates on paragraph-style resumes where it is difficult to create a clear column for the dates (pages 88, 89).

There is no single, preferred method for the positioning of dates on a resume. The key is to create a sense of balance by placing the dates in a position that is complimentary to the rest of your information, while keeping in mind how much importance you wish to give them.

METTE RIIS LERNER

Address
Møllegærdet 123
1234 Kolding, Denmark

Telephones
Tel: (75) 555-1234
Fax: (75) 555-1234

OBJECTIVE

A marketing management position with an internationally oriented firm that utilizes my marketing and finance skills

QUALIFICATIONS

- Degrees in Computer Management Science and International Business Management
- Demonstrated interpersonal skills, leadership qualities, and personal motivation
- Training and management experience
- Skilled administrator and communicator
- Broad multicultural and sociological knowledge

EDUCATION

MASTER OF BUSINESS ADMINISTRATION
European University, Antwerp, Belgium
Selected courses: Multinational Business Management, International Finance and Trade, International Marketing, International Consumer Marketing, International Business Policy

June 1995

CERTIFICATE OF ADVANCED STUDY
American Graduate School of International Management
Thunderbird Campus, Glendale, Arizona

Jan. 1995
– June 1995

BACHELOR OF SCIENCE *cum laude*   GPA 3.83/4.0
COMPUTER MANAGEMENT SCIENCE
Armstrong University, Berkeley, California
Selected courses: Risk Management, International Money and Banking, Operations Management, Managerial Finance, Marketing

June 1992

WORK EXPERIENCE

ASSISTANT RETAIL MANAGER
Popp Dress, Kolding, Denmark
- Achieved maximum sales potential through sales planning, merchandising, accurate inventory control procedures, and personnel management
- Supervised and trained department staff
- Exhibited high level of leadership and communication skills

June 1993
– Jan. 1994

COMPUTER CONSULTANT
Dun & Bradstreet Software Services, Inc., Los Angeles, California
- Successfully completed Career Development Program (four-month intensive management training program in Atlanta, Georgia)
- Trained customers to fully utilize the software programs
- Worked under very tight time schedules
- Ensured customer satisfaction by maintaining constant communication and solving technical problems
- Researched software programs and replaced existing software with new releases

Sep. 1992
– May 1993

ASSISTANT TO BUSINESS MANAGER (Part-Time)
Armstrong University, Berkeley, California
- Wrote letters suggesting student financial status and corresponded with other departments
- Received and processed tuition/fees and made bank deposits

Mar. 1991
– May 1992

HONORS & ACTIVITIES

- The National Dean's List 1990, 1991
- The Dean's List every semester of undergraduate study
- Member of Sigma Kappa Phi Honor Society

INTERNATIONAL EXPERIENCES

- Graduate education in Belgium and the United States
- College education in the United States
- High school education in Denmark
- Traveled extensively throughout Europe and the United States

LANGUAGES

Fluent in **Danish** and **English** • Highly proficient in **Norwegian** and **Swedish**
Working knowledge of **German** • Knowledge of **French**

DAVID J. WESTWOOD

EDUCATION	**MASTER OF INTERNATIONAL MANAGEMENT**	May '95

American Graduate School of International Management
Thunderbird Campus, Glendale, Arizona
- International Marketing, Finance, Negotiations

BACHELOR OF ARTS, INTERNATIONAL STUDIES — May '91

St. John's University, Collegeville, Minnesota
- Political Science, French, History

Collège International de Cannes, France — Autumn '89
- Intensive French language study program
- Member Alliance Française

Related Course Work
- Consumer Marketing, Multinational Business Management, International Negotiations, International Finance and Trade
- Marketing Projects:
  - InterAd – Advanced International Marketing and Advertising Workshop
  - International Market Research – Designed feasibility survey for Northwest Airlines

EXPERIENCE   **GRADUATE RESEARCH ASSISTANT** — Jan. '95 – May '95

The Thunderbird International Executive
- Researched 250 journals and 150 book publishers
- Wrote and edited bibliographical entries with synopses for inclusion in internationally circulated journal
- *International Executive* Outstanding Service Award

ASSISTANT MANAGER — Sept. '91 – May '93

The Westwood Restaurant Group, Boston, Massachusetts
- Managed staff of 15
- Generated and accounted for daily cash and credit sales
- Trained new personnel

STUDENT PROGRAM COORDINATOR — Sept. '90 – May '91

Office of International Studies, St. John's University
- Designed and implemented promotional and advertising campaigns for study-abroad programs
- Increased enrollment of overseas programs
- Wrote study-abroad newsletter

MODERN AND CLASSICAL LANGUAGE INSTRUCTOR — Autumn '90

Modern and Classical Language Department, St. John's University
- Selected from 50 candidates to teach college-level French course
- Developed course plan and evaluated student performance

LANGUAGES & COMPUTERS
- Highly proficient in French, working knowledge of Spanish
- Macintosh Desktop Publishing, Lotus 1-2-3, WordPerfect, Harvard Graphics, SPSSX

ACTIVITIES

Captain, Intramural Sports Team; Outdoors Club; Marketing Club; Amnesty International; Disc Jockey, KSJU FM; Awarded Photographer; Certified Scuba Diver; Theater

ADDRESS   123 Oak Grove Street, Minneapolis, Minnesota 55403   (612) 555-1234

DANIEL STEVEN OHIO

OBJECTIVE	A challenging position in international finance or marketing	

EXPERIENCE

Financial Analyst

Rothglen, Ltd., Evanston, Illinois   September 1991 – Present
- Analyzed client statements
- Calculated financial ratios
- Assisted in budgeting process

Marketing Representative

Jetline Development Group, Newport Beach, California   May 1989 – May 1990
- Identified and obtained new customer accounts
- Traveled extensively to update and generate accounts
- Represented corporation at numerous trade shows

Precious Metals Options Intern

Republic National Bank of New York, New York, New York   May – August 1988
- Recorded daily gold/silver trades
- Reviewed daily trades with floor brokers
- Reconciled all trades with London
- Reviewed all trades for accuracy

Financial Analysis and Control Intern

American Express Bank, Ltd., New York, New York   May – August 1987
- Assisted in international budgeting
- Created programs for various reports to controller
- Calculated various financial ratios on a daily basis

Reconciliation Intern

American Express Bank, Ltd., New York, New York   May – August 1986
- Reconciled interbank foreign exchange accounts
- Balanced weekly statements
- Participated in various corporate seminars including military banking, travel-related services, and brokerage

---

EDUCATION

MASTER OF INTERNATIONAL MANAGEMENT   GPA 3.45   May 1995
American Graduate School of International Management
Thunderbird Campus, Glendale, Arizona

BACHELOR OF SCIENCE IN MARKETING   GPA 3.20   May 1989
University of Dayton, Dayton, Ohio

LANGUAGES
- Knowledge of **Spanish** language
- Lotus 1-2-3, WordPerfect, IBM PS/1, and COBOL

ACTIVITIES & INTERESTS
- Lived overseas for 14 years – Liberia, Nassau, Jakarta, Hong Kong, and Singapore
- Phi Beta Alpha Fraternity, Sports Chairman 1988, Vice President 1987
- Treasurer International Winetasting Society
- Waterskiing, Travel, Softball, Reading

ADDRESS   123 Johnson #123, Evanston, Illinois 60202   (708) 555-1234

Patricia A. Boone

1234 Boone Avenue North
New Hope, Minnesota 55427
(612) 555-1234

OBJECTIVE

A career in Sales with an opportunity for continued growth and responsibility.

EXPERIENCE

REORDER & SALES REPRESENTATIVE   Sep. 1991 – Present
Farm & Home Foods, Inc., Phoenix, Arizona
Take reorders and bring inactive customers back to reordering in the West Phoenix territory. Perform in-home demonstrations.

FULL-SERVICE REPRESENTATIVE   Sep. 1988 – June 1991
R. J. Reynolds Tobacco Company, Phoenix, Arizona
Advanced from merchandiser, promotional specialist, and chain store representative to become full-service representative calling on chain, grocery, drug, and independent retailers.

SALES REPRESENTATIVE   Mar. 1987 – Sep. 1988
Pennington and Associates, Scottsdale, Arizona
Sales Representative for Arizona and New Mexico. Called on independent and chain drugstores selling hair ornaments, cosmetics, nail products, fragrances, and suntan products.

TERRITORY MANAGER   Sep. 1986 – Mar. 1987
Jonee' Nails, Inc., Pico Rivera, California
Managed territory for Arizona and Las Vegas, Nevada, selling to the drug and grocery trades. This company solicited my services but let me go due to their severe financial problems. Area was absorbed by two salespeople.

TERRITORY MANAGER   Mar. 1986 – June 1986
Fashion Sales, Inc., Division of Mercury Distributing, Chatsworth, California
Managed territory for Arizona and New Mexico. This division was dropped by its primary line, Jonee' Nails. Fashion Sales lost the area and position was eliminated.

TERRITORY MANAGER   Feb. 1978 – Jan. 1986
COTY Division, Pfizer, New York, New York
Responsibilities included increasing sales with established accounts, securing new accounts, solving credit problems, training retailers to sell the COTY line, and selling ads and displays. Major achievements included:
- No. 1 Territory Manager, District, 1985
- Consistently surpassed all sales quotas
- Sales trainer for new sales reps for seven years

SALES REPRESENTATIVE   Oct. 1975 – Feb. 1978
United Church Directories, Waco, Texas
Sold pictorial directories to churches within the state of Minnesota. Achievements included taking over a virgin territory and developing more than $600,000 in sales through cold calling.

BUYER   Prior to 1975
Donaldson's Department Stores & Target Stores, Minneapolis, Minnesota
Worked as a buyer of children's wear.

EDUCATION

- St. Louis Park High School, Minneapolis, Minnesota
- Minneapolis Vocational School
- Estelle Compton Modeling School

JOSEPH R. HERMANN

12 West 12th Street, Apt. 1 • New York, New York 10011 • (212) 123-4567

EXPERIENCE

BUSINESS WEEK, New York, New York   1993 – Present
Director of Conference Programming
- Identified, researched, and developed program themes and topics
- Recruited speakers for all keynote addresses, panel discussions, and workshops
- Designed marketing materials for prospective participants
- Coordinated logistics and operations for all aspects of event
- Assisted in selling of conference sponsorships
- Managed event team on-site

INSTITUTIONAL INVESTOR, INC., New York, New York   1988 – 1993
Conference Division/Money Management Group
Executive Director (1991 – 1993)
- Fully responsible for administration, audience development, programming, and sales of eight conferences a year, totaling $2.4 million in revenue
- Created sponsorship sales strategy and assisted in worldwide sales effort
- Developed four new conference projects into annual events
- Managed team of 10 in U.S., Europe, and Asia

Senior Program Manager (1988 – 1991)
- Responsible for creation and execution of international investment conferences in the U.S., Europe, and Asia
- Researched program topics, developed discussion sessions
- Assisted in target audience development process
- In charge of on-site management of conferences

INSTITUTE FOR INTERNATIONAL RESEARCH, INC.   1987 – 1988
New York, New York/Sydney, Australia
Conference Manager
- Responsible for complete development and marketing of product
- Prepared all brochure copy and press releases

PARK HYATT HOTEL, Chicago, Illinois   1984 – 1986
Assistant Manager
- Supervised front office operations
- Fulfilled guest service requests, coordinated group arrangements
- Trained and managed department staff of 20

COMPUSERVE, INC., Chicago, Illinois   1983 – 1984
Account Executive
- Devised sales strategy for team, reaching 100% of sales quota for year
- Prospected and acquired new business accounts
- Developed new applications for existing customers

EDUCATION

AMERICAN GRADUATE SCHOOL OF INTERNATIONAL MANAGEMENT   1987
Thunderbird Campus, Glendale, Arizona
Master of International Management
- Concentration in international marketing and advertising

UNIVERSITY OF NOTRE DAME, Notre Dame, Indiana   1982
Bachelor of Business Administration
- Marketing major, German minor

UNIVERSITÄT INNSBRUCK, Innsbruck, Austria   1979 – 1980
- Sophomore year abroad program

LANGUAGES   French, German: highly proficient • Italian, Spanish: working knowledge

83

LISA BIENSTOCK

EXPERIENCE

NEW TIMES, INC., Phoenix, Arizona   Jan. 1994 – Present
Account Executive – Sales and Marketing
- Generated new business through aggressive prospecting, resulting in 40 new accounts in nine months
- Managed all aspects of client accounts, including marketing plans, design and production of advertisements, and accounts payable
- Incorporated demographic information and media audit analysis in custom proposals and presentations
- Extensive experience in developing marketing strategies

THE GLOBAL TRADE DEVELOPMENT CENTER, Palatine, Illinois   1992 – 1993
Marketing Assistant
- Performed in-depth international market research
- Investigated and prepared reports on foreign markets
- Managed public relations materials and handled external communications

ARIZONA HOUSE OF REPRESENTATIVES, Phoenix, Arizona   1990
Legislative Intern, Transportation Committee
- Selected as one of 40 interns out of 800 applicants
- Prepared position statements for transportation committee chairperson
- Researched and drafted supporting arguments and defenses to advance committee directives throughout the legislative process

WESTIN LA PALOMA, Tucson, Arizona   1988 – 1990
Tennis Professional and Director of Junior Tennis Program
- Organized and ran corporate tournaments of over 100 players representing both domestic and foreign corporations
- Professional tennis instruction for both groups and individuals

EDUCATION

MASTER OF INTERNATIONAL MANAGEMENT   May 1992
American Graduate School of International Management
Thunderbird Campus, Glendale, Arizona

BACHELOR OF ARTS   May 1990
University of Arizona, Tucson, Arizona
- Major in English Literature
- Minor in Spanish Literature

INTERNATIONAL STUDIES
- Tours, France: 120 hours oral and written French   1990
- Geneva, Switzerland: French language and international relations   1987
- Guadalajara, Mexico: Spanish language and culture   1986
- Madrid, Spain: Spanish language and culture   1985

LANGUAGES & COMPUTERS

Fluent in Spanish • Proficient in French
WordPerfect, Lotus 1-2-3, dBASE

HONORS & AWARDS

- Honors Program Nominee for English Literature, 1988
- Received Humanities Honors Award, 1990

1234 West Mississippi Avenue, Apt. 10 • Phoenix, Arizona 85013 • (602) 555-1234

Catherine J. Degree

1234 Connecticut Street, Apartment 12
San Francisco, California 94109
(415) 555-1234

QUALIFICATIONS
- 2½ years of experience in Marketing
- Graduate degree in International Marketing and Management
- Able to conduct business in French
- Working knowledge of WordPerfect, Lotus, MS Word, and Freelance

EXPERIENCE

ASSOCIATE MARKETING MANAGER   Sep 1989 – Present
Continental Bank, San Francisco, California
- Assisted with the development, coordination, and implementation of marketing support activities for the Risk Management Marketing Department
- Implemented departmental seminars, presentations, and customer entertainment activities

MARKETING COORDINATOR   Jan 1993 – May 1993
Southwest Salon Products, Phoenix, Arizona
- Developed and implemented marketing materials for two lines of professional salon products
- Researched launch of a new salon product in the European market
- Coordinated events and publicity for current products

SALES ASSOCIATE   Nov 1992 – May 1993
The Gap, Inc., Phoenix, Arizona
- Consistently provide priority service to meet customer needs
- Gained knowledge of The Gap's store operations, merchandising, and selling techniques

SALESPERSON   June – Dec 1989
Bloomingdale's, Chicago, Illinois
- Successfully completed retail sales training program
- Worked part-time to supplement income

EDUCATION

MASTER OF INTERNATIONAL MANAGEMENT   May 1993
American Graduate School of International Management
Thunderbird Campus, Glendale, Arizona
Emphasis: Marketing and Management
- Developed corporate-sponsored international marketing plan for a Seattle company
- Analyzed the prospects for the retail industry in the European Community
- Researched and developed a marketing plan for introduction of a hair care product in two international markets

BACHELOR OF LIBERAL ARTS   May 1988
University of Iowa, Iowa City, Iowa
Emphasis: History and French

FOREIGN STUDY
Regents Program in Lyon, France – studied at the Institute Catholique   Summer 1986
American Institute of Foreign Study – studied and traveled in Europe   Summer 1984

ACTIVITIES
- Campus Ambassadors, International Marketing Club, Francophone Club
- Member and Officer of Kappa Alpha Theta Sorority
- Committee Chairperson, Students for Dole, national presidential campaign

Robert P. Monney

EXPERIENCE

INSTITUTE FOR INTERNATIONAL RESEARCH, Hartford, Connecticut   11/91 – Present
Free-Lance Conference Producer
- Developed three executive-level financial conferences for world's largest for-profit conference company
- Researched financial marketplace for industry trends and topics of concern
- Designed detailed forum agendas, including brochure copy and design
- Recruited 50 senior-level corporate executives
- Marketed individual conferences to the financial community through direct mail, advertising, and public relations

GERARD MONNEY INTERNATIONAL, Paris, France   1/91 – 10/91
Account Executive
- Analyzed distribution logistics and profit feasibility in the pharmaceutical industry
- Assisted in joint venture consultations
- Generated new-product publicity in local and trade press
- Defined corporate identity and designed corporate image promotional materials
- Initiated and oversaw all press conferences and trade shows

SHEARSON, LEHMAN, HUTTON, New York, New York   6/86 – 5/89
Account Executive Specialist
- Marketed and promoted new financial products in-house
- Supervised implementation of new computer system
- Conducted detailed seminars and training programs
- Served as corporate liaison to branch offices

GERARD MONNEY INTERNATIONAL, Paris, France   9/84 – 8/85
College Intern
- Researched U.S. and French pharmaceutical industry
- Interpreted drug descriptions and applications
- Performed various administrative tasks

EDUCATION

AMERICAN GRADUATE SCHOOL OF INTERNATIONAL MANAGEMENT   6/89 – 12/90
Thunderbird Campus, Glendale, Arizona
Master of International Management

Projects in International Marketing:
- Taco John's International/Taiwan
- Prima Diapers/Switzerland
- Tourism/Sri Lanka
- Gatorade/U.S.A.

BOSTON COLLEGE, Chestnuthill, MA   9/82 – 5/86
Bachelor of Arts
Major: Political Science/French

INSTITUTE DES ETUDES POLITIQUES, France   9/84 – 6/85
Junior Year Abroad Program

LANGUAGES   Highly proficient in **French**

ACTIVITIES   Travel throughout Europe, Africa, and the former Soviet Union
Treasurer/French Club, Toastmasters, Outdoor Adventure Club

ADDRESS   1234 Bentwood Drive, Hartford, Connecticut 06903   (203) 555-1234

China L. Black

123 Lariat Lane • Milwaukee, Wisconsin 78620 • (512) 555-1234

ABILITIES

Adaptable – Experienced at living in foreign countries
Multilingual – Able to conduct business in Spanish, French, Portuguese, and German
Creative – Helped launch multiple consumer-oriented products in South America
Analytical – Developed international marketing strategies for Universal Foods to increase sales
Resourceful – Effectively prioritized and organized projects to maximize efficiency

LANGUAGES

Highly proficient in **Spanish** • Knowledge of **Japanese**
Proficient in **French**, **Portuguese**, **German**

COMPUTERS

Highly proficient in **IBM** and **Macintosh** computer systems

EXPERIENCE

REGIONAL MANAGER, SOUTH AMERICA   9/92 – Present
Universal Foods Corporation, Milwaukee, Wisconsin
• Established worldwide partnerships with food processors and beverage manu-
  facturers providing flavors, flavor ingredients, and creative ingredient systems.
• Expanded direct account sales through restructuring existing customer service
  procedures and providing enhanced technical support.
• Managed and trained licensees and commissioned agents throughout South
  American region for Universal Flavors Division.
• Designed and implemented corporate transnational marketing materials.

INTERNATIONAL SALES & MARKETING MANAGER   6/89 – 9/92
Seven Bar Enterprises, Inc., Albuquerque, New Mexico
• Responsible for long-term risk management and strategic sales planning.
• Served as foreign government liaison and public relations coordinator.

CO-FOUNDER/CO-OWNER   9/86 – 5/89
Walkabout (T-Shirt Design and Sales Partnership), Dallas, Texas
• Profitably designed, manufactured, and sold current event T-shirts to students
  and various organizations while attending SMU.

EDUCATION

MASTER OF INTERNATIONAL MANAGEMENT (MIM)   *with honors*   12/91
American Graduate School of International Management, Glendale, Arizona
• Emphasis in both Marketing and Finance
International Sales Intern, M&M/Mars Incorporated, Hackettstown, New Jersey   6/91 – 8/91
• Prepared product health registrations and cost feasibility studies for export
  markets in Europe, Asia, Canada, and Latin America.
• Introduced new product to Latin American market.
• Developed internship training handbook to improve intern effectiveness.

BACHELOR OF ARTS   *cum laude*   5/89
Southern Methodist University, Dallas, Texas
• Emphasis in foreign languages: Spanish, French, German, and Japanese

FOREIGN STUDY
Center for International Studies, Madrid, Spain   Spring 1988
University of Paris, Paris, France   Fall 1987
Center for Bilingual Multicultural Studies, Cuernavaca, Mexico   Summer 1987
Ortega and Gasset Foundation, Toledo, Spain   Summer 1986

INTERESTS

• SMU Women's Varsity Golf Team
  (1985–89)
• Sun Country Junior PGA Champion (1985)
• New Mexico State High School Golf
  Champion (1985)
• Dallas Garden Society (1992–93)

• Dallas Junior League (1988–89)
• Albuquerque Junior League (1990–91)
• National DAR, Dallas Branch (1988–94),
  Co-Chairman (1988–89)
• Young Entrepreneurs of Dallas (1988–90)

RICHARD L. BOSWELL

1234 West Cinnabar
Glendale, Arizona 85302
(602) 555-1234

EXPERIENCE

EMERGENCY ROOM TECHNICIAN . . . . *11/88 – Present*
Boswell Memorial Hospital, Sun City, Arizona
Assist physicians and nurses in the care of patients. Sign in patients – obtain history and vital signs. Perform CPR and other emergency first-aid measures. Communicate with nursing staff and patient's family concerning patient's condition. Use computer to order lab work, EKG, x-rays, and other studies and services.

SITE SUPERVISOR . . . . *7/88 – 11/88*
Northwest Protective Services, Tacoma, Washington
Supervised activities of 20 Community Service Representatives (CSRs) in the Business Improvement Area of downtown Tacoma. Acted as liaison between the Tacoma Police Department, client members, Northwest Protective Services management, and the general public. Assisted Tacoma Police Department by identifying drug-related activity and reporting findings to the downtown task force. Provided security patrols of businesses, parking areas, and public areas such as parks. Responsible for assigning and scheduling the CSRs.

COUNTERINTELLIGENCE AGENT, U.S. Army . . . . *4/85 – 7/88*
Investigated national security crimes (espionage, sabotage, sedition, subversion, and mutiny). Conducted background investigations for security clearances. Interviewed personnel for subject and witness reports. Obtained sworn statements. Provided counterterrorist analysis and database services. Served on hostage negotiations team for base counterterrorist exercises. Conducted counterintelligence special operations. Advised supported commanders on matters of personnel, information, and physical security.

MEDICAL SPECIALIST (Combat Medic), U.S. Army . . . . *1/83 – 4/85*
Battalion Aid Station Medical Supply NCO/Senior Medic. Administered first-aid and other lifesaving measures. Triaged casualties and directed flow. Assisted battalion physician's assistant in care of patients. Set up procedures for medical resupply and evaluation.

EMERGENCY ROOM TECHNICIAN, U.S. Air Force . . . . *7/80 – 1/83*
Responsible for the care and treatment of patients, including but not limited to suturing as directed by the physician, interviewing patients to determine treatment priority, administering first-aid to injured and seriously ill patients, and administering inoculations and injections as prescribed. Responsible for the care and maintenance of emergency medical equipment. Performed as emergency ambulance driver and/or attendant.

OBSTETRICAL SPECIALIST, U.S. Air Force . . . . *8/79 – 7/80*
Assisted midwives, OB physicians, and nurses in labor and delivery rooms and postpartum areas. Assisted in newborn infant care and GYN pre- and postoperative care. Performed administrative duties and trained newly assigned personnel.

EDUCATION

1987   *16 credits toward a NURSING DEGREE with Community College of the Air Force*
1987   *BASIC KOREAN LANGUAGE COURSE, U.S. Army, 1 year*
1985   *COUNTERINTELLIGENCE AGENT'S COURSE, U.S. Army*
1985   *PRODUCTIVE INTERROGATION COURSE, U.S. Army*
1981   *PROFESSIONAL MILITARY EDUCATION, Management & Leadership Training, U.S. Air Force*
1981   *CPR INSTRUCTORS COURSE, U.S. Air Force, 2 weeks*
1981   *EMERGENCY MEDICAL TECHNICIANS COURSE, U.S. Air Force, 1 week*
1980   *BASIC PHARMACOLOGY, U.S. Air Force, 1 week*
1979   *MEDICAL SERVICES SPECIALIST COURSE, U.S. Air Force, 6 weeks*

JOAN M. VOLUNTEER

1234 W. Wescott Drive • Peoria, Arizona 85382 • (602) 555-1234

ARROWHEAD COMMUNITY HOSPITAL, Glendale, Arizona . . . . Three years
Organized the hospital Auxiliary, serving as President the first year. Succeeding years served as ex-officio member of the Auxiliary Board of Directors, working on special fund-raising projects, as well as serving on the hospital volunteer staff. In a volunteer position, was responsible for contacting all discharged patients for their comments on patient care while hospitalized at Arrowhead Hospital.

COLTER VILLAGE, Glendale, Arizona . . . . One year
As Volunteer Coordinator, developed and organized a volunteer program for both the nursing home and the independent living apartment complex, which included recruiting, training, developing policies and procedures and job descriptions for all volunteer positions needed for the complex.

CRICKET GIFT SHOP, Metairie, Louisiana . . . . Two years
Manager and Buyer for a gift shop in a 200-apartment complex for senior citizens under HUD and church-supported assistance and guidelines. This position included designing the shop, ordering supplies, purchasing the stock, obtaining and training volunteers, developing policies and procedures, conducting semiannual inventories, preparing an annual profit and loss statement, and budget planning. The profit from the shop was used directly or indirectly for the residents' care and activities.

PRESBYTERIAN CHURCH KINDERGARTEN & PLAY SCHOOL, Metairie, Louisiana . . . . Two years
As Manager, supervised all aspects of the schools, including hiring of teachers and directors and managing a $100,000 annual budget.

PARKWAY PRESBYTERIAN CHURCH, CAREER GUIDANCE PROGRAM, Metairie, Louisiana . . One year
Chairman of a program targeted at high school juniors and seniors. The scope of the program included: 1) individual counseling by business leaders; 2) regular monthly group meetings; 3) testing through the University of Southern Mississippi, Hattiesburg; 4) follow-up counseling by the University counselors; 5) Career Night, a forum chaired by business leaders with individual interviews available for the students.

EAST JEFFERSON HOSPITAL, Metairie, Louisiana . . . . Seven years
Hospital volunteer for this 350-bed hospital, including Unit Clerk Assistant, Emergency Room Hostess, and Information Desk Clerk.

GIRL SCOUTS OF AMERICA, Philadelphia, Pennsylvania and Dallas, Texas . . . . Sixteen years
Neighborhood Chairman with responsibility for 26 troops (560 girls) and more than 75 adult leaders. Conducted leadership training for both the Neighborhood and the Council, and planned Neighborhood and city-wide events. Responsible for all troop organization, recruiting leaders and sponsors, arranging for meeting places, and obtaining other types of volunteers – all following the guidelines of the national and state organizations.

OTHER ORGANIZATIONS . . . . Various years
Publicity Chairman for the League of Women Voters in Dallas, Texas. Scheduler (Appointment Secretary) for a candidate running for State Representative in the State of Louisiana. Volunteer for the National Cancer Foundation, Red Cross, United Way Campaign, and the Freedom Train Foundation.

AWARDS

Honored in 1982 as one of twelve recipients of the **"Carnation Award"** given annually in New Orleans, Louisiana, for outstanding volunteer service to the community at large

"Certificate of Merit" for outstanding service to the Jefferson Parish Community of Louisiana, 1982

"Volunteer of the Year" award for 1982 by the Newcomers Club of New Orleans, Louisiana

Awarded for over 5,000 hours of service as a volunteer for Louisiana hospitals

Recognition award from Colter Village, Glendale, Arizona, for Service to the Older Adult

"Volunteer of the Year" award for 1989 by Arrowhead Community Hospital

RODNEY G. PILOTS
12345 N. 21st Avenue
Coeur d'Alene, Idaho 85306
(208) 555-1234

OBJECTIVE CAREER PILOT EMPLOYMENT

FLIGHT RATINGS
- Airline Transport Pilot
- Type Rated: Short 330-360
- Airplane SEL/MEL
- Instrument Instructor SEL/MEL

- Flight Instructor
- Rotorcraft-Helicopter
- F.E.X. Written 82%
- Medical Certificate: FAA Class I

FLIGHT TIME
- TOTAL 5810
- Pilot in Command 4775
- Second in Command 701
- Multiengine 2050
- Single Engine 3762
- Instructor 1305

- Turboprop 2580
- Helicopter 50
- Cross Country 3776
- Actual Instrument 478
- Simulated Instrument 136
- Night 1101

EXPERIENCE

PILOT IN COMMAND, Empire Airways . . . . 4/90 – Present
12345 Airport Drive, Hayden Lake, ID
Pilot in command of C-208A/B, Shorts 330. First Officer on a Foker F-27.
Part 121 and Part 135 scheduled air freight for Federal Express. Operate
throughout the Southwest.

PILOT IN COMMAND, P.M. Air . . . . 12/84 – 4/90
1234 E. Airlane, Phoenix, AZ
Pilot in command of C-208A/B, Piper Navajo, Shorts 330. Part 135
scheduled air freight for Federal Express and United Parcel Service.
Operate throughout the Southwest.

REFUELING LINEMAN . . . . 9/84 – 12/85
City of Phoenix, Sky Harbor Airport, Phoenix, AZ
Lineman responsible for refueling aircraft.

PARTS MANAGER . . . . 1/80 – 9/84
Sunstate Equipment, 1234 E. Washington, Phoenix, AZ
Responsible for stocking and dispensing parts for a variety of
heavy equipment.

SECURITY POLICE SUPERVISOR . . . . 12/70 – 8/79
U.S. Air Force, various locations

EDUCATION

CESSNA AIRCRAFT, Wichita, KS 8/85
Caravan I Captain's Training

SHORTS TRAINING SCHOOL, Phoenix, AZ 4/87

WILLIAMSPORT COMMUNITY COLLEGE, Williamsport, PA . . . . 9/69 – 4/70
Welding Specialist

TROY AREA HIGH SCHOOL, Troy, PA . . . . 9/65 – 6/69

GEORGE N. COLONY

123 East Briarwood Drive • New York, New York 12110 • (518) 555-1234

QUALIFICATIONS
- *Extensive knowledge of international markets and product promotion*
- *Multinational commercial and trade consulting experience*
- *Developed experience in business planning and new business development*
- *Effective cross-cultural abilities in European and Asian business environments*

EDUCATION

AMERICAN GRADUATE SCHOOL OF INTERNATIONAL MANAGEMENT, *Glendale, Arizona*
Master of International Management *(January 1994)*

WESTERN NEW ENGLAND COLLEGE SCHOOL OF LAW, *Springfield, Massachusetts*
Juris Doctor *(May 1989)*

UNIVERSITY OF HONG KONG, *British Crown Colony of Hong Kong (June 1987 – August 1987)*
- *Legal study drawn from the resources of University of Hong Kong and Shanghai Institute of Foreign Trade focusing on the trade and commercial activities of the Pacific Rim*
- *Special emphasis on Chinese-Hong Kong Commercial Law, intellectual property rights, and the promulgation of joint venture law in the People's Republic of China*

UNION COLLEGE, *Schenectady, New York*
Bachelor of Arts, Political Science *(June 1984)*
- *Concentration in International Studies*
- *Senior thesis: The Cypriot Crisis and U.S. Strategic Interest in the Eastern Mediterranean*
- *Semester at **College Year in Athens**, Athens, Greece (December 1983 – March, 1983)*

EXPERIENCE

CIBA-GEIGY CORPORATION, *Summit, New Jersey*
Product Management Intern *(June 1992 – August 1992)*
- *Participated in the drafting and presentation of marketing plan for ethical pharmaceutical product with sales of $100 million annually*
- *Assisted in the preparation of patient/physician marketing materials, including multimillion dollar national direct-to-consumer print campaign*
- *Prepared and presented to marketing management a comprehensive multi-year sales forecast relative to proposed second generation drug treatment*

KELLEHER & FLINK, *Latham, New York*
Associate *(November 1990 – January 1992; October 1992 – May 1993)*
- *Commercial and corporate practice with emphasis in the areas of business planning, mortgage banking, commercial real estate, and bankruptcy*
- *Participation in all aspects of commercial litigation, including motion practice, pretrial conferences, and settlement negotiations*

ROEMER & FEATHERSTONHAUGH, PC, *Albany, New York*
Associate *(September 1989 – November 1990)*
- *General litigation with emphasis in the areas of insurance defense, personal injury, matrimonial, medical malpractice, and commercial matters*
- *Responsible for prosecution and defense of claims*

WILKINSON & GRIST, *British Crown Colony of Hong Kong*
Law Clerk *(June 1987 – September 1987)*
- *Assisted clients in intellectual property matters*
- *Researched Hong Kong legal considerations regarding foreign-based multinational corporations and the effects of labor, commerce, and trade issues*

SYSCO CORPORATION, *Albany, New York*
National Account Executive *(July 1984 – September 1986)*
- *Established and monitored national chain accounts that constituted 24% of branch sales*
- *Responsible for sales growth and procurement of additional volume accounts, with average annual rate of expansion over 105%*

LANGUAGES
*Native in **English**, Proficient in **German**, Knowledge of **Greek***

HONORS & ACTIVITIES
- *American Jurisprudence Award for Academic Achievement in Antitrust Law*
- *New York and American Bar Associations*
- *American Graduate School of International Management Import/Export Club*

RICHARD L. GRILLER

Current:
1234 North Martel Avenue #123
Los Angeles, California 90046
(213) 555-1234

Permanent:
1234 Canyon Road
Macon, Georgia 31210
(912) 555-1234

QUALIFICATIONS
- Extensive European travel, lived four years in Europe
- Two and one-half years of comprehensive international management and marketing experience
- Generated over 80% profit growth in one of the largest dollar volume districts overseas

EXPERIENCE

OWNER/COFOUNDER, Pharr Side Bar and Grill, Atlanta, Georgia
1988–Present: Owner of a successful establishment that is still in operation.
- Responsible for planning marketing theme, inventory control, hiring, daily sales statements, monthly profit and loss statements, and personnel management.
- Directed remodeling and all start-up procedures; met opening time schedule.
- Ensured that start-up and equipment costs were kept in line.

MARKETING MANAGER, S & K Sales Company, International Division, Munich, West Germany
1986–1987: Responsible for sales and merchandising of S & K's products in Germany and Italy.
- Increased promotion and distribution support, resulting in 40% volume increase.
- Responsible for hiring, training, payment, and field supervision of 30+ staff.
- Generated new accounts by cold calling.
- Responsible for successful preparation and presentation of quarterly business reviews covering distribution and sales, market share, key accounts, and operational/promotional budget analysis.
- Planned and coordinated sales demonstrations of products.

AREA MANAGER, Milbrands, Inc., Munich, West Germany
1985–1986: Responsible for sales and merchandising of Milbrands brokered products in Germany.
- Increased territory sales by 100%.
- Due to short-term sales volume and distribution increases in territory, company management doubled the territory size.
- Initiated a special ordering process to allow low-volume stores to obtain frequent deliveries of new or promotional items.
- Increased sales by 30% through implementation and maintenance of General Electric major appliance displays.
- Achieved outstanding territory sales growth ratio with European Division by increasing distribution from 40% to 90%.

SALESMAN, STORES CLERK, LABORER, Macon, Georgia
1978–1984: Positions with Shaw's Fine Clothiers, Armstrong World Industries, Inc., MacMillan Construction Company, and Beauregard's.

EDUCATION

AMERICAN GRADUATE SCHOOL OF INTERNATIONAL MANAGEMENT
Thunderbird Campus, Glendale, Arizona
Master of International Management, December 1990
GOETHE INSTITUTE, Munich, West Germany – German Language Course, 1987
UNIVERSITY OF GEORGIA, Athens, Georgia – BBA in Finance, 1983
NETHERLANDS SCHOOL OF BUSINESS, Breukelen, The Netherlands
International Finance & Marketing, 1982

LANGUAGES
Proficient in **German**

PERSONAL
- Single, born 1960, excellent health, willing to travel and relocate
- University of Georgia Activities: Sigma Chi Fraternity, Phi Eta Sigma, Freshmen Honorary Society, Pi Sigma Epsilon, Marketing Club, Finance Club
- Hobbies: Snow skiing, tennis, golf, drawing and architecture, history, reading

Sharon W. Kaler

12345 W. Peoria Drive • Glendale, Arizona 85307 • (602) 555-1234

OBJECTIVE   A position as a veterinary technician

QUALIFICATIONS
- **Friendly, outgoing, and personable** with well-developed interpersonal skills; interacts effectively with the public, coworkers and superiors.
- **Strong background in animal husbandry.**
- **Strong clerical/organizational skills**; knowledge of computer operations with experience in a variety of administrative/management functions.
- **Versatile and resourceful**; adapts easily to new environments, and requirements.
- **Conscientious and detail oriented**; reputation for dependability, integrity, and professionalism.

EXPERIENCE

HEAD VETERINARY TECHNICIAN
43rd Avenue Animal Hospital, Glendale, Arizona (9/93 – Present)
- Assisted doctor in surgeries, including preparation and postoperative care
- Responsible for ordering and maintaining inventory of supplies and drugs
- Drew blood and performed in-house blood tests, such as QBC, VEtTEST, PCV, TP, AZO, heartworm antigen test, and FeLV cite probe test; also set up and read fecals and parvo cite probe tests
- Administered injections and medications, treated wounds and abscesses, set IV catheters and fluids, performed dental scales and polishes, and made/processed radiographs
- Communicated post-surgery instructions to clients upon release of pet and followed up with telephone call the day after surgery or hospital release to check on patient and to answer any client questions
- Directed and trained kennel employees
- Assisted computerized front office during busy times by taking payments, making appointments, and receiving clients.

VETERINARY ASSISTANT
Agua Fria Animal Hospital, Avondale, Arizona (10/92 – 3/93)
- Rotated through all areas of the hospital, including front and back office duties
- Assisted in surgeries, including anesthesia, preparation, and postoperative care

MANAGER
Ethel M. Chocolates, Phoenix, Arizona (11/86 – 10/90)
- Managed all retail store operations, including hiring/training employees, inventory/cost controls, and customer relations
- Solicited corporate accounts and made presentations at trade shows
- Designed and conducted multi-store employee sales motivation and professionalism training seminars
- Increased sales and achieved outstanding performance level
- Utilized company central computer for all accounting and record keeping

JR. CATTLE COMMITTEE MEMBER
Arizona National Livestock Show, Phoenix, Arizona (1982 – 1992)
- Assisted in direction of show, acted as ring steward, managed setup, and nose printed cattle for I.D. purposes
- Provided trouble shooting and public relations skills
- Jr. Cattle Committee Secretary for four years

STABLE ATTENDANT
University of Arizona Horse Farms, Tucson, Arizona (1985 – 1986)
- Assisted in equine research, including breeding, grooming, training, exercising, administering medications, and assisting veterinarians

OPTOMETRIC ASSISTANT
Dr. John Doe, Phoenix, Arizona (1978 – 1982)
- Successfully developed retail selling skills: greeted customers and determined their specific needs; demonstrated and fit glasses; made repairs and adjustments; trained new contact lens wearers
- Responsible for both front and back office duties, handling billing and receptionist duties

EDUCATION   **LONG MEDICAL INSTITUTE**, Phoenix, Arizona   2/92 – 10/92
Graduate of Veterinary Assistant Program

UNIVERSITY OF ARIZONA, Tucson, Arizona   1984 – 1987
Major: Animal Science

93

Dawn M. Thomas

5244 Aspen Hills Way
Colorado Springs, Colorado 80917
(719) 555-1234

OBJECTIVE

A responsible administrative position where education and experience, combined with positive interpersonal skills, initiative, and the capacity to motivate others, can be utilized to mutual benefit.

QUALIFICATIONS

- Experienced in administration, accounting, customer service, and counseling.
- Willing to assume responsibility, self-motivated, possess a high degree of professional integrity.
- Well-rounded, flexible team player with the demonstrated capacity to learn quickly and apply that knowledge effectively.
- Skilled in applying a logical, common sense approach to seeking practical solutions.
- Well-organized, inquisitive problem solver who enjoys challenges and thrives in a "people" environment.
- Communicate effectively when dealing with people of diverse interests and levels of authority – develop rapport easily and motivate others to maximum openness and cooperation.
- Proficient in WordPerfect, FoxPro, Quattro Pro, JR-Link, and Print Master Gold computer software.

EXPERIENCE

1993 – Present

GOODWILL INDUSTRIES, Colorado Springs, Colorado
Administrative Associate . . . Assist the Vice President of Operations/Sales and Operations Director in office management and report preparation, including month-end statements, filing, retrieval of information, and communicating directives. Perform general administrative and secretarial duties. Calculate salvage records and compute quarterly salvage reports. Control requisition/purchase order system and organize bids for large dollar purchases. Calculate daily and weekly production records and process final numbers for the Accounting Department. Act as liaison between Operations/Sales, Store Managers, and Administration.

1991

U.S. ARMY TANK-AUTOMOTIVE COMMAND, Warren, Michigan
Secretary . . . Provided administrative support to the Section Chief. Prepared reports, entered contract revisions, answered telephones, and performed all clerical functions required.

1986 – 1989

AMERICAN RED CROSS, Kitzingen, Germany
Bookkeeper . . . Managed $100,000 operating budget. Maintained accounts payable records, reviewed invoices, and processed checks. Wrote and disbursed staff payroll. Implemented computerized accounting system and developed computerized inventory control/purchasing system for greater efficiency and cost effectiveness.
Counselor . . . Counseled service personnel and families requiring financial assistance and/or experiencing personal problems. Assisted in securing financial aid and making travel arrangements for emergency leaves. Outlined individual options and referred to other community resources.
Volunteer . . . Supervised up to 50 volunteers while serving as Hospitality Chairperson.

1974 – 1985

DEERE & COMPANY, Moline, Illinois
Customer Service Representative . . . Served as liaison between company, dealers, and customers. Researched and resolved customer problems, responded to information inquiries, located nearest dealer, advised of parts availability, and processed orders for customers in areas not serviced by dealers. Played a key role in conversion to new computer system and maintaining dealer and parts data, resulting in improved response time.

EDUCATION

Dec. 1994

BACHELOR OF SCIENCE DEGREE IN BUSINESS ADMINISTRATION
Regis University, Colorado Springs, Colorado

Feb. 1994

ASSOCIATE DEGREE IN BUSINESS
Northwood University, Mount Clemens, Michigan

CLEMENT ROBERT WIGGER

1234 Belden Drive • Los Angeles, California 90068 • Telephone: (213) 555-1234 • Fax: (213) 555-1234

QUALIFICATIONS
- Strongly motivated marketing professional with expertise in product development
- Excellent interpersonal and analytical skills
- Extensive customer service and consumer marketing experience
- Highly proficient in **Spanish**

EXPERIENCE

INDEPENDENT MARKETING & MANAGEMENT CONSULTANT (August 1993 – Present)

Los Angeles Times, Los Angeles, California
- Developing and implementing a promotional program with Delta Airlines to place the *Los Angeles Times* on all international flights, giving the newspaper a more global presence
- Assisting in the search for a new distributor for the *Los Angeles Times* in Mexico
- Helping to acquire sales for the *Nuestro Tiempo* Spanish language newspaper
- Developed five-year marketing and sales plan for the *Nuestro Tiempo* Spanish newspaper

Globe Media Incorporated, Mexico City
- Account Manager for the *Los Angeles Times* in Mexico
- Secured advertising and assisted in the development of client brand awareness
- Recommended and successfully implemented structural changes in the office's staffing and operation
- Developed a computer database system for Globe's sales force in order to access pertinent client information

Freeman Cosmetics, Beverly Hills, California
- Formulated a proposal and bid for the $6.5 million Delta Airlines first class and business class amenity kit project
- Blended Delta's idea of an all-natural amenity kit with Freeman's current international marketing strategy

Assistance in Marketing, Long Beach, California
- Developed a Hispanic marketing research project for McDonald's Corporation
- Modified the English and Spanish questionnaires to reflect cultural variations between the Hispanic ethnic groups living in Southern California
- Assisted in the formation of the research test sample
- Recruited Hispanic questioners and monitored their performance

DELTA AIRLINES (1987 – 1993)

District Marketing Analyst
- Assisted in designing public relations campaign to assure Delta's eventual approval of their application for the Los Angeles–Hong Kong route
- Analyzed markets, evaluating regional demand trends and customer satisfaction
- Assisted in the development of flight services quality assurance program
- Managed international flight attendants as an International In-Flight Service Coordinator

COMPUTERS WordPerfect, Word, Harvard Graphics, @ Risk, Paradox, PowerPoint, Lotus 1-2-3, FoxPro

EDUCATION

MASTER OF INTERNATIONAL MANAGEMENT (August 1992)
American Graduate School of International Management
Thunderbird Campus, Glendale, Arizona
- Emphasis in International Marketing and Sales
- Regional specialty in Latin America
- Analyzed Japanese airline industry for future growth patterns and outlook
- Winterim 1992 in Costa Rica and Nicaragua – Latin American Studies

BACHELOR OF ARTS (December 1990)
Antioch University, Yellow Springs, Ohio
- Major in Organizational Management
- Minor in Latin American Studies

JENNY L. HASKINS

Paraprofessional Accountant

1234 W. Rome Avenue, Phoenix, Arizona 85037

Phone: (602) 555-1234

EMPLOYMENT HISTORY

April 1989
to
Present

ASSISTANT CONTROLLER/CONTROLLER
Omni Adams Hotel, Phoenix, Arizona
(Formerly Sheraton Phoenix Hotel)
Hired as Assistant Controller but ended as one of five controllers in three years. Managed and projected cash flow, working daily with banks, corporate office, and vendors. Supervised accounts receivable and payable. Performed usual accounting duties, including financial statements, audit schedules, budgets, and numerous special projects for owners. Utilized Lotus 1-2-3, WordPerfect, Datanamics, and Lodging Systems software.

September 1987
to
March 1989

ASSISTANT CONTROLLER/CONTROLLER
Happy Trails Resort, et al., Surprise, Arizona
(Subsidiaries of Western Savings and Loan Association)
Produced bank reconciliations, journal entries, sales and property tax returns, financial statements, reports, and budgets. Reconciled intercompany accounts, including on the books at the bank. Utilized Lotus 1-2-3 and did trouble shooting on Lodgistix hospitality software.

January 1987
to
September 1987

CONTROLLER
Outdoor Enterprises/RoadVantage Corporations
Surprise, Arizona and Carson City, Nevada
(Sister companies to Happy Trails, divisions of Thousand Trails, Inc.)
Performed cleanup and original bookkeeping, journal entry, and analysis work for multifaceted companies involved in travel package sales, insurance, road service packages, and Visa credit cards. Produced all financial statements, reports, and tax returns. Changed accounting system and setup on Lodgistix. Also used Lotus 1-2-3.

February 1984
to
January 1987

PARAPROFESSIONAL ACCOUNTANT
Deloitte Haskins & Sells, Phoenix, Arizona
Gained multi-industry experience through the Emerging Business Department. Provided range of client services from accounting cleanup and setup to financial statements, tax returns, reviews, and projected financial statements used in public offering. Produced tax returns for individuals, partnerships, and corporations, manually and on Fast-Tax software. Trained DHS personnel on Lotus 1-2-3 and used it extensively for client and administrative work. Used various software, mostly CYMA.

August 1981
to
February 1984

STUDENT
Glendale Community College, Glendale, Arizona
Accounting studies toward A.A. degree

1971 to 1981

VARIED ACCOUNTING AND CLERICAL EXPERIENCE
Industries included wholesale, dairy, welfare, trucking, and insurance

REFERENCES AVAILABLE UPON REQUEST

JON M. SERGEANT

P. O. Box 1234, Clearlake Park, California 95424   *(707) 555-1234*

OBJECTIVE

*A position with growth potential where my discipline, positive attitude,
professionalism, and untiring efforts and interests can be used.*

WORK EXPERIENCE

**April 1990
to Present**

MERCHANDISER
Pepsi-Cola Bottling Company, *Clearlake Park, California*
Duties include restocking store shelves, building and taking down Pepsi displays, rotation of product according to code date, condensing and organizing stock in back rooms, inventory of product, and customer service.

**May 1985
to March 1990**

AIRCRAFT MAINTENANCE SPECIALIST
Sergeant, United States Air Force, *Luke Air Force Base, Glendale, Arizona*
Responsible for maintaining a safe and productive aircraft maintenance atmosphere. Duties included completion of maintenance in a timely and accurate fashion. Performed extensive preflight and postflight inspections, launch and recovery procedures. Maintained aircraft documentation with the Core Automated Maintenance System (CAMS). Duties also included supervision and computer operations. Demonstrated excellent verbal and written communication skills.

**July 1987
to December 1989**

MECHANIC
Sears and Roebuck Co., *Metro Center Parkway, Phoenix, Arizona*
Promoted after one year of service from tire installer to mechanic. Duties included brake service, computerized wheel alignments, safety inspections, removal and replacement of front end and suspension parts, re-service and trouble shooting air conditioner systems.

**June 1982
to October 1984**

COURTESY CLERK
Thrifty Drug and Discount, *Clearlake, California*
Responsible for the liquor and tobacco department. Duties included ordering and restocking shelves, managing and maintaining the liquor room, operating the cash register, and customer service.

**July 1980
to June 1981**

FOOD PREPARER
Treasure Cove Pizza, *Clearlake Oaks, California*
Duties included operating the cash register, running the bar, customer service, oven man, and general supervision of new employees.
Lakeshore Union 76 Station, *Clearlake, California*
Promoted from station attendant to supervisor. Supervised a small, independently owned station. Duties included opening and closing of station, minor repairs, and customer service.

EDUCATION

**February 1985
to March 1990**

ACADEMIC SPECIALTY
Community College of the Air Force
Studied aircraft maintenance technology. Credited with 17 semester hours.

BERNADETTE BARROW, RN

1234 West Northern Avenue, #1234 • Glendale, Arizona 85301 • Phone: (602) 555-1234

PROFESSIONAL OBJECTIVE

To broaden my nursing experience to include critical care and emergency room nursing while pursuing my BSN degree.

EXPERIENCE

Sep. 1991 – Present

ACUTE NEUROLOGICAL MEDICAL/SURGICAL CHARGE NURSE
Barrow Neurological Institute, St. Joseph's Hospital and Medical Center, Phoenix, Arizona
Responsibilities include evaluation and supervision of all unit patients, assignment of patient care based on acuity, staff resource person, doctor/patient liaison, implementation of nursing process, assisting with new employee orientation and evaluation of employee performance, implementation of JCAHO requirements, and total quality management.

May 1991 – Present

STAFF RN – ACUTE SEMI-INTENSIVE CARE UNITS
Barrow Neurological Institute, St. Joseph's Hospital and Medical Center, Phoenix, Arizona
Responsibilities include care of critical neuro patients with diagnosis of traumatic brain and spinal injuries, brain tumors, neurological disorders, cerebral vascular accidents, and pre- and post-operational medical/surgical patients. Patient care includes experience with tracheostomies, intubations and ventilators, basic EKG monitoring, lumbar drains, halo braces, spinal braces, tractions, patient teaching of self-care, and general nursing duties. Other duties include float nursing to oncology, orthopedics, spinal and brain rehab, pain clinic, and general medical/surgical nursing units, participating in nursing committee meetings, and community/education programs.

May 1990 – May 1991

NURSING ASSISTANT II
Barrow Neurological Institute, St. Joseph's Hospital and Medical Center, Phoenix, Arizona
Responsibilities included all student nurse functions with exception of administration of medication.

NURSING ASSISTANT

Sep. 1974 – Nov. 1974 **St. Benedicts Hospital**, Ogden, Utah
June 1974 – Sep. 1974 **Mercy Medical Center**, Durango, Colorado
Responsibilities at both facilities included general nursing assistant duties with orthopedic patients on orthopedic floors.

EDUCATION

Fall 1987 – Spring 1991

ASSOCIATE DEGREE IN NURSING
Glendale Community College, Glendale, Arizona
Nursing major. Graduated with honors, GPA of 3.90. Recipient of Pursuit of Excellence Award, Top Graduating RN, 1991. President of Glendale Association of Student Nurses, member of Student Honors Organization, elected to Who's Who Among American Junior College Students, and was a participant in Phi Theta Kappa "Out Reach" tutoring program.

Jan. 1986 – June 1986

COMPUTER CLASS
Western Wyoming College, Rock Springs, Wyoming
Basic computer programming.

Continuing Education Courses: 10th Annual BNI Nursing Symposium, 2nd Annual Neuro Rehabilitation Symposium, Smoking Cessation at the Bedside, Critical Care Pulmonary Workshop, Basic EKG Interpretation.

LICENSURE

Currently licensed in the state of Arizona as a Registered Nurse.

7 GEOGRAPHIC LOCATION

With my international clients, the fact that they have worked, studied, or traveled abroad strengthens their credentials for international jobs. Therefore, placing the geographic location of their work experience or schooling in a prominent location can be to their advantage.

Other times, it is only part of the overall design of the information. However, making it prominent does give it more importance, whether that was the intention or not.

When you really want the geographic locations of your past experience to stand out, the easiest way to accomplish that is to make them flush right (pages 102, 103, 104, and 106) or to place them in the left-hand column of the resume (page 100). Another alternative is to tab to a fixed place on the page for each location, as in the example on page 105.

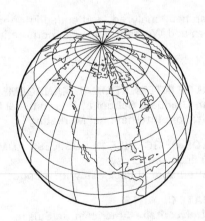

Rene Michelle Fritz

WORK EXPERIENCE

July 1993 – Present
Balboa, Panama

DUANE & ASSOCIATES, INC.
Account Executive
- Accounts: Radisson Resorts (Bahamas), Aeromexpress Cargo (Aeromexico, Aeroperu, Mexicana), Metro Bank, Barbachano Tours
- Work closely with clients to fulfill marketing and advertising goals
- Coordinate production of print advertising, radio/TV spots, and collateral material
- Organize and oversee direct mailings

Sep. – Dec. 1992
Glendale, Arizona

HEWLETT-PACKARD – INTERAD
Marketing Research Director
- Conducted an in-depth market research study of the scanner market in China
- Developed international marketing strategy for product line

Summer 1992
New York, New York

FRITZ COMPANIES, INC.
Intern
- Assisted branch manager with sales support activities, including scheduling, follow-ups, proposal preparation, and obtaining competitive price quotes
- Culled and analyzed documentation for potential trade lane-specific sales leads

Jan. – May 1992
Glendale, Arizona

UNIVISION AND TELEMUNDO COMPANY
Consultant – Thunderbird Corporate Consulting Group
- Researched the Hispanic market in Albuquerque and Santa Fe
- Produced a report to assist in the selling of TV and radio advertising space

Summer 1989
Balboa, Republic of Panama

PANAMA CANAL COMMISSION – MARINE BUREAU
Student Assistant
- Supported tugboat operations by handling daily purchase requests and materials

Summer 1988
Geneva, Switzerland

UNITED NATIONS – ECONOMIC COMMISSION FOR EUROPE
Intern
- Researched, analyzed, and coded information concerning contracts between Eastern and Western European corporations

EDUCATION

December 1992
Glendale, Arizona

MASTER OF INTERNATIONAL MANAGEMENT
American Graduate School of International Management – Thunderbird Campus
Concentration: International Marketing

May 1991
Washington, DC

BACHELOR OF SCIENCE IN BUSINESS ADMINISTRATION
The American University
Major: International Business with a concentration in Marketing

May 1989
Leysin, Switzerland

ASSOCIATE OF ARTS
Institut Universitaire Américain de Suisse
Focus: International Business

Prior to 1988

All other education in the Republic of Panama

LANGUAGES
COMPUTERS

Fluent in **English** and **Spanish**   •   Proficient in **French**
Paradox, WordPerfect, Lotus 1-2-3, BASIC

PERSONAL

Eligible to work in the United States and Latin America
Extensive travel experience to four continents

Address   •   Apartado 1234, Balboa, Republic of Panama   •   (507) 555-1234

100

Pamela Ann Bloomingdale

WORK EXPERIENCE

M&M Mars   Hackettstown, NJ
Media Buying Analyst. Reviewed media purchasing procedures at Mars, Inc., including an examination of Agency of Record capabilities. Researched media buying alternatives and interviewed independent media service groups and corporate media centers. Created a spreadsheet system for efficient transfer of agency reports. Developed and recommended a spot market test and procedural changes for potential competitive advantages in media buying.   (6/91 – Present)

Bloomingdale's   New York, NY
Executive Trainee and Assistant Department Manager. Assisted in merchandising a biannual merchandise volume of $19.3M in the Women's Coat Department and Leather Shop and managing a sales staff of 18 associates. "Superior" performance ratings led to assistant buyer responsibilities, including continued development of vendor relations and inventory reordering.   (8/89 – 7/90)

International Commission for Jurists (ICJ)   Geneva, Switzerland
Lawyer's Aide. Attended and reported on hearings of the Human Rights Commission at the United Nations. Synthesized proposals for a "right to communication" and presented summary to UNESCO. Internship was conducted in French.   (1/88 – 5/88)

Overseas Private Investment Corporation (OPIC)   Washington, D.C.
Marketing Intern. Researched and recruited U.S. companies to participate in investment missions to Third World countries. Prepared briefing books, researched talking points for countries, and updated all investment projects resulting from OPIC investment missions of 1981 through 1987. Position demanded rapid assimilation of complex information.   (6/87 – 8/87)

Provident Bank   Cincinnati, OH
Operations Assistant, Installment Loan Department. Computed home equity and debt to income equations for mortgage loan applications. Position demanded rapid assimilation of complex information and writing detailed correspondence to private U.S. companies.   (6/88 – 8/88)

Title Clerk, Installment Loan Department. Discharged liens, gave credit references, input computer data, typed correspondence, maintained files.   (6/86 – 9/86)

EDUCATION

American Graduate School of International Management (Thunderbird)   Glendale, AZ
Master of International Management, GPA 3.8/4.0 (with distinction)   May 1992

University of Michigan   Ann Arbor, MI
Bachelor of Arts in Political Science and French   May 1989

LANGUAGES
Highly proficient in **French**, working knowledge of **German**, and knowledge of **Spanish**
COMPUTERS
Lotus 1-2-3, dBASE, Harvard Graphics, PageMaker, Microsoft Word, WordPerfect, Excel, Quicken

ACTIVITIES
- *Front Line Forum*, Marketing Spokesperson
- *Das Tor*, AGSIM newspaper, Business Manager
- Ambassador Club, Campus Guide
- Recipient of Procter and Gamble Scholarship (NMSC)
- Kappa Kappa Gamma, Philanthropy Officer
- Ann Arbor Hunger Coalition

PERSONAL
Have spent seven years in Belgium and six months in Switzerland. Traveled extensively throughout Europe, the former Soviet Union, and Central America. Active in sports, in particular, horseback riding, skiing, and tennis. Art enthusiast.

ADDRESS   1234 Sandstorm Place, Cleveland, Ohio 45243   (513) 555-1234

MICHAEL J. GEORGE
12345 Highland Avenue
Wilmette, Illinois 60091
(708) 555-1234

EXPERIENCE

1992 – Present

PROGRAM DIRECTOR
International Development Exchange   Lodz, Poland
- Supported development and implementation of management training courses.
- Assisted in asset valuation of state-run companies preparing for privatization.
- Cooperated in development of seminar for several Polish interests on topic of alternative financing in the privatization process.

1991

MARKETING INTERN
Pascoe Nally International   New York, New York
- Supported arrangement of all television, sponsorship, supplier, and licensing agreements for the World University Games.
- Created proposal to promote development of sponsors for a sports medicine conference.
- Organized and directed promotional events.

1988 – 1990

LEGAL ASSISTANT   Chicago, Illinois
Clausen, Miller, Gorman, Caffrey & Witous, P.C.
- Responsible for organizing and maintaining a multidistrict litigation case file, which required full computerization of documents.
- Assisted attorneys in preparation for depositions and major litigation.
- Attended document productions, abstracted legal documents, and assisted in trial practice sessions.

1986 – 1987

MARKETING REPRESENTATIVE   Washington, D.C.
Anheuser/Busch
- Responsible for creation and distribution of promotional materials for school sports teams.
- Helped coordinated school-wide social events.
- Participated in national marketing seminar.
- Established campus alcohol-awareness events.

1987

FINANCIAL SERVICES INTERN   Chicago, Illinois
Continental Bank
- Researched corporations' cash management systems and created proposals for more efficient cash management.
- Assisted in establishing 1988 cash management market plans for the department.
- Gained experience in corporate customer relations.

EDUCATION

1991

MASTER OF INTERNATIONAL MANAGEMENT   Glendale, Arizona
American Graduate School of International Management (Thunderbird)
Relevant Course Work: Advanced Corporate Finance, Intermediate Accounting, International Finance and Trade, International Marketing Management

1988

BSFS INTERNATIONAL POLITICS   Washington, D.C.
Georgetown University
Concentration in International Relations, Law, and Organization

1986

SUMMER SESSION   Avignon, France
Institute of American Universities

ABILITIES

- French language: Proficient
- Computer: Working knowledge of all applicable business programs
- Extensive travel in and knowledge of Western and Eastern Europe

Samuel Fernando

OBJECTIVE	A position in finance/marketing leading to a career in International Management	

EDUCATION

MASTER OF INTERNATIONAL MANAGEMENT — *May 1995*
American Graduate School of International Management — *Glendale, Arizona*
Thunderbird Campus
Courses include:
- Import/Export Management
- Marketing to U.S. Hispanics Workshop
- International Marketing Research
- International Insurance Management

BACHELOR OF BUSINESS ADMINISTRATION — *May 1993*
The Wichita State University — *Wichita, Kansas*
Major: International Business
Minor: Economics
Courses include:
- Managerial Finance
- International Finance
- Cost Accounting
- International Purchasing

WORK EXPERIENCE

ASSISTANT AUDITOR (AIESEC Internship) — *Summer 1993*
Government of Comunidad Autónoma de la Rioja — *Logroño, Spain*
- Audited local wineries and presented report on financial status to management
- Assisted in government accounting process
- Sorted and filed local business proposals

ASSISTANT INVENTORY MANAGER — *Summer 1991*
Latin American Mission — *San José, Costa Rica*
- Managed inventory of construction materials
- Translated instruction manuals from English to Spanish
- Served as liaison between Costa Rican and U.S. work teams

CONFERENCE STAFF — *Summer 1990*
Billy Graham Association — *Amsterdam, The Netherlands*
- Supervised and coordinated activities for Latin American participants
- Served as English/Spanish interpreter
- Assisted with international human resources management

FOUNDER-PRESIDENT — *1985 – 1989*
Transportes Bello — *Bogotá, Colombia*
- Performed marketing/financial planning and analysis
- Managed human resources
- Directed public relations

ACTIVITIES

LATIN AMERICAN CLUB — *Fall 1994*
- Chairman Social Activities — *Glendale, Arizona*

WORLD TRADE CENTER OF WICHITA — *1992 – 1993*
The Wichita State University — *Wichita, Kansas*
- Assisted in organizing world trade meetings on behalf of the local business community

LANGUAGES

Native language **Spanish** ◆ Fluent in **English** ◆ Proficient in **Portuguese**

COMPUTERS

Lotus 1-2-3, WordPerfect, and dBASE III PLUS

School Address: P.O. Box 1234 ◆ Glendale, Arizona 85306 ◆ (602) 555-1234
Permanent Address: 1234 E. 13th Street ◆ Wichita, Kansas 67208 ◆ (316) 555-1234

Barbara J. Attorney

PROFILE
Diversified, outgoing professional who combines an excellent academic background with vast international experience. Ambitious and creative, enjoys challenging projects. Detailed and skilled in setting priorities.

OBJECTIVE
To utilize marketing, managerial, communication, and analytical skills in an entry-level position with a multinational firm leading to a senior executive position with increased levels of responsibility

EDUCATION

AMERICAN GRADUATE SCHOOL OF INTERNATIONAL MANAGEMENT — Glendale, AZ — 1995
Thunderbird Campus
Master of International Management – Marketing

ILLINOIS INSTITUTE OF TECHNOLOGY – CHICAGO KENT COLLEGE OF LAW — Chicago, IL — 1990
Juris Doctor – International Law and Business Law

NORTHWESTERN UNIVERSITY — Evanston, IL — 1987
Bachelor of Arts – German Studies

UNIVERSITÄT REGENSBURG — Germany — 1986
Completed courses toward German Studies degree

GOETHE INSTITUT — Germany — 1985
Zertifikat Deutsch als Fremdsprache

EXPERIENCE

CIRCUIT COURT OF COOK COUNTY — Chicago, IL — 1993
Office of the Chief Judge – Legal Research Division
Staff Researcher

SUNRISE VILLAGE APARTMENTS — Glendale, AZ — 1992
Residential Leasing Representative
- Conducted monthly market surveys of competing properties
- Marketed and leased apartment homes
- Increased and maintained occupancy levels at 97%

SHEA, ROGAL AND ASSOCIATES — Westchester, IL — 1989
Law Clerk

CIRCUIT COURT OF COOK COUNTY — Chicago, IL — 1988
Law Clerk

JAMES H. SCHREIBER, LTD. — Willow Springs, IL — 1987 – 1990
Administrative Assistant
- Performed monthly billing and accounting
- Purchased, stocked, and sold merchandise for retail operations
- Reorganized and maintained the bookkeeping and filing systems
- Translated international invoices and correspondence

CRATE AND BARREL — Skokie, IL — 1986
Salesperson

LANGUAGES
German – fluent • **French** – working knowledge

SKILLS
WordPerfect, IBM AS400, Lotus 1-2-3, dBASE, LEXIS/NEXIS, WESTLAW

12345 Woodbury Road • Chicago, Illinois 60521 U.S.A. • Eve (708) 555-1234 • Day (312) 555-1234

PIA POSADA

EXPERIENCE

INTERFACE ARNESSE INTERNATIONAL, INC.   **Puebla, Mexico**
MANAGEMENT TRAINEE   Sept. 1991 – Present
- Conduct cross-cultural research on protocols and business customs for U.S. companies doing business with foreign countries
- Produced research for a tourism and trade seminar focused on Canada and Mexico
- Translation and revision of technical documents in Spanish and German
- Voice-over for International Visitors Program

WORLD TRANSLATION SERVICES   **Phoenix, Arizona**   Sept. 1991 – Present
TRANSLATOR AND INTERPRETER
- Translation of documents in Spanish, German, and French
- Simultaneous translator for Spanish/English hearings

HOTEL POSADA DE LA MISIÓN   **Taxco, Mexico**
HOTEL MANAGEMENT TRAINING PROGRAM   Winter 1990 – 1991
- Received management training in the following departments: Reservations, Front Desk, Restaurant/Bar, Kitchen, Housekeeping, and Accounting
- Conducted public relations activities and served as an interpreter

GRAFIBA S.A., Subsidiary of Reynolds Aluminum   **Barcelona, Spain**
EXECUTIVE ASSISTANT TO THE GENERAL MANAGER   1989
- Negotiated sales of manufacturing equipment to foreign customers
- Contacted potential customers and suppliers in seven different countries
- Translated documents and correspondence in Spanish, English, German, and French

ZDF GERMAN TV – SOCCER WORLD CUP   **Mexico City, Mexico**
TECHNICAL ASSISTANT TO THE PRODUCTION MANAGER   Summer 1986
- Organized interviews with well-known public figures
- Served as interpreter between German and Mexican TV crews
- Coordinated transportation of office crew and studio guests

EDUCATION

MASTER OF INTERNATIONAL MANAGEMENT   May 1991
American Graduate School of International Management
Thunderbird Campus   **Glendale, Arizona**
- Academic emphasis in Marketing and Management
- Relevant course work included International Marketing Management, Marketing Research, Finance & Trade, Business-to-Business Marketing, Direct Foreign Investment & Technology Transfer, and Tourism and Economic Development

BACHELOR OF SCIENCE IN POLITICAL SCIENCE *cum laude*   1988
Oklahoma State University   **Stillwater, Oklahoma**
- Major in International Relations, Second Major in French, Minor in German

UNIVERSITÉ DE LA SORBONNE   **Paris, France**   Summer 1987
- Certificat de Langue Française

LANGUAGES

Fluent in Spanish, English, and German – Proficient in French

ACTIVITIES

- Member of Organizational Committee for two International Colloquiums on Latin American authors at Oklahoma State University
- Tae Kwon Do Instructor – Refereed and participated in tournaments; trained and supervised 15 students

INTERNATIONAL EXPERIENCE

- Resided four years in Germany, fifteen years in Mexico, five years in the United States, and one year in Spain
- Traveled extensively through Mexico, the United States, and Europe

ADDRESS   Apartado Postal 123, Puebla, Pue. 72000 Mexico   (22) 555-1234

PRABUDDHA NATH BENGALI

EDUCATION

1995 | **MASTER OF INTERNATIONAL MANAGEMENT**
American Graduate School of International Management | Glendale, Arizona

1990 | **SUBSIDIARY COURSES**
Royal College of Medicine | London, England
• Cardiovascular Diseases and Treatments

1990 | **Sandoz AG** | Weggis, Switzerland
• Quantitative and Qualitative Marketing Research

1988 | **BACHELOR OF ARTS IN INTERNATIONAL RELATIONS**
Pomona College | Claremont, California

1984 | **HIGH SCHOOL DIPLOMA**
Ecole d'Humanite | Hasliberg, Switzerland

EXPERIENCE

6/91 – 12/93 | **PROJECT MANAGER**
Infratest Health Research | Munich, Germany
• Initiated client contact with pharmaceutical companies in Europe and the United States
• Designed qualitative and quantitative research studies to client specifications
• Coordinated international studies and conducted research briefings
• Analyzed data and made recommendations and conclusions
• Presented research findings to client
• Experienced in the areas of hypertension, cerebral vascular disease, osteoporosis, cancer, and diagnostic imaging equipment

3/90 – 12/90 | **MARKET RESEARCH ANALYST**
Sandoz AG | Basel, Switzerland
• Performed qualitative and quantitative marketing research for mental health and cardiovascular products, both existing and in the research pipeline
• Participated in multinational repositioning exercise for important Sandoz product
• Interacted extensively with clinical research personnel

1/89 – 2/90 | **ASSISTANT MANAGER, NEW PRODUCTS DIVISION**
Progressive Technologies, Ltd. | Gurgaon, India
• Set the groundwork for a foreign collaboration with Bausch and Lomb
• Facilitated licensing, transfer of technology agreements, company structure agreements, etc., with Indian government
• Researched markets in principal Indian cities to estimate market size
• Attended marketing seminars in the Middle East and Europe
• Consulted with financial experts regarding 5-year profit and loss estimates
• Visited B&L factory in Waterford, Ireland, to determine manufacturing process and inventory calculation methods
• Sourced indigenous equipment for the Indian factory

9/88 – 11/88 | **PRAKTICUM, MARKETING RESEARCH**
Sandoz AG | Basel, Switzerland
• Conducted a multinational OTC study to identify high-growth areas and entry methods

LANGUAGES | English, German, Bengali, Hindi

INTERESTS | Extensive travel in Europe, U.S., Middle East, Kenya, and India
Acting, theatre lighting design, skiing, swimming

ADDRESS | Rush 1, 12 Carmichael Road, Bombay 123, India | (022) 555-1234

106

8 | PARAGRAPH STYLE

. . . versus bulleted phrases.

I have a personal preference for the bulleted style as opposed to the paragraph style, as you have probably noticed in these samples. Short phrases with bullets seem less intimidating to the reader. They are easy to read and get the point across quickly. It is a case of less is more.

However, there might be times when a paragraph style is preferable. It could be that there is just too much information to fit on one page with bullets. Again, a resume must reflect the personality of the one it describes and there are people who are just not short, sweet, and to the point.

If you choose to use the paragraph style, try to make each paragraph no longer than five lines after typesetting. Anything more is hard to read.

You should also use full justification (as in the first three paragraphs on this page), which I normally try to avoid in bulleted styles since it makes the information down the middle of the page look too much like a block. This paragraph and the next are set in left justification as an example. To further visualize the difference between a ragged right edge and full justification, see the resumes on pages 112 and 113.

You will find more paragraph-style resumes on pages 19, 21, 61, 64, 66, 69, 74, 75, 82, 88–90, 94, 96, 97, 98, 101, 119, 122, 127–129, 138, 140, 178, 181, 185, 188, 193, 214, 222, 224, 226, 228, 240, and 258.

Joseph E. Juris

EXPERIENCE

MANAGEMENT CONSULTANT

Standard Pipe Nipple Works, Garwood, New Jersey   September 1991 – Present
   Researched, planned, and promoted venture for new pipe fittings factory in Mexico. Developed contacts and negotiated with Mexican parties, including suppliers, lenders, government agencies, unions, lawyers, and real estate developers. Drafted comprehensive business plan. Made sales presentations across the country and overseas. Learned the entire technical manufacturing process. Able to operate, rebuild, and maintain all of the machinery in a pipe nipple factory.

Atlantic Imports, Miami, Florida   April – August 1991
   Structured and negotiated proposed sale of business. Prepared detailed company valuation. Analyzed current practices and future trends in the imported costume jewelry industry.

Summit World Trade Corporation, Taipei, Taiwan   May – August 1989
   Operated as sole contact in Taiwan for U.S. distributor of high-technology medical equipment. Assessed market opportunities and entry strategies in the Pacific Rim. Initiated relationships with Taiwan manufacturers, distributors, and government agencies.

ATTORNEY AT LAW   1987 – 1988
   McCarthy, Lebit, Crystal, and Haiman, Cleveland, Ohio
   Specialized in corporate, tax, and real estate law. Highlights included presenting case before Supreme Court of Ohio and negotiating major real estate transaction.

EDUCATION

AMERICAN GRADUATE SCHOOL OF INTERNATIONAL MANAGEMENT
THUNDERBIRD, Glendale, Arizona
   Master of International Management, With Honors (GPA 3.8)   December 1990
   Focus on International Industrial Marketing, Mandarin Chinese, and Asian Studies

UNIVERSITY OF INTERNATIONAL BUSINESS AND ECONOMICS, Beijing, China
   Exchange Student   Summer 1990
   Intensive Mandarin Language Study, Survey of Business Environment

GEORGE WASHINGTON UNIVERSITY, Washington, D.C.
   Juris Doctor   1987

VANDERBILT UNIVERSITY, Nashville, Tennessee
   Bachelor of Arts, *cum laude* in Psychology   1984

SKILLS

Proficient in Mandarin Chinese
Knowledge of personal computers, including Lotus 1-2-3 and WordPerfect

INTERESTS AND ACHIEVEMENTS

Admitted to practice law in Ohio and District of Columbia
Extensive international travel, particularly in East and Southeast Asia
Vanderbilt Rugby Team: competed in England and New Zealand

1234 Woods Blvd., Suite 123 • Independence, Ohio 44131 • (216) 555-1234 • Fax (216) 555-1234

JOSE L. SIEGLER

1234 N. 56th Lane
Phoenix, Arizona 85037
Home: (602) 555-1234

EXPERIENCE

LEAR SIEGLER MANAGEMENT SERVICES CORP.

Supply System Analyst . . . . 11/90 – Present
Provided data processing services to the Royal Saudi Air Force. Performed research and analysis to improve data systems. Assisted and provided technical support in the resolution of program problem areas. Processed and distributed reports for all supply customers. Coordinated with programmers to ensure quality products were furnished within specified time standards. Designed reports for customers. Resolved conflicts between customers and data services for all software and hardware problems.

U.S. AIR FORCE

Assistant Manager, Computer Operations Section . . . . 2/86 – 7/88
Managed data processing services for supply. Database manager. Data processing project coordinator. Prepared weekly/monthly utilization reports. Assisted and provided technical support in the resolution of system processing problems. Determined processing requirements between organizations. Reviewed, approved, and prepared 24-hour shift work schedule, daily/monthly reports, production schedules. Identified resources and monitored expenditures for data processing supplies, forms, and equipment. Trained personnel in the operation of the Sperry 1100/60 computer system and in the development/writing of QLP, SAL, SURGE, and COBOL programs.

Supervisor, Computer Operations Section . . . . 5/84 – 1/86
Assisted management of data processing section. Provided technical assistance in the resolution of system processing problems. Trained personnel in the operation of the Sperry 1100/60 and UNIVAC 1050-II computer systems and peripheral equipment. Submitted reports on equipment utilization, system operation, and a variety of correspondence. Determined processing requirements. Assisted in training personnel in the development and writing of SAL and QLP programs. Scheduled daily/monthly production and reports processing to ensure maximum use of computer system. Ensured compliance with operating instructions, rules, and regulations.

Computer System Analyst/Programmer . . . . 4/82 – 5/84
Analyzed workload schedules, computer utilization, business procedures, and problem areas in order to refine data and evaluate effectiveness. Studied existing data systems to evaluate and improve production or work flow as required. Prepared technical reports and instructional manuals relative to the resolution of problem areas and changes in programming and operational systems. Developed SAL computer programs to locate and retrieve documents, data, and other information to better serve the supply customer.

Computer Operator . . . . 4/75 – 3/82
Operated UNIVAC 1050-II mainframe computer system and peripheral equipment, console, tape/disc drives, and printer. Processed end-of-day, weekly, monthly, and special reports. Analyzed computer stops and problems and applied standard corrective procedures. Performed operator maintenance on all equipment. Trained personnel in computer operation. Maintained and updated computer utilization/tape library files and records. Performed distribution of computer products to all supporting organizations on a daily basis. Operated punch card automated machine (PCAM) equipment.

EDUCATION

Bachelor's Degree in Management/Computer Information Systems 12/89
Park College

Associate of Applied Science in Computer Science 12/88
Park College

Associate of Applied Science in Data Processing 3/88
Community College of the Air Force

Associate of Applied Science in Logistics 6/88
Community College of the Air Force

MICHAEL L. AVNET

1234 Moccasin
Wichita, Kansas 66049
(913) 555-1234

PROFESSIONAL OBJECTIVE

Personnel position as vice president, director, or manager. Prefer multi-location responsibility but would consider large facility assignment.

SUMMARY OF EXPERIENCE

Several years of multi-facility personnel experience with responsibilities for hourly and salaried employees in both non-union and union companies. Have an outstanding background as a generalist with proven skills in preventive labor relations.

EXPERIENCE

AVNET, INC.
May 1992 to Present

DIRECTOR HUMAN RESOURCES . . . Avnet is the world's largest distributor of electronic components. Responsible for all human resource functions for three non-union Phoenix locations employing 900.

ARIZONA PUBLIC SERVICE COMPANY
December 1990 to May 1992

SENIOR HUMAN RESOURCE POSITION . . . with nuclear division employing over 3,000. Responsibilities included employee relations, union contract negotiations, staffing, and countering a union-organization attempt for a major segment of the division.

ELECTROLUX CORPORATION
November 1989 to December 1990

DIRECTOR HUMAN RESOURCES . . . Electrolux is a premier non-union manufacturer of floor care products with three plants employing 1500.

Responsible for Human Resource functions at all manufacturing facilities. In addition, had HR responsibility for product/ manufacturing engineering, information systems, and the accounting functions.

The HR responsibilities included all of the traditional areas: Employee relations, employment, training, safety, environmental, wage/salary/benefits administration, policy/procedure development.

SAFELITE GLASS CORPORATION, LEAR SIEGLER, INC.
July 1980 to July 1989

VICE PRESIDENT HUMAN RESOURCES . . . Safelite is a $400M auto glass replacement company employing 4000 people in 4 manufacturing plants, 41 warehouses, and over 550 retail installation centers. *Responsibilities* included management of the personnel/legal/safety/training functions. Reported to the chairman.

Accomplishments included:

LABOR/EMPLOYEE RELATIONS:
- Implemented communication and organizational development programs to maintain non-union status.
- Directed company's strategy for all union elections, including decertifications.
- Negotiated and administered up to 16 union contracts—reduced to 3.
- Represented company in arbitrations with unions, state/local government, and special interest groups.

COMPENSATION & BENEFITS:
- Developed all wage and salary programs.
- Responsible for the development and administration of all benefit programs.

STAFFING/TRAINING/EEO:
- Implemented company's first management training program.
- Handled all compliance reviews.
- Directed staffing systems. Personally handled executive recruiting.

SAFETY/LEGAL:
- Directed safety program.
- Coordinated defense of legal cases.

STEVEN J. WILLIAMS

1234 W. Anderson Drive • Phoenix, Arizona 85023 • (602) 555-1234

PROFESSIONAL OBJECTIVES

Immediate Objective: To obtain a sales representative position within the consumer product market.
Long-Range Objective: To assume increased responsibilities and serve in various levels of management.

EXPERIENCES RELATING TO SALES/MANAGEMENT

1989 – Present FACTORY SALES/SERVICE REPRESENTATIVE
SHERWIN WILLIAMS COMPANY, Cleveland, Ohio
After completing college, was hired to service an area that includes the entire state of Arizona and the city of Las Vegas, Nevada. Primary customers include the three largest retail outlets in the area, i.e., Sears, Wal-Mart, Kmart, and other selected smaller retailers. Achieved total territory sales of over $704,000 and received Gold Shoe Award, among other achievement recognition rewards. Primarily responsible for factory orders, but also assist in merchandising, inventory control, and promotional activities. Conduct product knowledge sessions on an ongoing basis, including one-on-one and group sessions with customer personnel. Resolve end-user complaints. Responsible for company car, territory budget management, expense reporting, and other corporate paperwork.

1981 – 1990 SALES
SEARS, ROEBUCK & COMPANY, Phoenix, Arizona (Metrocenter)
Commission sales within the hardware and lawn and garden departments. Primary responsibilities include assisting customers in their purchasing process, overcoming their objections, closing the sale, and providing follow-up assistance. Assist management with inventory control and product display maintenance. Served on the Courtesy Committee in 1987. Three-time winner of the store's monthly Courtesy Award. Winner of the 1986 Courtesy Award of the Year. Recipient of the Vice President's Symbol of Service Award in 1985.

1979 – 1981 ASSISTANT STORE MANAGER
FOREMOST LIQUORS, Downers Grove, Illinois
Shared responsibility for the operation of a *franchised* retail store. Primary responsibilities included inventory control of wine and delicatessen goods. Assisted in billing, payroll, receiving, hiring, and training. Was direct supervisor of 10 employees.

1976 – 1979 ASSISTANT STORE MANAGER
FRANK'S NURSERY SALES, INC., Franklin Park, Illinois
Originally hired as a stock boy but later became manager trainee, co-assistant manager, and then assistant manager. Shared the responsibility for the entire operation of a retail *chain* store. As a working manager, primary responsibilities included bookkeeping, payroll, and inventory planning and control. Was also responsible for staffing, scheduling, and training new employees. In addition to management activities, secondary responsibilities included receiving, stocking, store maintenance, and constructing store displays. Directly supervised 25 employees.

EDUCATION RELATING TO SALES/MANAGEMENT

Dec. 1988 B.S. DEGREE, Arizona State University, Tempe, Arizona
Major in Marketing. Courses most related: Principles of Selling, Principles of Retailing, Consumer Behavior, Sales Management, Marketing Communications, Strategic Marketing, Human Behavior in Organization, Marketing Research, Business Policies.

1986 A.A. DEGREE, Glendale Community College, Glendale, Arizona
Major in Business Administration. Courses most related: Accounting, Business Communication, Data Processing.

Lou Farleigh

1233 West Kimberly Way
Glendale, Arizona 85308
(602) 555-1234

SUMMARY OF QUALIFICATIONS

Retail Manager with over 20 years experience in supermarket and department store operations with a major regional chain. Proficient in business planning and budgeting; employee training and motivation; enforcement of company standards and practices; and customer relations and services. Able to effectively delegate and monitor multiple employees and tasks concurrently.

ACCOMPLISHMENTS

- Consistently achieved bonuses for my store's operational profitability by careful attention to payroll budgets, gross profitability, inventory controls, and merchandise turnover.

- Recognized as a strong staff motivator able to develop a team attitude while enforcing company policies and procedures.

- Began with Smitty's as a courtesy clerk and progressed rapidly through the ranks to the position of supermarket manager.

PROFESSIONAL QUALIFICATIONS

SMITTY'S OF ARIZONA, Phoenix, Arizona   1971 – Present
Store Manager (6 years)
Store manager for six years prior to a company-wide reorganization and again at present, with responsibilities for both supermarket and department store operations with a total staff of 300-350 and gross revenues of over $35 million. Consistently met company standards of profitability and productivity while staying within budget guidelines and concurrently developing a loyal and dedicated employee team.

Supermarket Manager (7 years)
Manage all aspects of retail grocery operations at a busy store for this large regional grocery and department store chain. Direct the activities of 250 employees through delegation and supervision of eight subordinate managers. Departments include meat, bakery, produce, grocery, dairy, restaurant/snack bars, delicatessen, and floral department.

Key responsibilities include planning and executing budgets and business profit projections; developing and implementing employee motivation and training programs; delegating and ensuring company standards and practices; and instituting and maintaining ongoing customer relations and service activities. Also responsible for quality control and maintenance of the store and its facilities.

Key strengths include the ability to develop and control a profitable inventory mix and institute effective merchandising to serve those needs. This includes extensively training employees in customer service and public relations.

Prior positions held at Smitty's included: Assistant Supermarket Manager, Grocery Manager, Front End Manager, Night Manager, Department Manager, Receiving Manager, and Journeyman Clerk.

ROCHESTER HOUSING AUTHORITY, Rochester, New York   1967 – 1971
Housing Manager
Managed a staff of 30 people involved in renting and managing apartments and single-family housing in several locations. Collected rents. Handled evictions. Oversaw maintenance and repairs.

TWO GUYS DISCOUNT STORES, Harrison, New Jersey   1962 – 1966
Department Manager
Responsible for front-end operations with approximately 100 employees and the accounting department.

EDUCATION

FARLEIGH DICKINSON UNIVERSITY, Madison, New Jersey
Major: **Education/Mathematics**

Joseph A. Emberwood

12345 Circle Drive   Sun City, Arizona 85351   (602) 555-1234

PROFESSIONAL EXPERIENCE

PROGRAM REVIEW MANAGER
Neighborhood Reinvestment Corporation
Atlanta, Georgia (3/86 to 5/95)

Completely responsible for managing capacity-building activities among 75 community development organizations in 18 states. Supervised remote professional staff and organizational development consultants. Conducted or managed the conduct of intensive "organizational audits" under difficult conditions or in complex situations requiring the utmost sensitivity. Met stringent annual quota of "audits" conducted. Received many **compliments on the caliber of staff** hired.

PROGRAM MANAGER, CENTRAL INTAKE
Chicago Energy Savers Fund
Chicago, Illinois (12/84 to 3/86)

Directed operations for a city-wide program offering energy-related loan and construction assistance to homeowners. Ensured that production quotas were met and quality of work was maintained in a fast-paced environment. Supervised technical and clerical staff. Underwrote hundreds of good-quality loans originated by my office and fifteen others. Directed loan closing and escrow management operations, routinely solving staff, customer, and contractor problems every step of the way. Became known as the "damage control" specialist, called upon to deal with the most difficult personalities. My own employees made our office the **top producer** of all.

FIELD SERVICES OFFICER
Neighborhood Reinvestment Corporation
Chicago, Illinois (7/81 to 12/84)

Completely responsible for on-site management assistance to voluntary community development agencies in ten cities, three states. Independently conducted successful training in fund-raising, strategic planning, fiscal management, and personnel administration. Routinely intervened in crises ranging from critical cash shortfalls to impending litigation of construction jobs in trouble.

NEIGHBORHOOD DIRECTOR
Little Village Division
Neighborhood Housing Services of Chicago, Inc.
Chicago, Illinois (12/77 to 7/81)

Completely responsible for developing, then operating successful housing rehab program. Recruited, trained, and provided administrative support to Board of Directors and other volunteers. Prepared and managed annual budget and work plan. Recruited, selected, trained, and evaluated four-person staff. Provided credit analysis, financial counseling, and loan packaging services for primarily Spanish-speaking clients.

EDUCATION

Bachelor of Science in Economics, Illinois State University, 1975

Spanish Language Training, Berlitz School of Languages, 1980
(attained fluency with 2,000-word vocabulary in four weeks)

Sandra L. Enologist

1234 West Greenway Road #123, San Francisco, California 85306 • (602) 555-1234

Professional Experience

Communications Director
Sep. 1989 - Present
Vern Jones Oil and Gas Corporation (VJOG)
San Francisco, California
Lobbied for the oil and gas industry through the state legislature. Worked with state and county agencies to obtain permits. Ensured positive relations with investors through written communication and general meetings.

President
Feb. 1982 - Dec. 1988
Jones Four Corporation (JFC)
Healdsburg, California
Jones Four Corporation produced wine, marketed under the brand name Valfleur Winery. Developed the corporation's identity package, i.e., brand name, logo, brochures, trademark, bottles, and cartons. Determined wine styles, volumes, and varietals purchased from the vineyards. Researched potential markets. Developed and implemented marketing plan.

In 1987, Valfleur Winery produced 17,000 cases, 11,000 cases of Chardonnay from our Jimtown Ranch vineyard, 3,000 cases each of Sauvignon Blanc and Cabernet Sauvignon purchased from other vintners. The wines were marketed in approximately twenty (20) states. The company was sold in 1988.

Administrative Assistant
Jul. 1980 - Feb. 1982
Vern Jones & Associates
Sacramento, California
Established the accounting system, meeting all requirements of state and federal filing. Created and implemented a system for management of investments. Conducted research and feasibility studies on possible new ventures. From these studies emerged two companies: Jones Four Corporation in 1982 and Vern Jones Oil and Gas Corporation in 1985.

Education

Master of International Management
American Graduate School of International Management
Thunderbird Campus
May 1993
Glendale, Arizona

Bachelor of Business Administration
National University
January 1992
Sacramento, California

Language, Skills, and Affiliation

- Proficient in French (U.S. State Department Level 3)
- Extensive training in all aspects of the wine industry
- Elected Affiliate of American Society of Enologists
- Board of Director for Yolo County Child Sexual Abuse Treatment Center
- Member of San Francisco Ballet Auxiliary Association
- Outdoors enthusiast including skiing, running, mountain biking, hiking, and golf
- President of the International Wine Tasting Club – Thunderbird

International Exposure

- Summer study abroad in France 1992
- 1978-1980 lived in the Bahamas and France while employed with Club Med
- Extensive international travel

114

GREGG M. DIETHRICH

EDUCATION

Master of International Management　　　　　　　　　Glendale, Arizona **1993-1995**

AMERICAN GRADUATE SCHOOL OF INTERNATIONAL MANAGEMENT. Specializing in Financial Management, Marketing, and International Trade. Developed a Lotus 1-2-3 based accounting system for a small business and used computer-based modeling to determine optimal asset acquisition and investment strategies. Conducted international market research for consumer and industrial products and subsequently created appropriate marketing strategies and advertising campaigns.

Bachelor of Science in Commerce-Finance　　　　Santa Clara, California **1992-1986**

SANTA CLARA UNIVERSITY. Emphasis in Financial Decision Analysis and Investments with a minor in Asian Studies. Used computerized formulations of NPV, IRR, WACC, and risk and return analysis to determine alternative investment strategies and to support financial management decisions such as asset acquisition and lease/purchase evaluations.

Overseas Study Program　　　　　　　　　　　　　　Tokyo, Japan **1984-1985**

SOPHIA UNIVERSITY. Enrolled in Business and Asian Culture seminars. Exposed to international business environment through semiweekly visits to multinational companies. Worked directly with president of Inoue Art Products, assisting in development/implementation of public relations campaigns for international clients.

WORK EXPERIENCE

Project Director　　　　　　　　　　　　　　　　　　Poland **1995**

INTERNATIONAL DEVELOPMENT EXCHANGE. Coauthored program designed to introduce and support free-market economic operations in former centrally planned economies. Responsible for implementing pilot project in Poland. Duties included: Managing program development, supervising Western business consultants, assisting Polish managers and government personnel in their professional activities, developing a strong working relationship with business and education groups and government committees in order to ensure significant indigenous support and continued successful economic development.

Financial Manager　　　　　　　　　　　　　　　　Phoenix, Arizona **1991-1993**

THE DIETHRICH GROUP. Designed computerized reporting formats and evaluated business data, including: forecasts, operating cost/benefit analysis, cash flow estimates, budget requirements, financial statement projections, return analysis, and long-range planning.

General Manager/Partner　　　　　　　　　　　　Saudi Arabia **1990-1991**

SEA & SUN SPORTS. Conceived, designed, and successfully implemented/managed business plan serving sports and leisure market. Responsible for complete operations of three retail and training facilities for activities, including boating, fishing, martial arts, scuba diving, skiing, squash, surfing, tennis, and travel. Activities included international recruitment, purchasing, and charter services.

Managing Director　　　　　　　　　　　　　　　　Saudi Arabia **1987-1990**

LAKOS INTERNATIONAL. Responsible for entire joint venture operations, encompassing agricultural, industrial, and consumer products. Duties included: monitoring of manufacturing; overseeing shipping, customs clearance, and inventory control; supervising hiring/training and management of sales, installation, and service personnel; development of distribution channels/dealer network; reconciliation and compilation of relevant accounting and financial reports/statements; and distribution of profits. Also responsible for introduction of revolutionary well inspection and repair service.

TECHNICAL SKILLS

Foreign Languages: Proficient in Japanese. Knowledge of Arabic and Spanish.

ADDRESSES

Permanent • 12345 East Campus Drive • Mesa, Arizona 85282 • (602) 555-1234
Current • 12345 N. 59th Avenue, #123 • Glendale, Arizona 85306 • (602) 555-1234

RONALD V. DANIELS

1234 Stanley Avenue • Key Largo, Florida 34640 • (813) 555-1234

AREAS OF KNOWLEDGE AND EXPERIENCE

SALES AND MARKETING:
Sales Training & Motivation
New Home Marketing
Market Research
Product Development
Feasibility Studies

ADVERTISING:
Design/Layout
Copy Writing
Radio/TV Commercials
Film Production

REAL ESTATE:
Licensed Real Estate Broker
Property Acquisition
Land Development
Property Management

GENERAL CONSTRUCTION:
Residential
Commercial
General Contracting
Condo Conversions

FINANCE:
Licensed Mortgage Broker
Loan Packaging
FHA/VA Financing
Project Funding

EXPERIENCE

OWNER / MANAGER   Mar. 1985 - Present
Debron Group, Inc. (Builder Developer), Daytona Beach, Florida
Full responsibility for managing all aspects of our three companies: *Debron Realty* specializes in marketing new homes for area builders. We built a reputation as an aggressive and innovative sales group with over 1,500 new home sales to our credit. *Debron Development* purchases raw land and develops it into fully improved building lots for resale or our own use. *Debron Homes,* one of the top three volume builders of custom designed single-family homes in the Daytona Beach area.

SALES MANAGER   Apr. 1984 - Mar. 1985
ITT/CDC – Sheraton Corporation (Land Developer), Palm Coast, Florida
Headed up a new home sales division. Planned advertising and marketing programs for this 80,000 acre city on Florida's northeast coast. During our first year we sold $5,000,000 in new homes in a previously untapped market. Reason for change: Left to pursue an opportunity in Daytona Beach's growing housing market.

DIVISION MANAGER   Nov. 1982 - Apr. 1984
Beacon Homes (Builder Developer), Hudson, Florida
Managed "Beacon Woods," a 7,000-acre planned unit development. Was responsible for all sales activity for five model centers. Hired, trained, and motivated sales staff. Planned marketing programs to increase traffic and developed out-of-state broker contacts. Produced a company record of *500* new home sales in 1983. This represented a 300% increase over 1982, despite 21% interest rates. Reason for change: Offered position with ITT.

PROJECT MANAGER   Feb. 1978 - Nov. 1982
Deltona Corporation, Ocala, Florida
Managed all aspects of this 15,000-acre planned community called "Marion Oaks." Responsible for land sales, housing sales, golf course operations, advertising, marketing, sales training, and office operations. Reason for change: Economic cutbacks within corporate.

EDUCATION

BACHELOR OF ARTS IN BUSINESS ADMINISTRATION
John Carroll University, Cleveland, Ohio • Major in Management

SPECIAL STUDY
American Management Association Seminars • Dale Carnegie Sales Seminars
University of South Florida, Marketing & Psychology

PROFESSIONAL MEMBERSHIPS

National Association of Homebuilders, Daytona Beach, Florida
Daytona Beach Homebuilders Association, Chairman, Sales/Marketing Council
Sales/Marketing Executives, Tampa, Florida

9 | FUNCTIONAL VERSUS CHRONOLOGICAL

There are two basic types of resumes:

1. REVERSE CHRONOLOGICAL

A chronological resume arranges your experience and education in chronological order with the most recent dates first. It is important to list accomplishments, skills, and qualifications and not just job duties. Potential employers want to know what you can do for them. Use action verbs at the beginning of each sentence (see pages 3–4) and avoid personal pronouns (I, my, me).

You don't have to list every single position you have ever held. The trick is to pick and choose the ones that are relevant to your objective. You can also eliminate low-level positions and positions that duplicate later experience.

Most of the resumes in this book are chronological, but this section will show you what is possible with a functional type of resume in case that style better fits your needs.

2. FUNCTIONAL

A functional resume organizes your work experience by the functions you performed regardless of date. The functional resume highlights your skills and potential instead of your work history. It allows you to play down gaps in your experience and is especially good for those people entering the job market for the first time. If you are reentering the job market, for example, after raising children, this type of resume also allows you to list volunteer experience and community or school activities.

List your functional paragraphs in their order of importance, with the bulleted items listed first that will help you get the particular job you are targeting. At the bottom of the resume, you should still list a brief synopsis of your actual work experience with your title, employer, and the dates worked.

Outside of this section, you will find other functional resumes on pages 21, 36, 156, 184, 196, 198, 200, 208, 216, 236, and 259.

MARC BROOKLYN

1234 N. Maple Street, #123 • Tempe, Arizona 85201 • (602) 555-1234

**Objective: A sales management/training position
in the construction equipment industry**

HIGHLIGHTS OF QUALIFICATIONS

- Strongly self-motivated, enthusiastic, and profit oriented
- Outstanding communication and presentation skills
- Readily project a professional image
- A decision maker, well organized, resourceful, work well independently

RELEVANT EXPERIENCE

Sales, Public Relations, and Marketing
- Created sales and marketing programs for tool supplies and OSHA safety equipment in the construction industry
- Successfully generated half a million dollars in sales in 1990
- Developed a strong pattern of repeat sales and client loyalty; identified client needs and problems and found the right solutions; provided accurate and honest product information
- Eight-time recipient of top production award for monthly sales volume

Personnel Management, Motivation, and Training
- Interviewed and hired top sales people
- Trained sales representatives in presentation of product, selling benefits, handling objections, cold calls, closing, and other aspects of successful selling
- Directed all facets of personnel management, including employee scheduling, bonuses, payroll benefits, etc.

Administration and Management
- Managed the day-to-day business functions of personal Tele-Tool franchise, including everything from inventory control to bookkeeping, billings, and vendor relations
- Developed ideas for creating new business, prioritized work projects, designed and implemented follow-up procedures, resulting in more efficient and profitable work flow
- Developed and revised daily, weekly, and monthly sales strategies for the company
- Entered and retrieved computerized data; weekly and monthly sales statistics
- Expert in long distance communications vending, with vast knowledge of all major companies in the industry

EMPLOYMENT HISTORY

1986 – present	**Franchise Owner**	TELE-TOOL, CALIFORNIA CONTRACTORS SUPPLIES, INC. Satellite 666, Phoenix, Arizona
1985 – 1986	**Sales Manager**	CALIFORNIA CONTRACTORS SUPPLIES, INC.
1983 – 1985	**Sales Representative**	Satellite 777, Scottsdale, Arizona
1982 – 1983	**Advertising/Print Production**	LEVINE HUNTLEY SCMIDT PLAPLER & BEAVER
1981 – 1982	**Mail Room Supervisor**	New York

EDUCATION

BACHELOR OF SCIENCE IN MARKETING, MINOR IN BUSINESS MANAGEMENT
Brooklyn College, Brooklyn, New York
1979 – 1983

Gail B. Arif

OBJECTIVE   A career position in a progressive and creative environment with increased administrative responsibilities

EXPERIENCE   **Office & Clerical** . . . Experienced as an office manager, site supervisor, secretary, bookkeeper, and account clerk. Developed special interest college classes, researching subject matter, finding lecturers, scheduling classes, and assisting students with registration. Managed a city business license program. Organized and followed through with nonprofit fund raisers, including planning, assembling, pricing, advertising, and enlisting workers.

Skills . . . include public communication, accuracy, neatness, attention to detail, organization of work, time management, and ability to work on own with limited supervision. Have acquired skills in typing, word processing, filing, 10-key calculator, standard office machines, IBM System 36 computer, IBM personal computer, IBM and BPI software.

Public Relations & Communications . . . Positions held in the past have required extensive contact with the public, including good oral and written communications skills. Designed and distributed flyers, news releases, and worked on developing public relations between a college and its surrounding communities. Taught groups of 10 to 40 children or adults. Worked on large regional conferences involving up to 350 participants from conception to completion. Communicated information to employees regarding insurance benefits, payroll deductions, salaries, and leave balances. Researched, distributed, and explained revenue and expenditures to management to be used in budget projections.

Sales . . . Experienced in florist shop sales, fabric sales and cost estimation, furniture and appliance showroom sales, church and school fund raisers, garage sales, wholesale showroom sales of accessories, and sales to decorators. Served customers in a manner that would generate and/or continue their goodwill, satisfaction, and return business. Presented good showroom image by setting up and maintaining effective and attractive merchandise displays.

Bookkeeping & Inventory Management . . . Prepared payroll for a large staff. Have been responsible for accounts payable, accounts receivable, general ledger, record keeping, scheduling, computer setup and data entry, records management, bank deposits, purchasing, filing freight claims, research and retrieval of information, calendar and fiscal year-end reports, W-2s and 1099 preparation, quarterly and year-end tax reports, insurance benefits, payroll deductions, correspondence, and ordering, inventory, and distribution of office supplies. Responsible for estimating and expediting orders for supplies/merchandise, phone/wire orders, scheduling and delivery.

Creative . . . Adept in interior design, color coordination, textile design and selection, floral design and arrangement, handcrafts, layout of flyers and posters for sales and fund raisers, showroom displays of furniture and accessories, visual aids for teaching, designing and sewing clothing, assisting in wardrobe and accessory selection.

EMPLOYMENT
HISTORY

Site Supervisor, Rio Salado Community College, Surprise, Arizona	1/90 – 6/95
Chiropractic Assistant, Weathersby Chiropractic, Glendale, Arizona	1/89 – 5/89
Secretary/Bookkeeper, Maverick Masonry, Inc., Phoenix, Arizona	3/87 – 10/88
Account Clerk, City of Novato, Novato, California	4/74 – 10/86

EDUCATION   **Bachelor of Science in Home Economics**, University of New Hampshire

ADDRESS   1234 W. Athens Street • Peoria, Arizona 85382 • (602) 555-1234

Lucia de Carmen

12345 North 59th Avenue, #123 • Glendale, Arizona 85306 • (602) 555-1234

QUALIFICATIONS

- Talent for balancing long-range planning and attention to detail
- 3 years successful experience in program management and development
- In-depth knowledge of developing country social, political, and economic conditions
- Advanced degree in International Business Management

PROFESSIONAL EXPERIENCE

Program Management and Supervision

- Developed, administered, and secured $50,000-$300,000 in funding for development management training programs
- Prepared detailed training proposals for international development agencies; supervised 3-5 employees during planning and implementation of programs for Development Organization officers worldwide
- Arranged joint ventures with French companies; assisted with promotional efforts
- Upgraded staff skills and productivity: designed effective in-service training programs, assessed appropriate duties for new staff positions, interviewed, and participated in hiring decisions
- Assisted in start-up of new international consulting firm, including budgeting and client contacts

Research and Analysis

- Conducted business evaluations of two start-up businesses; determined present value and expected cash flows
- Coauthored a 125-page competitive intelligence study for a Mexican manufacturer
- Published, with M. Ingle and D. Brinkerhoff (1988), "Enhancing the Sustainability of A.I.D. Projects: Supplemental Guidance for Mission Managers." Washington, D.C.: Agency for International Development
- Published, with D. Brinkerhoff (1989), "Public Administration in Haiti: Background and Current Status." New York: UN

Written and Verbal Communication

- Compiled and edited comprehensive International Development conference reports for publication
- Conceptualized and authored descriptive brochure for an international consulting firm in Washington, D.C.
- Successfully mediated conflicts between management and staff, improving internal communications and cooperation
- Coordinated and updated training materials for international management seminar

International Experience

- Outstanding oral and written communication in Portuguese, Spanish, French, English; rudiments of Russian
- Born in Brazil and visit biannually; lived and/or attended school in Haiti, Algeria, Mexico, Argentina, and Paraguay
- Travel to Caribbean, Europe, Middle East
- Negotiated contract terms with agencies in France, Morocco, and Costa Rica in French and Spanish

EMPLOYMENT HISTORY

1988–1994	**Program Management Specialist**	Int'l Development Management Center	College Park, MD
1987–1988	**Document Editor**	World Bank	Washington, D.C.
1986–1987	**Executive Assistant**	DGA International/Pan Atlantic Consultants	Washington, D.C.
1986	**Project Coordinator**	Organization of American States	Washington, D.C.

EDUCATION

Master of International Management – 1995

AMERICAN GRADUATE SCHOOL OF INTERNATIONAL MANAGEMENT (Thunderbird Campus), Glendale, AZ

- International Business-to-Business Marketing
- International Purchasing and Countertrade
- Export/Import Management
- International Trade Strategies

Master of Arts – International Development Management – 1993

THE AMERICAN UNIVERSITY, Washington, D.C.

Bachelor of Arts – Government and Politics/French – 1990, *cum laude, with honors*

UNIVERSITY OF MARYLAND, College Park, MD

ANGELA C. CORVALLIS

12345 North 59th Avenue, #123 • Glendale, Arizona 85306 • (602) 555-1234

Objective: Position in International Operations
Focusing on Account Management, Customer Relations, and Credit Analysis

QUALIFICATIONS

- 5 years professional experience in high-pressure, customer-oriented environment
- Able to conduct business in English and Portuguese; native familiarity with U.S. and Brazilian culture
- Experience in both dealer and retail Account Management
- Graduate degree in International Management; specialized courses in International Marketing
- Experience in project management, with attention to detail

PROFESSIONAL EXPERIENCE

Account Management
- Responsible for over $60 million in accounts and inventories; reduced corporate loss exposure while strengthening customer base
- Developed proposals on account handling for decision-making analysis; maintained critical account records and control forms
- Co-authored a 125-page competitive intelligence study for a Mexican manufacturer; extracted valuable research data from U.S. government agencies
- Improved corporate account portfolio; identified, documented, and promptly reported audit irregularities and abnormal account activity
- Managed retail contracts and ensured their compliance with legal and corporate requirements
- Collected and concluded past-due accounts, using both telephone and field contacts

Customer Relations
- Established and maintained good rapport with over 30 dealers
- Resolved customer conflicts by applying diplomacy and assertiveness to reach mutually beneficial results
- Developed cooperative relationships with other financial institutions
- Promoted retail sales programs by assessing customer/dealer needs and anticipating problem areas
- Reestablished dealer trust on accounts that had been previously underserviced

Credit Analysis
- Supervised the transition to a computerized IBM financial analysis system; scheduled and trained managers on its use
- Analyzed business financial statements for accounts up to $5 million, and evaluated credit lines and loans; presented my recommendations to upper management
- Evaluated 80–100 retail credit applications daily while reducing average response time by 40%

EMPLOYMENT HISTORY

1988 – 1994	**Credit Supervisor**	General Motors Acceptance Corp. – St. Louis, MO
1987 – 1988	**Management Trainee**	General Motors Acceptance Corp. – Portland, OR
1985 – 1987	**Account Representative**	General Motors Acceptance Corp. – Portland, OR

EDUCATION

Master of International Management – 1995
AMERICAN GRADUATE SCHOOL OF INTERNATIONAL MANAGEMENT (Thunderbird Campus), Glendale, AZ

- Market research methodology
- Solving marketing management problems
- Export and import procedures
- Planning, organizing, and controlling marketing functions
- Consumer products and industrial market buying behavior
- International purchasing, negotiations, and countertrade

Bachelor of Science – Finance and International Business – 1985
OREGON STATE UNIVERSITY, Corvallis, OR

FRANK W. CAMPBELL

1234 West Campbell Avenue
Litchfield Park, Arizona 85340
Telephone (602) 555-1234

OBJECTIVE A career position in SALES, SALES MANAGEMENT, or PURCHASING

QUALIFICATIONS A dedicated, detail-conscious professional able to identify and solve problems, with special demonstrated skills in:

❖ **Management**
  ❖ **Sales / Purchasing**
    ❖ **Human Relations**
      ❖ **Persuasive Communications**
        ❖ **Analyzing / Organizing**
          ❖ **Determination / Foresight / Follow-Through**

ACHIEVEMENTS **Opened new territory for company sales**. Developed new accounts for company through determination and persuasive communication. Generated $1 million in new annual sales and established territory for additional expansion.

Rescued failing territory. Isolated problems and added improved customer service systems. Raised customer satisfaction level and account penetration. Secured market dominance and increased sales by 50% in first year.

Achieved position of top sales representative in local area. Determined company position was weak in certain areas. Initiated new prospecting techniques and developed target markets. Resulted in 30% increase in company sales in this territory.

Promoted to Marketing Director after one year in purchasing. Identified defects and instituted improved systems and product line. Resulted in increased inventory turns, fewer out of stocks, and 10% reduction in freight and product costs.

Organized system for inventory control. Analyzed current operation, made necessary changes in purchasing procedures to maintain optimum stock levels. Resulted in improved patient care and increased efficiency of pharmacy operations.

Established and administered new personnel department. Recognized need for employee evaluation system. Adopted necessary measures to formulate plan and implementation. Resulted in improved employee morale, reduced turnover, and increased productivity.

Howard Maggini

12345 West Glendale Avenue #1234, Phoenix, Arizona 85051
Home (602) 555-1234, Work (602) 555-1234

OBJECTIVE: BODY SHOP MANAGER OR ASSISTANT MANAGER

HIGHLIGHTS OF QUALIFICATIONS

- Extensive background in successful body shop management.
- Proven ability to maintain cost-effective operations.
- Excellent interpersonal and communication skills.
- Work effectively with customers, subordinates, and management.
- Organized, professional, and dedicated to the job.

AREAS OF EXPERTISE

Personnel Management	Supervision	Inventory Control
Customer Service	Purchasing	Sales
Forecasts	Cost Justification	Computer Operation
Administration	Scheduling	Systems

BODY SHOP MANAGEMENT

- Directed and oversaw operations in repair of damaged bodies and body parts of automobiles in both high-volume production shops and prestigious, high-quality performance shops.
- Experienced with European (BMW, Acura, Honda) and American (Oldsmobile, Pontiac, Chevrolet, GMC Pickup) models.
- Ensured all projects were completed within time and cost guidelines.
- Excellent results in assuring customer satisfaction and generating repeat business and referrals.
- Interfaced with customers to answer questions and resolve complaints or problems requiring management intervention.
- Provided cost-conscious purchasing of material, supplies, new and used parts.
- Worked closely with parts department to procure and expedite vehicle parts.
- Directed designated repair facility, managed All State Pro Shop.
- Skillful negotiations of estimated damages with insurance appraisers.
- Supervised and performed outside sales representative duties.

EMPLOYMENT HISTORY

1990 – Present	Body Shop Manager	Valley Dodge, Phoenix, Arizona
1988 – 1990	Body Shop Manager	Avery Green Motors, Vallejo, California
1986 – 1988	Body Shop Manager	Maggini Chevrolet, Oakland, California
1981 – 1986	Body Shop Manager	Courtesy Chevrolet, Phoenix, Arizona
1978 – 1981	Assistant Body Shop Manager	Northwest Auto, Phoenix, Arizona
1963 – 1978	Assistant Manager	Laclede Motors, Lebanon, Missouri

TRAINING

I-CAR Certified (in process of being qualified as instructor)
Lincoln Mercury Sales Course; Transmission and Management School

DIANA D. THOMSON

1234 West Villa Theresa
Phoenix, Arizona 85023
(602) 555-1234

OBJECTIVE	An accounting position allowing room for growth and the opportunity to advance

EXPERIENCE

SUPERVISION	■ Managed Student Account's Office during supervisor's two-month sick leave ■ Trained and supervised new student employees ■ Responsible for the dispatch of territorial representatives and maintenance men for Kinetic Concepts
LEADERSHIP	■ F.H.A. Treasurer for 1983 ■ Church Leader, Summer 1986 to Fall 1987 ■ Women's Hall Association Dorm Floor Representative ■ Business Undergraduate Society
PUBLIC RELATIONS	■ Answered inquiries concerning accounts ■ Took orders from hospitals for specialized equipment ■ Telephone receptionist
MONETARY	■ Responsible for petty cash and handled cash during student registrations
CLERICAL	■ Typing, mailing, filing, sorting, microfilming, photocopying

EMPLOYMENT HISTORY

1988 – Present	KELLY SERVICES, Phoenix, Arizona (Temporary) ABCO Markets, Inc., Personnel/Training Department Revco Drug, Warehouse Floor DeVry, Student Services Department, Bookstore SGS Thomson Microelectronics, Marketing Department
1988 – Present	BLUE ARROW PERSONNEL SERVICES, Phoenix, Arizona (Temporary) Arizona Bank, Corporate Communications, Bond and Real Estate Departments Arizona Bankers Association Phoenix General Hospital & Medical Center, Medical Records Department
1985 – 1988	TREASURER'S ASSISTANT, School of the Ozarks, Point Lookout, Missouri

EDUCATION	1988	B.A. IN BUSINESS ADMINISTRATION (Dean's List) The School of the Ozarks, Point Lookout, Missouri
	1983	Longview Community College, Lee Summit, Missouri (President's Honor Roll)
	1983	Graduate of Belton Senior High, Belton, Missouri (National Honor Society, Honor Roll, Certificate of Achievement for Outstanding Scholastic Achievement)

124

ROBERT CLEMENT ARAMIS

123 Belden Drive • Los Angeles, California 90068 • Telephone: (213) 555-1234 • Fax: (213) 555-1234

QUALIFICATIONS
- Strongly motivated marketing professional
- Excellent interpersonal and analytical skills
- Extensive customer service and consumer marketing experience

EXPERIENCE

Marketing Experience
- Managed Southern California roll-out of new, high-end consumer product, including liaison with head office, sales staff training, sales results analysis, and program evaluation and modification
- Increased unit sales by 20 percent in 18 months for men's fragrance and skin care product line
- Developed new marketing techniques
- Analyzed markets for major international transportation company, evaluating regional demand trends and customer satisfaction

Human Resource Management
- Responsible for managing 75 sales professionals in 25 retail locations
- Hired, terminated, and trained sales personnel
- Managed international flight attendants for Delta Airlines

EMPLOYMENT HISTORY

DELTA AIRLINES (1990 – 1995)
International In-Flight Service Coordinator
District Marketing Analyst

ARAMIS DIVISION OF ESTEE LAUDER (1988 – 1990)
Account Executive
Account Rotator

WESTERN AIRLINES (1981 – 1988)
Flight Attendant

EDUCATION

MASTER OF INTERNATIONAL MANAGEMENT (August 1995)
American Graduate School of International Management
Thunderbird Campus, Glendale, Arizona
- Emphasis in Strategic Management
- Regional specialty in Latin America
- Analyzed Japanese airline industry for future growth patterns and outlook
- Winterim 1995 in Costa Rica and Nicaragua – Latin American Studies

BACHELOR OF ARTS (December 1993)
Antioch University, Yellow Springs, Ohio
- Major in Organizational Management

LANGUAGES
Highly proficient in **Spanish**

COMPUTERS
Lotus 1-2-3, WordPerfect, Harvard Graphics, @ Risk, Paradox

SUZANNE NELSON

12345 N. 89th Lane
Peoria, Arizona 85382
(602) 555-1234

OBJECTIVE

Career position utilizing accumulated organizational, administrative, accounting, and personnel skills in a firm committed to growth and quality of product or services.

EXPERIENCE

ADMINISTRATIVE

- *Purchasing Coordinator and Buyer for Information Services*, City of Mesa, Arizona. Vendor selection following competitive bidding and quote preparation, receiving, asset management, invoice approval, and monthly purchasing reports.
- *Administrative Assistant* for Mesa Community and Conference Center. A staff position responsible for supervision of personnel for ticketed events, conducting financial settlements with event promoters and managers, and division accounting reports to the Director and City Manager.
- *Membership Coordinator* for the Colorado Medical Society. Investigated and processed potential physician members, maintained the organization's calendar, prescreened personnel, and conducted employee orientations.

ACCOUNTING

- *Accounting Clerk III* for City of Mesa Finance Department. Reconciliation and maintenance of several general operating accounts, audited golf course revenue receipts, maintained utility journals.
- *Administrative Assistant* for Mesa Community Center, including performance of all accounting functions for that department: accounts payable, accounts receivable, invoicing, collections, cash disbursements, purchasing, and appropriate computerized records.
- *Medical/Dental Office Management* for medical clinic and dentists in private practice.
- *Admission Secretary and Insurance Clerk* for three years with major Denver hospital; including billing, insurance claims processing, and collections.
- *Accounting Secretary* for Colorado Medical Society. Responsible for billing, collections, and maintaining revenue accounts and appropriate reports to management.

SALES

- *Real Estate* – Successful five years in sales and marketing of land and residential real estate. Advertising, conducted both market and cost replacement appraisals, prepared contracts, settlement forms, and conducted closings.
- *Employment Counselor* for two years with M.N. Nelson & Associates in Colorado.

SKILLS

Lotus 1-2-3, WordPerfect, Typing, 10-key, DOS, DataEase, Displaywrite IV

EDUCATION

BACHELOR OF SCIENCE IN ACCOUNTING in progress
Glendale Community College, 29 hours
University of Colorado, 17 hours

ROBERT H. TATUM II

PROFESSIONAL OBJECTIVE

To continue activities of a PGA Golf Professional and contribute my experience to promote and administer all phases of the golf profession. Seeking a long-term position with career and personal growth potential.

QUALIFICATIONS

Professional Standing . . . Apprentice of the Southwest Section PGA for four years.

Management Skills . . . Supervise and direct all golf operations in semiprivate, municipal, and real estate facilities. Responsibilities include:
- Interviewing, hiring, training, promoting, and recommending staff according to established policies and procedures.
- Planning day-to-day, weekly, and special event schedules for facility operation.
- Coordination and implementation of programs.
- Merchandising, inventory control, and purchasing of entire facility, including food and beverage operation.
- Collecting, depositing, and accounting for all monies involved in all operations.

Public Relations . . . Proven ability to successfully relate to people while continuing to maintain a high degree of professionalism. Adept in promoting the golf course and facility by creative advertising and effective communication within the community.

Golf Course Operations . . . Experienced in all areas of golf course maintenance, including mowing, irrigation, equipment maintenance, and budgeting. Supervised and directed golf shop, range, golf cart, and food/beverage operations.

Teaching . . . Ability to pass knowledge of techniques, swing mechanics, and fundamentals of the game of golf has led to a growing reputation as a teaching professional. Established and organized golf schools, clinics, various seminars, junior leagues, and schools.

EMPLOYERS

Aug. 1991 – Present	**JUNIOR GOLF ASSOCIATION OF ARIZONA** 12345 N. Tatum Boulevard, Suite 123 Phoenix, Arizona 85028
Oct. 1989 – Aug. 1990	**SECURITY FINANCIAL REALTY** dba Pueblo El Mirage Country Club El Mirage, Arizona 85123
Aug. 1986 – Oct. 1989	**COUNTRY MEADOWS COUNTRY CLUB** Managed by Design Master Homes 1234 W. Broadway Road, Tempe, Arizona 85282
Mar. 1975 – Sep. 1977	**APPLEWOOD GOLF COURSE** Gold, Colorado 80123

Jill K. Wolf

1234 West Dunlap #1234
Phoenix, Arizona 85021
(602) 555-1234

PROFESSIONAL OBJECTIVE

To attain a responsible and challenging position as an animal handler or keeper utilizing education and experience

EMPLOYMENT EXPERIENCE

Animal Technician   1990 – Present
Northern Animal Hospital, Phoenix, Arizona

Internship with Curator   1987 – Present
Wildlife World Zoo, Glendale, Arizona

Assistant and Technician   1988 – 1989
Sunburst Animal Hospital, Glendale, Arizona

EDUCATIONAL BACKGROUND

Bachelor of Science in Zoology   Dec. 1990
Arizona State University, Tempe, Arizona

QUALIFYING SKILLS

Animal Husbandry . . . Apprentice to head zookeeper and curator at the Wildlife World Zoo. Performed all duties pertaining to the care of wild and exotic animals, including cleaning, enclosure repairs, behavioral observation. Participant in behavioral research of the Maned Wolf. Assisted in the preparation of diets for carnivores, herbivores, primates, and aves. Demonstrated capture methods for the transference of animals.

Technical (Veterinary) . . . Executed daily medical procedures, such as obtaining vital statistics, administering vaccines, setting catheters, medicating, preparing for and assisting in surgery, performing various laboratory and blood work. Competent in handling all types of sick and injured animals.

Public Relations . . . Excellent writing and verbal skills. Prepared numerous experimental and research papers. Performed public presentations with parrots. Answered questions and supervised the public's proper handling of the animals.

Other Skills . . . Experienced in record keeping. Familiar with many types of computers. Skilled in typing. Some knowledge of the Spanish language.

AFFILIATIONS

- Member of the American Association of Zoo Keepers
- The Arizona Humane Society Auxiliary
- The World Wildlife Fund
- The Massachusetts Society for the Prevention of Cruelty to Animals

128

RICHARD H. ROOSEVELT
12345 North 8th Avenue
Glendale, Arizona 85308
(602) 555-1234

OBJECTIVE

MANAGEMENT POSITION offering major responsibility and opportunity for future growth.

SUMMARY OF QUALIFICATIONS

Business experience . . . Includes large business, small business, entrepreneur, profit responsibility, budgeting, and market planning. Understanding of all aspects of business and how they interrelate. Familiar with latest quantitative and management techniques.

Management experience . . . Responsible for planning and directing operations for a successful franchise building management organization. Have extensive experience in labor requirement planning and performance appraisals. Have managed large and small union and nonunion forces with production and management staff. Successfully started a customer contact and review program for our customers and managers.

Training . . . Trained and supervised workers in: new employee orientations, production, and time study techniques, standard working procedures, work scheduling, and job assignments. Set standards of performance.

Financial Controls . . . Responsible for total financial activities and complete P&L of each profit center.

Purchasing . . . Planned and implemented purchasing program, including expediting price and terms negotiation, and comparing vendor prices and terms.

ACCOMPLISHMENTS

- Increased sales 30% and penetrated new market areas.

- Opened up totally untapped market by convincing schools that in the past used only in-house forces to use our services.

- Organized operational team to begin new business. Identified and penetrated market, established accounting systems, etc.

- Trimmed $200,000 from company's budget without lowering quality or reducing personnel.

- Started large accounts to promote 40% growth rate within division.

- Won highest award for managerial excellence at Servicemaster Industries – a $1+ billion company.

EDUCATION

B.A. IN BUSINESS ADMINISTRATION, Roosevelt University   1992

Have completed ADVANCED COURSES in History and Political Science.

Completed MANAGEMENT AND LABOR RELATIONS COURSES at Servicemaster Industries.

MERRILL BRIARWOOD _____

1234 W. Greenway Road #1234
Phoenix, Arizona 85023
(602) 555-1234

OBJECTIVE   An increasingly responsible aviation operations position

_____

EXPERIENCE

SUMMARY
> A 20+ year career of responsible positions at all levels of aviation management.
> Firsthand experience in actively managing 6,000 aviation technicians in a large worldwide aviation operations organization.
> Gained an understanding of personnel management through application of human resource development/training programs.
> Federal Aviation Administration aviation facility examiner responsible for personnel and training scheduling, evaluation/standardization of four different military operations facilities.
> Experienced in aviation technical operations report preparation.
> Designed a new cost-saving aviation computer program.
> Overall job experience enhanced by aviation operations and educational background.

PERSONNEL MANAGEMENT AND AVIATION TRAINING
> Administrator solely responsible for the U.S. Air Force and Federal Aviation Administration air traffic control operations training, scheduling, facility rating, and certification programs for 6,000 aviation operations technicians.
> Facility administrator with hands-on managerial experience at seven different facilities, applying personnel management, aviation operations training programs, and firsthand experience in all aspects of human resources development.
> Superintendent responsible for training of 45 air traffic control operations specialists.

COMPUTER SYSTEM MANAGEMENT
> Conceived, justified, and implemented two new computer programs that saved the U.S. Air Force $30,000 annually and one man-year of labor.
> Hands-on experience operating a radar flight simulation system and National Airspace System computers.

_____

AVIATION EDUCATION & LICENSES

MASTER OF AERONAUTICAL SCIENCE, 1988
Embry-Riddle Aeronautical University

MASTER OF AVIATION MANAGEMENT, 1987
Embry-Riddle Aeronautical University

BACHELOR OF PROFESSIONAL AERONAUTICS, 1983
Embry-Riddle Aeronautical University

ASSOCIATE OF APPLIED SCIENCE ATC, 1983
Community College of the Air Force

FAA PRIVATE PILOT'S LICENSE with Aircraft Single-Engine Land Rating

Leslie Y. Wilson

Current:
1234 Druid Lane #123
Dallas, Texas 75205
(214) 555-1234

Permanent:
1234 W. 43rd Terrace
Kansas City, Missouri 64113
(816) 555-1234

ABILITIES
- Exceptional research, negotiating, and problem-solving skills.
- Resourceful – able to organize and prioritize multiple projects with divergent needs.
- Computer literate in both IBM and Macintosh computer systems.
- Proven ability to develop new markets and maintain profitable client relationships.
- Successful manager of diverse groups of people, utilizing strong communication skills.
- Empathetic listener and persuasive public speaker.

SALES ACHIEVEMENTS
- Settled a 3-year legal dispute utilizing a structured financial settlement that transferred all risk to a third-party guarantor.
- Created a Federal Estate Tax Return Case Study Book, which was extremely effective in motivating prospects to evaluate and take action on their personal estate conservation and business succession plans.
- Achieved qualification as a member in the Million Dollar Round Table, an international organization limited to the top 5% of insurance sales agents worldwide.
- Achieved a contract persistency rating of 99%.

MANAGEMENT HIGHLIGHTS
- Profitably co-managed a $500,000 EPA Superfund clean-up for dioxin contamination.
- Team member of 24-Hour Emergency Environmental Response and Cleanup Group.
- Diligent risk manager of liability and conventional loss exposures.

EXPERIENCE

THE PRUDENTIAL INSURANCE COMPANY OF AMERICA
Specialty Marketing Consultant, Kansas City, MO	6/90 – Present
Specialist, Advanced Estate Planning, Kansas City, MO	10/88 – 6/90
Insurance Agent and Registered Representative, Kansas City, MO	8/84 – 10/88

ENVIRONMENTAL SPECIALISTS INCORPORATED
Environmental Coordinator, Kansas City, MO	1/83 – 8/84

EDUCATION

MASTER OF INTERNATIONAL MANAGEMENT (MIM)	12/91
American Graduate School of International Management	
Thunderbird Campus, Glendale, Arizona	

FOREIGN STUDY PROGRAM	Summer 1991
Institut de Gestion Sociale, Paris, France	
European Integration Studies for the 1992 Initiative	

BACHELOR OF ARTS – ENVIRONMENTAL STUDIES	1982
University of Kansas, Lawrence, Kansas	

PROFESSIONAL TRAINING

CHARTERED LIFE UNDERWRITER (CLU)	
CHARTERED FINANCIAL CONSULTANT (CHFC)	
The American College	9/87 – 3/91
Courses: Investments, Personal and Corporate Taxation, and Employee Benefits	

ENVIRONMENTAL EMERGENCY RESPONSE TRAINING, EPA	1984
Hazardous Site Survey, Contaminate Identification, Emergency Response Protocol	

Michael A. Criscito

1234 Amstel Dr., Colorado Springs, CO 80907
Phone (719) 555-1234 • Fax (719) 123-4567

SUMMARY OF EXPERIENCE

MANAGEMENT
- Assisted in management of USAF Academy Video Store
- Three years of experience as business manager of an international secretarial service, including accounts payable, receivables, inventory, shipping, and customer service
- Established maintenance control and work flow procedures for Air Force shops
- Supervised and motivated subordinates to exceptional performance
- Coordinated 16 personnel, 4 vehicles, and thousands of food packs for Meals on Wheels
- Served for two years as Branch Technical Order and Training Monitor
- Augmented quality assurance teams in mobility and logistics planning

TRAINING MANAGEMENT
- Served four years as Unit Training Manager – made dramatic improvements in career development courses (CDC), upgrade training programs, class scheduling, and forecasting of training needs
- Overhauled the CDC course exam pretesting program, increasing completion rates by 400% with higher average test scores and no failures
- Developed pretesting appointment and tracking system and created flow charts
- Trained personnel in troubleshooting complex electronic components and use of associated test equipment, cockpit/explosive/flightline safety, radiation hazards, and other subjects

VEHICLE SUPERVISION
- Managed the largest vehicle program at Bitburg AB for three years with flawless inspections
- Coordinated vehicle maintenance and rotation; investigated accidents and abuse/misuse
- Commended for dramatically improving the squadron's vehicle management program
- Maintained $117,000 worth of radios at an exceptional operations rate

ARMAMENT & ELECTRONICS
- Inspected, maintained, installed, modified, and repaired bomb, rocket, and missile release, launch, suspension, and monitoring systems; gun and gun mount systems; and related munitions handling, loading, and test equipment for a total of 12 years
- Supervised and performed in-shop maintenance and functional checks on pylons, bomb racks, launchers, bomb release dispensers, guns, and other components
- Two years in the Component Repair Shop, troubleshooting electronic systems

LOADING
- Weapons Load Crew Chief – Launched and recovered aircraft, and loaded ordinance
- Performed integrated combat turnarounds
- Flightline Expeditor – assured that all aircraft on the flying schedule were configured as specified; supervised maintenance crew and four load crews

WORK HISTORY

Business Manager, ProType, Ltd., Colorado Springs		1991 – Present
Video Sales Associate, AAFES, USAF Academy, Colorado Springs		1994 – Present
Aircraft Armament Systems Technician, U.S. Air Force		1972 – 1992

EDUCATION

ASSOCIATE DEGREE IN ARMAMENT SYSTEMS TECHNOLOGY	in process
Community College of the Air Force	42 credits

RELEVANT TRAINING

Flightline Weapons Maintenance Management (34 hours)	1988
Section Supervisor OJT Course (12 & 24 hours)	1987
OJT Trainer Orientation (24 hours)	1980
Noncommissioned Officer Leadership School (Management) (191 hours)	1978
Maintenance Management and Data Collection System (30 hours)	1975

10 PERSONAL INFORMATION AND REFERENCES

PERSONAL DATA

There are very few times when personal information is appropriate on a resume. Usually such facts only take up valuable white space, especially details such as age, sex, race, health, or marital status, and other details that potential employers are not allowed to ask. Some exceptions to the rule might be:

If you are looking for a job in sales where you would need to travel a great deal, or overseas where relocating an entire family becomes expensive, showing that you are unmarried and willing to travel could be helpful.

Submitting a resume to a U.S. company doing business in certain foreign countries could be another example. On such a resume, an "Interests" section would show a prospective employer that your hobbies are compatible with the host country.

Students, or those who have recently graduated, often have a difficult time coming up with enough paid experience to demonstrate their qualifications. But, if they have held leadership positions in campus organizations or have supervised groups of people and organized activities on a volunteer basis, then an "Activities" section could strengthen those qualifications.

A list of sporting interests would be helpful for a person looking for a sports marketing position. And the list goes on. It is important to use your judgment, since you know best what qualifications are important in your field.

On the second example in this section, you will notice that the author was a minister. In that particular line of work, it is very important to list a great deal of personal information that most employers would not need to know or even want to know.

PHOTOGRAPHS

Photographs on a resume are required by companies in some foreign countries, although they are rarely used in the United States. However, if you were trying to test the waters in the fashion industry – before presenting a full-blown portfolio – a photograph might be appropriate. There is an exception to every rule in the resume business so, again, use your judgment.

REFERENCES

References are not usually presented on a resume since most employers will not take the time to check references until after an interview. By then, they will have your application form with a list of references. There is nothing wrong with taking a nicely printed list of personal references with you to an interview, however.

Stating on a resume that "references will be provided upon request" is not necessary since it is assumed you will provide them when asked. On rare occasions, however, I have been known to use that phrase as a filler on an extremely short resume (as you will notice on pages 17, 96, 211, and 250).

AHMAD A. EL-GUIZA

Training Department
Egyptian Hospitals Program
P.O. Box 123, Cairo, Egypt

Tel. 04-1234567
Ext. 12345 or
56789, 54321

PERSONAL

Date of Birth	15 October 1953
Citizenship	Egyptian
Languages	Arabic, English, French
Health	Excellent
Marital Status	Married

EDUCATION

MSC/Diploma in the Practice of Education
Surrey University, Guildford, United Kingdom
May 1994

Bachelor of Arts English Language
Faculty of Languages, Ain Shams University, Cairo, Egypt
May 1978

EXPERIENCE

Language Instructor
Training Centre, NWAF Hospital
P.O. Box 100, Cairo, Egypt
July 1990 – Present

- Develop teaching materials for medical terminology and conduct classes for on-the-job trainees and civilian hospital staff.
- Conduct classes in beginning and intermediate English, and develop teaching materials for special-purpose English.
- Teach beginning and intermediate Arabic, and develop teaching materials.

Language Instructor
Training Centre, GAMA
King Abdul Military Hospital
P.O. Box 123, Riyahd, Saudi Arabia
May 1987 – July 1990

- Developed teaching materials for special-purpose Arabic classes.
- Taught classes in beginning and intermediate Arabic for non-Arabs.
- Conducted classes in Arabic for long-term inpatient children.

Language Instructor
Training Centre
Allied Medical Group
Joint Venture
P.O. Box 123, Riyahd, Saudi Arabia
June 1984 – April 1987

- Developed teaching materials for special-purpose English and Arabic classes.
- Taught classes in beginning and intermediate Arabic for non-Arabs and for long-term inpatient children.
- Conducted classes in English medical terminology for new Nurse's Aide Interpreters.
- Translated materials for in-service education, as needed.

Language Instructor
Staff Development
Whittier Corporation
P.O. Box 123, Riyahd, Saudi Arabia
April 1981 – May 1984

- Developed teaching materials for special-purpose Arabic and English classes.
- Taught classes in beginning and intermediate Arabic for non-Arabic speaking personnel.
- Conducted classes in Arabic literacy for Saudi civilian staff.
- Translated for various hospital development classes related to Arabic culture and traditions.

Classroom Teacher
El-Guiza Preparatory School
Cairo, Egypt
December 1978 – April 1981

- Taught English language classes to preparatory students.
- Maintained all records of student progress.

ADDITIONAL INFORMATION

- TOEFL, April 1993
- Graduate Record Examination, April 1993
- Typing Skills in English and Arabic

Henry L. Deere

U.S. Mailing Address • ABC Unit 12345, APO AE 09812-1234 • Phone (966) (4) 555-1234
Saudi Arabia Address • ABC DEFG P.O. Box 12, Tabuk, Saudi Arabia • Fax (966) (4) 555-1234

OBJECTIVE

Supervisor of Heavy Equipment Maintenance or related role in an international setting.

SUMMARY OF QUALIFICATIONS

- *Achieved Master Craftsman status in the military/civilian heavy construction field.*
- *Over thirty years experience in mechanics, inspection, engineering, maintenance, and operation of dozers, graders, loaders/backhoes, forklifts, power generators, cranes, excavators, trucks, and cement mixers, including Caterpillar, Komatsu, John Deere, FMC Linkbelt, P&H, Galion, etc.*
- *Eleven years of active duty with the United States Armed Forces.*
- *U.S. Navy Construction Battalion (CB) experience for fourteen years, supervising and training CB units in all phases of the mechanics, maintenance, and operation of above-mentioned equipment.*
- *Over ten years of experience supervising and training Saudi Arabian Army construction engineers in all phases of mechanics, operation, and maintenance of construction and heavy equipment.*
- *Experienced in the supervision of multinational work forces, including Saudi Arabians, Americans, British, Philipinos, Koreans, and Jordanians.*

EXPERIENCE

MAINTENANCE WORKSHOP SUPERVISOR/INSPECTOR (June 1983 to Present)
Saudi Maintenance Corporation (SIYANCO SOCP), Saudi Operation & Maintenance Co., Ltd. (SOMC), Tabuk, Saudi Arabia
Supervise and train Saudi military work force and civilian multinational mechanics and technicians assigned to the heavy equipment maintenance workshop on a Saudi military base.
Primary Duties and Responsibilities:
- *Inspect, plan, direct, and supervise the operation and maintenance of all types of construction and heavy equipment and accessories.*
- *Organize and schedule heavy equipment repair shop operation to expedite completion of repairs.*
- *Analyze operational difficulties and provide corrective measures.*
- *Render technical assistance to subordinates.*
- *Conduct research, and requisition parts and supplies.*
- *Perform administrative functions, including payroll and timekeeping for subordinates, leave scheduling, and preparation of maintenance records and files.*
- *Directly supervise the work and performance of twelve mechanics and technicians.*
Achievements:
- *Greatly reduced turnaround time for repairs and overhaul of equipment under responsibility.*
- *Significantly decreased maintenance costs for repair parts and supplies to an acceptable level as a result of systematic planning, scheduling, and technical supervision of the maintenance and operation of heavy equipment.*
- *Enhanced the morale of subordinates through counseling and proper application of leadership.*
- *Promoted from Engineering Heavy Equipment Mechanic to Maintenance Workshop Supervisor in April 1994 because of exceptional technical skills and devotion to duty.*

HEAVY EQUIPMENT MECHANIC (Civil Service WG-10 & WG-11) (March 1968 to May 1983)
Public Works Transportation, Navy CB Detachment, U.S. Naval Air Station, Kingsville, Texas
- *Responsible for the maintenance, overhaul, and repair of all heavy and construction equipment, fire and crash trucks and equipment, and field and ground support equipment.*
- *Supervised and scheduled training of the Navy CB mechanics and operators on all heavy and construction equipment listed in the summary of qualifications section.*

HEAVY EQUIPMENT MECHANIC (June 1967 to February 1968)
Holders Equipment Rental Company, Corpus Christi, Texas
- *Maintained and repaired all heavy and construction equipment.*

ENGINEMAN FIRST CLASS PETTY OFFICER (E-6) (June 1956 to June 1967)
& FIREMAN APPRENTICE FA2, U.S. Coast Guard
- *Supervised mechanics and technicians aboard various ships (including five years of overseas tours) in maintaining engineering equipment, main propulsion engines and accessories, damage control, and the overhaul, repair, and operation of all heavy and construction equipment.*
- *Assignments also included various construction job sites and military base maintenance of heavy and construction equipment.*

OTHER SKILLS   Crane and machine shop equipment operator, welding, word processing, and office equipment

EDUCATION &   **Academic:** Diploma, Waskom High School, Waskom, Texas, 1956
TRAINING
Industrial and Military: Various Military Institute Correspondence Courses from E-2 to E-7 on Engineman Petty Officer ratings and Warrant Officer Engineering from the U.S. Coast Guard Institute, Groton, Connecticut. On-the-job training (OJT) in heavy equipment operation and maintenance, as well as shipboard training in turbine engine mechanic fundamentals, U.S. Army Aeronautical Depot Maintenance Center, Corpus Christi, Texas.

AWARDS
- Department of the Navy Federal Service Length of Service Award for completion of 25 years of service, June 1982.
- Meritorious Service Certificate from DS/GS Supervisor, Saudi Maintenance Corporation (SIYANCO), August 1989.

PERSONAL DATA
- U.S. Citizen with valid passport
- Eligible for United Kingdom residency
- Excellent health, married
- Interests include racquetball, jogging, yoga, and bowling
- Permanent address: 1234 Marshall Drive, Lawrence, Texas 75670, USA, Phone (903) 555-1234

REV. RANDY J. WREN

1234 North 10th Lane • Phoenix, Arizona 85019 • (602) 555-1234

PERSONAL INFORMATION

Born: February 19, 1961, Davenport, Iowa
Height: 6' 2"
Licensed: General Council Assemblies of God
Married: March 14, 1981
Wife: Sandra, born April 4, 1962, Milwaukee, WI
Son: Andrew, born November 8, 1982
Daughter: Candace, born September 19, 1984

FAMILY

My wife: Sandy is my best friend and support in our home and ministry. She is warm, friendly, hospitable, and gifted. She has served as Children's Church Director, Bible Quiz Coach, and Assistant Missionette Teacher. Presently she is the Junior Bible Coach and works as a Dental Assistant. She is a spirit-filled believer.

Andrew, our son, is presently in the 4th grade, attends the Honors program and has been on the principal's list since the first grade. He was saved at the age of four and filled with the Holy Spirit at the age of 9, baptized in water at 8 years old. He is a top Quizzer on the Junior Bible Quiz team. Andrew loves to sing for the Lord.

Candace, our daughter, is presently in third grade and has been on the Honor Roll list all the way through 2nd grade. She was born again at age 7 and filled with the Holy Spirit and baptized in water. She loves to sing for the Lord. She is presently in Junior Bible Quiz and doing very well for her first year.

BACKGROUND

I was born in Iowa and raised in Phoenix, Arizona. My parents have always served the Lord. My grandfather was a Pioneering Pastor (55 years). I was saved and filled with the Holy Spirit at age 8 and called into the ministry.

MINISTRY VISIONS AND GOALS

To utilize my experience, education, and ideas • To see God build His church through the power of the Holy Spirit • To preach, teach, and lead people into a balanced Christian lifestyle – this includes worship to God, growth in Christ, caring for one another, and evangelism to our world • To challenge Christians to find and use their gifts and be motivated by the Holy Spirit.

MINISTRY EXPERIENCE

1991 – Present   Since last year we have been on the evangelism field. We have been holding revivals and concerts. I have been teaching and preaching on the use of the power of the Holy Spirit for today's Christians. We have seen many lives changed through Christ. Pastors have been uplifted and encouraged and filled with a new drive.

MINISTRY EXPERIENCE (continued)

1989 – 1991   **ASSOCIATE/YOUTH PASTOR**, **South Mountain Assembly of God**, *Phoenix, Arizona*
Area of Ministry:
Coordinated, planned, and directed all Youth Ministries
- *Preached and taught weekly*
- *Planned curriculum and trained leaders*
- *Planned outings—youth retreats, family counseling camps*
- *Developed and directed fund raisers—Speed-the-Light*

Coordinate, plan, and direct all Sunday school programs
- *Taught Sunday school class*
- *Trained teachers, seminars, monthly meetings, visitation*
- *Taught new converts class, membership class*

Pastoral care and administrative areas
- *Assisted in preaching and pulpit ministries*
- *Performed counseling and visitation (family and one-on-one)*
- *Designed and produced special services—Western Round-up Sunday, Family Days*

1985 – 1988   **MINISTRY**, **North Freeway Assembly of God**, *Phoenix, Arizona*
Coordinated the children's church for two years
- *Recruited members*
- *Trained teams*

Taught Sunday school for two and a half years

Managed bus ministry
- *Visitation*
- *Recruited leaders*

EDUCATION

B.A. IN PASTORAL MINISTRY, **American Indian Bible College**, *Phoenix, Arizona*
Graduated 1989—Honor roll, Dean's List, Valedictorian, Mission President

REFERENCES

(listed here but removed for anonymity)

Leslie Y. Pruco

Current: 1234 W. Thunderbird Road, #1234 • Glendale, AZ 85306 • (602) 555-1234
Permanent: 1234 W. 3rd Terrace • Kansas City, MO 64113 • (816) 555-1234

OBJECTIVE

An international marketing position with a German company

PERSONAL

Birthdate: March 17, 1969
Citizenship: U.S.A.
Marital Status: Single
Languages: Proficient in German, working knowledge of French and Spanish
Licenses: Chartered Life Underwriter, Chartered Financial Consultant

EDUCATION

MASTER OF INTERNATIONAL MANAGEMENT (MIM)   12/94
American Graduate School of International Management
Glendale, Arizona

FOREIGN STUDY PROGRAM   Summer 1994
Institut de Gestion Sociale, Paris, France
European Integration Studies for the 1992 Initiative

BACHELOR OF ARTS—ENVIRONMENTAL STUDIES   1985
University of Kansas, Lawrence, Kansas

EXPERIENCE

THE PRUDENTIAL, PRUCO SECURITIES, Kansas City, Missouri
Specialist, Advanced Estate Planning   10/88 – 6/90
Designed solutions for complex estate conservation and business
succession problems. Created a Federal Estate Tax Return Case Study
Book that was extremely effective in motivating prospects to evaluate
their personal estate and business plans.

Insurance Agent and Registered Representative   8/84 – 12/94
Developed a personally selected clientele in the life, health, disability,
property, and casualty insurance markets. Evaluated personal and
corporate financial plans, defined loss exposures, and provided solutions for the problems discovered. Achieved qualification as a member
in the Million Dollar Round Table. Achieved a policy persistency
rating of 99%. Wrote first $2,000,000 permanent life insurance policy
in Kansas City Agency history.

ENVIRONMENTAL SPECIALISTS INCORPORATED
Environmental Coordinator   1/83 – 8/84
24 Hour Emergency Response Team Member for hazardous spills and
explosions, environment project procurement, management, and safety
quality control. Profitably managed a $500,000 EPA Superfund clean-
up for dioxin contamination.

**PROFESSIONAL
TRAINING**

ENVIRONMENTAL EMERGENCY RESPONSE TRAINING, EPA   1984
Hazardous Site Survey, Contaminate Identification, Emergency Response Protocol

11 FONTS AND BULLETS

FONTS

Fonts (aka type style or type face) set the tone for the entire resume. What is a font? It is that little bit of magic that enables humans to communicate in print. It is the alphabet set to music. It is art. Actually, a font is a set of curved, straight, or slanted shapes that your brain decodes into comprehensible information, but that sounds too boring for a subject as fascinating as type style.

Every font has its own designer and its own personality and projects a certain "feel." For instance, serif fonts (the kind with the little "feet" like the Souvienne font used on this page) are considered more traditional. They are usually used as **text** fonts in books and magazines. Some samples include:

- Times Roman
- New Century Schoolbook
- Padua
- Bookman
- See pages 163–165 for more serif fonts

Sans (meaning "without" in French) serif fonts, on the other hand, have no "feet" and are considered more contemporary, as in:

- **Helvetica**
- **Avant Garde**
- **CG Omega**
- **Univers**
- **See pages 166–167 for more sans serif fonts**

Although serif fonts are commonly used as text type for the main body of published works, you don't have to restrict yourself to these types of fonts for resumes. Either style produces equally impressive resumes.

Headline fonts and wild type faces have their place in design, but only in the headlines. Remember, you want your resume to be easy to read. You will find many samples of headline fonts on pages 168–174.

In all my years of designing resumes, I have discovered that my clients don't have to understand the science behind fonts or the difference between serif and sans serif fonts, and neither do you. It is more important that you look at samples of good resume fonts and then choose which one makes your eyes "feel good." In other words, choose the one you like the best. Again, it comes down to personality.

BULLETS

Bullets are special characters used at the beginning of indented short sentences to call attention to individual items on a resume. Short, bulleted sentences are easier to read and highlight the information you want the reader to see. Bullets also add some variety to a resume and make it just a touch more creative.

If you use WordPerfect, the Compose feature (Ctrl V or Ctrl 2 in 5.0/5.1 and Ctrl W in 6.0) allows you to enter special characters that are not found on your keyboard. That is how the bullets in this section were created. Your printing capabilities might not allow you to have access to all of these dingbats, but you can still be creative.

UNIVERS CONDENSED

123 South Otis Street   •   Lakewood, Colorado 80226   •   (303) 555-1234

QUALIFICATIONS

Marketing . . . Trained project managers to develop, manage, and implement export programs, resulting in 100% productivity. Developed training materials, achieving more efficient program implementation. Recognized by upper management for submitting "model" marketing plans and organizing an outstanding program.

Promotional Campaigns . . . Developed and directed promotions and advertising in major Asian, European, Canadian, and Saudi Arabian grocery and department stores. Produced promotional and educational brochures.

Trade Shows/Exhibitions . . . Coordinated food and agricultural exporters in nearly ten international trade shows per year. Trained interns to conduct research, evaluate programs, and manage trade show recruiting.

Public Relations . . . Coedited and wrote for a quarterly newsletter with a distribution of 4,000 worldwide. Initiated press release program, resulting in increased public awareness of export programs.

Client Relations . . . Counseled industry groups and private companies on export procedures, foreign markets, and product suitability. Presented trade programs at eight export seminars in 1993, increasing private company participation.

PROFESSIONAL EXPERIENCE

PROGRAM DIRECTOR
Southern U.S. Trade Association
1991 – 1995
New Orleans, LA
- Coordinated and implemented trade shows and export marketing projects in a nonprofit agricultural product export organization.
- Managed and internally audited a program budget, which tripled in 3 years to nearly $1 million.
- Served as liaison between public and private sector, adapting a federal program to fit the international marketing needs of over 15 agricultural industry groups.
- Researched, wrote, and edited marketing plans with set objectives and time-lines.

INTERN: COSMETICS MARKETING TEAM
Sunstar, Inc.
Summer 1990
Osaka, Japan
- Designed and presented to management a U.S. marketing plan for children's shampoo.
- Studied and applied Japanese marketing and advertising strategies.

HOST FAMILY RECRUITER
Aspect Foundation
1989
Seattle, WA
- Promoted organization to over 100 families.
- Coordinated recruitment, interviewing, and selection of host families for international high school students and counseled U.S. host families on cross-cultural issues.

ENGLISH TEACHER
Sapporo Sacred Heart School
1987 – 1988
Sapporo, Japan
- Taught English, speech, and drama to Japanese high school and junior college students.
- Co-directed a junior college play which won a city-wide drama competition.

EDUCATION

MASTER OF INTERNATIONAL MANAGEMENT
American Graduate School of International Management, Thunderbird Campus
1990
Glendale, AZ
- Concentration in International Marketing

BACHELOR OF ARTS, Honors
Gonzaga University
1987
Spokane, WA

STUDIES ABROAD
La Sorbonne, Université de Paris
1985 – 1986
Paris, France

LANGUAGES & COMPUTERS

- Fluent in French (earned Certificate of Proficiency in Business French, awarded by Chambre de Commerce et d'Industrie, Paris, 1993)
- Working knowledge of Japanese
- Competent in WordPerfect, Word, Windows, Lotus 1-2-3, Harvard Graphics, FoxPro

Helvetica Oblique

EXPERIENCE	**ADMINISTRATIVE MANAGER AND ACCOUNTANT**	*Apr. 1991*
	Inca World Imports, *Tampa, Florida*	*– Present*

Import-export company specializing in industrial products from the United States and handicrafts from Peru.

➡ *Developed operational, financial, administrative procedures for entrepreneurial adventure*
➡ *Installed and implemented computerized accounting system*

MANAGER OF EXPORT DEPARTMENT	*June 1989*
Establissements Marill, *Djibouti, East Africa*	*– Mar. 1991*

This 17 million dollar proprietorship, founded in 1896, is the exclusive importer of Toyota, Yamaha, Heinekin, and other products for the Djiboutian territory.

➡ *Hired by the proprietor to recover sales, which had deceased over past four years, and to repair Marill's damaged reputation with customers*
➡ *Managed exportation of company-represented products to neighboring countries (Ethiopia, Somalia, Sudan, Yemen)*
➡ *Supervised all stages of sales and ordering procedures*
➡ *Established standard operating procedures and improved job definition*
➡ *Reduced delivery time up to three weeks*
➡ *Supervised 12 Djiboutian staff; stimulated employee motivation and morale*
➡ *Increased sales by 30% and reduced operating mistakes by 60%*
➡ *Regained client confidence plus increased clientele by 10%*

PROJECT FINANCIAL MANAGER	*Aug. 1988*
Texas Instruments, Inc., *Dallas, Texas*	*– Feb. 1989*

➡ *Implemented financial operating requirements for five new cost centers*
➡ *Monitored and analyzed all financial transactions using integrated database, ledger, accounts payable, and charge-out systems for this five-million-dollar leasehold improvement project*
➡ *Monitored and analyzed all material and labor costs associated with the project*
➡ *Balanced cost transfers and general ledger on a monthly basis*
➡ *Responsible for project, cost center and space forecasts, and forecast reviews*
➡ *Provided financial support to cost center and project managers*

EDUCATION	**MASTER OF INTERNATIONAL MANAGEMENT**	*Jan. 1993*
	American Graduate School of International Management	

Thunderbird Campus, Glendale, Arizona
Emphasis: Marketing

BACHELOR OF SCIENCE IN FINANCE	*Apr. 1988*
Florida State University, *Tallahassee, Florida*	

LANGUAGES   *Bilingual in* **English** *and* **French**

COMPUTERS   *Working knowledge of Lotus 1-2-3, WordPerfect, WordStar, Harvard Graphics*

ACTIVITIES
& INTERESTS   *Born and lived in West Germany until 1983*
Lived in Africa two years
Lived in France six months
Golf, tennis, equestrian riding, swimming, travel

Address ➡ *1234 Wynwood Drive* ➡ *Tampa, Florida 33615* ➡ *(813) 555-1234*

HELVETICA

123 Michigan Avenue ⇢ Portsmouth, New Hampshire 03842 ⇢ (603) 555-1234

EXPERIENCE

HUSSEY SEATING COMPANY, North Berwick, Maine   May 1993 – Present
Credit Manager
↪ Manage all credit and collection activities for $50 million spectator seating company.
↪ Coordinate credit terms for $3 million international shipments.
↪ Direct bonding activity for all corporate bid and payment/performance bonds.
↪ Initiated and continue to manage sales tax billing and collection procedures.
↪ Cash management, including cash forecasting and payables.

CABLETRON SYSTEMS, INC., Rochester, New Hampshire   Nov. 1990 – Apr. 1993
Supervisor – Maintenance Contracts
↪ Created and developed a maintenance contract billing department to manage $10M contract base.
↪ Managed conversion of maintenance contracts to an automated billing system.
↪ Directed system development with MIS to enhance system capability and efficiency resulting in a 50% increase in productivity over a three-month period.
↪ Provided account management through identification and resolution of contractual issues, account reconstruction, and collection.
↪ Initiated corporate policies and reporting procedures encompassing Finance, Sales, and Technical Support departments.
↪ Trained contract administrators in accounts receivable, system, and audit procedures.

Senior Credit Analyst/Floorplanning and Leasing Coordinator
↪ Provided the credit management of all reseller accounts. Special emphasis on the negotiation of after-sale financing terms. Successfully accomplished such negotiations in balanced accordance with corporate credit policies and customer satisfaction.
↪ Developed floorplanning and leasing programs, including start-up of programs, marketing to customers and to sales force, and training of sales force.

WANG LABORATORIES, INC., Tewksbury, Massachusetts   Dec. 1987 – Nov. 1990
Collection Specialist – Contract Management Organization
↪ Managed $17M annual base with $1M contract maintenance receivables for Fortune 500 and state government accounts.
↪ Consistently exceeded collection goals, increased collection total by 12%.
↪ Regional leader, reduced aged receivables by 16% within one year.
↪ Coordinated regional cash and aging forecasts and variance reporting.
↪ Directed and prioritized administrative work flow; trained and developed new hires.
↪ Coordinated customer, field, and home office policies and procedures to maximize Wang goals and objectives while promoting customer satisfaction.
↪ Acted as liaison between user groups and MIS for the implementation of Wang Integrated Imaging Systems.

COMMUNITY EXPERIENCE

A SAFE PLACE, INC., Portsmouth, New Hampshire   Sep. 1991 – Oct. 1994
Board President
↪ Responsible for Board management of a $300,000 nonprofit social service agency serving Rockingham and Strafford Counties, New Hampshire.
↪ Steering Committee Coordinator responsible for long-term planning.

Finance Director
↪ Oversight included: grant funding; annual budgets; financial statements; capital expenditure review; and long-range financial planning.

EDUCATION

MASTER OF BUSINESS ADMINISTRATION   1991
New Hampshire College, Graduate School of Business, Hooksett, New Hampshire

BACHELOR OF SCIENCE, BUSINESS ADMINISTRATION   1981
University of New Hampshire, Durham, New Hampshire
Emphasis on Organizational and Human Resource Development

AVANT GARDE ITALIC

OBJECTIVE	*A position in economic development with a Christian nonprofit organization*

QUALIFICATIONS
- *Over two years work and living experience in Taiwan and China*
- *Proficient in Mandarin Chinese*

EDUCATION

MASTER OF INTERNATIONAL MANAGEMENT *GPA 3.84* 1995
American Graduate School of International Management
Thunderbird Campus, Glendale, Arizona
- *Researched and presented business prospects in Vietnam*
- *Represented the Philippines in a simulated ASEAN summit conference*

Course Work: Economic Development, International Finance and Trade, Export/Import Management, Modern China and Southeast Asia

BACHELOR OF BUSINESS ADMINISTRATION *GPA 3.65* 1989
Pacific Lutheran University, *Tacoma, Washington*
- *Market research project for Recreational Equipment, Inc., (REI)*
- *Researched Taiwan market for Washington wines*

Course Work: Strategic Marketing Management, International Financial Management, Management Accounting

FOREIGN STUDY

NATIONAL TAIWAN NORMAL UNIVERSITY
Intensive Chinese Language Program, 1991

CHENGDU UNIVERSITY OF SCIENCE AND TECHNOLOGY, *Sichuan, China*
University Exchange Program, 1988

EXPERIENCE

INTERNATIONAL DELEGATION COORDINATOR 2/93
International Exposition for Food Processors '93, *Chicago, Illinois*
- *Hired by Food Processing Machinery & Supplies Association to assist Chinese delegations attending the show and to consult companies interested in inviting the Chinese to tour their facilities*
- *Worked in the International Business Center assisting delegates from Eastern Europe, Russia, and Southeast Asia*

ENGLISH INSTRUCTOR 2/90 – 2/92
Jordan Language Systems International, *Taipei, Taiwan*
- *Instructed corporate classes for: AT&T, Schering Pharmaceuticals, Johnson & Higgins Insurance, and Scotiabank*
- *Developed and led seminars on business writing and case studies for international managers*

MARKETING ASSISTANT 10/89 – 2/90
American Pioneer, *Seattle, Washington*
- *Assisted company in developing initial marketing department*
- *Created database to maintain files of owners and leads*
- *Handled communications with customers, dealers, and sales representatives both domestically and internationally*

ADMINISTRATIVE ASSISTANT Summers 1985–89
Design Systems/Frigoscandia Inc., *Seattle, Washington*
- *Accounting preparation of invoice billing, A/P, A/R on Libra system*
- *Generated sales forecast reports on Lotus*

ACHIEVEMENTS & ACTIVITIES
- *Active in Thunderbird clubs: Vice President of Southeast Asia Club, China Club, International Christian Fellowship Club, Nonprofit Careers Club*
- *Volunteer organizer of first Girl's High School English Club, Taipei*
- *Thunderbird Continuing Student Scholarship Recipient, Summer & Fall 1992*
- *Pacific Lutheran University Presidential Merit Scholarship, 1985-1989*

ADDRESS	*12345 S.W. Mirror Place, Issaquah, Washington 98027*	*(206) 555-1234*

146

Avant Garde Book

OBJECTIVE	A rewarding career in International Management/Marketing/Consulting

QUALIFICATIONS
- Bilingual: English and Spanish
- Work experience in Mexico; in-depth knowledge of Mexican business structures
- Advanced degree emphasizing International Management and Marketing

---

EDUCATION

MASTER OF INTERNATIONAL MANAGEMENT May 1994
American Graduate School of International Management
Thunderbird Campus, Glendale, Arizona
Concentration: Marketing and Management
- Determined U.S. market entry strategy for Pepali Trading Co., a Mexican skin care company
- Developed marketing strategies for John Deere, Inc., in the U.S. and Mexico
- Prepared documentation in Spanish for exporting/importing bicycles to Spain
- Created business plan for starting a Mexican shrimp exportation company

BACHELOR OF ARTS 1991
Austin College, Sherman, Texas
Concentration: Business and Spanish

EXPERIENCE

IBM CAMPUS REPRESENTATIVE Aug. 1993
Phoenix and Glendale, Arizona – Mar. 1994
- Developed and implemented marketing strategies
- Sold PS/2 systems on three campuses

EXPORT CONSULTANT May 1993
Congeladora Marques, Campeche, Mexico – Aug. 1993
- Assessed organizational environment and made recommendations

EXECUTIVE ASSISTANT AND RESEARCH ANALYST Mar. 1992
Law Office of Robert Tobias, Santa Monica, California & Summer 1991

SUPERVISOR OF ACCOUNTING, PUBLIC RELATIONS, Aug. 1991
MARKETING, AND TRANSLATOR – Feb. 1992
Campeche Government, Public Works, Campeche, Mexico
- Appointed by Governor of Campeche to this position
- Assisted in creation of an historical tourist attraction
- Marketed the tourist attraction to Americans and Europeans

LANGUAGE INSTRUCTOR Aug. 1991
Universidad Autónoma del Sudeste, Campeche, Mexico – Feb. 1992
- Instructed Spanish to American university students
- Taught English to Spanish-speaking children

RESEARCH ANALYST Summer 1989
Campeche Government Administrative Offices, Campeche, Mexico & Jan. 1991
- Researched and analyzed government and employee relations for Public Relations Department

SKILLS

Language: Bilingual in **English** and **Spanish**
Computer: Lotus 1-2-3, Excel, dBASE, WordPerfect, Microsoft Word, Harvard Graphics

HONORS

Dean's List, Austin College ✿ Phi Sigma Iota: Foreign Languages National Honor Society

ACTIVITIES

Treasurer, Management Information Technology Society ✿ Mexico Club ✿ Co-Chair NAFTA Conference ✿ Public Relations Representative, International Career Opportunities

---

ADDRESS 1234 Encanto Park, Fort Worth, Texas 76109 (817) 555-1234

Arial

OBJECTIVE	A Career in International Sales, Import/Export, or Finance

QUALIFICATIONS

> ◇ Travel Abroad
> ◇ Sales Experience
> ◇ Production Experience
> ◇ Management Experience

EDUCATION

MASTER OF INTERNATIONAL MANAGEMENT   12/94
American Graduate School of International Management
Thunderbird Campus, Glendale, AZ   GPA: 3.55/4.00
Emphasis: Corporate Finance, Import/Export, Decision Models,
Commercial Spanish, Portuguese, Europe, Cross-Cultural
Communication, Financial Statement Analysis

BACHELOR OF ARTS, ECONOMICS   8/93
Brigham Young University, Provo, UT
Emphasis: Econometrics, Finance, Risk, International Trade,
International Development, Urban Economics

EXPERIENCE

AUTOMOBILE SALESPERSON   1990,1993
Criswell Chrysler, TX   • Washburn BMW, UT • Culiver Nissan, AZ   (Summers)
◇ Submitted credit applications and persuaded loan officers
◇ Achieved "highest gross profit," "highest sales" awards
◇ Utilized follow-up sales approach

LEAD OPERATOR/QUALITY INSPECTOR   1991–1993
Smith International (Megadiamond), Provo, UT   (Nights)
◇ Supervised four men and four diamond forming presses
◇ Analyzed diamond output for changes in dynamic program
◇ Submitted econometric research on product rejection
◇ Processed and expedited production/operation goals

PROPRIETOR   1989–1990,1994
Par Excellence Services, Houston, TX   •   Phoenix, AZ
◇ Operated small window-cleaning company
◇ Negotiated contracts, scheduled routes, organized labor
◇ Obtained 58 accounts in Houston and sold them

CHURCH REPRESENTATIVE   1987–1989
LDS Church Mission, Cordoba, Argentina
◇ Coordinated training, assignments, mail, allowances
◇ Lead and interviewed zones of 22 representatives over 10 cities
◇ Spoke at various forums and assemblies
◇ Interpreted for visiting authorities

LANGUAGE
TRAVEL
COMPUTER

Fluent **Spanish** • Proficient **Portuguese**
Lived in Argentina (2 years), Mexico
WP 5.1, Harvard Graphics, Lotus, @Risk, Lindo, QSB+, SPSS, SAS

ADDRESS   12345 W. Union Hills Drive #123, Glendale, AZ 85308   (602) 555-1234

148

UNIVERS

OBJECTIVE   To utilize my development experience and negotiation skills for an industrial manufacturer or business service provider committed to expansion into Asian and/or European markets.

QUALIFICATIONS
- Extensive development experience
- Graduate degree in International Management, with industrial marketing emphasis
- Exceptional research, negotiation, and analytical skills
- U.S. Air Force veteran with technical and supervisory experience
- Strong work ethic with high value placed on strategic planning

EXPERIENCE   *MIDWEST MARKET/TERRITORY DEVELOPMENT MANAGER*   1990–95
The Mangelsdorf Companies, Chicago, Illinois
- Sole responsibility for development of new Midwest market and corporate client base. Primarily offered negotiation assistance and placement of specialized tax-free annuities used in the settlement of litigated commercial claims.

TERRITORY SALES MANAGER, CORPORATE BENEFITS PLANS   1989–90
The Prudential Insurance Company, Chicago, Illinois
- Company-side sales of employee benefit plans to corporations. Brokerage houses and agencies serve as liaisons to firms seeking benefits for employees.

SETTLEMENT COORDINATOR, LITIGATED CLAIMS   1988–89
Liberty Mutual Insurance Company, Indianapolis, Indiana
- Negotiated commercial liability claims, with the objective of reaching the most equitable settlement value to both parties.

EDUCATION   *MASTER OF INTERNATIONAL MANAGEMENT*   GPA 3.7   August 1993
American Graduate School of International Management
Thunderbird Campus, Glendale, Arizona
- *Thunderbird Corporate Consulting Group* – Project leader of on-site market and organizational analysis for the new division of a Rosenheim, Germany-based industrial engineering firm. Structural changes are currently being implemented to reach the previously undefined new market.
- Created a research program designed to increase student exposure to all segments of the health care industry. Same information being used by the Marketing Department of Career Services.
- Emphasis on Industrial Marketing and Management with case study.

BACHELOR OF SCIENCE IN FINANCE   GPA 3.2   August 1988
Illinois State University, Normal, Illinois
- Finance internship, town of Normal, Illinois, Treasurer's Office – Treasury management analysis project.
- Lab Manager, Student Teaching Program – Taught students principles of business organization and management through real-life management projects.
- Campus Outdoor Program Trip Coordinator – Developed and led a wide range of outdoor excursions/adventures.

ESSCA – French Business Study Exchange   Summer 1987
Angers, France
- Examined French business concepts through interactive seminars and tours.

LANGUAGES   German: Proficient

Address ✧ *1234 Westshore Road, Cheyenne, Wyoming 82601* ✧ *(307) 555-1234*

CG Omega Italic

OBJECTIVE   *A career in marketing/strategic planning for a globally oriented company*

EDUCATION

MASTER OF INTERNATIONAL MANAGEMENT   GPA 3.76   Feb. 1994
American Graduate School of International Management   June 1995
Thunderbird Campus, Glendale, Arizona
- ☒ *InterAd (Advanced International Marketing & Advertising Workshop) – Designed and presented complete research, marketing, positioning, advertising, and sales promotion plans for the introduction of Dr. Pepper in Costa Rica*
- ☒ *International Trade Strategies – Studied the integration of business strategy into international competition and trade – Presented research and analysis of the international trade strategies of the Upjohn Company*
- ☒ *International Consumer Marketing – Explored procedures and techniques for marketing consumer products abroad*
- ☒ *Advanced Cross-Cultural Communication Seminar – Conducted a survey of 4,800 Thunderbird alumni women and their participation in international business worldwide*

BACHELOR OF BUSINESS ADMINISTRATION WITH HONORS   Aug. 1990
Oslo Business School, *Oslo, Norway*   June 1994
- ☒ *Salutatorian*
- ☒ *Major in Marketing – Minor in Internationalization*
- ☒ *Course work included: Business Policy, Marketing Strategy, Market Communication, Market Planning, and International Marketing*
- ☒ *Analyzed the effects of the Internal Market '92 on the Norwegian grocery business for E&B Partner A/S*

EXPERIENCE

PROJECT ASSISTANT   Sep. 1994
Den norske Bank A/S, Loan Collateral Department, *Nenset, Norway*   Jan. 1995
- ☒ *Processed the control and maintenance of collateral documents related to the merger of two Norwegian banking institutions*

TEACHING ASSISTANT   Aug. 1993
Oslo Business School, *Oslo, Norway*   June 1994
- ☒ *Assisted professors in semester-long courses in International Negotiations, Product Management, EEC/Internationalization, Consumer Behavior, Service Marketing, and Market Research*
- ☒ *Coordinated courses with six professors and provided student assistance*

MARKET RESEARCH   June 1993
Tele Control Communications A/S, *Oslo, Norway*   Dec. 1993
- ☒ *Chosen from among national business students by the Norwegian Export Council to write "The Export Mission"*
- ☒ *Conducted a survey of the purchasing system for air traffic control equipment within the Commonwealth of Independent States (Soviet Union)*
- ☒ *Met with various ministry officials on a study tour to Moscow*

SUMMER DEPUTY   1991
Den norske Bank A/S, *Porsgrunn, Norway*   – 1995
- ☒ *In Real Estate and Loan Collateral Department*

LANGUAGES   *Fluent in **English** and **Scandinavian** languages ☒ Proficient in **German***

Present Address ☒ 1234 North 29th Avenue #123 ☒ Glendale, Arizona 85306 ☒ (602) 555-1234
Permanent Address ☒ Enggravda 123 ☒ 1234 Skien, Norway ☒ 47-555-1234

CG OMEGA

QUALIFICATIONS
- ✓ Six years of finance and accounting experience
- ✓ Successfully managed US$100,000 futures portfolio
- ✓ Strong knowledge of international business environment

EXPERIENCE

INTERNATIONAL FINANCE INTERN (Liaison in Italy)   6/93 – 8/95
Active Noise & Vibration Technologies, Phoenix, Arizona
- ✓ Worked at Italian partner – FIAT Componenti e Impianti per l'Energia e Industria S.p.A. Torino, Italy
- ✓ Established relationships with Italian accounting personnel that could be transferred to ANVT Phoenix
- ✓ Developed system of timely financial reporting to U.S.
- ✓ Determined components and calculation of cost buildup and overhead rates
- ✓ Reviewed Italian capital requirements and transfer tax issues
- ✓ Analyzed Italian government and EEC subsidized financing contracts

SENIOR ACCOUNTANT   1/89 – 1/92
Arizona Heart Institute, Phoenix, Arizona
- ✓ Prepared and analyzed financial statements for $20 million company
- ✓ Performed daily cash management functions for $300,000
- ✓ Developed physician incentive compensation plans
- ✓ Organized staffing needs for yearly International Convention

JUNIOR FINANCIAL ANALYST   11/86 – 1/89
San Diego Unified School District, San Diego, California
- ✓ Broadened knowledge of financial systems and operations through projects involving Budgeting, General Accounting, Cost and Payroll Accounting
- ✓ Audited appropriated revenue and special projects for program compliance
- ✓ Reconciled in excess of $15 million cash to county treasurer
- ✓ Prepared monthly journal entries to assist the monthly close process
- ✓ Produced monthly financial statements
- ✓ Assisted in yearly bond issue cash flow schedules

EDUCATION

MASTER OF INTERNATIONAL MANAGEMENT   12/93
American Graduate School of International Management
Thunderbird Campus, Glendale, Arizona

Concentration in Finance – Capstone Courses
- ✓ *International Investment Banking* – analyzed and valued mergers and acquisitions
- ✓ *International Finance and Trade* – competed in foreign exchange simulation
- ✓ *Advanced Corporate Finance* – created venture capital private placement memos
- ✓ *Countertrade/Offset Seminar* – developed offset model for Republic of Slovenia
- ✓ *International Securities Investments* – analyzed IPOs as investment vehicle

CENTRO STUDI ITALIANI, Urbania, Italy   8/92
- ✓ Studied Italian business and culture in conjunction with the South Carolina Master of International Business School exchange program studies

BACHELOR OF BUSINESS ADMINISTRATION   5/87
University of San Diego, San Diego, California
- ✓ Awarded Tuscany Regional Scholarship to study Italian language and culture abroad

LANGUAGES   Native – English ✓ Proficient – Italian ✓ Knowledgeable – Spanish

1234 West Sweetwater ✓ Peoria, Arizona 85381 ✓ (602) 555-1234

HELVETICA NARROW

12345 W. Grisly Road ❑ Peoria, Arizona 85345 ❑ (602) 555-1234

OBJECTIVE   A career within the Financial Services Industry

QUALIFICATIONS
- Proficient on DLS and CPI systems for cashiering, customer service, letter writing, and payoffs
- New loan setup and documentation experience
- Excellent customer relations and problem solving skills; get along well with people
- Aptitude for numbers and skilled in math, organization, and reasoning
- Knowledge of DisplayWrite, Symphony, WordPerfect, and Lotus 1-2-3
- Type 50+ words per minute; 10-key by touch; microfiche experienced

EXPERIENCE   **MERIDIAN MORTGAGE CORPORATION**, Phoenix, Arizona (July 1991 to Present)
Payment Processor
- Prepared and posted all payments and payoffs to borrower accounts on both Data Link and CPI systems daily.
- Posted regular and modified payments, curtailments, reversals, special deposits, fees, and adjustments.
- Maintained daily suspense report, balanced batches, and prepared reports.
- Data entry for Investor Accounting Department.

Customer Service
- Answered phones and assisted customers by researching and completing histories, amortization schedules, credit verifications, payoff updates, letters of receipt, payment research, address changes, etc.
- Position required heavy emphasis on situations involving payments.

Receptionist & Other Duties
- First position was as Receptionist but quickly moved up to other areas.
- Letter Librarian duties included creation and maintenance of all office letters on both DLS and CPI systems.
- Prepared payroll and submitted biweekly; transferred payments to new servicers weekly.
- Operated and maintained various office machines.
- Maintained files for all monetary batch work and suspense reports.
- New loan setup and investor transfers.

SOUTHWEST SAVINGS & LOAN ASSOCIATION, Phoenix, Arizona (August 1989 to July 1991)
Vault Coordinator, Quality Control/Lending Operations Department
- Coordinated vault activities and supervised vault staff, including prioritization and delegation of daily work.
- Maintained vault records, documentation for other departments, monthly reports, and canceled files.
- Organized loan sales, RTC review projects, audits of loan files, and semiannual vault inventories.
- Managed retention procedures (preparation and shipping); created and utilized reports for files-out inventory.
- Ensured that department followed proper security guidelines.

Vault Clerk, Lending Operations/Loan Administration
- Retrieved, returned, maintained, logged, and microfiched files.

REPUBLIC AUTOMOTIVE PARTS, INC., Phoenix, Arizona (June 1986 to July 1988)
Front Office Secretary/Input Clerk
- Operated phone system (30 lines and intercom); typed letters and forms; sorted mail; maintained jobber files.
- Reconciled daily accounts for company store locations and input accounts payable.
- Maintained and input parts received in daily shipments; adjusted computer inventory.

File Clerk/Receiving Clerk
- Maintained accounts receivable files; purged invoice files; created and distributed monthly price sheets.
- Adjusted computer inventory; cross-referenced packing lists; ordered part shipments via computer; maintained receiving department files.

AMERICAN PAGING OF ARIZONA, Phoenix, Arizona (August 1987 to January 1988)
Administrative Assistant
- Handled customer complaints, solved problems, greeted clients, and answered phones.
- Prepared payroll, maintained employee files, scheduled meetings and appointments.
- Ordered supplies; typed invoices, charts, letters, memos; sorted and filed contracts.

HELVETICA NARROW OBLIQUE

OBJECTIVE   *A challenging position in finance with a multinational corporation*

EDUCATION

MASTER OF INTERNATIONAL MANAGEMENT *GPA 3.7*   *Dec. 1994*
American Graduate School of International Management
Thunderbird Campus, Glendale, Arizona

BACHELOR OF ARTS IN ECONOMICS & MANAGEMENT   *May 1992*
DePauw University, *Greencastle, Indiana*

GREAT LAKES COLLEGE ASSOCIATION PROGRAM   *Jan. – June 1991*
University of Freiburg, *Freiburg, West Germany*

EXPERIENCE

GLOBAL OPERATIONS ANALYST (Internship)   *Feb. – July 1994*
Goldman Sachs International Limited, *London, England*
- *Monitored trading accounts to assure the firm's trading positions were correct*
- *Reconciled differences between trading account positions and stock record positions*
- *Reviewed regulatory reporting process and developed and implemented new trade matching and reporting procedures*
- *Communicated with traders and sales staff to resolve differences in customer bookings*
- *Trained other individuals to process daily trade activity and to provide trading and sales staff support*

CREDIT ANALYST   *Feb. – May 1993*
First Colonial Bankshares Corporation
Michigan Avenue National Bank of Chicago, *Chicago, Illinois*
- *Analyzed financial statements, economic conditions, and industry trends to rationalize business transactions*
- *Conversed with clients' credit officers to obtain essential information for credit presentation to management*
- *Monitored lines of credit to accurately represent the bank's portfolio for senior management decision making*
- *Utilized and created computer spreadsheet models using Lotus 1-2-3 to facilitate the conversion of financial statements*

MANAGEMENT TRAINEE   *June 1992 – Jan. 1993*
First Colonial Bankshares Corporation, *Chicago, Illinois*
- *Participated in management program consisting of 15 different rotations within the holding company*
- *Evaluated products and services offered by the corporation and made proposals to upper management*
- *Generated reports for officers to evaluate procedures in different areas of the holding company*

LANGUAGES   *Proficient in* **German**

ACTIVITIES
- *Orientation Team, 1993*
- *ICO Germany Club; German Club*
- *Alpha Tau Omega Fraternity, 1988–1992, House Manager, Rush Committee, Social Chairman, Intramural Athlete*
- *DePauw Intramural Athlete of the Year, 1992*

ADDRESS   *12345 Saddle Crossing, Elkhart, Indiana 46514*   *(219) 555-1234*

CLASSIC TYPEWRITER

12345 W. Miramar Drive ¤ *Tucson, Arizona 85715* ¤ *(602) 555-1234*

EXPERIENCE

L.R. NELSON CORPORATION — Aix-en-Provence, France
International Marketing Assistant – Intern (8/94 – 12/94)
¤ Directed translations and production of International Product Catalogue
¤ Developed multilingual product packaging system for European distribution
¤ Worked at industrial trade shows in France, Germany, Italy, and Spain
¤ Acted as liaison between U.S. and European operations

AEON — Tokyo, Japan
English Language Instructor (8/92 – 7/93)
¤ Edited speeches, reports, and business documents
¤ Conducted specialized courses in: TOEFL, TOEIC, business terminology, medical terminology, and debate
¤ Engaged in direct marketing campaigns in Tokyo area

UP WITH PEOPLE – International Non-Profit Organization — Worldwide
Cast Member (7/90 – 7/91)
¤ **Marketing Intern:** Assisted in creating and implementing a marketing strategy for a musical production
¤ **Promotion Representative:** Organized logistics, solicited donations, and launched promotional campaign as part of advance team
¤ **Paris Program Coordinator:** Initiated and led a fashion study group to visit top design houses and learn merchandising techniques in Paris
¤ **Loges Coordinator:** Implemented corporate fund-raising program in The Netherlands

ROCHELLE K — Tucson, AZ
Sales Associate (1/90 – 7/90 and 10/91 – 7/92)
¤ Served as men's wear buyer
¤ Consistently maintained high-volume sales
¤ Translated for Spanish-speaking clientele

SUTTONS BOUTIQUE LTD. — Tucson, AZ
Manager/Buyer (4/87 – 1/90)
¤ Increased annual sales by 60%
¤ Appointed sole buyer for all store merchandise
¤ Directed fashion shows, photo shoots, and advertising layouts
¤ Represented company at apparel markets in L.A., Dallas, and New York

EDUCATION

MASTER OF INTERNATIONAL MANAGEMENT (1993 – 1995)
American Graduate School of International Management
Thunderbird Campus — Glendale, AZ
¤ Emphasis in International Marketing
¤ Paris Summer Program

BACHELOR OF ARTS IN LIBERAL STUDIES (1984 – 1988)
University of Arizona — Tucson, AZ
¤ Journalism/Spanish/Psychology

**LEADERSHIP &
SOCIAL SERVICE**

¤ **Muscular Dystrophy Association,** Volunteer Counselor
¤ *Arizona Daily Wildcat,* Staff Reporter
¤ Thunderbird Orientation Leader, Spring 1994
¤ Thunderbird ICO Francophone; Resume Book Chairman

BOOK ANTIQUA

1234 E. La View ✳ Tempe, Arizona 85284 ✳ (602) 555-1234

EDUCATION	**MASTER OF INTERNATIONAL MANAGEMENT** **American Graduate School of International Management** Thunderbird Campus, Glendale, Arizona ✳ Participated in International Banking Symposium concentrating on recent developments within the industry ✳ Traded currency futures through computer simulation ✳ Performed capital structure and cash flow analysis ✳ Analyzed and formulated business strategies for multinational companies	Aug. 1995
	BACHELOR OF SCIENCE IN BUSINESS **Arizona State University**, Tempe, Arizona Major in Finance	1993
	FOREIGN STUDY PROGRAMS **American Graduate School of International Management**, Paris, France **Université de Caen**, Caen, France	Summer 1995 Summer 1990
EXPERIENCE	**COOPERS & LYBRAND**, Phoenix, Arizona **Administrative Assistant, Tax Department** ✳ Managed time and expense reporting system ✳ Maintained tax calendar due date list ✳ Increased efficiency by implementing and maintaining software programs	Jan. 1993 – May 1994
INTERNSHIPS	**PHOENIX DEPARTMENT OF PUBLIC WORKS**, Phoenix, Arizona **Intern for Privatization Consultant** ✳ Organized and developed document center and contact network ✳ Researched global trends in privatization	Spring 1995
	ANCHOR NATIONAL FINANCIAL SERVICES, Phoenix, Arizona **Due Diligence Intern** ✳ Analyzed financial statements and 10K reports ✳ Reviewed and summarized prospectuses ✳ Assisted financial analysts in sponsor reviews	Jan. – Aug. 1992
LEADERSHIP	**AIESEC – INTERNATIONAL ASSOCIATION OF STUDENTS OF** **BUSINESS & ECONOMICS**, Tempe, Arizona **Vice President of Marketing** ✳ Coordinated marketing efforts to local business community for the International Traineeship Exchange Program ✳ Trained members of marketing committee	Spring 1993
AWARDS AND **ACTIVITIES**	✳ Co-chairperson for Thunderball Fundraising Event ✳ Social Consciousness Dinner Committee to Benefit the **Trickle Up Program** ✳ Friends of Thunderbird/Mavis Voris Partial Assistantship ✳ Teacher's Assistant for International Finance and Trade course ✳ Student Development Committee, Thunderbird Balloon Classic ✳ United Way volunteer for the elderly with visual impairments	Spring 1995 Spring 1995 Fall 1994 Fall 1994 Fall 1994 1993
SKILLS	**Languages**: Proficient in **French**, Knowledge of **Tagalog** **Computers**: Lotus 1-2-3, WordPerfect 5.1, Harvard Graphics	

155

TIMES ROMAN ITALIC

1234 W. Earll Drive ➤ *Phoenix, Arizona 85033* ➤ *(602) 555-1234*

HIGHLIGHTS OF QUALIFICATIONS
- ➤ *Community Health Nurse of two years*
- ➤ *Experienced CVICU/ICU nurse of nine years*
- ➤ *Able to work independently and as cooperative team member*
- ➤ *Certified critical care RN since 1983*

CERTIFICATION
- ➤ *Certified CCRN and ACLS from 1983 to present*

PROFESSIONAL EXPERIENCE

RELEVANT EXPERIENCE
- ➤ *Coordinated symptom management and community services for the home care client.*
- ➤ *Assessed patients requiring intensive care nursing, including patients requiring ventilatory support, IABP assistance, and hemodynamic monitoring.*
- ➤ *Performed venipunctures and/or IV therapy.*

MANAGEMENT & SUPERVISION
- ➤ *Served as Assistant Head Nurse in CVICU for two years*
- ➤ *Chaired Orientation Committee*
- ➤ *Supervised 34 nursing and ancillary personnel*

TEACHING
- ➤ *BCLS Instructor Course, 1991.*
- ➤ *Developed Imuran teaching packet for renal nursing staff at Good Samaritan Medical Center (GSMC).*
- ➤ *Planned primary nursing implementation of CVICU as member of Primary Nursing Care Committee.*
- ➤ *Designed chemotherapy administration record with the oncology critical nurse specialist presently under consideration for implementation at GSMC.*
- ➤ *Developed orientation/preceptor packet with committee members for orientation to CVU at GSMC.*
- ➤ *Instructed nursing students from Grand Canyon College in CVICU nursing and acted as preceptor during internship.*

EMPLOYMENT HISTORY

1989 – Present	CASE MANAGER, *Hospice of the Valley, Phoenix, Arizona*
1989 – 1990	STAFF NURSE, *Critical Care, Good Samaritan Medical Center, Phoenix, Arizona*
1985 – 1989	CVICU STAFF NURSE, *Good Samaritan Medical Center, Phoenix, Arizona*
1983 – 1988	*Pursued* BACHELOR OF SCIENCE IN NURSING *full time while nursing*
1982 – 1985	ASSISTANT HEAD NURSE, *Good Samaritan Medical Center, Phoenix, Arizona*
1980 – 1982	ICU NURSE, *St. Francis Hospital, Honolulu, Hawaii*
1976 – 1980	ONCOLOGY NURSE, *St. Francis Hospital, Honolulu, Hawaii*

EDUCATION

1988	BACHELOR OF SCIENCE IN NURSING *Arizona State University, Tempe, Arizona*	*magna cum laude*
1976	REGISTERED NURSE, *University of Hawaii, Manoa, Hawaii*	

Times Roman

1234 Bentley Drive * Stamford, Connecticut 06903 * (203) 555-1234

OBJECTIVE	To secure an internship position with an advertising firm	

EDUCATION

BOSTON UNIVERSITY, College of Communications, Boston, MA — 1995
Bachelor of Science — GPA 3.1
Major: Mass Communications with concentration in Advertising
Liberal Arts Concentration: Psychology
Courses of Study include:

* Communications Law
* Writing for Mass Communications
* Introduction to Advertising

* Child Development
* Social Psychology
* Problem Solving in Advertising

Marketing/Advertising Projects include:

* Mystic Valley Elder Services
* Ultra-Lite Beer

Greenwich Academy, Greenwich, Connecticut — 1991 – 1995

WORK EXPERIENCE

MARKETFORCE, Sydney, Australia — Spring 1994
DIVISION OF BACKER, SPIELVOGEL, BATES, INC.
Marketing Intern

* Accounts included Heineken, Stolichnaya (pitch), Thomas Cook Travel, and CPS Housewares
* Assisted in implementing ad campaigns for both television and radio commercial productions
* Involved in most account meetings, including new account pitches and brainstorming sessions
* Observed and analyzed focus group meetings
* Aided in merchandise promotion to both trade and consumer markets
* Researched and retrieved file tapes for clients

INGALLS, QUINN & JOHNSON, Boston, Massachusetts — Fall 1993
Marketing Information Services Intern

* Exposed to a variety of research and media functions
* Researched industries, product categories, and companies
* Maintained and improved the Information Research Center's data
* Investigated market trends for new business accounts

SELF-EMPLOYED AU PAIR, New Canaan & Greenwich, Connecticut — Summers 1990–1992

* Supervised young children and planned daily activities
* Responsible for all household duties

ACTIVITIES

ACCOUNT EXECUTIVE — Fall 1992
Boston University, Adlab, Boston, Massachusetts

* Mystic Valley Elder Services

DIRECTOR — Spring 1990
Brunswick School, Greenwich, Connecticut

* Sixth-grade play *Red Spy at Night*

STAGE MANAGER — Spring 1990 / Fall 1989
Brunswick School, Greenwich, Connecticut

* High school productions of *The Nerd, 42nd Street*

157

QUALIFICATIONS
- Well-developed skills in International Marketing and Finance
- Experienced in successful management of diverse groups of people, utilizing strong written, organizational, and communication skills
- Effective, aggressive market developer, and innovator
- Able to conduct business in **Arabic**; knowledge of **French**
- Computers: Fluent in various forms of business software

EXPERIENCE

ASLC, Thunderbird, Glendale, Arizona   1994 – 1995
President
- Elected to represent student concerns to administration and faculty for campus population exceeding 1,500
- Managed appointed and elected staff of 30
- Implemented customer satisfaction measurement tool through the use of focus groups, open forums, and marketing surveys
- Served as *Ex Officio* member, Board of Trustees
- Served as a member of the Thunderbird Alumni Association Board

DAS TOR, Thunderbird, Glendale, Arizona   1994
Managing Editor
- Responsible for content and weekly delivery of student-run newspaper
- Coordinated journalistic staff to cover campus and non-campus events
- Wrote news articles, commentaries, and editorials

MBNA AMERICA, Newark, Delaware   1991 – 1993
Telemarketing Manager (Health Care)
- Created a tele-sales unit responsible for canvassing health providers
- Increased national sales by 15% in first three months
Account Executive – Professional Payment Systems (Health Care)
- Acquired health-care providers to participate in HealthCap network, a medical-dental credit card financing program for patients

DESERT DELIGHTS, McLean, Virginia   1989 – 1991
President and Founder
- Created catering firm specializing in Middle Eastern foods
- Developed market, utilizing a successful direct mail campaign
- Managed kitchen and wait staff for parties of up to 300 people

EDUCATION

MASTER OF INTERNATIONAL MANAGEMENT   1995
American Graduate School of International Management
Thunderbird Campus, Glendale, Arizona
- Arabic Studies Scholarship

BACHELOR OF SCIENCE – FOREIGN SERVICE   1986
Georgetown University, Washington, D.C.
- Major in International Relations

CERTIFICATE OF ARAB STUDIES   1986
Georgetown, Center for Contemporary Arab Studies, Washington, D.C.

ACTIVITIES & INTERESTS

Student-Faculty Committee, Chair ♦ Middle East Club, Vice President ♦ Academic Honesty Task Force ♦ Campus Ambassadors ♦ Orientation Team ♦ Community Outreach ♦ Africa Club ♦ Volunteer Committee ♦ NCAA I Soccer

ADDRESS   1234 Poplar Place, McLean, Virginia 22101   (703) 555-1234

Bookman Light

1234 W. Charles Avenue ❖ Phoenix, Arizona 85023 ❖ (602) 555-1234

EXPERIENCE

About Time Shuttles, Flagstaff, Arizona   1989 – Present
- Owner/operator of tour company that catered to the needs of the white water raft industry
- Developed operational plan for 150 to 200 groups a season
- Administrated marketing, bookkeeping, advertisements, and advance booking programs
- Supervised staff of 8 to 10 employees on a seasonal basis

Worldwide Explorations, Inc., Flagstaff, Arizona   1989 – 1992
- Seasonal employee for white water river company – river guide and chef
- Wrote and produced via DTP system advertisements and brochures
- Responsible for public relations at travel and trade shows

High Country Express, Inc., Flagstaff, Arizona   1986 – 1989
- General Manager for a tour/transportation company
- Public relations liaison between board of directors and governmental and private entities
- Developed and wrote loan solicitations and financial proposals
- Filed monthly, quarterly, and annual reports for corporate, state, and federal review

Part-Time   1981 – 1986
- Seasonal/temporary employee for various firms primarily in the tourism and construction industries while in school

Air Illinois, Inc., Carbondale, Illinois   1978 – 1980
- A.M. customer service supervisor at St. Louis airport for Midwest's largest commuter airline
- Conducted new employee training and orientation
- Controlled daily cash receipts, ticket inventory, and arrivals/departures
- Operated station's communication network, teletype, computer, and ground-to-air radio

EDUCATION

Bachelor of Science Degree   1984 – 1989
Northern Arizona University, Flagstaff, Arizona
- Dual majors in Asian History and Physical Geography
- Curriculum included 8 hours of Chinese and 9 hours of English
- Worked 40 to 60 hours per week the entire duration of school
- Personally funded over 90% of educational costs – other 10% from scholarships, grants, and loans

Xian Foreign Language Institute, Xian, China   1984
- Language student in summer program in Shannxi province
- Personally funded 100% of cost of this program

Associate of Arts with distinction   1982 – 1984
Mesa Community College, Mesa, Arizona
- Maintained GPA 4.0 with 21 semester hours in spring 1983

The most important functions of a manager are to motivate and to teach. The effective manager is not the one who does the most but the one who fosters the environment that allows the most to be accomplished.

PALATINO

1234 West Mission Street ✳ *Scottsdale, Arizona 85021* ✳ *(602) 555-1234*

OBJECTIVES	Bilingual education instructor, with the ultimate goal of working into a position as instructor supervisor or director of special education services	
EXPERIENCE	**BOSTROM ALTERNATIVE SCHOOL**, Phoenix, Arizona	1993 – 1994
	✳ ASU Work Program	
	SPECIAL EDUCATION INSTRUCTOR, Phoenix, Arizona	1991 – 1992
	✳ Substitute teacher	
	HASBROOK INSTITUTE, Phoenix, Arizona	1987 – 1989
	✳ Volunteer telephone counselor and part-time drug and child/spouse abuse counselor	
	✳ Provide personal counseling in drug abuse, male violence intervention, and group child and spouse abuse groups (both male and female victims of abuse)	
	U.S. AIR FORCE	1988 – 1990
	✳ Electronics specialist	
	✳ Special air warfare training	
	✳ Linguistics training in Laotian and Thai (Kadai)	
	✳ Military advisor in Southeast Asia for three years	
	✳ Technical instructor of electronics	
	✳ Instructor supervisor	
	✳ Writer of text for technical instruction	
	✳ Two-year tour of duty throughout Europe, the Near East, Middle East, Africa, and Iran as an electronics advisor	
	✳ Quality control supervisor, five years	
	✳ Implemented a program to inspect factory-issued parts for frontline Air Force fighter and bomber aircraft not covered by technical order inspections	
EDUCATION	**BACHELOR OF SCIENCE DEGREE**	June 1991
	Arizona State University, Tempe, Arizona	
	✳ Major in bilingual education	
	✳ Minor in anthropology, sociology, mathematics, psychology, English, and political science	
	✳ National Honor Society	
	✳ Peer Counselor (1989) of Student Services	
	✳ School Yearbook Staff (1989–1990)	
PUBLICATIONS	Numerous technical and nontechnical articles for Air Force and military magazines. Article in teaching magazine in February 1991 on the gifted/special education student.	
PROFESSIONAL ORGANIZATIONS	✳ Kappa Delta Phi	
	✳ National Association of Retired Noncommissioned Officers	
	✳ National Federation of Teachers	
	✳ National Association of Personal Mathematics	

160

BASKERTON

EDUCATION

American Graduate School of International Management　　　1/93 – 12/94
Thunderbird Campus, Glendale, Arizona
Master of International Management
Concentration: Finance, Marketing, International Studies
- Conducted joint venture analyses to determine market potential for medical equipment in China, Singapore, and South Korea
- Participated in a marketing study for Smith & Nephew to determine market demand for an orthopedic knee brace in Japan
- Structured a countertrade/offset contract for the Republic of Slovenia

Golden Gate University, San Francisco, California　　　1/92 – 8/92
- Completed MBA course work in international business and finance

University of California, Santa Barbara, California　　　6/87
Bachelor of Arts in Political Science

University of Geneva, Geneva, Switzerland　　　6/85 – 12/85
- Studied International Relations and Economics
- Research project – Red Cross in the Middle East

EXPERIENCE

Direct Relief International, Santa Barbara, California　　　6/94 – 8/94
Marketing Consultant (Internship)
- Coordinated a marketing study with Frank N. Magid & Associates to increase name recognition on national and international levels
- Developed recommendations for design of the company name, position statement, logo, and all DRI materials
- Selected national spokesperson for DRI
- Established a public relations system to increase media attention on DRI's emergency relief assistance in Bosnia, Somalia, and the CIS

Attorney Service Firm, San Diego, California　　　8/92 – 1/93
Legal/Technical Agent
- Investigated, collected, and reproduced materials for litigation
- Developed teamwork skills through case preparation

Sara Lee Corporation, San Diego, California　　　5/89 – 5/91
Sales Representative
- Determined market potential for Hanes products by initiating market research and consumer surveys
- Forecasted and monitored area sales
- Improved product placement by negotiating with store management
- Recommended organizational changes that resulted in cost savings

Merrill Lynch, Pierce, Fenner & Smith, Inc., Geneva, Switzerland　　　6/86 – 12/86
Account Executive Assistant (Internship)
- Researched and organized investment vehicles
- Consulted clients regarding portfolio management

ACTIVITIES
- Extensive travel in Europe, Australia, and Mexico
- Volunteer for Special Olympics
- Health Care Assistant, CPR seminars for Save-A-Heart Foundation

---

P.O. Box 1234 ▸ 1234 North 39th Avenue ▸ Glendale, Arizona 85306-6017 ▸ (602) 555-1234

GARAMOND

QUALIFICATIONS
- Ability to converse and conduct business in four languages
- Eight years of experience living and working in Europe, Africa, and Latin America
- Proven adaptability to differing cultural and business environments

EXPERIENCE

UNHCR (U.N. High Commissioner for Refugees) through UNV   1993 – Present
Field Officer, Conakry, Republic of Guinea – Africa
- Assessed and monitored refugees' needs in various assistance sectors such as food, sanitation, and education
- Proposed and established new projects concerning camp management and distribution of supplies
- Developed and maintained working relationships with camp authorities, governmental organizations, and voluntary agencies to ensure the coordination of activities and provide technical guidance
- Followed up on logistics measures and prepared periodic reports

DAPP (Development Aid from People to People) with UNICEF   1990 – 1991
Project Officer for Community Health and Sanitation
Ombalantu, Namibia – Africa
- Developed and performed a rural sanitation needs assessment
- Designed and implemented a sanitation project affecting three communities
- Organized and carried out an education program focusing on primary health, hygiene, nutrition, and AIDS prevention utilizing original curriculum and support materials

BAYERISCHE HYPOTHEKEN-BANK, AG – Munich, Germany   1988 – 1990
Foreign Exchange Administrator
- Audited and processed interbank foreign exchange transactions
- Authorized million-DM payments via an international network
- Resolved account discrepancies with trading partners

Foreign Securities Department – Trader's Assistant
- Liaison to foreign bank representatives
- Processed security trade orders for all branch offices
- Analyzed international financial market trends and compiled daily reports

EDUCATION

MASTER OF INTERNATIONAL MANAGEMENT   1992
American Graduate School of International Management
Thunderbird Campus, Glendale, Arizona – USA

BACHELOR OF ARTS – **International Affairs/Psychology**   1984
University of Colorado, Boulder, Colorado – USA

FOREIGN STUDIES
- **Universidad Autonoma de Guadalajara** – Guadalajara, Mexico   1992
- **Ludwig-Maximilians-Universität** – Munich, Germany   1987 – 1988
  Abschlußprufung der Mittelstufe II – April 1988
- **Université d'Aix-Marseille II – Faculte des Sciences Economiques**   1985 – 1986
  Aix-en-Provence, France
- **Université de Paris, Sorbonne** – Paris, France   1981 – 1982
  Certificat de Langue Française – Degré Superieur Annuel – June 1982

LANGUAGES   Native in **English**, fluent in **French**, highly proficient in **German**, proficient in **Spanish**

ADDRESS   P.O. 1234, Conely, Guinea – Africa   (224) 555-1234

Serif Fonts

Albertus . . . . The quick brown fox jumps over a lazy dog
(pages 13, 129, 178)   THE QUICK BROWN FOX JUMPS OVER A LAZY DOG

Baskerton . . . . The quick brown fox jumps over a lazy dog
(pages 49, 161, 190)   THE QUICK BROWN FOX JUMPS OVER A LAZY DOG

Baskerton Italic . . . . *The quick brown fox jumps over a lazy dog*
(no samples)   *THE QUICK BROWN FOX JUMPS OVER A LAZY DOG*

Book Antiqua . . . . The quick brown fox jumps over a lazy dog
(pages 8, 131, 155, 205, 216)   THE QUICK BROWN FOX JUMPS OVER A LAZY DOG

Book Antiqua Italic . . . . *The quick brown fox jumps over a lazy dog*
(no samples)   *THE QUICK BROWN FOX JUMPS OVER A LAZY DOG*

Bookman . . . . The quick brown fox jumps over a lazy dog
(pages 25, 52, 54, 76, 79, 89, 95,   THE QUICK BROWN FOX JUMPS OVER A LAZY DOG
115, 123, 125, 159, 196, 263, 266)

Bookman Italic . . . . *The quick brown fox jumps over a lazy dog*
(page 184)   *THE QUICK BROWN FOX JUMPS OVER A LAZY DOG*

Capelli . . . . The quick brown fox jumps over a lazy dog
(page 42)   THE QUICK BROWN FOX JUMPS OVER A LAZY DOG

Capelli Italic . . . . *The quick brown fox jumps over a lazy dog*
(no samples)   *THE QUICK BROWN FOX JUMPS OVER A LAZY DOG*

Carnegie . . . . The quick brown fox jumps over a lazy dog
(page 80)   THE QUICK BROWN FOX JUMPS OVER A LAZY DOG

Carnegie Italic . . . . *The quick brown fox jumps over a lazy dog*
(no samples)   THE QUICK BROWN FOX JUMPS OVER A LAZY DOG

Center City . . . . The quick brown fox jumps over a lazy dog
(pages 10)   THE QUICK BROWN FOX JUMPS OVER A LAZY DOG

Center City Oblique . . . . *The quick brown fox jumps over a lazy dog*
(pages 128)   *THE QUICK BROWN FOX JUMPS OVER A LAZY DOG*

Classic Typewriter . . . . The quick brown fox jumps over a lazy dog
(pages 47, 58, 154)   THE QUICK BROWN FOX JUMPS OVER A LAZY DOG

Classic Typewriter Italic . . . . *The quick brown fox jumps over a lazy dog*
(no samples)   *THE QUICK BROWN FOX JUMPS OVER A LAZY DOG*

Garamond .... The quick brown fox jumps over a lazy dog
(pages 108, 162)   THE QUICK BROWN FOX JUMPS OVER A LAZY DOG

Garamond Italic .... *The quick brown fox jumps over a lazy dog*
(no samples)   *THE QUICK BROWN FOX JUMPS OVER A LAZY DOG*

Garamond Antiqua .... The quick brown fox jumps over a lazy dog
(pages 27, 44, 140)   THE QUICK BROWN FOX JUMPS OVER A LAZY DOG

Gazette .... The quick brown fox jumps over a lazy dog
(page 55)   THE QUICK BROWN FOX JUMPS OVER A LAZY DOG

Gazette Italic .... *The quick brown fox jumps over a lazy dog*
(pages 136)   *THE QUICK BROWN FOX JUMPS OVER A LAZY DOG*

Joulliard .... The quick brown fox jumps over a lazy dog
(pages 126)   THE QUICK BROWN FOX JUMPS OVER A LAZY DOG

Joulliard Italic .... *The quick brown fox jumps over a lazy dog*
(no samples)   *THE QUICK BROWN FOX JUMPS OVER A LAZY DOG*

Katrina .... The quick brown fox jumps over a lazy dog
(page 29)   THE QUICK BROWN FOX JUMPS OVER A LAZY DOG

Katrina Italic .... *The quick brown fox jumps over a lazy dog*
(no samples)   *THE QUICK BROWN FOX JUMPS OVER A LAZY DOG*

Lucinda Bright .... The quick brown fox jumps over a lazy dog
(pages 70, 177)   THE QUICK BROWN FOX JUMPS OVER A LAZY DOG

Lucinda Bright Italic .... *The quick brown fox jumps over a lazy dog*
(no samples)   *THE QUICK BROWN FOX JUMPS OVER A LAZY DOG*

New Century Schoolbook .... The quick brown fox jumps over a lazy dog
(pages 6, 33, 53, 75, 96, 122,   THE QUICK BROWN FOX JUMPS OVER A LAZY DOG
158, 195, 200, 236)

New Century Schoolbook Italic .... *The quick brown fox jumps over a lazy dog*
(no samples)   *THE QUICK BROWN FOX JUMPS OVER A LAZY DOG*

Oxford .... The quick brown fox jumps over a lazy dog
(pages 101, 254)   THE QUICK BROWN FOX JUMPS OVER A LAZY DOG

Oxford Italic .... *The quick brown fox jumps over a lazy dog*
(no samples)   *THE QUICK BROWN FOX JUMPS OVER A LAZY DOG*

Padua .... The quick brown fox jumps over a lazy dog
(page 11)   THE QUICK BROWN FOX JUMPS OVER A LAZY DOG

Padua Italic .... *The quick brown fox jumps over a lazy dog*
(no samples)   *THE QUICK BROWN FOX JUMPS OVER A LAZY DOG*

Palatino . . . . The quick brown fox jumps over a lazy dog
(pages 7, 40, 72, 74, 85, 114,   THE QUICK BROWN FOX JUMPS OVER A LAZY DOG
160, 188, 226)

Palatino Italic . . . . *The quick brown fox jumps over a lazy dog*
(no samples)   *THE QUICK BROWN FOX JUMPS OVER A LAZY DOG*

Rockland . . . . The quick brown fox jumps over a lazy dog
(page 232)   THE QUICK BROWN FOX JUMPS OVER A LAZY DOG

Rockland Italic . . . . *The quick brown fox jumps over a lazy dog*
(page 138)   *THE QUICK BROWN FOX JUMPS OVER A LAZY DOG*

Souvienne . . . . The quick brown fox jumps over a lazy dog
(page 111)   THE QUICK BROWN FOX JUMPS OVER A LAZY DOG

Souvienne Italic . . . . *The quick brown fox jumps over a lazy dog*
(no samples)   *THE QUICK BROWN FOX JUMPS OVER A LAZY DOG*

Times Roman . . . . The quick brown fox jumps over a lazy dog
(pages 19, 22, 23, 86, 90, 105,   THE QUICK BROWN FOX JUMPS OVER A LAZY DOG
157, 198, 265, 268)

Times Roman Italic . . . . *The quick brown fox jumps over a lazy dog*
(page 97, 156)   *THE QUICK BROWN FOX JUMPS OVER A LAZY DOG*

Top Hat . . . . The quick brown fox jumps over a lazy dog
(page 82)   THE QUICK BROWN FOX JUMPS OVER A LAZY DOG

Top Hat Italic . . . . *The quick brown fox jumps over a lazy dog*
(no samples)   *THE QUICK BROWN FOX JUMPS OVER A LAZY DOG*

Sans Serif Fonts

Aquiline Book . . . . The quick brown fox jumps over a lazy dog
(page 130)   THE QUICK BROWN FOX JUMPS OVER A LAZY DOG

Arial . . . . The quick brown fox jumps over a lazy dog
(pages 36, 38, 127, 148, 180)   THE QUICK BROWN FOX JUMPS OVER A LAZY DOG

Arial Italic . . . . The quick brown fox jumps over a lazy dog
(pages 37, 181, 191)   THE QUICK BROWN FOX JUMPS OVER A LAZY DOG

Arial Narrow . . . . The quick brown fox jumps over a lazy dog
(pages 9, 209, 222)   THE QUICK BROWN FOX JUMPS OVER A LAZY DOG

Arial Narrow Italic . . . . The quick brown fox jumps over a lazy dog
(page 14)   THE QUICK BROWN FOX JUMPS OVER A LAZY DOG

Avant Garde . . . . The quick brown fox jumps over a lazy dog
(pages 16, 28, 94, 106, 116,   THE QUICK BROWN FOX JUMPS OVER A LAZY DOG
121, 147, 224, 270)

Avant Garde Italic . . . . The quick brown fox jumps over a lazy dog
(pages 146, 193)   THE QUICK BROWN FOX JUMPS OVER A LAZY DOG

CG Omega . . . . The quick brown fox jumps over a lazy dog
(pages 26, 104, 110,   THE QUICK BROWN FOX JUMPS OVER A LAZY DOG
151, 202, 212)

CG Omega Italic . . . . The quick brown fox jumps over a lazy dog
(page 150)   THE QUICK BROWN FOX JUMPS OVER A LAZY DOG

Corporate Condensed . . . . The quick brown fox jumps over a lazy dog
(pages 43, 81)   THE QUICK BROWN FOX JUMPS OVER A LAZY DOG

Corporate Rounded . . . . The quick brown fox jumps over a lazy dog
(page 84)   THE QUICK BROWN FOX JUMPS OVER A LAZY DOG

Corporate Rounded Oblique . . . . The quick brown fox jumps over a lazy dog
(page 98)   THE QUICK BROWN FOX JUMPS OVER A LAZY DOG

Gibraltar . . . . The quick brown fox jumps over a lazy dog
(pages 45, 176)   THE QUICK BROWN FOX JUMPS OVER A LAZY DOG

Gibraltar Italic . . . . The quick brown fox jumps over a lazy dog
(page 112)   THE QUICK BROWN FOX JUMPS OVER A LAZY DOG

Helvetica . . . . The quick brown fox jumps over a lazy dog
(pages 12, 15, 17, 18, 21, 30, 32, 35, 50,   THE QUICK BROWN FOX JUMPS OVER A LAZY DOG
57, 62–66, 71, 83, 92, 113, 119, 120, 132,
145, 182, 185-187, 194, 197, 199, 206, 207,
208, 210, 213, 214, 234, 240, 258, 262)

Helvetica Oblique . . . . The quick brown fox jumps over a lazy dog
(pages 41, 51, 91, 144, 192, 205)   THE QUICK BROWN FOX JUMPS OVER A LAZY DOG

Helvetica Narrow . . . . The quick brown fox jumps over a lazy dog
(pages 68, 93, 135, 152, 228, 230, 264)   THE QUICK BROWN FOX JUMPS OVER A LAZY DOG

Helvetica Narrow Oblique . . . . The quick brown fox jumps over a lazy dog
(pages 20, 39, 73, 118, 153, 201, 204)   THE QUICK BROWN FOX JUMPS OVER A LAZY DOG

Lucinda Sans . . . . The quick brown fox jumps over a lazy dog
(pages 69, 183)   THE QUICK BROWN FOX JUMPS OVER A LAZY DOG

Lucinda Sans Italic . . . . The quick brown fox jumps over a lazy dog
(page 67)   THE QUICK BROWN FOX JUMPS OVER A LAZY DOG

Obelisk . . . . The quick brown fox jumps over a lazy dog
(page 56)   THE QUICK BROWN FOX JUMPS OVER A LAZY DOG

Obelisk Oblique . . . . The quick brown fox jumps over a lazy dog
(page 88)   THE QUICK BROWN FOX JUMPS OVER A LAZY DOG

Univers . . . . The quick brown fox jumps over a lazy dog
(pages 24, 48, 100, 149, 220)   THE QUICK BROWN FOX JUMPS OVER A LAZY DOG

Univers Italic . . . . The quick brown fox jumps over a lazy dog
(pages 109, 249)   THE QUICK BROWN FOX JUMPS OVER A LAZY DOG

Univers Condensed . . . . The quick brown fox jumps over a lazy dog
(page 143)   THE QUICK BROWN FOX JUMPS OVER A LAZY DOG

Univers Condensed Italic . . . . The quick brown fox jumps over a lazy dog
(page 103)   THE QUICK BROWN FOX JUMPS OVER A LAZY DOG

Weissach . . . . The quick brown fox jumps over a lazy dog
(page 46)   THE QUICK BROWN FOX JUMPS OVER A LAZY DOG

Weissach Oblique . . . . The quick brown fox jumps over a lazy dog
(page 61)   THE QUICK BROWN FOX JUMPS OVER A LAZY DOG

Headline Fonts

Aero
abcdefghijklmnopqrstuvwxyz
ABCDEFGHIJKLMNOPQRSTUVWXYZ

Agincort
(page 8)
abcdefghijklmnopqrstuvwxyz
ABCDEFGHIJKLMNOPQRSTUVWXYZ

Agincort Italic
abcdefghijklmnopqrstuvwxyz
ABCDEFGHIJKLMNOPQRSTUVWXYZ

Astaire
ABCDEFGHIJKLMNOPQRSTUVWXYZ

Avalon Quest Black
(page 56)
ABCDEFGHIJKLMNOPQRSTUVWXYZ

Blox
(page 9)
abcdefghijklmnopqrstuvwxyz
ABCDEFGHIJKLMNOPQRSTUVWXYZ

Blox Italic
abcdefghijklmnopqrstuvwxyz
ABCDEFGHIJKLMNOPQRSTUVWXYZ

Bodoni Poster
abcdefghijklmnopqrstuvwxyz
ABCDEFGHIJKLMNOPQRSTUVWXYZ

Bongo Black
abcdefghijklmnopqrstuvwxyz
ABCDEFGHIJKLMNOPQRSTUVWXYZ

Broadway
(pages 207, 224)
abcdefghijklmnopqrstuvwxyz
ABCDEFGHIJKLMNOPQRSTUVWXYZ

Brush Script
(page 100)
abcdefghijklmnopqrstuvwxyz
ABCDEFGHIJKLMNOP2RSTUVWXYZ

Buckingham
(page 34)
abcdefghijklmnopqrstuvwxyz
ABCDEFGHIJKLMNOPQRSTUVWXYZ

CARGO
(PAGE 213)
ABCDEFGHIJKLMNOPQRSTUVWXYZ

Cathedral
abcdefghijklmnopqrstuvwxyz
ABCDEFGHIJKLMNOPQRSTUVWXYZ

Certificate
(pages 53, 65)
abcdefghijklmnopqrstuvwxyz
ABCDEFGHIJKLMNOPQRSTUVWXYZ

Circus
abcdefghijklmnopqrstuvwxyz
ABCDEFGHIJKLMNOPQRSTUVWXYZ

COMIC STRIP
ABCDEFGHIJKLMNOPQRSTUVWXYZ

Commercial Script
(pages 49, 209)
abcdefghijklmnopqrstuvwxyz
ABCDEFGHIJKLMNOPQRSTUVWXYZ

Copperfield
(pages 19)
abcdefghijklmnopqrstuvwxyz
ABCDEFGHIJKLMNOPQRSTUVWXYZ

Coronation Script
abcdefghijklmnopqrstuvwxyz
ABCDEFGHIJKLMNOPQRSTUVWXYZ

Diner Script
(page 103)
abcdefghijklmnopqrstuvwxyz
ABCDEFGHIJKLMNOP2RSTUVWXYZ

Domenic
abcdefghijklmnopqrstuvwxyz
ABCDEFGHIJKLMNOPQRSTUVWXYZ

Don Casual
abcdefghijklmnopqrstuvwxyz
ABCDEFGHIJKLMNOPQRSTUVWXYZ

Empire Script
abcdefghijklmnopqrstuvwxyz
ABCDEFGHIJKLMNOPQRSTUVWXYZ

Exchequer Script
abcdefghijklmnopqrstuvwxyz
ABCDEFGHIJKLMNOPQRSTUVWXYZ

Frederick
abcdefghijklmnopqrstuvwxyz
ABCDEFGHIJKLMNOPQRSTUVWXYZ

Freestyle Script Italic
abcdefghijklmnopqrstuvwxyz
ABCDEFGHIJKLMNOPQRSTUVWXYZ

Gengis Kahn
ABCDEFGHIJKLMNOPQRSTUVWXYZ

Gengis Kahn Italic
ABCDEFGHIJKLMNOPQRSTUVWXYZ

Gravure
abcdefghijklmnopqrstuvwxyz
ABCDEFGHIJKLMNOPQRSTUVWXYZ

Guthrie
abcdefghijklmnopqrstuvwxyz
ABCDEFGHIJKLMNOPQRSTUVWXYZ

Harem
(pages 20, 24, 71)
abcdefghijklmnopqrstuvwxyz
ABCDEFGHIJKLMNOPQRSTUVWXYZ

Howlee
abcdefghijklmnopqrstuvwxyz
ABCDEFGHIJKLMNOPQRSTUVWXYZ

Ivy League Outline
ABCDEFGHIJKLMNOPQRSTUVWXYZ

Ivy League Solid
(page 201)
ABCDEFGHIJKLMNOPQRSTUVWXYZ

Kashmir
abcdefghijklmnopqrstuvwxyz
ABCDEFGHIJKLMNOPQRSTUVWXYZ

Knomen
ABCDEFGHIJKLMNOPQRSTUVWXYZ

Knomen Italic
ABCDEFGHIJKLMNOPQRSTUVWXYZ

Lalique
abcdefghijklmnopqrstuvwxyz
ABCDEFGHIJKLMNOPQRSTUVWXYZ

Lalique Italic
abcdefghijklmnopqrstuvwxyz
ABCDEFGHIJKLMNOPQRSTUVWXYZ

Logan
abcdefghijklmnopqrstuvwxyz
ABCDEFGHIJKLMNOPQRSTUVWXYZ

Logan Italic
abcdefghijklmnopqrstuvwxyz
ABCDEFGHIJKLMNOPQRSTUVWXYZ

Lucinda Blackletter
abcdefghijklmnopqrstuvwxyz
ABCDEFGHIJKLMNOPQRSTUVWXYZ

Lucinda Handwriting Italic
abcdefghijklmnopqrstuvwxyz
ABCDEFGHIJKLMNOPQRSTUVWXYZ

Lushlife Bold
(page 43)
abcdefghijklmnopqrstuvwxyz
ABCDEFGHIJKLMNOPQRSTUVWXYZ

Lushlife Bold Italic
(page 176)
abcdefghijklmnopqrstuvwxyz
ABCDEFGHIJKLMNOPQRSTUVWXYZ

Marigold
abcdefghijklmnopqrstuvwxyz
ABCDEFGHIJKLMNOPQRSTUVWXYZ

Moravian Italic
(page 35)
abcdefghijklmnopqrstuvwxyz
ABCDEFGHIJKLMNOPQRSTUVWXYZ

PITTSBURGH
ABCDEFGHIJKLMNOPQRSTUVWXYZ

Plage Tahiti
abcdefghijklmnopqrstuvwxyz
ABCDEFGHIJKLMNOPQRSTUVWXYZ

Quetzalcoatl
abcdefghijklmnopqrstuvwxyz
ABCDEFGHIJKLMNOPQRSTUVWXYZ

Quetzalcoatl Italic
abcdefghijklmnopqrstuvwxyz
ABCDEFGHIJKLMNOPQRSTUVWXYZ

Remus Italic
abcdefghijklmnopqrstuvwxyz
ABCDEFGHIJKLMNOPQRSTUVWXYZ

ROMULUS
ABCDEFGHIJKLMNOPQRSTUVWXYZ

ROMULUS ITALIC
ABCDEFGHIJKLMNOPQRSTUVWXYZ

Saddlebag
abcdefghijklmnopqrstuvwxyz
ABCDEFGHIJKLMNOPQRSTUVWXYZ

Scheherezade
abcdefghijklmnopqrstuvwxyz
ABCDEFGHIJKLMNOPQRSTUVWXYZ

SLAYER
ABCDEFGHIJKLMNOPQRSTUVWXYZ

Spinner
abcdefghijklmnopqrstuvwxyz
ABCDEFGHIJKLMNOPQRSTUVWXYZ

Stagecoach
abcdefghijklmnopqrstuvwxyz
ABCDEFGHIJKLMNOPQRSTUVWXYZ

Sterling
(page 16)
abcdefghijklmnopqrstuvwxyz
ABCDEFGHIJKLMNOPQRSTUVWXYZ

Stimpson
abcdefghijklmnopqrstuvwxyz
ABCDEFGHIJKLMNOPQRSTUVWXYZ

TRAJAN
ABCDEFGHIJKLMNOPQRSTUVWXYZ

University Ornate
(pages 7, 92, 188)
abcdefghijklmnopqrstuvwxyz
ABCDEFGHIJKLMNOPQRSTUVWXYZ

Waldorf Script
(pages 28, 216)
abcdefghijklmnopqrstuvwxyz
ABCDEFGHIJKLMNOPQRSTUVWXYZ

Write Bold
abcdefghijklmnopqrstuvwxyz
ABCDEFGHIJKLMNOPQRSTUVWXYZ

12 | GRAPHIC LINES

All of the resumes in this book were typeset using WordPerfect, and you will find that it can do anything you need to design a perfect resume. One of the most useful features of WordPerfect is its ability to draw lines of varying thicknesses and to create box borders.

Horizontal lines allow the reader to focus on each section separately and draw the eye from section to section, especially when there is little room for extra white space (which can serve the same purpose).

Vertical lines add pizzazz to the design of a resume and can be used very creatively. See, for example, the resumes on pages 181–183.

Lines can be used to set the name and address section(s) apart from the text so the eye can be drawn to the most important information first.

It is important, however, to avoid the use of too many lines with different thicknesses on the same page. The resume can get "busy," which makes the reader work too hard. It is a good idea to use no more than two line widths per resume. For instance:

This line is .02 inch thick.

And this one is .005 inch thick.

You might combine the two together.

*And you could reverse them at the
bottom of the resume to give it balance.*

The samples that follow will give you some ideas for ways to use lines in a resume. There are lines on almost every resume in this book, but the ones on pages 15, 57, 58, 62, 69, 81, 109, 111, 114, 135, 204–210, 212, 213, 216, and 262 might offer you even more unique ideas.

CAROLYN B. VANDERBILT

OBJECTIVE	A fulfilling position leading to a career in International Business Development	

EDUCATION

MASTER OF INTERNATIONAL MANAGEMENT — May 1995
American Graduate School of International Management
Thunderbird Campus, Glendale, Arizona
↪ Designed international market research study for Arizona company
↪ Analyzed the economic development of India during the 1980s
↪ Researched international environmental policies
↪ Extensively surveyed the changing political and economic climate of Hong Kong

BACHELOR OF ARTS: PSYCHOLOGY AND FINE ARTS — May 1990
Vanderbilt University, Nashville, Tennessee
Vanderbilt-in-France, Fall Semester 1988

**EMPLOYMENT
PROFILE**

INTERN, SOUTHEAST ASIA PROGRAMS — June 1994 – Aug. 1994
The Asia Foundation, San Francisco, California
↪ Evaluated grants to assure fulfillment of stated goals and objectives
↪ Conducted consultant searches and organized international itineraries
↪ Wrote project descriptions, program highlights, and contractual letters of agreement

FOUNDER/MANAGER — Feb. 1992 – Nov. 1992
Professional English Services, Taipei, Taiwan
↪ Created and managed an English language service company tailored to the needs
of local Chinese businesses
↪ Marketed services and negotiated contract terms
↪ Designed curricula and instructed classes

EXECUTIVE ASSISTANT — Feb. 1992 – Aug. 1992
Yao-Teh International Real Estate Development Co., Ltd., Taipei, Taiwan
↪ Contacted government offices and private agents to locate real estate projects in Asia
↪ Responsible for international correspondence
↪ Wrote company presentations and proposals

ENGLISH AS A SECOND LANGUAGE (ESL) INSTRUCTOR — July 1991 – Nov. 1992
Taiwan Normal University, Gram English Center, Taipei, Taiwan
↪ Created syllabi, instructed writing, business, and conversational English classes

HOTEL RECEPTIONIST — Sep. 1990 – Feb. 1991
Tower Thistle Hotel, London, England
↪ Greeted international guests, handled complaints, and utilized computer system

BUSINESS MANAGER/ADVERTISING STAFF — Jan. 1989 – Dec. 1989
Vanderbilt Hustler Student Newspaper, Weekend Section, Nashville, Tennessee
↪ Established business department – responsible for layout, billing, and accounting
↪ Sold display advertising space, fully funding special topics section

**LANGUAGES
& COMPUTERS**

Proficient in **Mandarin Chinese** ↪ Working Knowledge of **French** ↪ Knowledge of **Spanish**
Lotus 1-2-3, Word Star, WordPerfect, Quattro Pro, Harvard Graphics

ACTIVITIES

↪ **"Growing Our Future" an NGO Symposium on Food Security and the Environment**, Rapporteur
↪ **Thunderbird Nonprofit Careers Club**, President, Resume Book Editor
↪ **Toastmasters International**
↪ **India Subcontinent Club**, Treasurer, Social Coordinator
↪ Traveled extensively throughout Europe, Mexico, Guatemala, Egypt, India, and Southeast Asia

ADDRESS

1234 Jennifer Street, New Orleans, Louisiana 70115   (504) 555-1234

176

FRANÇOIS DOVENMEUHLE

OBJECTIVE

A position in International Marketing

QUALIFICATIONS

> *International* – Extensive cross-cultural experience in Europe, North America, Africa, Japan
> *Multilingual* – Able to conduct business in four languages
> *Creative* – Experienced in developing marketing and business strategies
> *Analytical* – Skilled at evaluating options and generating solutions

EDUCATION

MASTER OF INTERNATIONAL MANAGEMENT (Dec. 1994)
American Graduate School of International Management, Thunderbird, Glendale, Arizona
> Corporate Consulting Associate – Developed a *marketing plan* for SeaBeam Instruments
> Engineered transactions during *countertrade,* offset and barter seminar
> Adapted Ben & Jerry's Ice Cream *marketing mix* for Japan
> Perfected political risk analysis skills
> Recipient of Friends of Thunderbird/Mavis Voris Scholarship

BACHELOR OF BUSINESS ADMINISTRATION (Dec. 1990)
University of Texas at Austin
> Designed a *national marketing plan* for Dynapult (baseball pitching machine)
> Designed a mail-order *sales strategy* for an instructional videotape

INSTITUT D'ETUDES POLITIQUES DE PARIS (Oct. 1988)
Graduate College of Economics & Finance, alumnus
> Concentration in political science, economics

LANGUAGES

Fluent in **French, English,** and **Serbo-Croatian**
Working knowledge of **German, Portuguese,** and **Spanish**
Knowledge of **Japanese**

EXPERIENCE

TRANSLATOR, Equipment Development Command, Versailles, France (1991 – 1992)
> Prepared and delivered bilingual presentations on equipment capabilities to foreign buyers
> Supervised a team of six translators
> Served as interpreter and assisted U.S. military officials in France
> Translated documents for joint European weapons programs

CONSULTANT, Dovenmuehle Mortgage Bank, Schaumburg, Illinois (Spring 1989)
> Audited the organization and procedures of the residential marketing department
> Improved product tracking by developing a database for FNMA/GNMA mortgages

INTERN, Enterprise Savings Bank, Chicago, Illinois (Summer 1985)
> Assisted Executive Vice President in merger negotiations and board meetings
> Instituted and conducted in-house training for software applications
> Studied and recommended locations for new branches

HONORS & ACTIVITIES

Awarded Scholarship: The International Budo University, Chiba, Japan (Summer 1994)
Founded and elected President, Circle of Conservative Students (1985 – 1987)
Elected Secretary, Austin Kendo Doshikai (Japanese fencing) (1992 – 1993)
Worked 18 months as agricultural volunteer in Angola

COMPUTERS

Word for Windows, EXCEL, Harvard Graphics, WordPerfect, dBASE

PERSONAL

Eligible to work in the U.S. and the E.C.

Address ➤ *123, Cité Condorcet* ➤ *75009 Paris, France* ➤ *(33) (1) 555-1234*

ANTHONY S. McDONALD

1234 W. Cactus Avenue
Peoria, Arizona 85345

Home: (602) 555-1234
Fax: (602) 555-5678

- QUALIFICATIONS -

The entrepreneurial spirit, dynamic energy, and sagacity to help plan and lead a good business opportunity to its optimum profit, value, growth, synergism, and success. Extensive experience in financial planning, budgeting, negotiations, control, analysis, and reporting. An in-depth knowledge and extensive experience in general and cost accounting; computer operations, data processing and management information systems; billing, credit and collections; purchasing and inventory control. Creative skills in marketing, sales, new product development, pricing, and customer service. Excellent communication, organization, and problem solving skills and the leadership, discipline, enthusiasm, and ethics to effectively direct, develop, and motivate human resources.

- EXPERIENCE -

McDONALD GROUP, INC., Birmingham, Alabama
Corporate Construction Analyst/Manager, from November 1993 to March 1995, for sixteen cable television systems operated in Louisiana, Alabama, and Georgia. Major responsibilities/contributions:
- managed $20 million capital budget including negotiating, purchasing, and tracking of fixed assets and of materials and labor for the construction of cable extensions, upgrades, rebuilds, and fiber optic projects;
- development of automated systems to project costs, determine feasibilities, track capital expenditures, analyze variances, and control inventory.

AMERICAN TELEVISION AND COMMUNICATIONS CORPORATION, BIRMINGHAM DIVISION
(Subsidiary of TIME, INC.) Birmingham, Alabama
Financial Vice President, Board of Directors, from June 1989 to April 1993, for major metropolitan cable television systems and advertising business. Major responsibilities/contributions:
- strategic business planning with detailed capital and operating budgets, reestimates and cash flow forecasts;
- effective management and accurate reporting of balance sheet position, P&L performance and source and use of funds, with supplemental reporting to SEC, FCC, franchising authorities, and other regulatory agencies;
- development and direction of general and cost accounting, billing, credit and collections, purchasing, inventory, computer and management information systems;
- development of strong internal control, audit, and accountability procedures;
- development and direction of human resources department, policies, and wage and benefit plans;
- analyses of demography, critical success factors, ROI, IRR, NPV, and cost variances;
- initiation and implementation of substantial revenue enhancement and cost containment programs;
- successful rate increase and re-franchising negotiations;
- due diligence and successful negotiations for acquisition of Bessemer Cable.

AIRWEST CORPORATION, Fort Collins, Colorado
Financial Vice President, from December 1981 to December 1989, for aviation services company providing: helicopter support for seismic energy exploration and offshore drilling operations; air-ambulance services for major hospital systems; and rebuild and repair services for crash-damaged aircraft; in addition to operating the Fort Collins/Loveland municipal airport. The company filed for reorganization and eventually bankruptcy as a result of the "Energy Glut" of 1982.

AIRWEST CORPORATION (continued)
Major responsibilities/contributions were much the same as above with the addition of:
- ▸ development of an automated project cost accounting system for the re-manufacture and repair of crash-damaged aircraft;
- ▸ development and defense of Plan of Reorganization under Chapter 11 of the Bankruptcy Act.

IMPORTS INTERNATIONAL, INC., Denver, Colorado
Financial Vice President, from March 1977 to November 1981, for international wholesale ski accessories distributor. Major responsibilities/contributions were much the same as above with the addition of:
- ▸ implementation of fully integrated, automated sales order entry, accounts receivable, inventory and general accounting computer system;
- ▸ financing imports and exports.

U.S. ARMY, 4TH INFANTRY DIVISION (MECH), Fort Carson, Colorado
Commissioned Officer, July 1973. Served to First Lieutenant as transportation platoon leader and assistant adjutant. Honorably discharged July 1976.

GEO. J. MEYERS MFG., Akron, Ohio
Cost Accountant, from June 1972 to June 1973, for heavy bottling equipment manufacturer.

- EDUCATION -

BACHELOR OF SCIENCE DEGREE, ACCOUNTING
University of Akron, Ohio (June 1973)
Member Reserve Officers Training Corps (ROTC)

ASSOCIATE DEGREE, GENERAL SCIENCE
Marion Military Institute, Marion, Alabama (June 1969)
U.S. Air Force Academy nominee - 1968
Annapolis Naval Foundation Scholarship - 1969
Commandant's List, track, and football

CPA REVIEW COURSE – 1976

COLORADO REAL ESTATE LICENSE – 1976

PRIVATE PILOT LICENSE – 1976

John P. Firefighter
1234 West Bell Road, #1234
Phoenix, Arizona 85023
(602) 555-1234

OBJECTIVE	TEMPE FIREFIGHTER RECRUIT	

PERSONAL DATA

Date of Birth: March 17, 1964	Health: Excellent	
Height/Weight: 6'4" / 200 lbs.	Marital: Married	

EDUCATION

MIRAMAR FIRE ACADEMY, Miramar, California	
Basic E.M.T.	Spring 1994
Fire Apparatus	Fall 1993
Fire Tactics and Strategy	Fall 1993
PHOENIX COLLEGE, Phoenix, Arizona	
E.M.T. – Defibrillator	Fall 1990
Basic E.M.T.	Fall 1986
Introduction to Fire Science & Fire Suppression	Fall 1986
NORTHERN ARIZONA UNIVERSITY, Flagstaff, Arizona	
Major: Special Education	9/85 – 6/86

ADDITIONAL CERTIFICATES

Firefighter I and II	Spring 1993
C.P.R. Instructor	Fall 1993
EMT-D	Fall 1993
Hazardous Materials/First Responder	Fall 1993
Level I Para-Professional (Special Education)	Fall 1986

WORK HISTORY

FIREFIGHTER	10/89 – Present
Rural Metro Fire Department	
VIDEOGRAPHER	4/89 – Present
Video Porter Productions	
• Training films for small businesses and wedding videos	
CUSTOMER SERVICE REPRESENTATIVE	8/89 – 4/90
Colonial Penn Insurance, Phoenix, Arizona	
FOOD SERVER	
Hungry Hunter Restaurant, Scottsdale, Arizona	5/86 – 1/90
Bennigan's Restaurant, Glendale, Arizona	11/84 – 9/85
TEACHER'S AIDE	9/83 – 6/84
Kilgore Center, Baytown, Texas	
• Worked with autistic children and adults with hearing disabilities	
COUNSELOR (Volunteer)	1979 – 1985
Muscular Dystrophy Association Camp, Sedona, Arizona	

SUMMARY OF QUALIFICATIONS

- Three-and-one-half years experience with Rural Metro Fire Department
- E.M.T. certified since 1986
- CPR Instructor Certified
- Hazardous Materials First Responder Certified
- EMT-D certified
- Fluent in sign language

AVOCATIONS Scuba diving, cycling, basketball, racquetball

LEE J. IRVING
7139 W. Turnkey
Phoenix, Arizona 85033
(602) 555-1234

EXPERIENCE

ELIGIBILITY INTERVIEWER I   12/92 – Present
Department of Economic Security (DES), Peoria, Arizona
Interviewed applicants face to face and over the telephone for government food
stamps, AHCCS medical and cash benefits. Following verification of all information
received, determined eligibility according to state and federal guidelines. Authorized or
denied benefits in a timely manner, and advised ineligible clients of alternative
programs available. Ran computer checks on current employment and unemploy-
ment. Documented case files and entered data into computer. Routinely worked with
private and confidential financial information. Maintained and monitored assigned
caseload, complying with established policies, procedures, regulations, statutes, and
client confidentiality laws. Answered questions concerning eligibility requirements and
status. Provided general information and advised clients of assigned program
provider, provider function, client responsibility, and appeal rights. Updated and
maintained manuals.

ASSISTANT MANAGER   10/92 – 12/92
Jiffy Lube, Phoenix, Arizona
Responsible for opening and closing retail store on a daily basis. Dealt directly with
customers and handled customer complaints. Delegated employee responsibilities.
Handled banking, sales, inventory management, cash sales, and auto maintenance.
Entered customer and inventory data into main terminal computer.

ASSISTANT REGIONAL MANAGER   7/91 – 9/92
Speedee Oil Change & Tune-up (aka Auto Care Corporation), Glendale, Arizona
Responsible for inventory control, accounting, interviewing potential employees, cash
management, employee and customer relations, sales and marketing. Trained new
store managers. Supervised approximately 50 employees in 13 chain stores.

DIRECTOR OF OPERATIONS   7/84 – 6/91
Classic Photo Promotions, Glendale, Arizona
Designed marketing campaigns and generated new accounts. Assured customer
satisfaction. Supervised 20 employees. Purchased inventory and maintained books.
Trained photographers and sales staff. Interviewed and hired all employees.

OPERATIONS DIRECTOR   1982 – 1983
Irving Oil, Ltd., of Canada
Leased and operated two full-service gas stations. Responsibilities included payroll,
customer relations, accounting, purchasing, inventory control, personnel
management, advertising, and other management functions.

EDUCATION

HONORS STUDENT
KENNIBICASIS VALLEY HIGH SCHOOL   1981
New Brunswick, Canada

CONSUMER CREDIT COUNSELING, Scottsdale, Arizona   1989
Three-week course in credit counseling

BIZARRE FINANCING, Scottsdale, Arizona   1990
Business Financing Strategies – 3-day workshop

COMPUTERS

Familiar with IBM PC computers, IDEAL, AZTEC, APIS, Lubesoft, check writing
and accounting programs

Charles Bernard Block, Jr.

1234 Camino Fuente Drive
El Paso, Texas 79912
(915) 555-1234

OBJECTIVE

A challenging position in international marketing leading to a senior management career

QUALIFICATIONS

- Graduate degree emphasizing international marketing, finance, and trade
- Five years of successful professional sales experience
- Project management skills
- Proven leadership abilities
- Experience and interest in working on multicultural teams
- Highly proficient in Spanish

EXPERIENCE

ROCHE LABORATORIES, El Paso, Texas
Professional Products Representative

Nov. 1993
to Present

- Plan and organize territory in order to increase market share and dollar growth of promoted products
- Consistently meet or exceed sales goals

Division Sales Representative

Oct. 1992
to Nov. 1993

- Promoted an institutional and retail pharmaceutical product line to Columbia Healthcare System in El Paso, government accounts, and rural customers
- Achieved and maintained formulary status of all promoted products in El Paso Healthcare System and William Beaumont Army Medical Center

DEAN WITTER & PRUDENTIAL-BACHE SECURITIES, Tucson, Arizona
Investment Broker

Oct. 1987
to June 1990

- Coordinated formation of nonprofit research foundation for Veteran's Administration Medical Center
- Served as regional specialist for retirement planning and corporate and executive services
- Opened 150 new accounts during first year and increased number of new accounts to 400 during second year

EDUCATION

MASTER OF INTERNATIONAL MANAGEMENT (MIM)
American Graduate School of International Management
Thunderbird Campus, Glendale, Arizona

Aug. 1991

- Relevant course work included: International Market Research, International Finance and Trade, International Trade Strategies, International Health Care Systems, Multinational Business Management, Cross-Cultural Communications, Intermediate Accounting, Advanced Corporate Finance
- As a member of an eight-person team, developed a successful trade strategy for Grupo Visa S.A. de C.V., facilitating the sale of chemical adhesives to Anheuser-Busch
- Participated in an international market research group project to determine the U.S. market entry potential for an all-natural skin care product to be imported from Mexico
- Brought an improved skin care product to market by managing all development and marketing aspects from conception to distribution

BACHELOR OF SCIENCE, BUSINESS ADMINISTRATION
University of Arizona, Tucson, Arizona

Aug. 1987

- Concentration in finance, marketing, economics
- Extracurricular activities included: Pledge Class President and Philanthropy Chairman of Sigma Phi Epsilon Fraternity, intramural sports, Student Union Activities Board, and Speakers' Board

Julie E. Ludwig

EMPLOYMENT	**Administrative Support** Norrell Temporary Services	1990 to Present Phoenix, Arizona

Administrative Support
Norrell Temporary Services
- Arizona Economic Council: An organization that promotes and markets the state of Arizona to potential business people and investors across the U.S. and abroad
  - Assisted the marketing personnel in drafting correspondence
  - Initiated and completed an international business resources bibliography for the Vice President, International
  - Performed secretarial and receptionist duties
- U.S. Bankruptcy Court – Clerical
- Arthur Andersen & Co. – Data entry (payroll), Wang Computer

Research Library Assistant   1989 – 1990
Barton Kyle Yount Memorial Library   Glendale, Arizona
- Assisted in organizing the computerized processing and manual organizing and documenting of requests for materials not located in the library

Receptionist, Edward S. Cook, D.D.S.   1988 – 1989
- Computer control of 500 patient accounts   Santa Fe, New Mexico
- Transferred approximately 500 hard-copy records to computer files
- Processed month-end reports and monthly statements
- Processed 10+ insurance transactions per day
- Posted 10–20 receivables per day
- Entered procedures and fees for approximately 25–30 patients per day

Teller/Bookkeeping Assistant, Kiowa State Bank   1985
                                                    Kiowa, Colorado
Intern, U.S. Senator William Armstrong   1983
- Constituent correspondence   Washington, D.C.
- Campaign volunteer

EDUCATION   **Master of International Management** GPA 3.4   1990
American Graduate School of International Management   Glendale, Arizona
Relevant courses:
- International Trade Administration
- Cross-Cultural Communication for International Managers
- International Marketing Management
- International Finance and Trade
- Regional Business Environment of Europe
- International Marketing Research
- Cost and Managerial Accounting
- Managerial Finance

Bachelor of Arts, German/History   GPA 3.8   1988
Colorado State University   *magna cum laude*   Fort Collins, Colorado

Albert Ludwigs Universität   1987 – 1988
                                                        Freiburg, Germany

ACTIVITIES   German Club • Entrepreneur's Club • Pi Beta Phi: Membership
Chairman, Alumni Coordinator, Reporter • Phi Alpha Theta (History
Honor Society), President

HONORS   **Phi Beta Kappa**
Mortar Board
Phi Sigma Iota, Foreign Language Honor Society

ADDRESS   1234 Vondelpark Drive, Phoenix, Arizona 85382   (602) 555-1234

183

Personal Resume of

HARVEY BURK EGLIN

Present Address
12345 N. 43rd Avenue #123
Phoenix, Arizona 85029
(602) 555-1234

Permanent Address
Post Office Box 123
Alabaster, Alabama 35007
(205) 555-1234

– OBJECTIVE –

A challenging position as an Aircraft Junior Mechanic.

– QUALIFICATIONS –

Seasoned Crew Chief on T-38, F-111, F-15, and F-16 aircraft with ten years of experience in:

- *Performing preflight, thru-flight, postflight, phase, and calendar inspection of aircraft, including skin, structures, landing gear, engines, instruments, cockpits, flight controls, and surfaces.*
- *Inspecting aircraft components for cleanliness, corrosion, alignment, proper clearance and operation, evidence of wear, cracks, and looseness according to applicable technical orders.*
- *Removal and installation of major flight control surfaces, engines, wings, landing gear, wheels, brakes, panels, and doors.*
- *Launching and recovering of aircraft and debriefing air crews.*
- *Servicing oil, fuel, hydraulics, liquid oxygen, liquid nitrogen systems.*
- *Obtaining samples of fuel, oil, and hydraulic fluids for analysis.*
- *Operating flight line support equipment.*
- *Interpreting diagrams and applicable publications.*
- *Documenting and maintaining maintenance data forms.*
- *Performing duties of maintenance operation control supervisor.*
- *Supervise trainees in their duties.*
- *Write progress reports on all trainees assigned under my supervision.*
- *Order and receive parts; turn in parts for repairable maintenance.*

– EXPERIENCE –

TACTICAL AIRCRAFT MAINTENANCE SPECIALIST

United States Air Force, *Luke AFB, Arizona* . . . . *October 1989 to Present*
United States Air Force, *Ramstein AB, Germany* . . . . *September 1985 to October 1989*
United States Air Force, *Eglin AFB, Florida* . . . . *April 1981 to October 1985*

– PROFESSIONAL EDUCATION –

U.S. AIR FORCE TRAINING . . . . *1981 to 1991*

- *Technical School – Tactical Aircraft Maintenance Specialist (600 hours)*
- *Air Frame License and Power Plant License (March 1991)*
- *220 Engine On Maintenance Course (18 hours)*
- *Dedicated Crew Chief (80 hours) and Advanced Dedicated Crew Chief (50 hours) Courses*
- *Field Training Development Courses (225 hours)*
- *Professional Military Education School (Management) (75 hours)*
- *Seven-Level Trouble Shooting Course (40 hours)*
- *Flex Scope, Bore Scope (8 hours)*

– PERSONAL DATA –	– AWARDS & HONORS –
Born January 16, 1962	*The Air Force Commendation Medal*
Nonsmoker	*The Air Force Achievement Medal*
Excellent Health	*The Air Force Good Conduct Medal (3)*

TIMOTHY A. PROCTER

1234 W. Tulip Drive
Glendale, AZ 85306
(602) 555-1234

OBJECTIVE: To pursue unique and challenging opportunities in the Industrial/Technical Field

---

SUMMARY OF QUALIFICATIONS:

- Background encompasses more than 10 years experience in manufacturing production, reflecting knowledge and expertise in:

  - industrial robotics
  - quality control
  - trouble shooting
  - people management
  - logistics

  - pneumatics
  - hydraulics
  - new equipment start-ups
  - statistical process control
  - safe practices

- Excellent supervisor with strong documentation and communication skills; able to maintain a positive teamwork environment by developing mutual respect and rapport.

- Proficient in tracking and analyzing statistical data through computer for maximum efficiency, productivity, and profitability (just in time concept).

- Conscientious and detail-oriented, lending to an earned reputation for dependability, efficiency, integrity, and professionalism.

EXPERIENCE:

1980 - Present   PROCTER & GAMBLE   Phoenix, Arizona
Production Technician/Supervisor

Oversaw production in the conversion of raw materials into finished paper products. Trained, supervised, and evaluated a production crew. Determined need and ordered raw materials for production with attention to proper documentation.

Tracked and analyzed statistical data to foresee problems, to schedule staff and machinery efficiencies, and to analyze convertible waste. Conducted regular employee safety and affirmative action meetings and developed safety projects. Maintained machinery with attention to preventive maintenance to maximize run time efficiencies and minimize down time and preventable outages.

Developed a training program and training manual related to understanding robotics. Conducted training sessions for technicians. Recognized for 11 years of safe employment and five years of perfect attendance. Consistently #1 of three shifts in quality and production numbers.

TRAINING:
- Industrial Robotics
  - Cincinnati Milicron operational and maintenance courses for industrial robotics
  - Glendale Community College for industrial robotics
  - Knowledge of M.C.L. machine language for medium technology robots
- Knowledge of vibration analysis/laser alignment
- Analytical trouble shooting (A.T.S.)
- Statistical Data Tracking and Control
- Bearings and Lubrication
- Total Quality Approach (T.Q.A.) Quality Training
- People Management/Affirmative Action/Safety
- Basic Logistics   • Basic Pneumatics   • Basic Hydraulics

Christopher Taunton

SUMMARY

A **Professional Engineer** and **Project Manager** with eleven years experience in Consulting, Project Engineering and Contract Administration. Major strengths include:

- ♦ Program Management
- ♦ Problem Solving
- ♦ Innovator

PROFESSIONAL EXPERIENCE

06/94 - 06/95   **PACIFIC CONSULTANTS INTERNATIONAL**   Tokyo, **Japan**

Consultant to one of the largest private Japanese consultant firms. Assigned to infrastructure and development programs in Southeast Asia funded by Japanese agencies and the World Bank.
- ♦ Assisted with feasibility studies, project evaluations, and proposals

09/94 - 06/95   **Contracts Advisor** for the Jakarta-Merak Tollway project   Jakarta, **Indonesia**
- ♦ Formulated and amended contract specifications, documents, and drawings
- ♦ Enhanced communications between our design team and site managers

01/94 - 05/94   **INTERNATIONAL EDUCATION SERVICES**   Tokyo, **Japan**

English Language Instructor to Japanese corporations, banks, and finance houses. Taught technical English to Japanese engineers and managers.

09/93 - 12/93   **C.H. ENGINEERING SERVICES**   Taunton, **U.K.**

Independent Consultant to the construction industry. Established my own business in order to finance my move to Tokyo.

10/89 - 09/93   **PICK, EVERARD, KEAY & GIMSON**; Consulting Engineers   Taunton, **U.K.**

Project Manager of a multidisciplinary team engaged in environmental engineering. Responsible for project appraisal, costing, design, contract specification, tender evaluation, and contract administration. Public and private sector, $0.2 million to $2.5 million value.
- ♦ Produced civil, electrical, and mechanical contract documents
- ♦ Designed and supervised a major water pipeline diversion, value $1 million
- ♦ Coordinated structural, hydraulic, and biological designs of wastewater plants
- ♦ Established contract periods and specified key contract requirements
- ♦ Rescheduled design and services work to achieve project deadlines
- ♦ Monitored contractor performance on site, produced financial evaluations, and reported progress to the client

01/87 - 09/89   **TAYLOR WOODROW**; Project Managers   Heysham Nuclear Power Plant, **U.K.**

Acting Section Engineer on one of the largest construction projects in Europe. Responsible for site supervision, operations planning and resourcing, and the design, manufacture, and implementation of site engineering systems.
- ♦ Supervised subcontractors and trained six graduate engineers on site
- ♦ Ordered materials, outlined bonus proposals, drafted progress reports
- ♦ Formulated strategic work programs from critical path analysis
- ♦ Documented information used to pursue financial claims for contract delays
- ♦ Devised tests, models, and method statements to verify construction techniques and quality assurance
- ♦ Supervised night shift operations and improved liaison between day and night shifts to achieve program completion

ADDRESS   123 Broadway Chadderton, Oldham 0699JH Lancashire, England   (061) 555-1234

186

Christine L. Scenturas

OBJECTIVE

A responsible position in marketing that requires utilization of problem solving and presentation skills, and a knowledge of foreign markets

EDUCATION
May 1993

MASTER OF INTERNATIONAL MANAGEMENT
American Graduate School of International Management
Thunderbird Campus, Glendale, Arizona
Emphasis on International Marketing
- Researched, coordinated, and presented market feasibility study for frozen yogurt in Germany
- Created a marketing plan for Virginia Kitchens entry into Canadian markets

May 1992

Autónoma Universidad de Guadalajara, Mexico
- Studied Mexican political system and country risk
- Extensive travel throughout Mexico

May 1990

BACHELOR OF SCIENCE BUSINESS ADMINISTRATION
Loyola University of Chicago, Watertower Campus, Chicago, Illinois
Marketing Specialization

January 1989

Loyola University, Rome Center, Italy
- Accepted into International Studies Program
- Extensive travel throughout Western Europe

EXPERIENCE
1992

GRADUATE ASSISTANTSHIP IN MARKETING
American Graduate School of International Management
- Coordinated logistics for visiting presenters
- Publicized upcoming presentations in campus newspaper
- Performed administrative duties

1991

ASSISTANT STORE MANAGER, Wohl Shoe Company
Carson Pirie Scott, Mount Prospect, Illinois
- Trained and supervised personnel
- Motivated staff through sales contests
- Participated in managerial training program

ADMINISTRATIVE ASSISTANT, Fasco Industries, Inc.
North American Headquarters, Lake Forest, Illinois
- Developed computerized indexing system
- Assisted in the creation of in-house tax department
- Planned full company convention

1990

SALES OFFICER, Scentura Creations
Perfume Sales, Elk Grove, Illinois
- Demonstrated success in cold call selling
- Trained sales personnel
- Led sales excursions

INTERNSHIP, August, Bishop, & Meier, Inc.
Sales Promotion Agency, Chicago, Illinois
- Assisted Account Supervisor in account service
- Participated in establishment of print media placement department

COMPUTER SKILLS
- Proficient in Spanish, knowledge of Italian
- Skilled in WordPerfect and Lotus 1-2-3
- Experience with Macintosh SE

ACTIVITIES & INTERESTS
- Active member of Hoplology Adventure Society
- Active member of International Hash House Harriers Club

Current Address: 1234 Oriole Road, Orinda, California 94563, (510) 555-1234
Permanent Address: 1234 RFD, Long Grove, Illinois 60047, (708) 555-1234

OBJECTIVE	A position as Purchasing Manager in the office supply industry either in the retail or the wholesale side.	

EXPERIENCE

PURCHASING MANAGER AND GENERAL MANAGER
V.I.P. Suppliers, Inc.
Also known as Belfair Office Supply, Inc.
Los Angeles, California
1983 - Present

Created a sales team, which was then able to acquire Twentieth Century Fox Films Corporation as one of its largest clients, thereby increasing sales. Designed and implemented warehouse layout. Purchased all merchandise for both commercial and retail purposes. Established and maintained all inventory levels and buyouts, including special orders. Established all selling prices. Responsible for all input and programming on DDMS computer system. Trained employees on DDMS system. Backed up computer system at end of day and performed end of week, month, and year procedures. In charge of all costs, markup, and selling input.

STORE MANAGER, SALES MANAGER, WAREHOUSE MANAGER, PURCHASING AGENT
Campbell-Tolstad Stationers, Inc.
Los Angeles, California
1973 - 1983

Supervised 31 employees, including hiring and firing. Opened and closed retail store and warehouse. Managed accounting department, including opening and closing of safe and files for payables and receivables. Purchased all merchandise for commercial department, and approved payables in all departments. Established and maintained all merchandise stock levels and buyouts, including special orders. Established and maintained selling prices and approved any costs for overhead, salaries, etc.

AFFILIATIONS

ADVISORY STAFF
Data Distributions Management System
1984 - 1991

One of the first persons trained on the DDMS Office Supply System, now the most widely used system in the world for office supply companies. Later served as an advisor at several National and Regional Meetings, as well as various seminars.

EDUCATION

CLASSES AND SEMINARS
Data Distributions Management System
1983 - 1991

Completed classes on Purchasing Management, Inventory Control, Shipping, Receiving, Payables, Receivables, System Analysis, and Programming.

CERTIFICATE OF COMPLETION
Harbor Occupational Center, Long Beach, California
1973

Air conditioning course.

BUSINESS MANAGEMENT MAJOR
El Camino College, Redondo Beach, California
1972

One semester. Varsity basketball.

ADDRESS   1234 W. Maxwell Avenue, Phoenix, Arizona 85033, (602) 555-1234

13 | GRAPHIC DESIGN ELEMENTS

The following resumes aren't extremely elaborate in their use of graphic design elements. They are still basically conservative resumes with just a little something added to make them stand out.

Keep in mind that the graphic should maintain the theme of the resume. You wouldn't put a world globe on a waitress's resume or drafting tools on a doctor's. In some more conservative professions (banking, accounting, upper management, etc.), graphics on a resume are not recommended, even if they are small and conservative. For those in more creative industries (i.e., arts, entertainment, advertising), please see the resumes on pages 204–214 for more ideas.

Pages 190 through 193 use graphics that reflect an international focus (as do pages 20, 50, 73, and 80), whereas the graphics on pages 194–199 and 201 reflect the person's industry.

By becoming a little more inventive, you can incorporate scanned letters or figures that reflect your personality more than the industry (see pages 200 and 202 in this section and pages 29 and 30 elsewhere).

Jessica Lee Titus

EXPERIENCE

President, Associated Students Legislative Council November 1994
American Graduate School of International Management May 1995

- Managed and supervised 25 officers
- Supervised application of a $70,000 budget
- Made presentation to Board of Directors
- Liaison to Board of Trustees
- Member of the Academic Council
- Conducted meetings on a weekly basis

Vice President, Associated Students Legislative Council August 1994
American Graduate School of International Management November 1994

- Supervised publication of campus directory
- Regulated club activities
- Allocated over $10,000 of student funds
- Organized all campus elections
- Coordinated school-sponsored activities
- Organized charity ball for Red Cross

Customer Service Counselor July 1993
BancFlorida, Sarasota, Florida January 1994

- Opened and closed accounts
- Responsible for training of new tellers
- Received and resolved customer complaints
- Controlled access to safety deposit boxes
- Balanced bank records of negotiables
- Participated in numerous training programs

Bank Teller May 1991
BancFlorida, Sarasota, Florida August 1991

- Operated cash drawer of $10,000
- Maintained positive customer relations
- Verified commercial deposits
- Balanced branch records

Bank Teller May 1990
Dauphin Deposit Bank & Trust Company, Harrisburg, Pennsylvania August 1990

- Participated in a 6-week training program
- Developed customer service skills
- Replaced vacationing employees
- Operated and balanced cash drawer

EDUCATION

Master of International Management May 1995
American Graduate School of International Management, Glendale, Arizona
Concentration: International Marketing and French

Bachelor of Arts May 1993
Eckerd College, St. Petersburg, Florida
Major: French ▪ Minor: Management
Completed comprehensive exams in major with a 4.0/4.0

LANGUAGES

Proficient in **French** and **Danish**
Knowledge of Lotus 1-2-3, WordPerfect, BASIC, dBASE III, and MS Word

OVERSEAS EXPERIENCE

Youth for Understanding Exchange Student, Borup Skole, Borup, Denmark 1987 – 1988
Eckerd College Independent Study, Paris, France January 1993

ACTIVITIES

Vice President of Women's Rugby Club, Co-Coordinator for Career Services
Fashion Show, Development and Volunteer Committees, French Club

ADDRESS

12345 Casey Key Road, Nokomis, Florida 34275 (813) 555-1234

Julie L. Starkel

EXPERIENCE

APV LATIN AMERICA   *1992 – Present*
International Food and Beverage Processing Equipment Manufacturer
Business Development/Marketing Manager, *São Paulo, Brazil*
• *Responsible for developing new business in all of South America*
• *Set up a component distribution network and optimized the agent network*
• *Created and managed advertising campaigns and trade shows*
• *Developed a continent-wide customer service program, inquiry and quotation system, and inside sales plan*
• *Organized and conducted company capabilities seminars for top multinational companies, including Nestlè and General Foods*
Market Analyst, *Chicago, Illinois*
• *Played integral role in creating Business Development Plan with Managing Director*
• *Coordinated sales into Latin America of over 30 subsidiaries in the U.S. and Europe*
• *Prepared market research reports for APV's industries throughout Latin America*

WORLD HEALTH ORGANIZATION, United Nations   *1990*
Finance Assistant, *Geneva, Switzerland*
International Task Force on Social and Behavioral Determinants of Fertility Regulation
• *Responsible for the administration and finance activities of the task force*

HONEYWELL LUCIFER, S.A.   *1989*
Assistant to Europe and Asia Sales Manager, *Geneva, Switzerland*
• *Exported valves and analyzed sales statistics for the entire plant*
• *Prepared export sales and marketing reports*

CREDIT SUISSE BANQUE, S.A.   *1987 – 1988*
Geneva Stock Exchange Broker, *Geneva, Switzerland*
• *Cofounded the International Institutional Service*
• *Dealt Swiss securities for large international institutional companies*
Logistics and Planning Management Trainee, *Lausanne, Switzerland*
• *Created and tested programs using various methods to forecast five-year projections of several of the bank's products*

E. F. HUTTON, INC. (now Smith Barney Shearson)   *1985 – 1986*
Sales Assistant, *Ann Arbor, Michigan*
• *Aided brokers dealing on the American exchanges*
Traders Assistant Intern, *Paris, France (Summer 1985)*
• *Assisted a top currency trader on the world's exchanges for E. F. Hutton, France*

EDUCATION

THUNDERBIRD, *Glendale, Arizona*   *Dec. 1991*
AMERICAN GRADUATE SCHOOL OF INTERNATIONAL MANAGEMENT
Master of International Management
• *Concentration in international trade and marketing*

THE UNIVERSITY OF MICHIGAN, *Ann Arbor, Michigan*   *1987*
Bachelor of Arts in International Commerce
• *Emphasis on international politics, economics, and languages*

ACTIVITIES

INTERNATIONAL CAREER OPPORTUNITIES – FRANCOPHONE   *1991*
Chairperson – *Student group interested in pursuing careers in French-speaking countries*

AIESEC (*The International Association of Students in Economics and Management*)   *1984 – 1987*
President (*1986*), **Reception Director** (*1985*)

LANGUAGES & SKILLS

French – *highly proficient (France, Switzerland)* • **Spanish** – *proficient (Spain, Guatemala)*
Portuguese – *proficient (Brazil)* • **Computer** – *Spreadsheet, graphics, and word processing programs*

---

*Brazil Tel/Fax: +55-11-555-1234 • USA Tel: (810) 555-1234 • USA Fax: (810) 555-1234
USA Mailing Address: 1234 W. Fordham, Bloomfield Hills, Michigan 48302*

Fernando F. Barbosa

1234 Boulevard East, Apt. 123, Weehawken, New Jersey 07087   *(201) 555-1234*

QUALIFICATIONS
- Masters degree in International Management with a focus in Marketing and Strategic Planning
- Experience in consumer brand management, advertising, sports marketing, and finance
- Extensive knowledge of Latin American markets
- Multilingual—Fluent in **Spanish, Portuguese,** and **English**; proficient in **French**
- Strong analytical ability

EXPERIENCE

GOLDMAN, SACHS & CO., New York, New York   *1994 – Present*
Associate, Latin American Equity Group
- Managed instruction, settlement, and reconciliation of Latin American equities
- Interact with traders, sales reps, clients, and managers in all areas of equities trading, including prime brokerage, arbitrage, and derivatives trading
- Develop procedures and system enhancements for reducing failed transactions
- Plan and develop information flow to assist risk arbitrage desk
- Liaison between the Latin American Equity Group and custodian banks
- Contribute strategic, financial, risk management, and operational solutions to the opening of a regional office in Mexico
- Led the investigation and resolution of failing transactions
- Monitor agency and proprietary accounts

CURTIS MANAGEMENT GROUP, Indianapolis, Indiana   *1993*
Account Executive—Latin America (Sports & Entertainment Industry)
- Coordinated international marketing campaign and maintain close contact with clients
- Investigated markets for product expansion and managed promotional/marketing efforts of licensing

PHILIP MORRIS INTERNATIONAL, KRAFT GENERAL FOODS, Mexico City, D.F.   *1993*
Assistant Brand Manager
- Researched the possibility of brand cannibalization among Kraft powdered soft drinks
- Orchestrated the development and improvement of the Kraft brand image in Mexico through a million dollar ad campaign entitled "Stars in the Kraft Kitchen"
- Developed a profit per square meter analysis on the three largest supermarket chains in Mexico City for KGF major brands
- Forecasted sales quotas for all regional divisions
- Developed a brand development index and created a sales history presentation for KGF powdered soft drinks (Kool-Aid, Tang, Frisco)

IASA, Houston, Texas & Veracruz, Mexico   *1991 – 1992*
U.S. Marketing Representative
- Contacted and established long-term relations with U.S. industrial manufacturers
- Developed and implemented U.S. marketing strategies

MONTAUK YACHT CLUB, The Hamptons, Long Island, New York   *Summers 1989 – 1992*
Co-Director of Tennis
- Organized and coordinated camps, clinics, and celebrity exhibitions

EDUCATION

MASTER OF INTERNATIONAL MANAGEMENT   GPA 3.80/4.0   *May 1994*
American Graduate School of International Management   with honors
Thunderbird Campus, Glendale, Arizona
- Conducted extensive marketing research and created advertising program for Pepsico's introduction of Mirinda soft drinks in the Phoenix area
- **International Consumer Marketing Seminar; Marketing for U.S. Hispanics Seminar**

BACHELOR OF BUSINESS ADMINISTRATION   GPA 3.81/4.0   *July 1992*
Southern Arkansas University, Magnolia, Arkansas   magna cum laude
Major: Business Administration (Outstanding Business Student Award)   Minor: French

ACTIVITIES   Academic All-American (Tennis), 1991–1992 • Member of the SAU Tennis Team, 1988–1992 • Captain of the soccer team at SAU for four straight years, 1989–1992 • Competitive triathlete • Active member of the AGSIM Latin America, Marketing, Triathlon, Tennis, and Soccer Teams • Vice President of Finance of Phi Beta Lambda, 1991 • Treasurer of the International Student Association, 1991

EVERETT C. ATHERTON JR.

EDUCATION

Thunderbird, American Graduate School of International Management
   Master of International Management   *May 1994*
      Emphasis on Mandarin Chinese, Asian Studies, International Marketing and Trade

Stanford University
      Intensive Modern Chinese language program   *Summer 1993*

Menlo College, *Atherton, California*
   Bachelor of Arts   *1992*
      Major: Philosophy • Minor: Business Administration
      Honors: Dean's List (five semesters) • Most Outstanding Humanities Major, 1992

INTERNATIONAL STUDY PROGRAMS

Southeast Asia Today   *Winter 1992*
Selected to represent Menlo College in a student delegation to Hong Kong, Malaysia, Thailand, Singapore, and China. Formally conferred with leaders in both public and private sectors. Analyzed foreign and economic policies to assess the relative significance of uncertainty in the region and evaluate both market and resource opportunities of multinational endeavors in the East.

Semester in Paris   *Spring 1988*
Resided in Paris as a full-time student, studying French language, the humanities, and contemporary politics. Took advantage of the intellectually stimulating environment through extracurricular pursuits and immersion in Parisian culture.

WORK EXPERIENCE

Malke-Sage Galleries – *Installation Manager*   *1988 – 1991*
Head of corporate sales installation department for a prominent San Francisco bay area firm specializing in fine art and limited edition work. Approximately $1.8 million in annual sales with five locations on the peninsula. Successfully devised and implemented program to handle record level of corporate sales. Personally responsible for coordination of $60,000 in installations and general client satisfaction.

et sequens

Language:	*Proficient in Mandarin Chinese and French*
Computer Skills:	*MS Word, WordPerfect, Lotus 1-2-3, Excel, dBASE IV, and BASIC*
Eastern Thought:	*Authored thesis investigating the relationship between Lao Tzu's Tao Te Ching and the Western philosophical problem of freewill versus determinism*
Martial Arts:	*Five years of Tae Kwon Do study; rewarded both in rank and competition*
Travel:	*Extensive international travel, particularly in Europe and Asia*

Present Address • P.O. Box 1234 • Glendale, Arizona 85306 • (602) 555-1234
Permanent Address • 123 Albino Way • Woodside, California 94062 • (415) 555-1234

KARALIE K. DRAFTING

12345 North 54th Drive, Glendale, Arizona 85306
Phone: (602) 555-1234

OBJECTIVE	A career in Architectural Drafting/Space Planning/Store Planning/Interior Design where design talent can be used
QUALIFICATIONS	• Four years of design/drafting/space planning experience • Residential designing and planning • AUTO CADD and VERSA CADD experience as well as manual • Two Associate Degrees: Design and Drafting Engineering Technology and Architectural Drafting Technology

EXPERIENCE

FREELANCE DESIGNER   1991 – Present
St. Louis, Missouri and Phoenix, Arizona
• Designed and drafted floor plans and elevations for residential additions

STORE PLANNER/FIXTURE DESIGNER   1989 – 1991
The NU-ERA Group, St. Louis, Missouri
• Designed an athletic shoe display rack for KEDS
• Responsible for the design of metal and wood fixtures for Dillards, Target, Edison Brothers, Venture, and specialty shops
• Planned and designed stores including children's, men's, and women's retail stores, pro shops, and various showrooms
• Provided concept sketches, renderings, construction drawings, and assembly instructions
• Presented oral and visual recommendations to clients, advised clients on their needs, and created solutions to planning problems
• Office space planning and designing

ARCHITECTURAL DRAFTSPERSON   1987 – 1988
Stevenson & Turner Asia, Taipei, Taiwan
• Acted as the space planner for a regional hospital
• Operated AUTO CADD drawing site plans, elevations, and plan views

ARCHITECTURAL DRAFTSPERSON   1986 – 1987
Price Development Company, Salt Lake City, Utah
• Layout and design of regional malls and strip centers in six states
• Coordinated the remodeling design and space planning of commercial tenant and executive office spaces
• Presented rendering illustrations and designs in general conferences with Project Managers and Directors
• Created site plans and checked legal descriptions on the VERSA CADD systems

EDUCATION

ASSOCIATE DEGREE IN ARCHITECTURAL DRAFTING TECHNOLOGY   1986
AND DESIGN AND DRAFTING ENGINEERING TECHNOLOGY
Ricks College, Rexburg, Idaho

COMPUTERS

Proficient in the use of AUTO CADD and VERSA CADD

194

JOHN ERIC FIREMAN

1234 W. Cactus, Phoenix, Arizona 85029

Home: (602) 555-1234
Work: (602) 555-4321

OBJECTIVE	A professional firefighter position	
EDUCATION	**ASSOCIATE OF ARTS DEGREE, General Studies**	Fall 1994
	Glendale Community College, Glendale, Arizona	1990 – 1994
	Honors Program	1993 – 1994
	Relevant Course Work:	
	• Basic EMT	
	• EMT Refresher Course	
	• Introduction to Fire Suppression	
	• Introduction to Spanish	
	• Reading, Communication, Critical Thinking	
	(40 credits of general studies)	
	Arizona State University, Tempe, Arizona	1985 – 1994
	• 54 credits completed toward engineering degree	

CERTIFICATES & HONORS	**FIREFIGHTER I & II**, Arizona State Certification	1994
	HAZARDOUS MATERIALS AWARENESS	1993
	EMERGENCY MEDICAL TECHNICIAN (EMT)	1991
	CPR CERTIFIED, Arizona Heart Association	1989 – Present
	ARIZONA CHAUFFEUR'S LICENSE #123456789	1989 – Present

EMPLOYMENT HISTORY	**FIREFIGHTER RESERVE**	
	Surprise Fire Department, Surprise, Arizona	Sep. 1992 – Present
	Tolleson Fire Department, Tolleson, Arizona	May 1992 – Sep. 1992
	RECRUIT FIREFIGHTER	
	Tolleson Fire Academy, Tolleson, Arizona	Sep. 1991 – May 1992
	PRODUCTION MANAGER	
	Sun City Sun Control, Peoria, Arizona	1986 – Present
	• Fabricate sun screens	
	• Construct awnings and patio enclosures	
	ASSISTANT STORE MANAGER	
	Bill's Sight & Sound, Phoenix, Arizona	1985 – 1986
	• Sales of audio and video equipment	

PERSONAL	Social Security Number: 555-12-3456
	Date of Birth: June 29, 1966
	Marital Status: Single

INTERESTS	Favorite Sports: Body building, volleyball, bicycling
	Hobbies Include: Restoring furniture and automobiles, and
	interior design

195

Donny W. Medtech

1234 N. 37th Avenue #123 • Glendale, Arizona 85301 • (602) 555-1234

QUALIFICATIONS
- 10 years as a Medical Technician
- Experienced in Medical, Surgical, Family Practice, Dermatology, Allergy, and Emergency Room Medicine
- CPR Certified and EMT-Basic Licensed

EXPERIENCE

MEDICAL SERVICE SPECIALIST, U.S. Air Force   1981 – Present
- Assisted professional medical personnel in planning, providing, and evaluating patient care, including inpatient, outpatient, emergency services, and disaster preparedness
- Served as ambulance driver and emergency medical technician
- Performed aeromedical evacuation duties

PATIENT CARE
- Triage, vital signs, venipuncture for IVs, controlling hemorrhage, resuscitation, emergency management of burns and shock
- Dressing changes, casting, splinting
- Assisted in minor surgery (suturing, anesthetics)
- Administered oxygen and respiratory treatments
- Eye and ear irrigation, Foley catheterization, enemas
- Trained to assist physicians with chest tube insertion, paracentesis/thoracentesis, lumbar puncture, external and internal cardiac pacemakers, cricotracheotomy, central line or subclavian IV line insertion

TESTING
- Drew blood, performed urine strains, computerized PT counts
- Performed tympanograms, pulmonary function studies, and throat cultures
- Immunizations and testing for social diseases
- Allergy testing and injections
- Accomplished well-baby checks (vitals, weight, head circumference, length)

EQUIPMENT
- EKG, code cart, defibrillator, vitals monitoring, intubation and airway equipment
- Cleaned instruments, sterile setup, infection control
- Prepared minor surgery packs and PAP packs

MANAGEMENT
- Scheduled appointments and received patients at reception desk
- Supervised more than six workers at any given time
- Obtained, stored, and disposed of supplies and linens
- Maintained medical records, observing and reporting observations in patient progress notes and team conferences

EDUCATION

ASSOCIATE DEGREE IN ALLIED HEALTH SCIENCES   in process
Community College of the Air Force   38 credits
Rio Salado Community College, Phoenix, Arizona
Southwest Virginia Community College, Richlands, Virginia
Ferrum College, Virginia

TRAINING

Medical Service Specialist, Sheppard AFB, Texas (240 hours)   1982
Pharmacology Course, Luke AFB, Arizona (20 hours)   1982
I.V. Therapy Course, Luke AFB, Arizona (20 hours)   1983
Noncommissioned Officers Preparatory Course (191 hours)   1985
Noncommissioned Officers Leadership School (in residence)   1990

Joe Golfer

12345 N. 91st Avenue
Peoria, Arizona 85345
(602) 555-1234

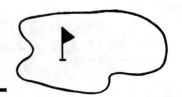

**SUMMARY OF
QUALIFICATIONS**

Diverse and accomplished individual offering an established track record in all aspects of a PGA golf professional. Expertise includes all facets of management, wholesale/retail, golf lessons, club design and repair, cart maintenance, tournament operation, and public relations. Excellent liaison and troubleshooting skills.

**EMPLOYMENT
OVERVIEW**

ESTRELLA GOLF CLUB
Goodyear, Arizona

Assistant Golf Pro   12/84 – 8/91
High-visibility position involving operations of assisting golf director, shipping, receiving inventory control, merchandising, golf club repair, tournament operations, starter, tee times/reservation, cashier responsibilities/deposits.

WHISPERING PALMS COUNTRY CLUB
Rancho Sante Fe, California

Golf Instructor   4/84 – 6/84
Position requiring strong leadership to individuals seeking beginning, intermediate, and advanced training, also golf club repair.

DIXON LAKE PARK
Escondido, California

Ranger Aide   6/83 – 6/84
Maintained direct involvement in enforcing park policies, general maintenance, reservations, and collecting monies.

DUNHAM HILLS GOLF CLUB
Milford, Michigan

Greenskeeper   3/82 – 10/82
Duties included inspection of equipment, repairs, turf grass grooming, and maintenance.

EDUCATION

PGA BUSINESS SCHOOL II   10/88
Phoenix, Arizona

PGA BUSINESS SCHOOL I   11/85
Phoenix, Arizona

SAN DIEGO GOLF ACADEMY   2/83 – 11/84
Rancho Santa Fe, California

**SPECIALIZED
ACCOMPLISHMENTS**

PLAYERS ABILITY TEST (PAT)   5/86
Arrowhead Ranch Golf Course

197

D. L. Journeyman
Painter

EXPERIENCE

PAINTING
- Journeyman with 15 years of experience
- Experienced in all phases of painting from preparation of surfaces to spray/brush/roll
- Drywall repairs, texturing, taping, popcorn finish
- Furniture and wood finishing/refinishing
- Repainting of all types
- Industrial and commercial jobs
- New construction, custom and tract homes
- Government contract work
- Insurance painting – water and smoke damage repair
- Experienced with all types of interior and exterior paint – latex, oil, varnish, lacquer, stains, synthetics, primers, epoxy, Elastimeric coatings, etc.

EQUIPMENT
- Scaffolding, man lifts, scissor lifts, ladders
- Airless sprayers with extension wands and all other associated equipment
- Air compressors
- Texturizing guns
- Electrostatic machines
- All hand tools and sanders used for painting and wood finishing

MANAGEMENT
- Foreman – directed seven workers for government contracts; four workers for 70-home subdivision tract project
- Experienced in all aspects of company ownership, including job bidding and planning, personnel management, marketing, public relations, budgeting, and bookkeeping

WORK HISTORY

1994	Master Group Project Management
1985 – 1994	Self-Employed, D. L. Journeyman Painting, Visalia, CA, and Phoenix, AZ

- McDonald Construction, General Contractors
- Fistelaro Construction, General Contractors
- Ghaster Painting, Inc.
- John Doe, Realtor
- Jane Doe, Realtor
- Grand Painting

1984 – 1985	Atkins Construction, Visalia, CA
1983 – 1984	Shy, Inc., Builder, Visalia, CA
1982 – 1983	Parker Painting Contractors, Visalia, CA
1980 – 1981	Roache Painting Contractors, Visalia, CA
1978 – 1979	Price Painting Contractors, Visalia, CA
1977	Visalia Unified School District, Visalia, CA
1976	Furniture Stripping Shop, Van Nuys, CA

1234 Port Lane • Indianapolis, Indiana 46517 • (219) 555-1234

KEVIN W. CIRCUIT
1234 Academy Drive
Colorado Springs, CO 80910
(719) 555-1234

Objective

To obtain a full-time position as a Printed Circuit Board Designer.

Experience

- Three years experience in the layout of single-layer, double-layer, multi-layer, thru-hole, surface-mount, analog, and digital printed circuit boards.

- Thorough knowledge of **P-CAD Master Designer Ver. 4.5 and 5.0** design process, including schematic capture, packaging placement, routing, fabrication drawings, and photoplot output. Specialties are high-speed, padded traces and dense, SMT, prototype boards.

- Extensive knowledge of schematics, schematic symbols, and electronic components. Have previously created a complete, P-CAD compatible, custom part library with matching padstacks and special symbol file.

- Experience in Mechanical Design and Drafting using **Autocad Rel. 10**.

Employment History

PCB DESIGN, MECHANICAL DRAWING   11/89 – Present
Digital Computer Corp., 1234 Union Drive, Colorado Springs, Colorado 80906
Supervisor: John Doe   (719) 555-1234

PCB DESIGN   9/88 – 11/89
HP Research Inc., 1234 Academy Boulevard, Colorado Springs, Colorado 80906
Supervisor: Bob Doe   (719) 555-1234

Education

OCCUPATIONAL ASSOCIATES DEGREE IN DRAFTING TECHNOLOGY   6/86 – 1/88
National Education Center, A.A.I. Drafting Division, 1234 North 46th Avenue, Glendale, Arizona 85301

Electro-Mechanical Drafting and Design. Subjects included: Emphasized Printed Circuit Board Package Design, both analog and digital, Sheet Metal Packaging and Detail conforming to ANSI Y14.5M and DOD 100 standards, and Computer Aided Drafting.

 **argie N. Manager**

1234 E. Redfield Road
Scottsdale, Arizona 85254
(602) 555-1234

CAREER OBJECTIVE

A challenging supervisory position with potential growth.

PROFESSIONAL EXPERIENCE

Jan. 1967 – Present　　**SEARS ROEBUCK AND COMPANY**

Acting Manager
- Protected and reduced losses
- Evaluated, conducted, reviewed, and prepared reviews of 20 associates

Collections Supervisor
- Determined and controlled daily production
- Trained and motivated 20 associates
- Conducted, administered, and supervised all policy and system changes
- Analyzed, negotiated, and resolved problem accounts

Special Accounts Correspondent
- Worked seriously delinquent accounts
- Coordinated legal and bankruptcy accounts
- Operated computers, credit bureau, 10 key

Assistant Customer Convenience Manager
- Received manager complaints
- Supervised cashier and daily receipts (15 employees)
- Determined and controlled daily production

Installation Manager
- Coordinated installation jobs
- Calculated and supervised installation pricing
- Hired and terminated subcontractors (30 employees)

Home Improvement
- Implemented systems for purchasing and stocking

Assistant Manager
- Prepared sales reports
- Provided customer service to clients in store and via telephone
- Received manager complaints and found solutions to the problems

Collections Manager
- Protected and reduced losses
- Coordinated office services
- Coached and developed each associate to his or her highest potential
- Reviewed 25 credit associates

Adjustment Supervisor
- Solved large volume of special problems
- Trained employees and provided consultations
- Utilized bookkeeping skills

EDUCATION

Scottsdale Community College, Computer and English Courses
Management Seminars

LORI MANSON

1234 South Overview Drive, San Ramon, California 94583, Phone (510) 555-1234

OBJECTIVE   *A challenging teaching career utilizing my motivation, creativity, and desire to educate*

EXPERIENCE

TEACHER/CENTER SUPERVISOR   *Oct. 1991 – Present*
Turtle Mountain Head Start, *Belcourt, North Dakota*
- *Manage six center employees and evaluate job performance through biannual reviews*
- *Complete comprehensive monthly reports to reflect inventory control, accounts payable/receivable, and adherence to federal health and safety regulations*
- *Design learning environment to meet educational development objectives*
- *Educate handicapped and nonhandicapped students in both individual and group sessions according to their needs*
- *Document assessment findings and review with central staff and parents*
- *Assist coordinator for handicapped children with preparation of individual education plans (IEPs) in accordance with PL94-142*
- *Participate in Comprehensive Developmental Team (CDT) staffing meetings to review IEPs*
- *Screen, assess, and record observations and evaluations of child development, including referrals for cognitive, language, fine/gross motor, vision, health, and social development*
- *Responsible for classroom schedule, subject matter, selection of materials and media, development of learning activities, and documentation of plans*

DAY CARE FACILITATOR   *May – Oct. 1991*
Tykes Daycare, *Belcourt, North Dakota*
- *Provided day care services to children ages infant to eight years*
- *Processed customer invoices and calculated payment schedules*

CROP INSURANCE CLERK   *Jan. 1987 – June 1988*
Agricultural Stabilization and Conservation Service (USDA-ASCS), *Rolla, North Dakota*
- *Assessed and processed client insurance claims*
- *Distributed crop insurance payments to ASCS members*
- *Monitored damage claims and revised records to reflect adjustments*

EDUCATION

BACHELOR OF SCIENCE   *GPA in major 3.47*   *May 1994*
University of North Dakota, *Grand Forks*
Major: Elementary Education with emphasis in Science/Bilingual Education

ASSOCIATE OF SCIENCE, cum laude   *GPA 4.0*   *May 1991*
Turtle Mountain Community College, *Belcourt, North Dakota*
Major: Early Childhood

HONORS
- *Bureau of Indian Affairs Scholarship*   *1990 – 1994*
- *North Dakota Indian Affairs Commission Scholarship*   *1991 – 1994*
- *Who's Who in Junior and Community Colleges*   *1990 – 1991*
- *President's List and Dean's List (UND and TMCC)*   *1989 – 1994*

ACTIVITIES
- *American Indian Higher Education Consortium (AIHEC) Member*   *1989 – 1991*
- *North Dakota Association for the Education of Young Children (NDAEYC)* *1991 – 1994*
- *University of North Dakota Indian Association*   *1991 – 1994*
- *Head Start Council Member*   *1991 – 1994*

LANGUAGES   *Knowledge of **Michif** • Communication skills in **Spanish***

COMPUTERS   *Microsoft Works, Microsoft Windows, WordPerfect, Lotus 1-2-3*

SARI BOSTON

Current Address:
1234 W. Greenway Road #123
Glendale, Arizona 85306
(602) 555-1234

Permanent Address:
1234 E. Vista Avenue
Scottsdale, Arizona 85250
(602) 555-1234

EDUCATION

MASTER OF INTERNATIONAL MANAGEMENT (MIM) 01/94 – 05/95
American Graduate School of International Management
Thunderbird Campus, Glendale, Arizona
- Concentration: International Finance and the European Continent
- Summer Semester at the Institut de Gestion Sociale, Paris, France

BACHELOR OF ARTS IN ART HISTORY 08/86 – 05/90
Brandeis University, Waltham, Massachusetts
- Concentration: Twentieth Century American Painters
- *cum laude*

INSTITUTE FOR EUROPEAN STUDIES 01/89 – 05/89
Madrid, Spain
- Concentration: Spanish history, politics and culture

EXPERIENCE

SOCIAL SERVICE AGENT AND DIRECT CAREGIVER 06/90 – 12/94
Mirim Associates, Chicopee, Massachusetts
- Received training in crisis management
- Served as a liaison between clients and physicians
- Responsible for all aspects of welfare and care of mentally and physically impaired elderly persons, including psychological observation and behavior modification

EXHIBITION COORDINATOR 09/89 – 05/90
Rose Art Museum, Waltham, Massachusetts
- Planned and installed fine art exhibitions for a nonprofit facility
- Responsible for inventory control, preservation of art objects, and catalogue research

CURATORIAL INTERN 09/88 – 12/88
Rose Art Museum, Waltham, Massachusetts
- Aided in curating a photography exhibit
- Responsible for research, writing, and compilation of exhibition catalogues

TELEMARKETER 05/89 – 08/89
American Renewal Service, Phoenix, Arizona
- Learned personal selling and developed customer service skills

GALLERY ASSISTANT / INTERN 05/88 – 08/88
Mills Gallery at Boston Center for the Arts, Boston, Massachusetts
- Interviewed artists for future exhibitions
- Responsible for planning, budgeting, publicity, and promotion of art exhibitions

LANGUAGES

Spanish: highly proficient
French: working knowledge

IBM Computers: Lotus 1-2-3, WordPerfect, dBASE III
Macintosh: Microsoft Word, Quicken

14 CREATIVE RESUMES

How fun to be in an industry where almost anything goes! The arts and advertising fields are like that.

Whether or not you choose to use graphics or a special designer paper for a resume is determined to a large extent by the type of industry that is being targeted. For instance, an accountant or a banker would want a more conservative resume on a conservative color of paper. On the other hand, a graphic artist or an advertising executive could make a real statement with an artsy resume or a designer paper. However, it takes a very special type of person to use these resumes. They aren't for everyone.

No matter how creative you want to be, you must still keep readability in mind. The only exception might be a resume designed for the arts, since creativity is as important as experience. But . . . your audience must still be able to read your resume or you won't get that all-important interview.

Here I most gratefully acknowledge the work of Gregg Berryman[1]. I have in my library a copy of his book, *Designing Creative Resumes*, and the clients on pages 210, 211, and 214 chose their styles from his examples. It is a great resource for creative resume ideas and, although it is out of print at this writing, it can be found in many city libraries.

---

[1]Gregg Berryman, *Designing Creative Resumes* (Menlo Park, CA: Crisp Publications, Inc., 1985).

Mason Michael Brooklyn

Languages

Native in English
Highly proficient in German
Working knowledge of Spanish
Computers: Apple, IBM, Wang

Activities & Awards

- Phi Sigma Kappa, 4 years
  Offices: Pres., Secr., Social
  Terrill Graduate Fellowship
  1991 Brother of the Year
- 1991 WMU Homecoming Co-Chair
- Advertising Club, Secr./Treas.
- Advertising Explorer Outpost
  Leader

Education

December 1994, with honors
Master of International Management
American Graduate School of International Management,
Glendale, Arizona
- Includes semester at the European Business School, Schloss Reichhartshausen, Germany (conducted in German)

April 1993, magna cum laude
Bachelor of Business Administration
Western Michigan University, Kalamazoo, Michigan
- Major: Advertising
- Minor: German, General Business
- 1993 Michigan Association of Governing Boards of State Colleges and Universities Outstanding Student
- 1993 WMU, AMA Chapter, and Detroit Ad Club Outstanding Student
- Board of Trustees Scholarship

Experience

6/94 – 8/94
adidas, AG
Marketing Racketsport Germany
Herzogenaurach, Germany
Marketing Associate (Intern)
- collected, analyzed, and disseminated information to the German sales force concerning rollout of the 1994 Racketsport collections
- translated and proofread promotional and company material including the 1994 textile catalog

8/91 – 4/92
William R. Biggs/Gilmore Assoc.
Advertising Associate (Intern)
- supervised company promotional material through all phases of development
- coordinated the redevelopment of the traffic function
- placed print media

1/91 – 4/92
University Theatre, WMU
Assistant to the Publicist
- supervised "front of house," i.e., ticket audits and sales receipts
- trained and managed usher corps
- coordinated maintenance of master mailing list
- created and developed promotional materials

1/92 – 4/92
Department of Fine Arts, WMU
Student Coordinator
Michigan Youth Arts Festival
- promoted MYAF working with various university, local, and state media
- assembled and managed student staff (two previous years on student staff)

4/91 – 12/91
WMU, Dept. of Student Services
Orientation Leader
- oriented the WMU freshman class using a working knowledge of all areas of the university
- organized, wrote, and directed skit as a part of the program
- conducted follow-up interviews to monitor progress and advice

12 Doug Street #123, Brooklyn, New York 11231, (718) 555-1234

RCH

Robert C. Hollywood
2nd Assistant Cameraman
1234 North 50th Place
Phoenix, Arizona 85014
(602) 555-1234

EMPLOYMENT HISTORY

1990 - Present	*Free-Lance Camera Assistant* *Cinematography Camera Assistant*	*Hollywood, CA*

1990 - June 1991   Sunrise Sets, *Scenery Designer*   *N. Hollywood, CA*

1988 - 1990   Clairmont Camera, Inc.   *Studio City, CA*
Operations
- Personally assisted production companies on nationwide and international film projects
- Position required complete knowledge of all equipment on premise, which included: Arriflex • Fries • Stedicam • Norris • MovieCam • Mitchell • Zeiss • Cooke • Angenieux
- Prepared over 1,000 commercial packages and 150 feature film units
- Inspected and evaluated all equipment on a continual basis
- Shipping and receiving

1987 - 1988   Setefex, Inc.   *Hollywood, CA*
Shop Foreman
- Promoted to supervise building crews for commercial and theatrical scenery company
- Responsible for hiring, training, and directing an average crew of 25 carpenters, painters, welders, and drivers
- Estimated costs and prepared bids on potential projects
- Acquired and completed over 100 sets and special effects for film, television, and theater
- Established a 38% profit margin, which exceeded all previous years

1984 - 1987   KNAZ-TV   *Flagstaff, AZ*
Production Department/News/Commercial
- Technical Director News 2Night Productions
- News and Sports Photographer
- Package Editor
- Master Control Operator

EDUCATION

1982 - 1986   Northern Arizona University   *Flagstaff, AZ*
Degree: B.S. of Telecommunications
- Film/T.V. emphasized

BETH L. IRVING

123 W. Irving Park Rd. #1234
Chicago, Illinois 60613
Home (312) 555-1234

Office (708) 555-1234
Fax (708) 555-1234

SKILLS	Proficiency in Spanish and Japanese
	Strong public speaking and written communication
	IBM – WordPerfect and Lotus 1-2-3
	Macintosh – Microsoft Word and Excel
	Pagemaker, Harvard Graphics, AlphaFour

EXPERIENCE

Baxter Convertors
Custom Sterile
Sr. Market Analyst – Int'l
May 1993 – Present

- Continued previous responsibilities
- Added responsibility for supporting growth in Latin America
- Assisted Mexican management with key customer targeting, product offering, evaluation of pricing strategies, and sales focus

Baxter Convertors
Custom Sterile
Market Analyst – Int'l
May 1992 – May 1993

- Facilitated information flow between domestic functional departments and international personnel
- Trained international sales personnel and conducted customer tours
- Assisted country managers with new product design and production
- Managed implementation of multilingual packaging

M&M/Mars, Incorporated
Int'l Sales Internship
Fall 1990

- Prepared cost and feasibility reports for international packaging changes in Canada, Latin America, and Asia
- Coordinated orders and shipments for overseas subsidiaries
- Supported regional directors in development of international marketing programs utilizing displays, sweepstakes, and premiums
- Prepared report on new product introductions and line extension activity for Asian Market Manager

Thunderbird Corporate
Consulting
Summer 1990

- Developed feasibility study on business seminar industry in Japan
- Conducted primary research through phone interviews with Japanese businessmen
- Presented marketing plan for a direct mail program to client

Associated Students
Legislative Council
Vice President
Spring/Summer 1990

- Elected by student body to this salaried position
- Worked closely with administrators to enhance student life
- Chaired: Graduation Committee, Thunderball Charity Formal Committee, Program Board, Election Committee
- Held budgetary responsibility to allocate funds for campus activities

EDUCATION

Master of International
Management
May, 1991

American Graduate School of International Management
Thunderbird Campus, Glendale, Arizona
- Emphasis in Marketing and Asian Studies

Bachelor of Business
Administration
May, 1989

Southern Methodist University
Dallas, Texas
- Major in Marketing

ACTIVITIES AND
INTERESTS

- Toastmasters International – President, Thunderbird Chapter
- Marketing Club – President
- Japan Club – Member
- Delta Sigma Pi – Professional Business Fraternity
- Speakers Committee
- AFS exchange student – Norway
- *Das Tor* Columnist (campus newspaper)

Stephanie Selig

PROFILE
- Master of International Management
- Three years of working experience in management and sales
- Proven leadership and organizational abilities
- Strong cross-cultural communication skills

EXPERIENCE

INTERNATIONAL TRADE SPECIALIST June 1993 – Present
World Trade Center, Phoenix, Arizona
- Promoted and expanded world trade by facilitating import/export activities
- Provided international market research and trade information to both local and worldwide companies
- Team player in coordinating an international business symposium consisting of 400 to 500 business leaders

SALES REPRESENTATIVE 1990 – 1991
Selig Chemical, a division of National Service Industries, Ft. Myers, Florida
- Sold industrial chemicals to several different markets
- Maintained and developed accounts
- Reestablished southwest Florida territory and exceeded sales forecasts
- Consistent high achiever for sales of new accounts
- Made effective sales presentations involving technical product details to many levels of decision makers
- Thoroughly familiar with techniques for generating new business in industrial and commercial markets

MANAGER 1988 – 1990
Door Store of Florida, Ft. Myers, Florida
- Top sales manager for 1989
- Analyzed market and coordinated relocation of store resulting in a steady increase in sales of 20% per month
- Computerized operations of the store
- Responsible for hiring, training, and supervision of employees
- Managed inventory control, shipping, receiving, and deliveries
- Prepared accounts receivable, banking transactions, daily accounting, and payroll

EDUCATION

MASTER OF INTERNATIONAL MANAGEMENT May 1993
American Graduate School of International Management
Thunderbird Campus, Glendale, Arizona
- Relevant Course Work: Import/Export Management, International Marketing Management, International Finance & Trade, Countertrade
- Provided Funds for Education: Teaching Assistant, Thunderbird World Business Department; Campus Pub Bartender

BACHELOR OF ARTS 1988
St. Mary's College, Winona, Minnesota
- Business administration with concentration in marketing

EUROPEAN STUDIES Jan. – June 1987
West London Institute of Higher Education, London, England

ACTIVITIES
- Personnel Advisory Committee – one of two students appointed
  - Participated on committee charged with recommending finalist candidates for faculty appointment at St. Mary's College
  - Evaluated resumes and conducted interviews of prospective candidates
- Thunderbird Campus Ambassadors

ADDRESS 1234 West Greenway Road #123, Glendale, Arizona 85306 (602) 555-1234

207

Christine Lynn Watertower

OBJECTIVE	A responsible position within the marketing/consulting industry that requires utilization of research, problem solving and presentation skills, and a knowledge of foreign markets

EDUCATION
May 1995

MASTER OF INTERNATIONAL MANAGEMENT
American Graduate School of International Management
Thunderbird Campus, Glendale, Arizona
Emphasis on International Marketing
- Researched, coordinated, and presented marketing feasibility study for frozen yogurt in Germany
- Created a marketing plan for Virginia Kitchens entry into Canadian markets

May 1994

Autónoma Universidad de Guadalajara, Mexico
- Studied Mexican political system and country risk
- Extensive travel throughout Mexico

May 1992

BACHELOR OF SCIENCE BUSINESS ADMINISTRATION
Loyola University of Chicago Watertower Campus, Chicago, Illinois
Marketing Specialization

January 1991

Loyola University, Rome Center, Italy
- Accepted into International Studies Program
- Extensive travel throughout Western Europe

EXPERIENCE
1994

GRADUATE ASSISTANTSHIP IN MARKETING
American Graduate School of International Management
- Coordinated logistics for visiting presenters
- Publicized upcoming presentations in campus newspaper
- Performed administrative duties

1993

ASSISTANT STORE MANAGER, Wohl Shoe Company
Carson Pirie Scott, Mount Prospect, Illinois
- Trained and supervised personnel
- Motivated staff through sales contests
- Participated in managerial training program

ADMINISTRATIVE ASSISTANT, Fasco Industries, Inc.
North American Headquarters, Lake Forest, Illinois
- Developed computerized indexing system
- Assisted in the creation of in-house tax department
- Planned full company convention

1992

SALES OFFICER, Scentura Creations
Perfume Sales, Elk Grove, Illinois
- Demonstrated success in cold call selling
- Trained sales personnel

INTERNSHIP, August, Bishop, & Meier, Inc.
Sales Promotion Agency, Chicago, Illinois
- Assisted Account Supervisor in account service
- Participated in establishment of print media placement department

LANGUAGE & COMPUTER SKILLS
- Proficient in Spanish, knowledge of Italian
- Skilled in WordPerfect 5.1 and Lotus 1-2-3
- Experience with Macintosh SE

ACTIVITIES & INTERESTS
- Active member of Hopology Club
- Active member of International Hash House Harriers Club

Current Address: Box 1234, 12345 N. 59th Ave., Glendale, Arizona 85306, (602) 555-1234
Permanent Address: 1234 RFD, Long Grove, Illinois 60047, (708) 555-1234

Tanya Lansing

OBJECTIVE

Position in international sales, marketing, or advertising that will provide the opportunity for a continual learning experience and career growth.

QUALIFICATIONS   A graduate degree in international marketing, two internships, and seven years of progressively responsible part-time work experience gained financing my education.

ACHIEVEMENTS

- Supervised, designed, and actively engaged in all aspects of production, advertising, and publicity of the 1994 issue of THUNDERBIRD's class annual, *Fortune*.

- As an intern with Priss Prints, Inc., established international licensing department, collaborated on product development, and developed ads and press releases.

- As an intern with a London firm, designed and implemented job evaluations used to establish new job classification system.

- Planned and supervised all aspects of production, advertising, and publicity for 1994 Career Services Fashion Show.

- As a junior achiever in a statewide program embodying 44 companies with 700 participants generating over $138,700 annual sales, won best sales technique contest and "President of the Year" runner up. Company ranked as one of the top five.

LANGUAGES

Proficient in **French**
Knowledge of **Spanish**

EDUCATION

MASTER OF INTERNATIONAL MANAGEMENT   May 1994
American Graduate School of International Management
THUNDERBIRD, Glendale, Arizona
Concentration: International consumer marketing

BACHELOR OF ARTS   August 1992
Michigan State University, Lansing, Michigan
Concentration: International marketing

EMPLOYMENT HISTORY

1993	Co-Editor: *Fortune*, A.G.S.I.M.
1992	International Licensing Coordinator: Internship with Priss Prints of Dallas, Texas
1992	Executive Assistant: Huntsman Container Lancashire, England
1992	Salesperson: Coreys Jewel Box, Lansing, Michigan
1991	Salesperson: Sherwin Williams, Grand Rapids and Lansing, Michigan
89/92	Performer: Grand Rapids Singing Telegram, Grand Rapids, Michigan
86/89	Customer Service: Instructional Fair, Inc., Grand Rapids, Michigan

COMPUTER SKILLS

Lotus 1-2-3, WordPerfect, dBASE III, Microsoft Word

Present Address • P.O. Box 1234 • Glendale, Arizona 85306 • (602) 555-1234
Permanent Address • 12345 S. 117th Avenue • Orland Park, Illinois 60462 • (708) 555-1234

Resume

Education

Employment History

Personal

Dianne D. Quad

12345 North 61st Drive
Glendale, Arizona 85304

(602) 555-1234

1987
Bachelor of Arts
Communications and English
Rutgers University
New Jersey

Continuing education classes at UCLA

1994
Advertising Sales Representative
Scottsdale Progress
Scottsdale, Arizona

1992 – 1994
Account Executive
KC Design, Advertising and Promotion
Phoenix, Arizona

1988 – 1992
Customer Sales and Service
Representative
Quad/Marketing, Inc.
Los Angeles & New York

1987 – 1988
Marketing Assistant
BBDO Advertising
New York

Qualifications

- Excellent oral and written
  communication skills
- Creative
- Problem solver
- Self-starter
- Strong organizational and
  coordinating skills

Goals

To join energy and insight with
business experience to be part
of a productive work environment

Interests

Reading, athletics, family, social
well-being

Reference available upon request.

Dianne D. Rutgers
12345 North 61st Drive
Glendale, Arizona 85304
(602) 555-1234

Education

1987
Bachelor of Arts
Communications and English
Rutgers University
New Jersey

Continuing education classes at
UCLA

Employment History

1994
Advertising Sales
Representative
Scottsdale Progress
Scottsdale, Arizona

1992 – 1994
Account Executive
KC Design
Advertising and Promotion
Phoenix, Arizona

1988 – 1992
Customer Sales and Service
Representative
Quad/Marketing, Inc.
Los Angeles and New York

1987 – 1988
Marketing Assistant
BBDO Advertising
New York

Qualifications

- *Excellent oral and written communication skills*
- *Creative*
- *Problem solver*
- *Self-starter*
- *Strong organizational and coordinating skills*
- *Strategic thinker*

Goals

To join energy and insight with business experience to be part of a productive work environment

Interests

Reading, athletics, family, social well-being

References available upon request

$\mathcal{D}$AY PAPILLON

1234 Lakeshore Drive
Stockton, California 95204
(209) 555-1234

STRENGTHS

- Very talented studio artist with superb capabilities in graphic design
- Comfortable working with all personality types
- Extremely reliable, considerate, and organized
- Ability to grasp new ideas and integrate them into desired results

EXPERIENCE

LA PAPILLON, Dallas, Texas   1990 - Present
Display Coordinator
- Prepared displays in showroom for major holiday markets
- Performed all general office duties

ALMAY COSMETICS, Stockton, California   1992
Sales Associate
- Conducted test market evaluations for new product line
- Maintained inventory in eight stores throughout city
- Attended monthly sales meetings to discuss progress and consumer response

CRABTREE & EVELYN, Dallas, Texas   1987 - 1992
Account Executive
- Maintained inventory for three retail stores and showroom
- Participated in seasonal markets for retail customers
- Responsible for devising new marketing strategies to increase sales

EDUCATION

BACHELOR OF ARTS   May 1994
University of the Pacific, Stockton, California
- Major: Studio Art

HIGH SCHOOL DIPLOMA   May 1990
Highland Park High School, Dallas, Texas
- Awarded photography scholarship

PHOTOGRAPHY

- Photo technician at University lab (1991)
- Internship with Haggin Museum – hired to document the collection (1992)
- Commissioned to photograph several faculty members' artwork (1993)

ACTIVITIES & HONORS

- Co-Chairperson for 1994 Senior Arts Show
- AFS International Studies Program Member
- Member of Omega Phi Alpha – President 1993-1994, Social Chairman 1993
- Omega Phi Alpha Little Sister of the Year 1993-1994
- Highland Belles Drill Team
- Hi Lites Girls Club Member

MARK M. MILITARY

OBJECTIVE   Seeking employment as an Aircraft Mechanic with an upwardly mobile company

OVERVIEW
- Aircraft mechanic skills acquired from training and firsthand experience with the United States Air Force for 10 years
- Available for employment June 2, 1991

EXPERIENCE

UNITED STATES AIR FORCE   June 1981 – Present
Tactical Aircraft Maintenance Specialist
Tyndall A.F.B., Florida, March 1982 – March 1984
Kadena A.B., Japan, March 1984 – September 1985
Luke A.F.B., Arizona, September 1985 – Present
- Performed preflight, postflight, and calendar inspections of aircraft (including structures, landing gear, engines, instruments, cockpits, flight surfaces, and controls)
- Serviced oil, fuel, hydraulic, and oxygen systems
- Obtained engine oil samples for analysis
- Operated flight line support equipment
- Interpret diagrams and applicable publications
- Rigged flight control surfaces
- Removed and installed engines
- Stator and rotor inspections
- Engine electronic controller removal and installation
- Backup fuel control removal and installation
- Augmentor igniter flame holder removal and installation
- Events history recorder removal and installation
- Engine analyzer unit hook-up (static/dynamic)
- Engine throttle linkage removal and installation
- Engine throttle rigging

EDUCATION/ TRAINING

U.S.A.F. Basic Leadership School for Supervisors	December 1989
U.S.A.F. Aircraft Maintenance Technical School	262 hours
Field Training Detachment Upgrade Courses	244 hours
Air Frame License Candidate	June 1991
Power Plant License Candidate	June 1991

36 hours towards an Associates Degree in Professional Aeronautics
Community College of the Air Force

ADDRESSES

Present: P. O. Box 1234, Luke A.F.B., Arizona 85309   (602) 555-1234
Permanent: 123 Lorel Drive, Middletown, New York 10940   (914) 555-1234

Elena Valerie Latis
1234 W. Olive Avenue #123
Glendale, Arizona 85302
(602) 555-1234

Elena Latis

OBJECTIVE

A position with a multinational firm in the field of marketing/advertising

EDUCATION

MASTER OF INTERNATIONAL MANAGEMENT, MIM (5/94)
The American Graduate School of International Management
THUNDERBIRD Campus, Glendale, Arizona

INTERNATIONAL ADVERTISING (INTERAD) SEMINAR,
Thunderbird, Account Executive (9/93–12/93)
Served as a liaison between Kellogg's Corporation and 7-member
marketing team. Developed advertising strategy for Kellogg's Corn
Flakes in Russia.

BACHELOR OF ARTS, Indiana University, Bloomington, IN (8/92)
Majors: Journalism and Slavic Studies
Minors: German and Spanish Languages and Culture
International Media Law Graduate Seminar – Emphasis on GATT,
constitutional rights, political barriers to media

FOREIGN STUDY
Barcelona, Spain – ESADE Abroad Program, Thunderbird (1993–94)
Graz, Austria – Indiana/Graz University Exchange Program (1991)
Thessaloniki, Greece – Study Abroad Program (1987, 1990)

PROFESSIONAL EXPERIENCE

RUSSIAN ECONOMIC COUNCIL, Thunderbird Convention (5/93)
Translated for city councilmen from Moscow, Leningrad, and
Novgorod on the subjects of local government reforms, decision
making, and conflict resolution between ethnic and racial groups.

MANACO SYSTEMS INTERNATIONAL, LTD., Northfield, IL
Account Executive (8/92–1/93)
Intern, Assistant Account Executive (5/91–8/91)
Presented products to prospective clients from Argentina, Chile,
Mexico, and Turkey via news releases, brochures, advertisements,
and public speaking. Assisted in preparing trade agreements. Created
and coordinated exhibit booths at trade shows. Selected and pur-
chased garment lines and gift items; budget of $750,000.

M & N TRANSPORTATION, INC., Morton Grove, IL
Intern, Administrative Assistant (5/90–8/90)
Wrote copy and laid out of brochures for prospective clients. Solicited
business; assisted dispatcher; computerized filing systems (database)

NEW LIFE BROADCASTING CO., WVVX FM
Highland Park, IL
Copy Editor (5/89–8/89)
Wrote commercials in English and Russian; edited copy. Solicited air
time advertisements.

LANGUAGES

Fluent in Russian, German, Spanish, and English
Conversational in Greek, Czechoslovakian, and Polish

214

15 | LONG RESUMES AND CURRICULUM VITAE

As a general rule, a resume should be limited to one page. Carefully select your information to provide a synopsis and don't try to include everything.

But there are exceptions to every rule! In certain industries, the longer a resume is, the better your chances of getting the job. You will generally find those resumes in the medical or academic fields. A successful resume in these cases should include not only experience and education but also publications, certifications, grants, professional associations, awards and honors, presentations, and/or courses taught. The resume on pages 240 through 246 is a perfect example. Such a resume is called a *curriculum vita* from the Latin meaning "course of one's life" (literally like running a race—and you just *thought* your life was a rat race!).

Another interesting variation on the two-page resume is to present a cover page that summarizes your career highlights (page 220) and then continues with an in-depth, chronological description of experience (page 221).

The resume on pages 216 through 219 is an adaptation of that same idea. In Beverly's case, she has a stand-alone one page resume (page 216), which can then be supplemented by a detailed work history when the prospective employer requires more information.

The most important thing to keep in mind with multiple-page resumes is that your name must appear on each page in case the second page becomes separated from the first.

(For those of us who have trouble knowing how to spell the word, *vita* is singular, *vitae* is plural!)

$\mathcal{B}$everly $\mathcal{A}$nn $\mathcal{S}$olver

1234 West Mariposa Grande
Peoria, Arizona 85345
(602) 555-1234

Dynamic, results-oriented problem solver offers highly refined leadership skills; management, marketing, and systems expertise; and a commitment to accuracy and effectiveness to a progressive, quality-driven organization.

EXPERIENCE SUMMARY

- Marketing Management
- Product and Program Development
- Market Analysis and Strategic Planning
- Business Development
- Account Management
- Direct Sales
- Communications – Event Management
- Pre/Post-Sales Support
- Customer Service – Training

- Enterprise-wide Management Consulting
- Business – Systems – Process Analysis
- Information Systems Planning
- Systems and Application Integration
- Project Management
- Software Engineering and Development
- Systems/Network Operations and Administration
- Hardware, Software, and Communications Support
- Installation – Implementation – Training

Health Care ◆ Manufacturing ◆ Telecommunications ◆ Banking ◆ Retail
Insurance ◆ Government ◆ Education ◆ Aerospace ◆ Engineering
IBM ◆ Bull ◆ Tandem ◆ Digital ◆ UNISYS ◆ Wang ◆ Hewlett-Packard ◆ SUN ◆ 3COM

ACHIEVEMENT HIGHLIGHTS

- Managed product programs for $250 million operation with seven districts, covering the full spectrum of hardware, software, and communications products and services.
  - Cultivated third-party solution partnerships
  - Developed comprehensive UNIX marketing plan
  - Initiated focused team sales approach and training program

- Earned a reputation for outstanding account management through creative business partnerships, a management consulting presence, the effective orchestration of resources, and consistent growth.

- Designed and developed innovative marketing information system.

- Managed consulting team, converting network management control system from a Tandem to IBM processing environment.

- Directed proposal of a UNIX object-oriented prototyping workstation.

- Redesigned claims front-end processing, netting 30% staff reduction.

- Led analysis team to successfully resolve a $2 million payment error.

- Assisted in acquisition of a $2 million seed investment to initiate the development of a 600-gigabyte national health care database.

- Coordinated district-wide health care systems and services.

- Deployed CAD system for facilities management.

- Established a proven track record in complex project management.

- Integrated IBM/Wang/Novell/PC environment.

- Provided technical support to diverse multivendor environments.

EMPLOYMENT HISTORY

CAP GEMINI AMERICA, INC.
Seattle, Washington (1993 – 1994)
- **Client Services Executive**

BAY STATE HEALTH CARE, INC.
Cambridge, Massachusetts (1992 – 1993)
- **Senior Business Systems Analyst**

BULL HN INFORMATION SYSTEMS, INC.
Boston, Massachusetts (1989 – 1992)
- **Marketing Manager, Eastern Operations**
- **Account Manager, Mid-States District**
- **Marketing Support Representative, TN/AK**

BLUE CROSS OF WESTERN PENNSYLVANIA
Pittsburgh, Pennsylvania (1988 – 1989)
- **Senior Systems Analyst, System Integration**
- **Micro Computer Information Specialist**

CORPORATE INFORMATION SYSTEMS, INC.
Pittsburgh, Pennsylvania (1986 – 1988)
- **Consultant to Westinghouse Electric**

WESTINGHOUSE ELECTRIC CORPORATION
Pittsburgh, Pennsylvania (1984 – 1986)
- **Marketing Systems Analyst, Robotics**
- **Office Automation Specialist, Wang**

INDEPENDENT CONSULTANT
Rockwell International, AMS Engineering, Community College of Allegheny County

ASSOCIATIONS

Vice President, Pittsburgh Chapter, Women in Computing ◆ President's Club, Seattle Chamber of Commerce
Micro Curriculum Advisory Committee, Community College of Allegheny County
Northwest DB2 and CASE users groups ◆ ASM ◆ DPMA

RESUME SUPPLEMENT
DETAILED WORK EXPERIENCE

CAP GEMINI AMERICA, INC. (CAP GEMINI SOGETTI GROUP, Paris, France)
1993 – 1994

CLIENT SERVICES EXECUTIVE, Seattle, Washington

Chartered with account management and business development from a historically contract-programming oriented market position to enterprise-wide consulting, systems integration, and project management service offerings. Managed 16 existing customers, opened 3 new major accounts. Industries included High Technology, Telecommunications, Aerospace, Banking, and Retail with predominantly IBM, Tandem, and UNIX processing environments.

- Earned a reputation for outstanding account management and control, development of creative and cooperative business partnerships, exceptional analytical and consulting skills, a talent for achieving a team commitment, effective project management, and orchestration of resources to yield optimal growth and customer satisfaction.
- Opened and managed new telecom account replacing IBM SID with a consulting team to convert/develop a network management control product from Tandem-Guardian-COBOL and Digital-UNIX-Informix-C platforms to an IBM MVS-CICS-DB2-C/AIX-Informix-C processing environment. Also provided specialized, high-level consulting support in Engineering, Architecture, and Operations and completed enterprise-wide IS planning, product strategy, and configuration/change control studies for executive management.
- Proposed a UNIX-based, object-oriented prototyping workstation to a major cellular client.
- Supported ongoing conversion projects to assist mergers and acquisitions for major national bank.
- Developed target market programs for IBM-DB2, Computer Aided Software Engineering (CASE), telecommunications, and retail industries.

BAY STATE HEALTH CARE, INC.
1992 – 1993

SENIOR BUSINESS SYSTEMS ANALYST, Cambridge, Massachusetts

Internal consultant to Vice President of MIS and Claims. Provided business and information systems analysis in support of existing operations for this 300,000-member HMO. Served as technical liaison among executive management, MIS, various operating units, and vendors. Participated in the analytical phase of the "Systems of the Future" project addressing all internal and external business processes and available technologies.

- Defined Integration Strategy and Information Systems Plan.
- Coordinated market research and analysis of point-of-service systems. Addressed the integration of providers, clinics, laboratories, and practice management systems with the payor for electronic submission of claims, episode of care indicators, and on-line access for eligibility, authorization, and claims status information.
- Redesigned claims front-end processing resulting in staff reduction of 30% with a forward view toward a paperless image-oriented solution.
- Lead analysis for resolution of $2,000,000 payment error.
- Vendor interface for UNIX-based corporate decision support system.

BULL HN INFORMATION SYSTEMS, INC. (formerly Honeywell Bull)
1989 – 1992

MARKETING MANAGER, PRODUCT PROGRAMS, Eastern Operations, Boston, Massachusetts

Managed product programs for $250 million operation comprised of seven districts. Reporting to the Vice President of Marketing, developed and executed operations target market programs covering mainframe, mini and micro computer hardware, software, and communications products. Acted in liaison role to corporate product marketing and strategic development.

- Developed comprehensive UNIX marketing plan based on an operations and district specific market analysis, published in 50-page document and adopted throughout the operation. A two-pronged market approach was indicted, targeting large volume commodity sales and solution-oriented opportunities. Included was the definition of porting centers, solution partnerships strategies, management, sales and technical training, customer education programs, program requirements, critical success factors, and recommendations to product marketing.
- Defined vertical and target market strategies and programs.
- Cultivated third-party solution partnerships (Oracle, UNIX).
- Promoted effective use of networking products and services.
- Initiated focused team sales approach and training program.
- Key consultant in critical account situations.
- Supported extensive analysis, reporting, and presentation requirements.

BULL HN INFORMATION SYSTEMS, INC. (continued)

ACCOUNT MANAGER, Nashville Branch, Nashville, Tennessee

Responsible for the direct sale of information systems solutions based on a full range of hardware, software, and communications products and services. Managed eight customer accounts. Developed new-name sales opportunities, focused on Healthcare, Database, Office Automation, and Networking target markets.

- Reactivated six customer accounts.
- Cultivated ten new-name opportunities into active campaigns.
- Promoted weekly seminar program for customers and prospects.
- Prepared and presented presentations, proposals, and contracts.
- Effectively directed local and national resources.

MARKETING SYSTEMS REPRESENTATIVE, Tennessee/Arkansas District

Provided pre- and post-sales marketing and technical support for branch offices throughout the district. Technical support for hardware, software, and communications, local and wide area networks, including systems and configuration analysis and design, installation, administration, training, and troubleshooting. Marketing assistance through program definition, coordination, delivery of demonstrations, presentations, training programs, and communications tools.

- Coordinated district-wide health care and office automation marketing.
- Developed and implemented successful health care marketing plan.
- Managed Tennessee Hospital Association trade show.
- Provided product development consulting and trade show presentation and demonstration support to corporate Healthcare Product Marketing Organization for departmental medical records, radiology, and time management solutions, and hospital-wide information systems.
- Project manager, on-line medical records system integrated with UNISYS-based central hospital system for a 800-bed teaching hospital.
- District Specialist, office automation products and technologies.

BLUE CROSS OF WESTERN PENNSYLVANIA   1988 – 1989

SENIOR SYSTEMS ANALYST, SYSTEMS INTEGRATION

Optimized utilization of newly purchased hardware, software, and communications systems for start-up of health care cost management subsidiary. Addressed integration issues relating to the development of managed care and utilization research software for in-house use and outside sale. Facilitated efficient information access, improved processing, and effective decision support through the progressive application of technology. Managed training, systems administration, and support staffs.

- Integrated IBM/Wang/Novell/PC environment including multiple IBM hosts.
- Led a corporate-wide multi-platform status reporting system project.
- Evaluated new technologies for IS planning efforts.
- Commended for proactive user support philosophy and effective management skills in handling mushrooming requirements and organizational growth.

MICRO COMPUTER INFORMATION SPECIALIST

Managed installation, implementation, administration, support, and training for mini/micro/network solutions for local and remote sites. Responsible for evaluation, justification, and recommendation of computer hardware, software, and network acquisitions. Applications included database, CAD, graphics, project management, spreadsheet, word processing, electronic mail, facilities management, conversion, and communications software. Hardware included Wang VS, IBM AT's, Novell LAN, and associated peripherals.

- Provided "help-desk" support for local and remote user community.
- Established PC/Novell/Wang VS conventions, standards, and procedures.
- Reduced costly on-site support through remote diagnostics and administration.
- Successfully implemented AUTOCAD system.
- Assisted in development of inter-plan marketing campaign for 600-gigabyte national database leading to investments of $2 million in seed money.

CORPORATE INFORMATION SYSTEMS, INC.

1986 – 1988

<u>CONSULTANT</u>, Pittsburgh, Pennsylvania

Consultant to Westinghouse, supporting contracts requiring systems and network management, analysis, design, development, programming, database administration, implementation, training, and documentation efforts. Additionally, played an active role in CIS software development efforts and provided marketing support, including presentation, demonstrations, advertising, and communications design, training, and customer support.

- Managed Westinghouse, Unimation marketing information system.
- Productized and promoted Marketing IS for outside sale (OPTIMARK).
- Designed IBM 5520 network and implementation plan for Westinghouse Nuclear Center to replace Wang VS systems with IBM host and Tymnet integration requirements.
- Assisted in development of Accident Information Management System for GM.
- Specialist, office automation products and technologies.
- Provided ongoing consulting support for Wang VS systems.
- Project Manager for large Wang VS critical upgrade for Westinghouse R&D.

WESTINGHOUSE ELECTRIC CORPORATION

1984 – 1986

<u>MARKETING SYSTEMS ANALYST</u>, Industry Automation Division, Pittsburgh, Pennsylvania

Provided business and systems analysis to the marketing department. Managed the design, development, and support of an innovative marketing information management system to streamline departmental operations and serve as a decision support system. The system included inquiry specific response, advertising reach, frequency analysis, geographic/trend analysis, ad hoc query, and extensive reporting capabilities for management and international field sales support. Utilized database software, COBOL programming, productivity, development, query and reporting tools on Wang VS and Hewlett Packard hardware.

- Created innovative marketing system to support robotics sales effort.
- Developed marketing communications tracking/inventory system.
- Provided systems and database support for national trade shows.
- Specialist corporate electronic mail system (Tymnet).

INDEPENDENT CONSULTING

<u>ROCKWELL INTERNATIONAL, INC.</u> – Systems Administrator

Managed International Wang VS network providing user support, training, hardware/software/communications trouble shooting and vendor management.

<u>AMS ENGINEERING</u> – Software Engineer

Designed UNIX/Informix information system for three merging engineering firms.

<u>COMMUNITY COLLEGE OF ALLEGHENY COUNTY</u> – Instructor/Curriculum Developer

Developed and delivered various Personal Computing courses.

TRACY F. CARD

CURRENT ADDRESS
1234 NORTH 18TH STREET #123
PHOENIX, ARIZONA 85020
(602) 555-1234

PERMANENT ADDRESS
12345 PARKWOOD DRIVE NORTH
GULFPORT, MISSISSIPPI 39503
(601) 555-1234

CAREER HIGHLIGHTS

- Majority of career in banking, including credit card fraud processing support.

- Experienced and skilled in development, planning, organization, launching and administrating a centralized bank function.

- Comprehensive knowledge of design, production, and supervision requirements, procedures, methods, and report formats for management information.

- Special skills in de nova setup, internal bank mergers, consolidations, and acquisitions – both in employee training and internal systems.

- Expertise in bank reconciliation, accounting, audits, and security controls, budgets, electronic data processing systems, financial reporting, profitability, production control and scheduling, records and inventory controls, and cash handling and controls.

- Thoroughly trained in all phases of operations with a strong record of performance in each phase.

- Highly successful in personnel hiring, training, employee development, and salary administration.

- Extensive practical experience and training in employee orientation, public relations, productivity reviews, counseling and grievances, and manpower planning and development. This includes OSHA compliance requirements, personnel policy and procedure, and State/Federal equal opportunity regulations.

- Particularly dedicated to and effective with staff relations, morale, and staff teamwork.

- Known for being reliable and responsible, innovative, willing and capable of learning new things.

- Able to conceptualize and implement broad, complex programs to meet new goals.

- Possess competent leadership and management qualities.

TRACY F. CARD

EXPERIENCE

BANK OF AMERICA, Credit Card Division, Fraud Processing Department, Phoenix, Arizona

Operations Manager 4/92 – Present
- Promoted from an analyst position to oversee the personnel processing areas, including all payroll-related issues.
- Manage and administer all salary actions for the department, including establishing an annual salary plan.
- Supervise a staff of 18 personnel providing support for the fraud processing department.
- Audit dollar and non-dollar activity for cases relating to fraud.
- Manage the areas of reward processing and return plastics.
- Monitor the warning bulletin for both Visa and MasterCard, domestic and international.
- Responsible for managing general ledger for two cost centers, including suspense control and the auditing of these areas.
- Process all monetary and non-monetary dollar transactions for all fraud and counterfeit cases.
- Manage departmental supplies and monitor all record inventories concurrent with outlined retention schedules.
- Responsible for the merger of Security Pacific Bank's personnel and procedures into these areas.

Operations Analyst Officer 1/92 – 4/92
- Supervised personnel processing area for the administrative department for a staff of 170 employees, involving all payroll related issues for officers and all hourly, part-time and full-time employees.
- Assisted in the Bank of America/Security Pacific National Bank merger.
- Acted as the communications officer for the department, coordinating all incoming internal communications, as well as all incoming communications from Visa International and MasterCard, Inc.

EAGLE ENERGY, INC., Gulfport, Mississippi

Bookkeeper (Temporary) 6/91 – 11/91
- Posted and processed daily status reports for ten convenience stores and gas stations.
- Maintained inventories; posted receivables and payables.
- Assisted with fuel orders.
- Provided backup to credit card processing and EFT payments on invoices.

BILOXI HOUSING AUTHORITY, Biloxi, Mississippi

Secretary (Temporary) 2/91 – 5/91
- Provided clerical and secretarial support to the Maintenance Director and Maintenance Department.
- Coordinated and implemented annual unit inspections.
- Prepared all work orders pertaining to these inspection reports for computer input.

SUNBURST BANK, Gulf Coast Division, Gulfport, Mississippi

Operations/Personnel Coordinator 5/88 – 7/90
- Responsible for overseeing and servicing operations for four Kroger grocery store branches in a de nova situation.
- Concurrent with operational functions, was responsible for hiring and development of all bank personnel.

SECURITY PACIFIC NATIONAL BANK, San Francisco, California 12/76 – 1/88

Assistant Vice President
- Responsible for 60 staff members engaged in servicing of 130 banking offices for operational support and the coordination of bank acquisitions.
- Also served as Special Assignment/Consolidation Team Leader, Branch Operations Assistant, Supervisor, and Convenience Center Branch Manager.

EDUCATION

Special Courses: Intro to Lotus 1-2-3, Intro to WordPerfect, Intermediate WordPerfect, and Managing Human Resources

Banking Courses: New Accounts, Safe Deposit, Performance Appraisals, Staff Utilization, Counseling, Customer Profitability Reports, Staff Relations/Labor, BAI, Modern Teller Training, Selling Skills for Bankers, Sunburst Teller Training

Michael F. Richards

U.S. Address • 1343 Albert Packer Drive • Colorado Springs, Colorado 80907 • Qatar Tel. 974-555-9810

EDUCATION	**POSTGRADUATE STUDIES, INTERNATIONAL MANAGEMENT** **American Graduate School of International Management** Thunderbird Campus, Glendale, Arizona	January to August 1994
	MASTER OF EDUCATION, ADULT AND CONTINUING EDUCATION **University of Texas at Austin**, Texas	1978
	BACHELOR OF ARTS IN POLITICAL SCIENCE **Chesser College**, Minot, North Dakota Emphasis in International Relations	1974
HONORS AND PROFESSIONAL DEVELOPMENT	**ARABIC LANGUAGE STUDY SCHOLARSHIP** **American Graduate School of International Management**	January 1994
	FELLOW (F.Coll.P.) **College of Preceptors**, United Kingdom	July 1993
	AMERICAN SOCIETY FOR TRAINING AND DEVELOPMENT	1984 to Present
	OUTSTANDING YOUNG MEN OF AMERICA U.S. Jaycees	1981
LANGUAGES	Spanish, Arabic	

EMPLOYMENT HISTORY

TRAINING CONSULTANT, PROGRAM ADMINISTRATION — September 1994 to Present
MidMed Limited, Doha Es-Salaam Medical Complex, Doha, Qatar

Following an eight-month residency in the study of international management and Arabic language, returned to Qatar to serve as Training Consultant, Program Administration, in a 2,500-employee hospital project. As the project's senior training administrator reporting to the CEO, participate in program management's strategic planning and advise on the development, implementation, and operation of professional, technical, and vocational training programs for Qatar and expatriate staff. Provide guidance and support to hospital training departments in the development of goals and objectives, curricula, resource material, and staff needs for all nonmedical training programs. Supervise a cross-functional/ multinational faculty of allied health and English language instructors and support staff. Advise and give direction to the formulation of performance monitoring criteria. Coordinate with Human Resource Development and appropriate Qatari officials in determining institutional training. Liaise with various local, national, and international bodies. Review and recommend appropriate out-of-country training for various nonmedical staff. Perform periodic needs assessments. Participate in various hospital professional committees.

International Travel and University Study — September 1993 to August 1994

COORDINATOR, STAFF EDUCATION SERVICES — January 1990 to August 1993
CONSULTANT, QATAR MOBILIZATION PROJECT — July 1992 to December 1992
MidMed Limited, Al-Haleej Medical Center, Al-Manama, Bahrain

Returned to Qatar as part of the initial Qatar Mobilization Team. In January 1990, assumed the position of Coordinator, Staff Education Services. In this position, planned and coordinated the overall activities of a comprehensive education and training department in a 3,000 staff, acute tertiary care teaching hospital project, managed by MidMed Limited. Supervised a multinational staff of 25 in the provision of new-hire testing and orientation; medical library services; instructional development, including English (ESP-TOEFL), Arabic, and computer-assisted learning; and nationalization programs, including technical institute and university internships; medical photography, audiovisual services; video production; and medical illustration. Participated in the logistical planning of international medical conferences, symposia, and workshops. Served on various committees and task forces. Proctored extension examinations for hospital staff.

STAFF DEVELOPMENT COORDINATOR   July 1984 to August 1987
Compania Tula Ryan, S.A., Hospital Delmita Juarez, México, D.F.
Coordinated and supervised a competency-based on-the-job training program in Allied Health for Mexican military personnel in a 2,000-employee Ministry of Defense Project. Trained Allied Health trainers in the development of linguistically appropriate, non-culturally biased competency-based teaching strategies. Assessed hospital department needs. Developed and implemented in-hospital training programs for multinational, multilingual staff. Evaluated military trainee progress, as well as the effectiveness of the Allied Health Trainers. Liaised with Military Administrative personnel. Conducted extensive training sessions in cross-cultural communications. Supervised curriculum development and teaching of special-purpose English language programs. Implemented a basic Spanish Literacy program for Mexican civilian employees. Taught English as a Second Language and GED. Participated with medical, patient, and nursing in-service education programs. Managed orientation of all new foreign-hire staff. Assisted staff with correspondence work.

Interim Employment

DIRECTOR OF ADULT EDUCATION SERVICES   May 1988 to July 1989
Newcomer-Fuller School of Continuing Education, Ignatius Reiley College, Natchitoches, Louisiana
Coordinated comprehensive bilingual Adult Basic Education, English as a Second Language, and Computer-Assisted Instruction programs. Served as a voting member on Classification Committee. Evaluated students. Liaised with management. Supervised and trained contract teaching and bilingual teaching staff. Developed program needs. Participated in Quality Assurance program.

ASSISTANT DIRECTOR, ADULT EDUCATION   April 1980 to June 1984
Erath County Adult Education Co-op, Packersville, Colorado, USA
Co-administered and supervised a five-county public school Adult Basic and Secondary Education program with over 50 instructors. Conducted search, hiring, and pre-service and in-service for teaching staff. Edited training manuals and program newsletters. Counseled and screened clients in English and Spanish. Developed services for state hospitals, a sheltered workshop, a senior citizens center, libraries, factories, adult probation departments, a battered women's shelter, and jails. Trained teachers statewide. Liaised with local, state, and federal programs. Wrote proposals for discretionary funding. Developed teaching materials. Developed advertising. Served on various local community advisory committees.

ASSISTANT TO DIRECTOR   September 1979 to September 1980
The Ray Clark Center, Sarah Combs College for Women, Swanson, Colorado, USA
Participated with the Director in the planning and implementation of a continuing education program for business, industry, and the community, in an urban community college serving a multiethnic clientele. Liaised with a wide range of community groups, developed radio and newspaper advertisements, and catalogues. Supervised clerical staff. Enrolled students. Coordinated teaching schedules. Taught GED preparation and conducted staff training.

PUBLICATIONS & PRESENTATIONS

Coauthor, "Putting Class in Your Evenings: A Marketing Strategy for Community Education." *Community College Digest,* Volume 1, Number 6, Summer 1978.

Co-Presenter, "Health Care Training in Qatar: A Cross-Cultural Approach." Presented at the Annual Conference of the International Society of Healthcare Training, San Diego, California (May 1991).

Coauthor with Carol McNeely, "Stopping Off at the Roadside Diner on the Information Superhighway: The Implications for Cross-cultural Trainers." *Cross-Cult: The International Journal of Cross-Cultural Training and Development,* Volume 10, Number 1, April 1995.

Larry O'Keefe

12345 60th Drive • Sun City, Arizona 85351 • (602) 555-1234

QUALIFICATIONS

- Production Control
- Inventory Control
- Production Planning
- MRP Implementation

- Real Estate Sales
- Property Evaluation
- Market Forecasting
- Budget Control

EXPERIENCE

1992 – 1994   REAL ESTATE AGENT, O'Keefe Realty

As a licensed agent, sold residential real estate in the Sun City/Sun City West area. Successfully sold both single-family homes and condominiums/apartments. Also was proficient in developing comparative analysis reports and sales forecasting plans for both home buyers and sellers, using advanced computer software programs.

1990 – 1991   OPERATIONS MANAGER, AAA Transport Company

Responsible for all freight loading and unloading into and out of the terminal, both long haul and local delivery. Also served as terminal dispatcher. Worked with both local and national representatives to acquire contracts for inbound and outbound rail and truck freight.

1988 – 1989   PRODUCTION PLANNER, ITT Cannon

Responsible for the production and shipment of major cables and harnesses for customers such as McDonnell and Hughes. This included the initial staging, production tracking, parts storage control, and final assembly. The above requirements were initiated through the use of an MRP system, which required continual input of data and control of production parameters. Product line represented shipments valued at approximately $8 million per year.

1986 – 1988   PRODUCTION CONTROL SUPERVISOR, Advanced Semiconductor Materials America

Supervised and trained subassembly planners and expeditors, which included timely and accurate staging, reviewing MRP guidelines and monitoring scheduled receipts and allocations. Previous responsibilities as a Senior Planner for the low pressure/diffusion wafer processing systems involved the implementation of two MRP II systems, proper control of allocations, and timely staging at the top assembly level. Improved delivery performance to better than 95% on major systems.

1984 – 1986   INVESTIGATOR/ANALYST, Subcontractor to Law Firm

Investigated and analyzed law firm property and assets held in various trusts and estates. Position involved contact with local and state government agencies, real estate brokers, and financial institutions. Prepared reports to provide information for estate heirs and for the preparation of tax returns. Arranged financing for various investment and construction projects. Served as registered process server for legal documents.

1983 – 1985   MANAGER, RAW MATERIALS AND BULK SCHEDULING, Revlon, Inc.

Ordered and controlled all materials needed for the production of bulk used in all Phoenix-produced products. Also determined the quantity and dates for the production of all bulk to correspond with product requirements. Supervised three executives and five clerical personnel. Prior position was Supply/Demand Manager, which included analysis of marketing forecasts, calculation of production frequency, and auditing of inventory positions.

1982 – 1983   PRODUCTION PLANNER, Sperry Flight Systems

Planned, covered, and master scheduled programs for Boeing, Hughes, McDonnell, and Grumman. Also involved in preproduction and production plans and schedules to assure a smooth transition of new products from design to production. Position included contact with Engineering, Manufacturing, and Marketing. Customer contact and presentations were also required.

1981 - 1982   PRODUCTION CONTROL MANAGER, Simplicity Pattern Company

Responsible for the production and inventory planning of all patterns produced for the United States and Canada. Also responsible for determining inventory levels for the factory and six branches, developing and implementing EDP programs for production and inventory control, forecasting future sales, and auditing line production output and efficiency.

1978 - 1981   ASSISTANT BUSINESS DEVELOPMENT ADMINISTRATOR, The Bank of California, N.A.

Coordinated business development and marketing efforts between 37 branch offices and head office management. Position required calling on corporate customers and prospects, analyzing branch marketing efforts, and administering the bank's advertising and promotion programs for the branches.

1975 - 1978   SUPPLY CORPS OFFICER, United States Navy

Duties included disbursing, commissary, and stores. Served as division officer for 35 men. Honorable discharge.

EDUCATION

Master of Business Administration • Indiana University, South Bend, Indiana • 1978
Bachelor of Arts, Economics • Hanover College, Hanover, Indiana • 1963

PATRICIA A. DOMINICAN

OBJECTIVE

A key management position in an international environment with responsibilities for strategic planning, new business development, and international marketing management.

QUALIFICATIONS

- Thirteen years sales, marketing, and general management experience
- Advanced Degree in International Management
- Proven management skills in new product development and expansion
- Skilled in negotiations, people management, and interpersonal skills
- Excellent communication, analytical, and leadership abilities

PROFESSIONAL EXPERIENCE

CONSULTANT .... 1986 – 1995
Trosclair Marketing, San Rafael, California
Consultant to small/medium firms. Strategic business planning; sales/marketing planning; service and product packaging; new business development; television production planning and implementation.

REGIONAL SALES MANAGER, WESTERN UNITED STATES ...... 1984 – 1986
Showtime Networks, Inc., San Francisco, California
Within first 9 months negotiated $19+ million in new revenue. Within first 12 months increased distribution by 10.2%. Key strategist for 11 Area Managers in financial and sales negotiations; key strategist for introduction of new pay-per-view service. Training and development of management team.

NATIONAL SALES MANAGER .... 1983 – 1984
Varicom, Inc., San Francisco, California
National Sales Manager, promoted from Western Regional Manager, San Francisco, California. Managed national distributor sales; managed sales to Western Region television stations, both network and independent.

CONSULTANT 1983
Trosclair Cable Marketing, San Rafael, California
Consultant to cable television management, specializing in marketing management, public/community affairs, and employee training. Analyzed a proposed California legislative bill, and designed and directed the campaign to the bill's defeat.

REGIONAL MANAGER, NORTHWEST .... 1979 – 1982
Home Box Office, San Francisco, California
Regional Manager, Northwest, promoted from Regional Coordinator: Sales to and marketing planning for 150+ cable television managements. Directed cooperative product promotion campaign for 20+ metropolitan cable firms. Analyzed and planned multi-product positioning. Managed field representatives. Conducted numerous client training programs.

DIRECTOR/EXECUTIVE PRODUCER OF TELEVISION STATION ... 1976 – 1979
Marin 11, Viacom Cablevision, Inc., San Rafael, California
Designed and directed start-up, and managed award-winning television profit center for a community television station. Created and programmed 300+ television programs. Established community/media support and participation. Hired, trained, and managed employees; developed and managed three college intern programs. Nine national awards for excellence awarded within first three years of operation.

DIRECTOR OF DOMINICAN DAY CAMP . . . . 1974 – 1976
Dominican College of San Rafael, California
Creator and strategist for the foundations and operations of a recreational day camp. Directed the camp, which attracted capacity attendance the first year. Wrote procedures/ operations/programming manuals. Hired/trained staff. Developed sales/marketing campaign and materials. Awarded the coveted *American Camping Association* accreditation in record time.

SAVINGS & LOAN INSTITUTIONS / BANKING / EDUCATOR . . . . 1968 – 1976

EDUCATION

MASTER OF INTERNATIONAL MANAGEMENT . . . . May 1990
American Graduate School of International Management
Thunderbird Campus, Glendale, Arizona
Emphasis: International Marketing Management; Asia
Special Projects:
- Developed market feasibility study for entry of new product into the Japanese market
- International Consumer Marketing Seminar
- Market research survey for development of new service between Japan and U.S.A.
- Study of telecommunications in the Pacific Rim

BACHELOR OF ARTS, SPEECH COMMUNICATION, *cum laude* 1975
Dominican College of San Rafael, San Rafael, California

LANGUAGES

Knowledge of Japanese

AWARDS/HONORS

Ace Award for Cable Television Excellence 1977
Ace Award for Cable Television Excellence 1978
Who's Who in Cable Television 1978–79
1975 Outstanding Senior Student Nominee, Dominican College

PROFESSIONAL ACTIVITIES

Women In Cable, San Francisco Chapter – President, Vice President, PR Chair 1979–85
Bay Area Cable Club – Program Chair 1985
American Women in Radio and Television – Executive Board 1977–83

COMMUNITY ACTIVITIES

Mother Lode Musical Theatre, Inc. – Executive Board
San Rafael Chamber of Commerce – Executive Board
Marin Ballet – Executive Board
Cultural Affairs Service League – Charter President

INTERESTS

Travel in United States, Mexico, Canada, Asia

ADDRESS

Current Address:
1234 W. Greenway Road, #123
Glendale, Arizona 85306
(602) 555-1234

Permanent Address:
1234 Lincoln, #123
San Rafael, California 94901
(415) 555-1234

RONALD L. MAILHOT

12345 West Carole Lane
Glendale, Arizona 85303
(602) 555-1234

PROFILE

Fifteen years in the field of Maintenance Engineering, including seven years as Nuclear Power Plant Technician with supervisory duties and experience as follows:

- Crew supervision
- Federal guidelines
- Motor actuators
- Reactor system removal and installation
- Nuclear plant process systems

- Management information systems
- Hazardous and radioactive material handling
- ANSI/ASME codes
- Specialty machinery
- Blueprints, flow diagrams

EXPERIENCE

4/94

FIELD ENGINEER ASSOCIATE, Babcock & Wilcox
McGuire Nuclear Station, Duke Power
Duties Entailed: Removal of a stuck thermal sleeve from the in-core guide tubes in the bottom of the lower grid assembly of the reactor core barrel using a remote control robotic arm and video monitoring. Also debris removal from fuel assemblies using the B&W Faris station and long poles with video monitoring.

3/94 – 4/94

SUPERVISOR / TECHNICAL ADVISER, Babcock & Wilcox
David Bessi Nuclear Station, Toledo Edison Power
Supervised union craft personnel performing maintenance on the B&W reactor head to include control rod drive mechanism (CRDM) component maintenance and installation. In-core instrumentation installation. Reactor vessel head and component reinstallation. Documentation and interdepartmental coordination for the work performed.

1/93 – 3/94

SENIOR MOTOR ACTUATOR TECHNICIAN, Babcock & Wilcox
Indian Point II, Con Edison Power
Duties Entailed: Removal and reinstallation into service of 90+ motor actuators, SMB-000 through SMB-2.

10/92 – 11/92

SENIOR REACTOR COOLANT PUMP TECHNICIAN, Babcock & Wilcox
Millstone Nuclear Generation Station, Northeast Utilities
Duties Entailed: Removal of the motor and rotating assembly of the Byron Jackson N9000 Reactor Coolant Pump. Installation of a new rotating assembly and mechanical seal replacement. Reassembly of all associated components.

8/92 – 9/92

SENIOR MOTOR ACTUATOR REFURBISHMENT TECHNICIAN, ITI Movats
Laguna Verde Nuclear Generating Station, Veracruz, Mexico
Duties Entailed: Removal from service and electrical determination. Mechanical refurbishment of SMB 000-SMB 3 motor actuators. Approximate 90% of work was performed while on critical path.

4/92 – 6/92

SENIOR REACTOR COOLANT PUMP TECHNICIAN, Babcock & Wilcox
Crystal River Nuclear Generating Station, Fla Power Company
Duties Entailed: Removal of the motor and rotating assembly of the Byron Jackson N9000 Reactor Coolant Pump. Installation of a new rotating assembly and mechanical seal replacement on three of four pumps. Reassembly of all associated components.

2/92 – 4/92

SENIOR REACTOR MAINTENANCE TECHNICIAN, Babcock & Wilcox
Palo Verde Nuclear Generating Station, Arizona Public Service
Duties Entailed: Destack/restack of the Combustion Engineering System 80 Reactor Head and its associated components. Design modification installation of quick-release vents for the Control Element Drive Mechanisms (CEDM). In-core instrumentation cut up and disposal, and cavity seal ring installation.

9/91 – 11/91

MOTOR ACTUATOR TECHNICIAN, ITI Movats
Comanche Peak Nuclear Station, Texas Utilities
Motor actuator refurbishment and inspection in accordance with NRC generic letter 89-10. Determination/retermination; mechanical refurbishment of SMB/SB 000 through 4 actuators and HBC units. Electrical inspection of limit and torque switches; Raychem and lug repair; gearbox inspection; documentation of all work performed.

3/91 – 5/91

REACTOR MAINTENANCE TECHNICIAN, Shearon Harris Nuclear Station, Carolina Power & Light
Reactor destack/restack, cavity seal ring installation/removal, reactor seal ring replacement, instrumentation seal replacement, stud cleaning, repair and maintenance of various pumps and valves, Limitorque motor operator maintenance, documentation of work performed, interdepartmental coordination.

EXPERIENCE (Continued)

9/90 – 12/90 **MOTOR ACTUATOR TECHNICIAN, Surry Nuclear Station, Virginia Power Co.**
Removal PM and overhaul inspection, reinstallation and documentation of motor actuators. Working with engineering and maintenance departments providing information and analysis of problems resulting from use of actuators. Providing corrective action, procedure correction.

3/90 – 5/90 **REFUELING TECHNICIAN, Trojan Nuclear Station, Portland General Electric**
Member of refueling crew; destack and restack of reactor head and associated equipment; fuel transfer and replacement, new fuel receipt, and replacement of flux thimble instrumentation.

4/89 – 2/90 **OUTAGE MANAGEMENT TASK GROUP SUPERVISOR, Palo Verde Nuclear Generating Station**
Arizona Public Service
Coordinated shift and monitored Mechanical Maintenance crew. Lead technician for Reactor Coolant pump disassembly/reassembly, Control Element Drive Mechanism (CEDM) coil stack modification, reactor destack/restack, reactor refueling equipment maintenance and Integrated Leak Rate Testing (ILRT) support. Shift supervisor responsibilities include shift maintenance documentation and turnover, parts/material requisitioning, interdepartmental coordination, system walkdown, post-maintenance testing and work order close out.

3/89 – 4/89 **LEAD TECHNICIAN/SHIFT SUPERVISOR, Grand Gulf Nuclear Station, Mississippi Power & Light**
Duties included the set up and inventory, as well as procurement of tools and equipment to be issued during outage. Also responsible for records of tools, measuring and test equipment (M&TE) and consumables.

1/89 – 2/89 **LEAD TECHNICIAN/SHIFT SUPERVISOR, Millstone Nuclear Station, Northeast Utilities**
Duties included the set up and inventory, as well as procurement of tools and equipment to be issued during outage. Also responsible for records of tools, measuring and test equipment (M&TE) and consumables.

10/88 – 12/88 **MACHINIST, Chin Shan Nuclear Plant**, Republic of China, Taiwan
Using the Mac-Tech machines 410, 616, and 812. Cut out and remove recirculation pipes on General Electric BWR reactor.

5/88 – 11/88 **SENIOR TECHNICIAN REACTOR COOLING PUMPS, McGuire Nuclear Station, Duke Power**
Removal and replacement of reactor coolant pump seals during refueling outage.

5/88 – 7/88 **CRANE OPERATOR**
Pendant and boom truck operator for equipment removal to induce safe rigging practices.

2/88 – 5/88 **LEAD TECHNICIAN/SUPERVISOR, Possum Point Coal Plant, Virginia Power Plant**
Unit 3 maintenance crew supervisor for unit 3 outage.

TRAINING

- **ITI Movats:** Motor actuator refurbishment course
- **Portland General Electric:** Refueling equipment training and qualification
- **Northeast Utilities:** Firefighting and safety, rigging
- **Arkansas Power & Light:** Overhead crane operation, rigging
- **Duke Power/Westinghouse:** Reactor cooling pumps and motor course
- **Duke Power:** Procedure documentation control; mechanical maintenance orientation; pendant crane, boom truck operation, rigging courses. Independent verification
- **APS/Combustion Engineering; Siemens Allis/KSB:** Reactor coolant pump overhaul and repair training
- **APS/B&W:** Multi-stud tensioner training
- **General Electric:** Overhaul of steam feed water pumps and resurfacing machines; hydraulic cutting machines
- **Chesterton:** Live load repack of valves
- **Babcock & Wilcox:** Certified motor actuator technician, ANSI 3.1 current
- **Babcock & Wilcox:** Byron Jackson reactor coolant pump training
- **Babcock & Wilcox:** Nozzle dam installation training, manway cover removal, channel head decontamination
- **U.S. Army:** Mechanical maintenance of army vessels watercraft engineer 61B30 course
- **U.S. Army; Coast Guard:** Shipboard firefighting school

Michael L. Banyan, CBI, CBE

1234C West Jackrabbit Drive
USAF Academy, CO 80840-1220

Office: (719) 555-1234
Residence: (719) 555-1234

Objective   To make the transition from military computer network applications as a Certified Banyan Engineer (CBE) and Certified Banyan Instructor (CBI) to a commercial network design and integration company, using experience and training that is universal to both sectors.

Experience

United States Air Force .... 1973 to Present
Twenty-one years of progressively more responsible service and training positions, which included contact with manufacturers, service contractors, and major computer suppliers. Extensive specialized training at both Department of the Air Force and manufacturers' schools.

CHIEF, HARDWARE SERVICES DIVISION, ACADEMIC COMPUTING SERVICES
Department of the Air Force, Dean of Faculty, USAF Academy, Colorado (1993 to Present)
- Supervised an office of 10 technicians, with a wide range of responsibilities including the installation of a 65-server Banyan VINES network with 6000+ clients.
- Prepared and conducted training for group and building VINES administrators for the USAF Academy.
- Worked with the Dual Broadband system for distribution of VAX cluster output and connections.
- Engineering functions for projects included design and trade-off studies.
- Supported base-level contracting with technical information needed to complete purchase requests.
- Assembled and distributed systems to operational users.
- Improved process methods, reducing expenditures and minimizing total man-hours for all projects.

PROGRAM MANAGER FOR COMPUTER INFORMATION SYSTEMS
Training System Program Office, Wright-Patterson AFB, Ohio (1990 to 1993)
- Managed and provided engineering support for a 12-server Banyan VINES network with 400+ clients.
- Completed an upgrade of the network from 10base2 client wiring to 10baseT wiring, which included WAN connections to an off-site work location during the upgrade with no loss of work time.
- Designed and deployed an extension of the network to a Utah division of the organization, using Internet for connectivity.
- Engineered design and trade-off studies; supported base-level contracting with technical information.

ASSISTANT TO THE PROGRAM MANAGER
Training Systems Program Office (SPO), Wright Patterson AFB, Ohio (1987 to 1990)
- Assisted in leading a team of 13 functional experts in defining, acquiring, and fielding a family of maintenance training devices.
- Managed the Support Equipment Requirement Development list for the C-17 Maintenance Training Devices program in coordination with HQ Air Mobility Command, HQ Air Training Command, C-17 Airlifter SPO, and the contractor.

FIELD ENGINEER, DEFENSE METEOROLOGICAL SATELLITE PROGRAM (DMSP) GROUND SYSTEM
1000 Satellite Operations Group, Offutt AFB, Nebraska (1983 to 1986)
- Evaluated proposals for any changes to the Satellite Ground Control Facility.
- Lead Engineer on embedded microcomputer applications for controlling the DMSP Ground System links and equipment
- Test Engineer for installation of new electronic systems.
- Limited project costs to $250,000 in time and materials, while an alternate proposal was provided for $2,500,000.
- Controlled equipment failures and coordinated with DMSP SPO, three contractors, and two detachments when failure trend analysis indicated needed action.

MASTER INSTRUCTOR & SCIENTIFIC MEASUREMENTS TECHNICIAN (1978 to 1980)
- Instructor for three key areas of the Scientific Measurements Technician School: Introduction to Programming and Computers, Seismic Analysis, and Seismic Field Station Operation.
- Responsible for 12–15 students per class.
- Updated portions of the course for new requirements and technologies, resulting in manpower and resources savings and more effective learning.

AIR TRAFFIC CONTROL RADAR TECHNICIAN & INSTRUCTOR (1973 to 1978)
- Instructor for the Video Signal Processor (VSP) course with responsibility for 12–15 students per class.
- Installed and maintained air traffic control radar systems.

Education

College Degrees

- Master of Science, Systems Management, Air Force Institute of Technology
- Bachelor of Science, Electrical Engineering, Texas A&M University
- Applied Associate of Science, Instructor of Technology, CCAF
- Applied Associate of Science, Electronics Engineering Technology, CCAF
- Applied Associate of Science, Ground Radar Systems Technology, CCAF
- Applied Associate, General Studies, Mississippi Gulf Coast Junior College

Certifications and Honors

- Certified Banyan Instructor, 1994
- Certified Banyan Engineer, 1993
- Certified Banyan Specialist, 1993
- Inducted into Sigma Iota Epsilon, 1987

Banyan Courses

- Train-the-Trainer for VINES Administration (VINES 5.5), Banyan, 1994
- Advanced VINES Administration & Planning (VINES 5.5), Banyan, 1994
- Basic VINES Administration (VINES 5.5), Banyan, 1994
- VINES 5.5 Engineering Update (VINES 5.5), Banyan, 1993
- Technical Tools II (VINES 5.0), Banyan, 1993
- Technical Tools I (VINES 5.0), Banyan, 1992
- Introduction to VINES 5.0, Banyan, 1992
- VINES Gateways, Banyan, 1992
- Advanced VINES Administration & Planning, 1991
- VINES Communication Architecture, ABUI Training Institute, 1991
- StreetTalk Design & Operation Synchronization, ABUI Training Institute, 1991
- Basic VINES Administration, Blue Chip Computers Inc., 1990

Other Courses

- Systems Engineering Course, Systems Management & Development Corp, DSMC, 1992
- Computer Resources Acquisition Course, AFMC SAS, 1992
- Defense Data Management, AFIT, 1991
- Total Quality Management Corrective Action Team Leader Training, 1991
- Squadron Officer School (Residence), 1989
- Advanced Systems Acquisition Management Course, AFSC SAS, 1989
- Government Contract Law, AFIT, 1988
- Introduction to Systems Acquisition Management Course, AFSC SAS, 1988

Activities

Banyan Users In Colorado (BUIC) . . . . 1993 to Present
Vice President of the Regional Banyan user group and currently assisting in the development of the user group.

Association of Banyan Users International (ABUI) . . . . 1990 to Present
Chairman for Asynchronous Technical Wizards Interface Group (TWIG) with the responsibilities of overseeing session content at the semiannual conferences, conducting session, and coordinating the tracking of member requirements with a Banyan representative as related to asynchronous and WAN issues.

Lyleth M. Merex

1234 50th Street
Lubbock, Texas 79416
(806) 555-1234

TEACHING EXPERIENCE (ADULT)	*Effective Reading Centers*, Lubbock, Texas • Instruction in speed/comprehension of reading and study skills	1993 – Present
	Merex Corporation, Lubbock, Texas • Information processing and mathematics instruction • Curriculum development • Developed testing and reading materials for information processing and thinking strategies for math instruction	1992 – Present
	Goodwill Industries, Lubbock, Texas • Workplace skills instruction, upgrading in reading, writing, and math • Instruction in workplace communication – A staff development project for City of Lubbock Operations/Maintenance personnel • Planned and developed a communication curriculum based on reading/writing connections	1992 – 1994
	Big Bend Community College, Germany • Basic skills educational program • Designed and developed materials for reading courses	1979 – 1980
	City Colleges of Chicago, Iceland • Communication Development I	1979
	U.S. Navy, Iceland • Dantes Pilot Videotaped High School Studies	1977 – 1978
	Los Angeles Community College, Iceland • English 64 (4 terms); Developmental Communications (3 terms); Oral Communications for Supervisors (1 term); Written Communications for Supervisors (1 term) • Designed and developed material for developmental and communication courses	1976 – 1979
	Ruetten Learning Center, Phoenix, Arizona • Individualized remedial math and reading for disabled veterans	1975
	Big Bend Community College, Azores • Basic Reading 009; Basic Writing 002; Developmental Reading 003; Reading Improvement, Basic Communications 100; Music Appreciation 244; Power Reading 101; English as a Second Language	1974 – 1975
	Minato Commercial School, Yokohama, Japan • Conversational English	1971

TEACHING EXPERIENCE (ELEMENTARY)	*Second-Fifth Grades*, DoD Schools, Germany
	• Chaired social studies committee and designed and spearheaded multicultural activity week
	• Set up a cultural exchange day with German partner school
	• Chaired language arts committee of 800-pupil school which:
	  - sponsored a ten-day Language Arts Festival involving 30 guest presenters from the military, foreign community, and other Department of Defense schools
	  - produced and published an anthology of students' written works
	• Sponsored/directed several dramas and musicals
	• Sponsored the Student Council and the gifted/talented programs
		1980 – 1991

	First Grade, Hokkaido International School, Japan	1968 – 1969
	Reading Improvement, ESEA Title I, Corcoran, California	1966 – 1968
	Fourth Grade, Ash Fork, Arizona	1965 – 1966

EDUCATION   **POSTGRADUATE STUDIES**   1974 – 1989
Portland State, Boston University, U.S.C.,
Central Michigan extensions

MASTER OF ARTS, EDUCATION   1968
Northern Arizona University, Flagstaff, Arizona
- Major in Reading/English

BACHELOR OF SCIENCE, EDUCATION   1965
Arizona State College, Flagstaff, Arizona
- Major in Elementary Education

ASSOCIATE OF ARTS   1964
Phoenix College, Phoenix, Arizona

CARMAN Y. PRINCIPAL

Home Address:
12345 W. Alice Avenue
Peoria, Arizona 85345
(602) 555-1234

Work Address:
1234 W. Indian School Road
Phoenix, Arizona 85037
(602) 555-1234

OBJECTIVE

A teaching position

EXPERIENCE

PRINCIPAL, Christian School, Phoenix, Arizona   8/90 – Present
- Organized and implemented an effective Parent-Teacher Organization
- Initiated school-wide reward system to recognize good behavior
- Launched and supervised before and after school care program
- Experienced in site-based management
- Implement and manage policies and procedures regarding classroom and campus behavior
- Enforce attendance and discipline policies
- Meet with parents, teachers, and students with regard to discipline problems
- Supervise maintenance of discipline records
- Interview potential candidates and make staffing decisions
- Prepare reports for School Board and attend monthly School Board meetings
- Evaluate teachers
- Organize and teach in-service workshops for teachers
- Supervise events; plan and organize school activities and fund-raisers
- Initiated Read-a-Thon, Fall Festival, and Grandparents Day
- Coordinate summer school
- Supervise reporting of grades

TEACHER, Christian School, Phoenix, Arizona   1986 – Present
- Taught all basic subjects for:
  - 7th/8th grade combined class (1992–Present)
  - 6th/7th/8th grade combined class (1991–1992)
  - 6th/7th grade combined class (1990–1991)
  - 5th/6th grade combined class (1989–1990)
  - 2nd grade (1987–1989)
  - 2nd/3rd grade combined class (1986–1987)
- High school cheerleading sponsor (1987–1989)
- Music teacher, K-6 (1987–1988)
- Served on committees to organize and plan fund-raisers

TEACHER, Southeast Missouri Christian Academy, Sikeston, Missouri   1980 – 1986
- Taught all basic subjects for:
  - 3rd grade (1982–1986)
  - 1st/2nd combined class (1980–1982)
- High School and Junior High Cheerleading Sponsor
- Treasurer for "Band Aides" (band fund-raiser support group)
- Yearbook Sponsor

TEACHER, Jack & Jill Schools, Inc., San Antonio, Texas   1972 – 1973
- Taught first grade

SUBSTITUTE TEACHER, Public School Districts, San Antonio, Texas   1971 – 1976

EDUCATION

MASTER OF EDUCATION IN EDUCATION ADMINISTRATION   (15 hours)   1992 – Present
Arizona State University, Tempe, Arizona   GPA 3.83

BACHELOR OF SCIENCE IN EDUCATION   GPA 3.5   1980 – 1982
Southeast Missouri State University, Sikeston, Missouri

UNDERGRADUATE STUDIES   (95 hours)   1967 – 1970
Oklahoma Christian College, Oklahoma City, Oklahoma

CERTIFICATIONS
- Arizona Teaching Certificate (K-8)
- Missouri Teaching Certificate (K-8)
- Illinois Psychiatric Aide II (certified to work with mentally retarded children)

HONORS & AWARDS
- Four-year scholarship in Music and Speech from Oklahoma Christian College
- Letter of commendation from Dr. Mary Tablada for course work during Reading Practicum

GRADUATE HOURS

EX 572	Psychology/Education of the Exceptional Child	A	3 hours
COE 501	Introduction to Research and Evaluation in Education	B	3 hours
COE 504	Learning and Instruction	A	3 hours
EDA 526	Instructional Supervision	A	3 hours
ECI 661	Administration & Supervision of Reading Program	A	3 hours
EDU 596	Reading, Writing & Speaking – Spalding Method	A	3 hours

CATHERINE CLEVELAND, RNC, BSN, CCRN

123 West Siesta Lane • Glendale, Arizona 85308 • (602) 555-1234

HIGHLIGHTS OF QUALIFICATIONS

- Masters candidate in Critical Care Nursing at Arizona State University
- Five years experience in hospital education department
- Current Critical Care experience spanning from emergency department nursing to coronary/medical intensive care and cardiovascular/surgical intensive care since 1974

PROFESSIONAL EXPERIENCE

TEACHING

- Delivered classes for implementation of new documentation system at Del E. Webb Memorial Hospital
- Served as Education Specialist for Nursing in the Training and Development Department of Sun Health for five years
- Position responsibilities included design, development, and delivery of the nursing orientation program for Walter O. Boswell Memorial Hospital
- Designed, developed, and implemented programs for corporate mandatory education based on JCAHO guidelines and recommendations
- Updated and presented nursing and unit secretary preceptor programs
- Team teaching member for Series in Aging
- Gerontological nursing and aspects of death/dying presented as part of critical-care class
- ACLS and BLS instructor

Conference planning committee member for:
- "Geriatric Syndromes: Prevention and Management," October 1992
- "The Forgotten Priority: Cancer in the Elderly," April 1992
- "Your State Board of Nursing," February 1992
- "Practical Approaches for Behavior Problems in Older Adults," October 1991
- "Aging Perspectives and Possibilities: Issues in Gerontology," June 1988

CLINICAL

- Critical Care nursing experience spans nineteen years and includes emergency department nursing, coronary/medical intensive care nursing and cardiovascular/surgical intensive care nursing skills
- Currently responsible for coordinating and delivering all aspects of care for critically ill adult medical and surgical intensive care patients and their families
- Qualified to care for patients requiring mechanical ventilatory assistance, IABP support, and all types of invasive and noninvasive hemodynamic monitoring
- Experience caring for immediately postoperative cardiac surgery patients
- Qualified to remove pulmonary artery catheters and discontinue temporary transvenous pacer wires

MANAGEMENT & SUPERVISORY

- Assisted with advertisement, interview process, review of resumes and served as committee member for selection of training and development staff
- Actively participated in initiation and formulation of nursing, critical-care and emergency department policies and procedures
- Chaired Critical Care Policy and Procedure Committee
- Served as Charge and Resource nurse

CONSULTANT

- Consultant for the BLS Training Center of Del E. Webb Memorial Hospital
- Member of the BLS Training Center review team of the American Heart Association
- Served as a nursing consultant in the Education Specialist position for the Training and Development Department and all entities of Sun Health
- Training and Development representative on nursing policy and procedure committee and product review committee
- Consulted with Sun City Fire Department for fire safety training of hospital staff

RESEARCH

- Conducting research for thesis entitled "Relationships among preoperative affect, extubation outcome and length of intensive care after elective cardiac surgery"

EMPLOYMENT HISTORY	**STAFF NURSE, CRITICAL CARE** Del E. Webb Memorial Hospital, Sun City West, Arizona	1992 – Present
	EDUCATION SPECIALIST, TRAINING AND DEVELOPMENT Sun Health, Sun City, Arizona	1989 – 1992
	STAFF NURSE, CCU/MICU and CV/SICU Walter O. Boswell Memorial Hospital, Sun City, Arizona	1989 – 1992
	EDUCATION SPECIALIST, NURSING Sun Health, Sun City, Arizona	1987 – 1989
	STAFF NURSE, CCU/MICU Walter O. Boswell Memorial Hospital, Sun City, Arizona	1985 – 1987
	STAFF NURSE, EMERGENCY DEPARTMENT Walter O. Boswell Memorial Hospital, Sun City, Arizona	1982 – 1985
	STAFF NURSE, CCU/MICU Walter O. Boswell Memorial Hospital	1980 – 1982
	STAFF NURSE, TELEMETRY Mesa Lutheran Hospital, Mesa, Arizona	1977 – 1980
	STAFF NURSE, URGENT CARE UNIT Arizona Health Plan, Phoenix, Arizona	1975 – 1976
	STAFF NURSE, EMERGENCY DEPARTMENT Deaconess Hospital, Cleveland, Ohio	1974 – 1975
EDUCATION	**MASTER OF SCIENCE CANDIDATE IN CRITICAL CARE NURSING** Arizona State University, Tempe, Arizona Thesis to be completed by December 1995	1995
	BACHELOR OF SCIENCE IN NURSING Arizona State University, Tempe, Arizona	1985
	DIPLOMA IN NURSING Lutheran Medical Center School of Nursing, Cleveland, Ohio	1974

CERTIFICATIONS

- ANA Gerontological Nursing Certification from 1991 to present
- BLS Affiliate Faculty from 1988 to present
- ACLS instructor from 1983 to present
- AACN Critical Care Nursing Certification from 1983 to present
- ACLS provider from 1982 to present

AWARDS AND ACTIVITIES

- Member of ARISTA Honor Society
- Mended Hearts Scholarship – 1991
- Corresponding Secretary for AACN-GPAC – 1991
- Interim VP AzNA Gerontological Chapter – 1989 – 1991
- Member ANA since 1988
- Member of AACN since 1987
- Nursing Trainee Scholarships 1971 – 1974

VIVIAN MALCOLM, B.Ed., M.Ed., Ed.D.

12345 Ridgeway Drive • Sun City, Arizona 85351 • (602) 555-1234

SYNOPSIS:

Twenty-eight (28) years in adult, college, primary, elementary, and high school in the gamut of: lecturer, core professor, classroom teacher, student counselor, educational researcher, and public speaker.

Demonstrated ability encompassing a broad spectrum of skills involving training sessions with student teachers and psychology interns, conferences, workshops, social, civic, religious, and public relations activities.

Years of successful experience in establishing and maintaining rapport with students, teachers, administrators, and community leaders. Speaker and lecturer with experience in the direction of educational, cultural, church programs, community, business, and public relations activities throughout the United States, the Caribbean Islands, France, and England.

ACADEMIC TRAINING:

1974	***Doctor of Education, Administration and Supervision*** – University of Illinois, Champaign
1964	***Master of Education, Counseling and Guidance*** – Chicago State University, Chicago
1959	***Bachelor of Education, Kindergarten and Primary*** – Chicago Teachers College

ADDITIONAL GRADUATE STUDY:

1980–81	Illinois Institute of Technology
1978	Roosevelt University, Chicago, Illinois
1977–78	University of Illinois, Circle Campus, Chicago, Illinois

PROFESSIONAL EXPERIENCE:

1994	***Instructor*** – Essentials of Psychology, Gateway Community College, Phoenix, Arizona
1990–94	***Psychologist*** – Dysart Unified School District #89, El Mirage, Arizona
1990	***Instructor*** – Applied Education Psychology, Spring Semester, Northern Arizona University, Coolidge
1990	***Instructor*** – Introduction to Psychology, Spring Semester, Central Arizona College, Eloy and Coolidge, Arizona
1989–90	***Contractual Psychological Testing*** – Pinal County Special Education Program, Casa Grande, Arizona
1989	***Contractual Psychological Testing*** – Proviso Area for Exceptional Children, Maywood, Illinois
1988	***Contractual Psychological Testing*** – Chicago Board of Education
1988	***Student Teacher Supervisor*** – Winter Trimester, Northeastern University, Chicago
1971–86	***School Psychologist*** – Chicago Board of Education

Description: The scientific study and evaluation of the behavior of children, their educational problems, with the purpose of facilitating learning and total human adjustment. Duties and responsibilities included:

- Performance of psychological diagnosis and evaluations.
- Writing educational prescriptions.
- Recommending instructional goals and approaches.
- In cooperation with multi-disciplinary team, serving as resource person to teachers, administrators, students, and parents.
- Providing support and guidance in mainstreaming program.
- Providing short-term individual counseling and guidance to the child.
- Interpreting psychological findings and counseling parents regarding pertinent recommendations and possible courses of action.

- Consulting with and interpreting psychological findings and recommendations to individual teachers, teacher discussion groups, school counselors and administrators regarding individual differences, discipline, remedial programs, and psychological aspects of working with exceptional children.
- Participating in selection of suitable curricula for special programs such as perceptually and emotionally handicapped children (as well as gifted), et al.
- Serving as liaison with community organizations, hospitals, and institutions on referral services and necessary follow-up.
- Supervising psychologist interns when programs are operant.
- Conducting in-service for schools and institutions.
- Conducting stress workshops for Desegregation Institute under Title IV (Chicago Board of Education and Northeastern University).
- Participant: Operation Higher Achievement, Grant School and District Nine (motivational program for better achievement).

ADDITIONAL PROFESSIONAL EXPERIENCE:

1980–82	**Core Professor** – Graduate Field Experience Program, National College of Education, Evanston, IL
1970–71	**Interned as School Psychologist** – Chicago Board of Education
1965–70	**Kindergarten Primary Teacher** – Gresham Elementary School
1959–65	**Kindergarten Primary Teacher** – Beale Elementary School

SUPPLEMENTAL EXPERIENCE:

Consultant – Malcolm X College
Travel Agent – Trains, Boats & Planes Travel Agency

WORKSHOPS CONDUCTED:

- Strategies for Successful Teaching in a Culturally and Ethnically Diverse Classroom – Dysart School District, El Mirage, Arizona, October, 1990
- Discipline, Your Child and School Success – Pinal County Special Programs, Eloy, Arizona, January, 1990
- Can I Live Longer by Managing Stress? – Illinois Park and Recreation State Convention, Hyatt O'Hare, Chicago, November 1987
- Stress and Burnout – Northeastern University, Desegregation Institute, '80 to '83

PUBLICATION:

Dissertation: *An Evaluation of Gains Made by Chicago Public and Catholic School Students Who Were Serviced by the Summer Diagnostic Clinic in Area B*, 1974

AFFILIATIONS AND MEMBERSHIPS:

- Member, National Sorority of Gamma Phi Delta
- International School Psychology Association
- National Association of School Psychologists
- Chicago Association of School Psychologists
- National Sorority of Phi Delta Kappa, Mu Chapter
- Phi Delta Kappa, Fraternity - Education Honors Society
- Kappa Delta Pi - Education Honors Society
- Member, Board of Directors - Englewood Community Health Organization
- Member, Illinois Council for Exceptional Children
- Member, Advisory Board - Primary Health Care Services

**PROFESSIONAL
EXPERIENCE**

ONCOLOGY NURSE SPECIALIST/CANCER PROGRAM COORDINATOR 1990 – Present
Maryvale Samaritan Medical Center (MSMC)
Responsible for developing, coordinating, implementing, and evaluating the oncology programs and services of MSMC. Provide community and staff education. Serve as a nurse consultant for inpatient and outpatient services and patients. Coordinator for Samaritan Health System (SHS). Coordinate oncology screening programs. Coordinator for SHS oncology education programs. Director of SHS Clinical Oncology Nursing Council. Director and nurse practitioner for SHS mobile cancer services.

FAMILY NURSE PRACTITIONER   **1991 – 1992**
Palo Verde Hematology/Oncology
Coordinated family/patient plan of care. Directed symptoms management as related to disease, chemotherapy, and psychosocial needs. Followed long-term cancer survivors for routine health maintenance and long-term needs.

RADIATION ONCOLOGY NURSE AND TECHNOLOGIST   **1976 – 1990**
Maryvale Samaritan Medical Center
Coordinated and delivered nursing care and radiation therapy to oncology patients. Designed and conducted patient and family education programs and support groups. Designed and implemented community cancer prevention and detection programs. Resource person for oncology unit.

CONSULTANT (Part-Time)   **1984 – Present**
Medical/Radiation Oncology
Act as a consultant to hospitals, home health agencies, and private practices related to oncology services.

SENIOR CHEMOTHERAPY NURSE (Part-Time)   **1980 – 1991**
Palo Verde Hematology/Oncology
Responsible for mixing and administering chemotherapeutic agents to oncology patients in the office setting. Coordinated overall patient services, education, and counseling. Responsible for initial history on all new patients. Provided in-services for staff on new advances and technology in oncology.

HOME I.V. THERAPY NURSE (Part-Time)   **1984 – 1985**
Home Health Care of America
Provided home I.V. therapy, nutritional therapy, and chemotherapy in the home setting.

CLINIC CHEMOTHERAPY NURSE (Part-Time)   **1979 – 1980**
Dr. Alex Denes
Mixed and administered chemotherapy in a hospital clinic setting as a research nurse.

STAFF NURSE (Part-Time)   **1975 – 1976**
Nurses Central Registry
Provided nursing care (med/surg) for Phoenix area hospitals.

**CURRENT
HOSPITAL
SERVICES**

- SHS Steering Committee, 1992 – Present
- SHS Wellness Committee, 1993 – Present
- Oncology Clinical Nursing Council Chairman, 1991 – Present
- Samaritan Oncology Education Committee Chairman, 1991 – Present
- Samaritan Screening/Detection Committee Chairman, 1990 – Present
- MSMC Cancer Committee Coordinator, 1989 – Present
- MSMC Tumor Board Coordinator, 1976 – Present
- Samaritan Mobile Cancer Services Coordinator, 1992 – Present
- Samaritan Outreach Committee, 1991 – Present
- Samaritan Oncology Subcommittee, 1990 – Present
- Samaritan Research Committee, 1987 – Present
- MSMC Radiation Safety Committee, 1976 – Present
- MSMC Radiology Committee, 1976 – Present

RESEARCH EXPERIENCE

Data Manager/Nurse
- SWOG, GP-CCOP, and RTOG studies, 1979 – Present
- Ondansetron study by Glaxo, 1990
- ONS Radiation Therapy Documentation Tool Study, 1992

Contributing Writer
- CDC grant for Arizona Breast and Cervical Cancer Study/DHS, 1992
- GP-CCOP grant, 1990

Principal or Collaborating Investigator
- The Breast Cancer Experience – Quantitative Study, 1994
- Post-Breast Cancer: A Woman's Lived Experience – phenomenological study – 1993
- The Influence of Educational/Information Support Groups on the Quality of Life Scores of Cancer Caregivers – Master's thesis, 1990
- Individual Perceptions of Cancer (McCaffrey, Pelusi, and Keith), 1984

EDUCATIONAL BACKGROUND

University of Arizona College of Nursing Tucson, Arizona	1992 – Present	Doctoral Program Major: Nursing Minor: Public Admin. & Policy
Arizona State University College of Nursing Tempe, Arizona	1990 – 1991 1987 – 1990 1983 – 1987	FNP MS (Community Health) BSN
Scottsdale Community College Scottsdale, Arizona	1990	General Electives
Phoenix Community College Phoenix, Arizona	1984 – 1985	General Electives
Glendale Community College Glendale, Arizona	1979 – 1983	General Electives
Northern Arizona University College of Radiologic Technology College of Nursing Flagstaff, Arizona	1972 – 1976 1972 – 1975	Associate Degree Associate Degree in Nursing

MASTERS THESIS

The Influence of Educational/Informational Support Groups on the Quality of Life Scores for Cancer Caregivers. Chairman: Juanita Murphy, RN, Ph.D.

LICENSES & CERTIFICATIONS

FNP – Arizona #351
RN – Arizona #RN-032327
RT – Arizona #CRT-2727 (Radiology and Radiation Therapy)
OCN – Oncology Certified Nurse (National)
CPDP – Cancer Prevention/Detection Certification

GRANTS OBTAINED

1994 **MSMC EDUCATION GRANT, Mead Johnson**
$1,500 – Education Grant
1993 **CANCER CARE GRANT, Samaritan Health Services**
$350,000 – Project coordinator for Mobile Service portion of grant
1993 **VICTORIES IN CANCER CARE GRANT, Samaritan Health Services**
$300,000 – Samaritan Charitable Trust (SCT). Project coordinator for cancer mobile services and oncology education (portion of grant)
1992 **CANCER CARE GRANT, Samaritan Health Services**
$450,000 – Samaritan Charitable Trust (SCT). Project director for caregivers program and prevention and detection program (portion of grant)

GRANTS OBTAINED (continued)	1992	**ARIZONA BREAST AND CERVICAL CANCER STUDY, DHS**

GRANTS OBTAINED (continued)

1992   **ARIZONA BREAST AND CERVICAL CANCER STUDY, DHS**
$270,000 – CDC. Patient and Family Support Committee chairman and grant Executive Committee member

1991   **MOBILE CANCER PROGRAM STUDY, Samaritan Health Services**
$100,000 – SCT. PI and clinical director/practitioner

1991   **ONCOLOGY EDUCATION GRANT, Samaritan Health Services**
$25,000 – SCT. Clinical director/educator

1990   **CANCER PROGRAM DEVELOPMENT GRANT, Maryvale Samaritan Medical Center (MSMC)** – $10,800 – SCT. Program director

1990   **CANCER PREVENTION AND DETECTION GRANT, MSMC**
$35,980 – SCT. Program director

1989   **BREAST CANCER AWARENESS/DETECTION GRANT, MSMC**
$90,000 – SCT. Program director

1988   **FIGHTING CANCER IN OUR SCHOOLS, MSMC**
$2,000 – SCT. Program director/educator

1988   **ONCOLOGY EDUCATION – TELECONFERENCE GRANT, MSMC**
$7,500 – SCT. Program director/educator

1988   **CANCER PREVENTION AND DETECTION GRANT, MSMC**
$4,000 – SCT. Program director

1988   **ONCOLOGY ADVANCEMENT GRANT, MSMC**
$6,500 – SCT. Program consultant

1988   **COMMUNITY CANCER EDUCATION GRANT, MSMC**
$1,000 – SCT. Program director/educator

1987   **KIDS CAN COPE GRANT, MSMC**
$1,400 – SCT. Program director/educator

1987   **COMMUNITY SCHOOL EDUCATION GRANT, MSMC**
$1,500 – SCT. Program director/educator

ASSOCIATION MEMBERSHIPS

- **Oncology Nursing Society**, 1978 – Present
  - Board of Directors, Director at Large, 1994 – 1997
  - Multicultural Task Force Member, 1992 – Present
  - Radiation Therapy SIG Editor, 1989 – 1991
  - Radiation Safety Committee, 1992 – 1993
  - Cancer Rehabilitation SIG, 1992 – Present
  - Transcultural Nursing SIG, 1994 – Present
  - ONC Test Development Task Force, 1990
  - Role Definition Task Force, 1989
- **Phoenix Oncology Nursing Society**, 1977 – Present
  - President, 1986 – 1990
  - Newsletter Editor, 1984 – 1988
  - Special Project Chairman, 1990 – Present
  - Annual Conference Chairman, 1989, 1990
- **International Society of Nurses in Cancer Care Member**, 1986 – Present
- **Arizona Society of Radiologic Technologist Member**, 1976 – Present
- **American Society of Radiologic Technologist**, 1967 – Present
- **Arizona Nursing Network**, 1985 – 1990
  - Secretary, 1986 – 1988
- **Arizona Nurses Political Action Committee Member**, 1985 – 1989
- **Sigma Theta Tau Member**, 1987 – Present
- **Southwest Oncology Group**, 1979 – Present
  - Nursing Committee, 1988 – Present
  - Breast Cancer/Radiation Committee, 1990 – Present

VOLUNTEER ACTIVITIES

- *Arizona Women's Cancer Network*, 1992 – Present
  - Patient and Family Support Committee Chairman
  - Service Delivery Committee Chairman, 1993 – Present

VOLUNTEER ACTIVITIES (continued)

- *American Cancer Society – Arizona*, 1966 – Present
  - Breast Cancer Core Team Chairman, 1994 – Present
  - Vice President, Maricopa County, 1992 – Present
  - Service/Rehabilitation Chairman, Division, 1989 – 1992
  - Board of Directors, Division, 1988 – Present
  - Committee membership (Service/Rehabilitation, Professional Education, Public Issues, Development, Field Services), 1990 – Present
  - Board of Directors, Unit (G/P/M), 1986 – Present
  - ONCOPA Chairman, 1987, 1988, 1989
  - Medical Director and Practitioner – childhood cancer programs and women's program, 1985 – Present
  - Service and Rehabilitation State Chairman, 1989 – 1991 (have served on all unit committees during last 27 years)
- *City of Phoenix Parks & Recreation – Special Population*, 1991 – Present
  - Nursing Director for White Water Raft Trip through the Grand Canyon for people with disabilities
- *Kids Can Cope*, 1985 – 1988
  - Board of Directors
- *Our Lady of Perpetual Help Catholic Church*, 1975 – Present
  - Religious Education Teacher, 1975 – 1990
  - Home Eucharist Minister, 1983 – Present
  - Lay Eucharist Minister, 1983 – Present
  - Parish Council, 1984 – 1988
  - Teen advisor, 1978 – 1984

AWARDS & HONORS

1994	Helen Misco Scholarship – Ph.D. Studies
1993	Special Volunteer Award, American Cancer Society – Arizona Division
1992	Distinguished Service Award, American Cancer Society – Arizona Division
1991	Lane W. Adams Award, American Cancer Society – National
1990	Special Service Award, American Cancer Society – Arizona
1989	Paul Singer Award for Outstanding Community Service – Arizona
1989	Women Helping Women Award, Soroptimist – Golden West Region
1988	Outstanding Achievement Award, American Cancer Society – Arizona
1988	Life Saver Award, American Cancer Society – Arizona
1987	Distinguished Service Award, American Cancer Society – Arizona
1987	Sigma Theta Tau
1987	Life Saver Award, American Cancer Society – Arizona
1985	Employee of the Year, Maryvale Samaritan Medical Center
1984	Helen Misko Nursing Scholarship
1973	Raymond Foundation Nursing Scholarship

PUBLICATIONS

- Case Study – Cancer Practice, June 1994.
- Working Within the Circle – Treating Breast Cancer in the Native American Population, *Innovations in Oncology*, October 1994 (pending publication).
- Editor, *1992 and 1993 Annual Cancer Report, Maryvale Samaritan Medical Center*, Samaritan Health Services, 1994.
- Contributing Editor, "Handbook of Therapeutic Interventions," *Chemotherapy*. Springhouse, PA: Springhouse Corporation, 1993, pp. 170–176.
- Editor, "3rd Annual Cancer Report," Maryvale Samaritan Medical Center, Phoenix, AZ: Samaritan Health Systems, 1993.
- Contributing Editor, "Radiation Therapy," *Nursing Procedures*. Springhouse, PA: Springhouse Corporation, 1992, pp. 205–210.
- Editor, *Second Annual Cancer Report, Maryvale Samaritan Medical Center*. Phoenix, AZ: Samaritan Health System, 1990 – 1991.
- Editor, *First Annual Cancer Report, Maryvale Samaritan Medical Center*. Phoenix, AZ: Samaritan Health System, 1989.

PUBLICATIONS
(continued)

- Levine, Pelusi, & Steinway, *Kids Can Cope Manual.* Phoenix, AZ: Kids Can Cope Foundation, 1989.
- Editor, *The Boost* [Newsletter of the National Radiation Oncology Special Interest Group, Oncology Nursing Society] (1988 – 1990).
- Pelusi, Pinckard, & Hilger, "Radiation Therapy and You," [a patient education video]. Phoenix, AZ: Samaritan Health Services Publication, 1987.
- Haber, B., & Pelusi, J. "Cancer is a Scary Word" [a patient education pamphlet for children whose parents have cancer]. Phoenix, AZ: Samaritan Health Services Publication, 1987.
- Editor, *Phoenix Oncology Nursing Society Newsletter,* 1984 – 1988.

ACCOMPLISHMENTS

- Panelist, "Reduce Your Risk" (Special on cancer prevention), 1993
- Panelist, "Samaritan Presents – Taking Control" (TV special on cancer prevention and early detection), 1992
- Panelist, numerous TV interviews on cancer-related issues, 1991 – 1994
- Panelist, numerous radio talk shows related to cancer issues, 1991 – 1994
- Development of Arizona OCN Review Program, 1988
- Development of Oncology Nurses Bed/Breakfast Program – Arizona
- Development of "Because We Care For You" – caregivers program
- Development of "Upbeat Retreat" – retreat for women with cancer
- Development of "New Beginnings" – support group for women with cancer
- Development of "A Time for Survivors" – support group for cancer survivors
- Development of SHS Oncology Education Programs (Chemotherapy Validation Courses – Basic, Revalidation, and Home Health)
- Development of SHS Prevention and Detection Program for Nurses

PRESENTATIONS

INTERNATIONAL:

| 5/1994 | *Because We Care For You – Addressing the Needs of Caregivers*, 2nd Annual International Patient Education Conference, Tempe, Arizona. |
| 6/1994 | *Women's Stories of Struggle: Post Breast Cancer Treatment*, 2nd Annual International Quantitative Research Conference, Hershey, Pennsylvania. |

NATIONAL:

9/1994	*Caregivers*, Veterans Administration's Patient Health Education, "Patient Centered and Health Care Reform," Las Vegas, Nevada
5/1994	*Changing Paradigms in Oncologic Urology Nursing*, American Urology Association, San Francisco, California
5/1994	*Cultural Competence: Facing the Challenges of Our Changing World*, Oncology Nursing Society 19th Annual Congress, Cincinnati, Ohio
5/1993	*Radiation Therapy – Transcultural Issues for the Native American*, Oncology Nursing Society Congress, Orlando, Florida
4/1993	*Sexuality: A Forgotten Dimension of Transcultural Patient Education*, National Cancer Institute, Pasadena, California
5/1992	*The Silent Attacker of Men: Prostate Cancer*, Oncology Nursing Society, San Diego, California
5/1991	*When a Parent Has Cancer*, Oncology Nursing Society, Washington, D.C.
5/1990	*Role of the Radiation Oncology Nurse*, Oncology Nursing Society, San Antonio, Texas
5/1990	*Influence of Informational/Education Support Group on Quality of Life Scores of Cancer Caregivers*, WSRN, Albuquerque, New Mexico

REGIONAL:

9/1994	*The Impact of Cancer and Its Treatment on Sexuality*, American Oncology Nursing Society/ACS
9/1994	*Cancer Survivorship*, Cancer Registry Association of Arizona, State Meeting, Phoenix, Arizona
9/1994	*What Every Woman Should Know About Cancer: A Wellness Approach*, Phoenix, Arizona

PRESENTATIONS
(continued)

9/1994	*What Every Man Should Know About Cancer: A Wellness Approach*, Phoenix, Arizona
7/1994	*Circle of Life – Breast Cancer Education for Native Americans*, Scottsdale, Arizona
6/1994	*Chronic Lymphocytic Leukemia and Its Treatment*, Boise, Idaho.
4/1994	*Chemotherapy: What to Know about Patients On and Off Treatment*, Arizona Family Planning Council – 1994 Spring Pharmacology Update for Nurse Practitioners, Phoenix, Arizona
4/1994	*Breast Cancer Update*, Arizona Operating Room Nursing Society Annual Meeting, Tempe, Arizona
10/1993	*Women's Health Issues and Breast Cancer*, YWCA State Meeting, Phoenix, Arizona
9/1993	*Men's Health Issues – Prostate Cancer (Keynote)*, Mercy Care Cancer Symposium, Cedar Rapids, Iowa
8/1993	*Rehabilitation and Long-Term Survivorship Issues*, St. Patrick's Hospital Symposium, Lake Charles, Louisiana
6/1993	*Childhood Cancer*, American Cancer Society, Phoenix, Arizona
6/1993	*Understanding Sexual Changes Caused By Cancer and Its Treatment*, Visiting Nurse Service, Yuma, Arizona
5/1993	*Behavioral Approach to Cancer Pain Management*, Hospice, Phoenix, Arizona
5/1993	*Breast Cancer – From Prevention To Long-Term Follow Up*, Arizona Family Planning Counsel, Phoenix, Arizona
4/1993	*Changing Paradigms in Oncology Care*, Mission Cancer Symposium, Ashville, North Carolina
4/1993	*The Role of the Operating Room Nurse in Cancer Care*, Arizona Association of Operating Room Nurses, Phoenix, Arizona
2/1993	*Because I Am the Man: Sexuality Issues for the Individual with Cancer and Their Partner*, Fifth Annual Southwest Oncology Symposium, Phoenix, Arizona
10/1992	*The Challenge of Long-Range Planning: Cancer Survivorship*, Phoenix Oncology Nursing Society and Arizona State University Annual Conference, Phoenix, Arizona
10/1992	*Cancer: What It Means to You*, Arizona Society of Radiologic Technologists, Flagstaff, Arizona
9/1992	*Sexuality in the Ostomate*, Regional Ostomy Association, Phoenix, Arizona
3/1992	*The Impact of Cancer and Its Treatment on Sexuality*, Sixth Annual Southern Arizona Oncology Nursing Society Conference, Tucson, Arizona
2/1992	*The Impact of Cancer and Its Treatment on Sexuality*, Fourth Annual Southwest Oncology Symposium, Phoenix, Arizona
10/1991	*Cancer: It's a Family Disease*, Arizona State University and Phoenix Oncology Nursing Society Conference, Scottsdale, Arizona
9/1991	*La Paz County Health Assessment Project*, Rural Health Conference, Phoenix, Arizona
8/1991	*Cancer Caregiver: Intervention Study Review*, Phoenix Oncology Nursing Society Conference, Phoenix, Arizona
7/1991	*Overview: Cancer and Young Adults*, Street Teen Program, Phoenix, Arizona
6/1991	*Cancer Rehabilitation*, Arizona Physical Therapist Conference, Phoenix, Arizona
5/1990	*Cancer in the Elderly*, Maricopa County Long-Term Care (Director of Nurses) Conference, Phoenix, Arizona
5/1990	*Overview of Inpatient Cancer Chemotherapy*, Health Service Advisory Group, Scottsdale, Arizona
4/1990	*Prevention and Detection: The Role of the Nurse*, American Cancer Society Conference, Tempe, Arizona
LOCAL:	Provided numerous lectures to community and health care professionals on cancer-related topics. List furnished upon request.

COURSES TAUGHT   1993 – 1994   ***Breast Cancer*** education course. An eight-week course focusing on prevention and detection, disease trajectory, treatment options, long-term survivorship issues, family assessment, patient and family education, spirituality, sexuality, nutritional concerns. Phoenix, Arizona. Enrollment = 25

1993 – 1994   ***Cancer Prevention & Detection Course for Nurses***. A one-day course focusing on educating nurses about risk factors, warning signs, and screening techniques for common cancers as well as issues related to prevention and detection. Phoenix, Arizona. Enrollment = 50

1993 – 1994   ***Group Facilitation Course***. A one-day course focusing on group facilitation techniques and strategies related to support groups. Phoenix, Arizona. Enrollment = 45

1990 – 1994   ***Cancer Core Course***, a three-day course. Phoenix, Arizona. Enrollment = 35 (offered twice a year)

1987 – 1994   ***ONCC Review Course***, a five-day course reviewing basic oncology issues—by ONS guidelines. Phoenix, Arizona. Enrollment = 30 (offered once a year)

*1987 – 1994   ***Chemotherapy Revalidation Course***, a six-hour course. Phoenix, Arizona (and other regional sites). Enrollment = 50. (offered five times a year)

*1986 – 1994   ***Chemotherapy Validation Home Health Course***, an eight-hour course. Phoenix, Arizona (and other regional sites). Enrollment = 40 (offered three times a year)

*1984 – 1994   ***Chemotherapy Validation Course***, a three-day course. Phoenix, Arizona (and other regional sites). Enrollment = 45 (offered five times a year)

* *These courses also provided throughout the State of Arizona as a consultant*

PRECEPTOR   1982 – 1990   Radiation Oncology and Radiological Technology Students (as needed)
1980 – Present   Student Nurse, AND, BSN, MS, NP; Glendale Community College, Phoenix Community College, Grand Canyon University, Arizona State University, Northern Arizona University, and University of Phoenix

16 | WHEN IS 11" x 17" PAPER APPROPRIATE?

If you fold an 11" x 17" piece of paper in half, you will have four 8½" x 11" sheets of paper for your multiple-page resume. For a three- or four-page curriculum vita, it is a convenient way to present all the information without shuffling a lot of paper. For a resume that takes up two pages, you can design a cover page that has only your name, address, phone number, etc., and use the two inside pages for your resume. If you have a clean, one-page resume, don't use 11" x 17" paper. This is only an alternative for people who must have resumes longer than one page.

Some readers don't think to turn the paper over to see the very back of the folded 11" x 17", so make sure that any information you put on that page is not critical to your overall qualifications.

Since the pages never become separated from each other, it is not necessary to put your name on every page. However, your name should be on the first page of the inside text so it sticks in the reader's mind.

There is one problem with paper of this size. There are few laser printers that are capable of handling 11" x 17" paper, so your only alternative is a copy machine. Laser-printed masters make such a striking statement that you can't really beat them, but there is nothing wrong with a good copy. As with any copying process, the better the machine, the better the results, so be certain you get the best copy machine available in your area.

JUDY P. PROBATION

PRESENTATION OF QUALIFICATIONS

12345 W. Union Hills Drive #123
Phoenix, Arizona 85027
Home: (602) 555-1234
Work: (602) 555-1234

JUDY P. PROBATION

OBJECTIVE

Seeking a challenging and rewarding career position in the SOCIAL SERVICE/ COUNSELING field, utilizing educational background as well as professional and volunteer experience.

OVERVIEW OF CAPABILITIES

Offers college degree, continuing education, and more than 10 years of experience in positions requiring the following abilities:

- *Interpersonal Relationships*
- *Family Counseling*
- *Court Procedures*
- *Report Preparation*

- *Crisis Intervention*
- *Parenting Skills*
- *Supervision/Training*
- *Computer Use*

- *Extensive experience in a voluntary capacity in Adult Probation, Child Protective Services, TEROS, and Planned Parenthood with numerous social service agencies.*
- *Establishes and maintains productive rapport with people of all backgrounds and socio-economic levels.*
- *Communicates clearly and concisely in language anyone can understand.*
- *Possesses sound judgment and excellent decision-making skills.*
- *Noted for organizational skills, ability to prioritize and meet deadline requirements.*
- *Works efficiently under pressure and remains calm in stressful situations.*

EDUCATION/ TRAINING

ARIZONA STATE UNIVERSITY *Tempe, Arizona*
B.S. Degree in Justice Studies
Master Degree Candidate: Justice Studies

PHOENIX COLLEGE
Degree: Associate in Applied Science – Counseling
- *Graduated with Distinction*

Courses included: Communication Skills; Supervised Practice (Intern Program); Report Preparation; Ethnic Counseling; Counseling Methods and Procedures; Individual/Group Counseling; Psychology; Reality Therapy; Personality Analysis; Emergency Medical Technology.

Activities:
- *Phi Beta Kappa – Honor Society*
- *Advisory Committee Counseling*

Additional Studies: Child Abuse; Stress in Law Enforcement; Gestalt Workshop; Stress Management; Take Charge of Life; Growth and Development; Becoming Naturally Therapeutic

---

SPECIAL SKILLS

- *CRT: Data Entry/Retrieval*
- *Switchboard*
- *Microfiche: Filming/Retrieval*
- *Other Office Machines/Equipment*

- *Remote Computer Terminal*
- *Teletype*
- *Two-way Radio*

REFERENCES

References and additional data available upon request

EXPERIENCE

ADULT PROBATION, FIELD OFFICER
Maricopa County

1991 – Present
Phoenix, Arizona

Provide correctional casework services; conduct pre-sentence investigation; supervise probationers; counsel clients or refer them to various social agencies; visit probationers at home, work, or in treatment facilities; conduct urinalysis supervision of drug addicts; investigate alleged violations of probation; enforce court-mandated terms of probation; present written reports and recommendation to the court; maintain case records; testify in court. Able to apply principles and methods of correctional casework; able to analyze and evaluate home situation and family conflicts; able to speak and write effectively; able to maintain and utilize case files effectively.

COURT SERVICES
Phoenix Municipal Court

1980 – 1991
Phoenix, Arizona

Meets or exceeds all requirements of this position and others held with this extremely active arm of the law. Demonstration of ability and in-depth knowledge of the inner workings of the court system resulted in advancement to positions of increasing responsibility. Utilized organizational skill to clear three-month correspondence backlog and resolved numerous problems involving defendants. Processed personnel into system, providing training and supervision as required. Used computer to update defendant background information as well as data entry and retrieval. Frequently called upon to assist other departments, serving virtually every department in the court system. Heavily involved in courtroom activities, recording proceedings and assisting bailiff.

- Selected to serve as Acting Bailiff for a 15-month period. Duties encompassed assistance to judges, attorneys, and defendants, processing required paperwork, and holding defendants in protective custody prior to jail booking.
- Commended by presiding judge for ability in dealing with jurors.
- Recipient of letters of appreciation for outstanding assistance.

MAIL ROOM SUPERVISOR
North American Coin & Currency

1980
Phoenix, Arizona

Within three weeks of hire by this brokerage firm, was promoted to supervisory position with full responsibility for maintaining efficiency of staff, personnel training, and effective scheduling of work loads. Established office supply department to control expenditures while maintaining proper inventory of supplies and equipment. Provided accurate journal, detailing incoming revenue and bank deposits. Consistently met all requirements on dated material.

CUSTOMER SERVICE REPRESENTATIVE
United Parcel Service/Western Temporary

1979 – 1980

Developed excellent relations with customers, via telephone, serving as Customer Service Representative for this major shipping/receiving company. Services included arranging for pickup/delivery of orders, serving as a problem solver with regard to tracing lost parcels, and extensive telephone work.

RADIO DISPATCH OPERATOR
Maricopa County Sheriff's Office

1974 – 1979
Phoenix, Arizona

Utilized ability to function efficiently under pressure in service to the community. As the central core of this active office, was responsible for coordinating incoming calls and dispatching same, via two-way radio, to the appropriate field officers. Relayed emergency messages to other agencies throughout the county.

COMMUNITY SERVICE

- Parent/Teachers Association: Various offices – 10 years
- Boy Scouts of America and Campfire Girls: Leader, etc. – 8 years
- Child Protection Services: Volunteer Case Worker – 6-month practicum
- Planned Parenthood: Volunteer Counselor – 1½-year practicum
- TEROS: Volunteer Phone Crisis Intervention – 6-month practicum

GENE C. VAN WATERS

12345 Tropicana Circle
Sun City, Arizona 85351
Phone (602) 555-1234
Fax (602) 555-1234

CAREER OBJECTIVE

A challenging career position in the industrial chemical/chemical specialties industry as a technical sales representative, field sales manager, or branch office manager with sales responsibilities.

CAREER SUMMARY

- Account Manager/Technical Sales Specialist in electronics, aerospace, and related industries utilizing surface finishing. Advanced to product line manager—electronics plating for a leading international chemical specialties corporation. Interfaced with leading electronics manufacturers, the military, and corporate R&D to develop and market state-of-the-art processes and establish company as industry leader.

- A twenty-year track record of sales growth, new product introduction, and satisfied customers.

- Strengths include sales/communication skills, technical knowledge, industry association, and success in meeting new challenges.

- Developed considerable technical expertise in development, optimization, and automated control of chemical processes for electronics and finishing industries.

PROFESSIONAL EXPERIENCE

CYPRESS CHEMICAL COMPANY, Anaheim, California   1991 – 1995
Technical Sales Representative – Industrial Chemicals
- Tripled sales within first six months.
- Acquired new major accounts and regained business with inactive major accounts.

SHIPLEY COMPANY, INC., Irvine, California   1983 – 1991
Senior Account Manager (2 years), West Coast Electronics Finishing Sales
- Sales and technical service to Shipley's electronics finishing clients throughout the Western United States. More than $2 million in annual sales, 50 percent plus gross margin.
- Recommended, installed, and maintained chemical processes and automated control equipment.

Senior Product Line Manager (2 years), Electronic Plating Products
- Developed and implemented business and marketing plans for growth of electronics plating department.
- Promoted worldwide sales by implementing advertising, trade show participation, staff technical training, and technical sales/training literature.
- Visits, presentations with sales department nationwide to develop major accounts.
- Initiated new product development, process control equipment to meet industry needs.

Senior Technical Sales Representative (4 years), Arizona, New Mexico, Utah, Nevada
Account sales and technical services for all electronics and plating products within region.
- Established company presence at all electronics, aerospace, and other companies utilizing surface finishing.
- Technical responsibilities included recommendation, installation, and optimization of chemical processes and automated process control equipment.
- Doubled sales first year in territory; gained over 50% market share during second year.
- Field tested and introduced many new products to customers; led company in new product sales.

M&T CHEMICALS, Pico Rivera, California 1979 – 1983
Technical Sales Representative, Arizona, New Mexico, Utah, Nevada
Responsible for sales and technical services of printed circuit and metal finishing products.
- Increased business 50 percent.
- Appointed Senior Sales Specialist, Electronics.
- Introduced many new products to area customers.

VAN WATERS & ROGERS, Los Angeles, California 1975 – 1979
Technical Sales Representative
Sales of industrial chemicals to all industries within assigned territories.
- Developed growth in three different territory assignments: South Bay, San Gabriel Valley, and San Bernardino and Riverside Counties.
- Specialized in certain product lines: chlorinated and Freon solvents, bulk installations, hydrogen peroxide for wastewater treatment, and specialties for the electronics and plating industries.
- Area *Salesman of the Month* award for growth.

ROY'S RADIO & TV, Ontario, California 1973 – 1975
Manager
Managed this television and electronics service business.
- Increased business volume 40 percent in less than two years.
- Leased ownership of family business with option to purchase (elected not to purchase).

VAN WATERS & ROGERS, Brisbane, California 1967 – 1973
Technical Sales Representative (2 years), East San Francisco Bay
Sales of industrial chemicals to industries within territory.
- Grew business 40 percent within two years.

Operations Supervisor (2 years), Fresno, California
- Supervised inside sales, inventory control, warehousing, and shipping for Southern Valley area.

Inside Sales Supervisor (6 months), Brisbane, California
- Supervised Order Department, inventory control, and other functions for the laundry and dry cleaning supplies division.
- Implemented VW&R system in newly acquired division.
- Developed inventory control systems.

Purchasing, Inside Sales (1 year), Pico Rivera, California
- Maintained inventory of local and satellite warehouses.
- Developed a Corporate Purchasing Procedures Manual and Source Book for laundry and dry cleaning supplies department.

HONORS, AWARDS, AND PROFESSIONAL AFFILIATIONS

- Van Waters, *Salesman of the Month*, 1976
- Shipley, *Salesman of the Year*, 1984
- American Electroplaters, Certified Electronics Specialist
- Member and Past Officer, American Electroplaters and Surface Finishers Association
- Member, International Institute of Connector and Interconnect Technology, Inc.

JONN FABRICATOR

an idea can do anything...

1234 South Clementine Court
Tempe, Arizona 85282

Telephone: (602) 555-1234

JONN FABRICATOR

EDUCATION:

1983 – 1984, 1990	Mesa Community College, Arizona	General Technology
1975 – 1978	Arizona State University	Mechanical Engineering
1873 – 1975	Western Illinois University	Industrial Technology

EXPERIENCE

1992 – Present

ROB GORDON RACING   Orange, California
Team Manager/Co-Driver
Managed off-road racing team, including resolution of start-up issues. Maintained relationships with major sponsors (Ford, BF Goodrich, Tecate, La Victoria). Organized race support volunteers and managed three mechanics/fabricators. Utilized computer (database and word processing), and purchased parts and supplies.

1990 – 1991

VENABLE RACING   Hemet, California
Race Team Fabricator/Head Mechanic/Co-Driver
Venable Racing was the recipient of Ford Motor Company's main off-road race project with the most sensational driver in off-road racing behind the wheel. Responsible for mechanical and structural integrity of the vehicle. As co-driver, won the Class 8 Championship for 1990, including an overall victory at the Baja 500. Along with Venable's designer, was contracted by a factory Jeep team to build an unlimited Cherokee for a prominent driver.

1988 – 1989

VECTOR PROMOTIONS, INC.   Orange, California
Race Team Fabricator/Mechanic/Co-Driver
Through skills and experience in the off-road field, aided in the racing of a factory Chevrolet Class 7 truck (S-10) for a winning season. Working with an engineer, played a major part in the fabrication and assembly of an exotic unlimited race truck. Organizing skills were sharpened by the many facets of this prominent off-road race team.

1986 – 1988
1982 – 1983

PALMER CUSTOM SPEED   Phoenix, Arizona
Race Car Fabricator/Mechanic/Co-Driver
Extended my fabrication skills through many forms of vehicles and accessories. Special projects included heading up the design, fabrication, and race prep of a state-of-the-art off-road car.

1986

LAZE R. TRON
Car Show Entertainer
Designed Laze R. Tron as a stage show involving a high-tech robot costume similar to a "Transformer" toy. Was contracted by various "World of Wheels" car shows in Canada and the Western U.S., including Hawaii.

1978 – 1981

BRANDWOOD CARS   Phoenix, Arizona
Foreman/Head Fabricator
Gained valuable knowledge and skills in the race car and metal fabrication industry. Designed jigs, templates, and special tools pertaining to custom metal fabrication.

**SKILLS/
ACTIVITIES**

Artistic and Technical Creations
- Designed and built many forms of indoor and outdoor art.
- Assembled and experimented with low-power lasers.
- Experimented with and used many specialized electronic devices and lighting systems.
- Constructed and performed in unique costumes.
- Utilized gadgetry and special effects for theme parties.
- Decorated lavish cakes and floral arrangements.

Staging and Light Setup
- Designed trade show displays for race car products.
- Set up car show displays for customers.
- Designed and built theatrical stage displays.
- Controlled theatrical audio and visual equipment, including multi-scene light boards.
- Operated pyrotechnical stage equipment.
- Hired by various movie companies as a carpenter and metal fabricator.

Performances
- Performed in numerous plays and musicals.
- Danced for a jazz performance group.
- Performed as a clown at public events.

Racing
- Raced off-road cars, 3-wheelers, bicycles, and outhouses.
- Completely built and prepped own race car for winning season.
- (See "Experience")

Miscellaneous
- Drove vehicles in two nationally televised commercials.
- Familiar with farm equipment, from tractors to combines.
- Worked with young people as a summer camp counselor.
- Graduated from a certified bartender's school.
- Completed a certified floral design school.
- Additional hobbies include photography, volleyball, camping, ATVs.
- Enjoying life.

ORGANIZATIONS:

Honor Society – Mesa Community College
MCC Dance Performance – Jazz Dance Troupe
Arizona Dirt Off-Road Club

17 FOREIGN LANGUAGES

I have designed resumes in many different languages, including Spanish, Portuguese, German, French, Swedish, Norwegian, Russian, Dutch, among others. All of them were created using WordPerfect's soft keyboards (where you assign certain characters to the keys in Setup F1) or the Compose feature (Ctrl V or Ctrl 2 in 5.0/5.1 and Ctrl W in 6.0). WordPerfect comes standard with character sets that allow you to access letters for most character-based languages, as well as ancient and modern Greek, Hebrew, Cyrillic (Russian, Ukrainian, Serbian, Macedonian, Byelorussian, Bulgarian), and Japanese (Hiragana or Katakana). Special modules are available for many other languages and can be purchased from WordPerfect or other software dealers.

Needless to say, typing in languages that use characters similar to our English ones is easier than keying in the less-familiar characters of, say, Greek, Japanese, or Russian, but it can be done.

Companies in many countries outside the United States either require or prefer more personal information on a resume than we in the United States are used to seeing. That may include:

- Nationality
- Citizenship
- Birth date
- Place of birth
- Sex
- Marital status
- Health condition
- Photograph

It is important for you to research the requirements of the international company to which you will be applying and lay out your resume in a format that meets its criteria. Often you can request sample formats from the company itself or inquire of your associates who have experience applying for jobs in your target country.

Françoise WENDLING

Vorstweg 123
1234 NV Velden
Pays-Bas
Tél: (31) 555-1234

FORMATION

Décembre 1995 — **Master of International Management**
AMERICAN GRADUATE SCHOOL OF INTERNATIONAL MANAGEMENT
Thunderbird Campus, Glendale, Arizona (Etats-Unis)
Spécialisation en marketing et commerce
- Participation dans un séminaire de publicité et marketing; développement stratégie de marketing et publicité (McIlhenny Company, U.S.A.) pour relancer Tabasco en Italie

Août 1992 — **Bachelor of Business Administration**
Ecole Supérieure de Commerce de Nijenrode, Breukelen, Pays-Bas
Spécialisation en marketing et stratégie commerciale

EXPERIENCE PROFESSIONNELLE

Juin 1995 — **PT AMERICANA, Jakarta, Indonesia**
Marketing Consultant
- Direction de séminaires pour 500 cadres marketing et publicité asiatiques
- Instruction de la création d'un plan de marketing et de publicité international

Août 1993 – **KNIGHT WENDLING, Amsterdam, Pays-Bas**
Juillet 1994 **Junior Consultant**
- Développement d'un procédé logistique et suivi des clients pour un producteur allemand de piles
- Mise au point d'une étude de stratégie pour une Chambre de Commerce hollandaise

Mars 1993 – **TOPDATA SOFTWARE, Copenhague, Danemark**
Juillet 1993 **Stagiaire (AIESEC)**
- Recherche et analyse du marché du Benelux
- Mise au point de la stratégie commerciale pour introduire des nouveaux logiciels sur le marché du Benelux

Août 1992 – **OCE-FRANCE, Paris, France**
Février 1993 **Assistante du chef de marketing**
- Evaluation d'un système informatique de marketing, analyse des besoins des utilisateurs et présentation des recommandations
- Analyse de la concurrence et participation dans les activités promotionnelles

Eté 1991 — **CHAMBRE DE COMMERCE HOLLANDE-SUISSE, Zürich, Suisse**
Stagiaire en marketing
- Analyse du marché Suisse pour les produits hollandais

LANGUES

Hollandais	Langue maternelle
Anglais, Français	Courant
Allemand	Lu, écrit et parlé
Espagnol	Bonnes notions

DIVERS

- Hollandaise (permis de travail français), 24 ans, célibataire
- Diplôme de Français Commercial et Economique de la Chambre de Commerce et d'Industrie de Paris (1994)
- Bourse du Rotary Foundation pour suivre des cours à l'étranger
- Présidente du Conseil Universitaire, Haute Ecole de Commerce de Nijenrode
- Stage d'espagnol intensif à Antigua, Guatemala (Juin - Août 1995)
- Loisirs: Equitation, badminton, musique, voyages

Jaime Vista Hermosa

OBJETIVO Trabajar en una posición administrativa en una compañia internacional en México, Canada o E.E.U.U.

CALIFICACIONES
- Excelentes contactos de negocios en México, asi como muy buen conocimiento de politica y negocios en México y E.E.U.U.
- Experiencia en el extranjero, incluyendo cinco años en E.E.U.U. y cuatro veranos en Inglaterra
- Disponibilidad de viajar constantemente

EDUCACION

MAESTRIA EN ADMINISTRACION INTERNACIONAL Agosto 1994
American Graduate School of International Management
Thunderbird Campus, Glendale, Arizona
Concentración Academica: Contabilidad, Finanzas, Finanzas y Comercio Internacional, Mercadotecnia Internacional, Ambiente de Negocios Norteamericano

LICENCIATURA (BACHELOR OF ARTS) 1990
Tufts University, Medford, Massachusetts
Concentración en Economia e Historia

BACHILLERATO 1985
Colegio Vista Hermosa, México D.F.

EXPERIENCIA

SUBDIRECTOR DE MERCADOTENIA 1990 – 1993
Colchones de Mexico S.A., México D.F.
- Creación de una campaña de mercadotenia para introducir Englander Sleep Products en México (joint venture)
- Organizar evento promocional para presentar el producto a las cadenas comerciales mas importantes de la Republica, asi como desarrollo de campañas promocionales en radio y television
- Responsable de promoción de ventas y supervisión de agentes comerciales

ASISTENTE DEL DIRECTOR DE MERCADOTECNIA 1989 – 1990
Colchones de Mexico S.A., México D.F.
- Promoción de ventas a nivel nacional
- Supervisión de agentes comerciales
- Promoción de ventas a las cadenas comerciales mas importantes de la Ciudad de México

DIRECTOR GENERAL Y SOCIO 1988 – 1989
Tienda de Ropa Infantil, México D.F.
- Experiencia empresarial
- Responsable de todas las areas del negocio: diseño de ropa, manufactura, importación, compra y arreglo de local comercial, contratación de empleados, y asuntos legales del negocio

ENTRENAMIENTO EN VENTAS Y ADMINISTRACION 1983 – 1984
Colchones de Mexico S.A., México D.F.

IDIOMAS **Ingles** y **español**, algo de **frances**

COMPUTACION WordStar, WordPerfect, Lotus 1-2-3, Harvard Graphics, dBASE

DATOS PERSONALES Actividades: Club Español, Club de México (AGSIM)
Intereses: Tennis, natacion, buceo, futbol, viajar
Fecha de Nacimiento: Julio 10 de 1964
Ciudadania mexicana

DIRECCION Auvernia Montes 1234, México 11000, D.F., México (915) 555-1234

SANDRA LIESELOTTE OSWEGO

STUDIENADRESSE
12345 N. 9th Avenue #123
Glendale, Arizona 85306 USA
Tel: (602) 555-1234

HEIMATADRESSE
1234 E. Cortez
Phoenix, Arizona 85028 USA
Tel: (602) 555-1234

PERSÖNLICHE DATEN
Geburtsdatum:	14. Juni 1965
Geburtsort:	New York, New York USA
Staatsangehörigkeit:	amerikanisch
Familienstand:	ledig

AUSBILDUNG

09/1979 – 06/1983
Lake Oswego High School
Lake Oswego, Oregon USA
Abschulß: High School Diploma

08/1983 – 08/1987
Oregon State University
Corvallis, Oregon USA
Abschluß: Bachelor of Arts – Business Administration
Schwerpunkt: Finanzwesen

09/1992 – 12/1994
American Graduate School of International Management (Thunderbird)
Glendale, Arizona USA
Abschluß: Master of International Management (MIM)
Fächer: Internationales Management und Marketing

02/1994 – 06/1994
Europa-Studium, Deutsch
European Business School, Schloß Reichartshausen
Fach: Internationales Marketing

BERUFS-ERFAHRUNG

09/1987 – 06/1988
Allstate Enterprises, San Diego, California USA
Sachbearbeiterin für Versicherungen und Kredite

07/1988 – 05/1989
John Burnham & Company, San Diego, California USA
Research Assistant für kommerzielle Immobilien

06/1989 – 12/1990
John Burnham & Company, San Diego, California USA
Makler für kommerzielle Immobilien

01/1991 – 07/1991
Koastal Kids, San Diego, California USA
Verkauf und Großhandel für Kinderbekleidung

08/1991 – 07/1992
Ocean Pacific Sunwear, Ltd. ("OP"), San Diego, California USA
Verkauf und Großhandel für Herrenbekleidung

06/1994 – 07/1994
New Balance Germany, München
Marktforschung, Vertriebstätigkeiten, Repräsentationen

SPRACHKENNTNISSE
Mutterspache Englisch • Deutsch fließend in Wort und Schrift

EDV-KENNTNISSE
Lotus 1-2-3, dBASE IV, WordPerfect, BASIC, Harvard Graphics

HOBBIES/INTERESSEN
Reisen, Skifahren, Aerobics, Jogging
Mitglied des deutschen Clubs und der International Career Opportunities (ICO)
in Germany – Gesellschaft, Thunderbird

264

Joyce B. Hinsdale

Adresse:	Neustraße 123	
	6000 Frankfurt am Main 123	
	Telefon: 069/555-1234	
Persönliche Daten:	Geburtsdatum: 3. Mai 1964	
	Geburtsort: Chicago, Illinois USA	
	Staatsangehörigkeit: amerikanisch	
	Familienstand: ledig	

Ausbildung:	1983–1987	HINSDALE CENTRAL HIGH SCHOOL
		Hinsdale, Illinois USA
		Diploma
	1987–1991	NORTHWESTERN UNIVERSITY
		Evanston, Illinois USA
		Abschluß: Bachelor of Arts
		Fächer: Germanistik, Politikwissenschaft
	SS 1990	UNIVERSITÄT REGENSBURG
		Regensburg
		Fächer: Germanistik
	1991–1994	ILLINOIS INSTITUTE OF TECHNOLOGY
		CHICAGO KENT COLLEGE OF LAW
		Chicago, Illinois USA
		Abschluß: Juris Doctor
	1994–1995	AMERICAN GRADUATE SCHOOL OF
		INTERNATIONAL MANAGEMENT
		Glendale, Arizona USA
		Abschluß: Master of International Management
		Fächer: Marketing, Management
Beruflicher Werdegang:	1991–1992	JAMES SCHREIBER, LTD.
		Willow Springs, Illinois USA
		Sekretärin, Verkäuferin und Käuferin
	SS 1992	DONALD P. O'CONNELL
		Vorsitzenderrichter der Rechtsabteilung,
		First Municipal District, Circuit Court of Cook County
		Chicago, Illinois USA
		Rechtspraktikantin
	SS 1993	SHEA, ROGAL AND ASSOCIATES
		Westchester, Illinois USA
		Rechtspraktikantin
	1994	SUNRISE VILLAGE APARTMENTS
		Glendale, Arizona USA
		Vermarketerin und Vertreterin
	1995	CIRCUIT COURT OF COOK COUNTY
		Chicago, Illinois USA
		Juristin
Weiterbildung:	SS 1989	GOETHE INSTITUT BREMEN
		Intensiv-Sprachkurs (DaF – Zertifikat)

Sprachen:	English – Muttersprache
	Deutsch – fließend
	Französisch – Grundkenntnisse
Besondere Kenntnisse:	WordPerfect, IBM AS400, Lotus 1-2-3, dBASE IV, LEXIS, WESTLAW
Aktivitäten/ Interessen:	Presidentin und Kassenverwalterin des Deutschen Klubs; Mitglied der ICO-Germany, Chicago Council on Foreign Relations, Chicago Bar Association, American Bar Association; Reisen; Photographie; Tauchen

MONA SARPSBORG

ADRESSE Stm. Kolstadsvei 123, 1234 Sarpsborg, 09 555-1234

FØDT 17.07.69

UTDANNELSE **MASTER OF INTERNATIONAL MANAGEMENT** Mai 1994
American Graduate School of International Management
Thunderbird Campus, Glendale, Arizona
International Corporate Consulting: Konsulentoppdrag for
Vitro – Mexico. Utviklet markedsføringsplan for introduksjon av
Vitro calcium chloride i USA.
International Business-to-Business Marketing: Utførte
markedsanalyse og utviklet markedsføringsplan for introduksjon
av **Natterman** lecithin i Canada.
European Integration: Studier av EF og virkningene av 1992 på
det europeiske samarbeid.

SIVILØKONOM Juni 1993
Bedriftsøkonomisk Institutt, Oslo
• Hovedvekt på Internasjonal Bedriftsledelse.

FAGKURS I ØKONOMI OG DATABEHANDLING 1988 – 1989
Bedriftsøkonomisk Institutt, Oslo

ERFARING **Ramstad Veiservice**, Oslo 1990 – 1994
• Deltidsansatt som ekspeditør.
• Fungerte som kontormedarbeider i sommerferier med ansvar
  for daglig drift når daglig leder hadde ferie.

Haneborg Finne, Oslo 1988 – 1989
• Praktikant med daglig ansvar for tre barn i alderen 3 til 12 år.

Sarpborg Idrettslag, Sarpsborg 1986 – 1988
• Fri-idrettsinstruktør med ansvar for utvikling og
  implementering av treningsprogram.

ANNET **Orientation Team – AGSIM**, Glendale, Arizona 1994
• Planla agenda for 400 nye studenter og hjalp dem i
  tilpasningen av et nytt miljø.

Ballkomite – BI, Oslo 1993
• Organiserte avslutningsball for siviløkonomkullet av 1989–1993.

BI – Studentenes Idrettslag, Oslo
• Planla og organiserte felles idrettsdager for BIs høyskole og
  lokalavdelinger.

National Kunstløpsklubb, Sarpsborg 1974 – 1983
• Topputøver av kunstløp på nasjonalt nivå.

SPRÅK Engelsk, tysk og spansk.

PC – SPRÅK **Apple Systemer:** WordPerfect, MS Word, Excel, SuperPaint, MacDraw
DOS Systemer: WordPerfect, Minitab, DataBase

Todd DeWitt

Studienadresse:	Thunderbird Campus Box 1234 Glendale, Arizona 85306 Telefon: 001-602-555-1234
Heimatadresse:	123 15th Avenue DeWitt, Iowa 52742 Telefon: 001-319-555-1234
Persönliche Daten:	Geburtsdatum: 3. Mai 1963 Geburtsort: Rock Island, Illinois Staatsangehörigkeit: amerikanisch Familienstand: ledig

---

Ausbildung:

08/1986 – 05/1989 DEWITT COMMUNITY HIGH SCHOOL, DeWitt, Iowa (USA)
08/1989 – 12/1993 UNIVERSITY OF NORTHERN IOWA, Cedar Falls, Iowa (USA)
Bachelor of Arts
Hauptfach: Finanzwesen   Nebenfach: Deutsch
Zertifikat in Internationaler Betriebswirtschaft
02/1994 – 05/1995 AMERICAN GRADUATE SCHOOL OF INTERNATIONAL
MANAGEMENT, Glendale, Arizona (USA)
Abshluß als "Master of International Management"

Berufserfahrung:

08/1986 – 05/1989 BARNES FOODLAND, DeWitt, Iowa (USA)
Lagerarbeiter im Lebensmittelgeschäft
05/1992 – 09/1992 MICHAEL J's, Cedar Falls, Iowa (USA)
Verkäufer in einem Kleiderwarengeschäft
05/1993 – 08/1993 FIRST BANK, Davenport, Iowa (USA)
Durchführung von Kreditgeschäften
02/1994 – 12/1994 AMERICAN GRADUATE SCHOOL OF INTERNATIONAL
MANAGEMENT, Glendale, Arizona (USA)
Career Services Center – Forschungsassistent

Weiterbildung:

02/1990 – 05/1990 Intensiv Sprachkurs in Deutsch
Universität Klagenfurt, Klagenfurt, Österreich

Sprachkenntnisse: Deutsch in Wort and Schrift fließend

Computerkenntnisse: Lotus 1-2-3, WordPerfect, BASIC

**Außercurriculare
Aktivitäten:**
Aktives Mitglied im Deutschen Klub
Freiwillige Mitarbeit beim Roten Kreuz
Mitglied in der Leichtathletik – Mannschaft an der "University of Northern Iowa"

Hobbies: Skifahren, Golf, Fitness, und Basketball

**Berufliche
Zielvorstellungen:**
Internationale Tätigkeit im Bereich Marketing

Lydia San Juan

12345 North 9th Avenue #1234, Glendale, Arizona 85306 U.S.A.   (602) 555-1234

OBJETIVO

Una posición en el campo académico, en administración internacional, la cual haga uso de mi educación y experiencia de una manera efectiva, además de proveer lugar para crecimiento tanto profesional como personalmente.

EDUCACION

Mayo 1995   **MASTER OF INTERNATIONAL MANAGEMENT**
American Graduate School of International Management, Glendale, Arizona
Completé cursos en "International Banking, Money and Banking, Internatinal Trade Administration, International Insurance y Cross-Cultural Communications" además de los requisitos del programa.

1991   **SEMINARIO PARA GERENTES INTERNACIONALES**
Bozell, Jacobs, Kenyon, & Eckhardt, New York, New York

1987   **PROGRAMA DE ENTRENAMIENTO AVANZADO EN PUBLICIDAD**
Foote, Cone, & Belding, Chicago, Illinois

1983   **BACHELOR OF SCIENCE IN GENERAL STUDIES**
Louisiana State University, Baton Rouge, Louisiana
Concentración: Humanidades-Historia del Arte

1979 – 1982   **ESCUELA DE ARQUITECTURA**
Universidad de Puerto Rico, Rio Piedras, Puerto Rico

EXPERIENCIA PROFESIONAL

1995   **ARIZONA STATE UNIVERSITY, WEST CAMPUS**, Phoenix, Arizona
Profesora Sustituta en el Departamento de Artes y Ciencias

1983 – 1993   **OMEGA ADVERTISING**, Hato Rey, Puerto Rico
SUBSIDIARIA DE SAATCHI AND SAATCHI COMMUNICATIONS
Directora de Medios, miembro de la Junta Ejecutiva y del Comité de Nuevos Negocios

1988 – 1992   **CPV/BOZELL, JACOBS, KENYON, & ECKHARDT**, San Juan, Puerto Rico
Comencé como Directora de Medios y Supervisora de Cuentas. Fuí promovida a Vice-Predidente, Directora de Servicios de Mercadotécnia; a Vice-Presidente Senior, Directora de Servicios a Cuentas; a Gerente General en funciones, miembro de la Junta de Directores. En estas posiciones me reportaba directamente al Presidente de la Compañía, quien a su vez era Director de Area para Latinoamérica. Desde 1984 a 1987 formé parte del Comité Latinoamericano de Nuevos Negocios reportando directamente al Presidente Internacional. En estas funciones tuve la oportunidad de trabajar para la oficina Mexicana en varias presentaciones.

1987 – 1988   **FOOTE, CONE, & BELDING**, San Juan, Puerto Rico
Ejecutiva de Cuentas. Manejo de la cuenta del mayor distribuidor de Perfumes y Cosméticos franceses y norteamericanos y de cuatro productos para el Cabello de Clairol Caribe, para quien diseñé y conduje seminarios en las universidades de la Isla sobre "El Secreto del Exito en tu Entrevista de Trabajo".

1987   **PUBLICIDAD SIBONEY**, Isla Verde, Puerto Rico
            Supervisora de medios de paso luego del "merger" de Publicidad Siboney con Norman, Craig &
            Kummel, Inc.

1985 – 1986 **NORMAN, CRAIG & KUMMEL, INC.**, Santurce, Puerto Rico
            Comencé como Directora Asociada de Medios y fuí ascendida a Directora de Medios.

1983 – 1985 **ULISES CADILLA AND ASSOCIATES/BBDO**, Santurce, Puerto Rico
            Comencé como asistente de Medios y fuí ascendida a Planeadora de Medios

1983   **MARTI, FLORES, PRIETO, INC.**, San Juan, Puerto Rico
            Trabajo de verano y temporero como analista de encuestas de medios

1975 – 1982 **J. WALTER THOMPSON COMPANY**, Santurce, Puerto Rico
            Trabajo temporero y de verano en varios departmentos de la Agencia mientras asistía a la Escuela
            Superior y Universidad.

1979 – 1980 **SEARS ROEBUCK**, Hato Rey, Puerto Rico
            Departamento de crédito. Trabajo temporero mientras asistía a la Universidad de Puerto Rico.

ACTIVIDADES EXTRACURRICULARES

Socia de los Clubes de Portugués, Español y Newman de la "American Graduate School of International Management"
Coleccionar frascos de perfume
"National Association of Underwater Instructors"
Pertenecí al Equipo de Ajedrez de la Universidad de Puerto Rico. Gané el premio de
Mejor Suplente Femenina en las Conpetencias Intramurales de 1979
Navegación y Pesca por las Islas del Caribe

DATOS PERSONALES

Lugar de Nacimiento: San Juan, Puerto Rico
Ciudadanía: U.S.A.
Fecha de Nacimiento: 31 de Marzo de 1962
Estado Civil: Soltera, Sin dependientes
Idiomas: Inglés y Español – Completamente Bilingüe
Programmación de Computadoras
Conocimiento del Idioma Francés

ANNE MARSEILLE

Détails Personnels:	• Date de Naissance: 24 Août 1969 • Nationalité: française • Situation de Famille: célibataire

Adresse:

1234, Boulevard du Roi René (33) 42 555-1234
12345 Aix-en-Provence (33) 42 555-1234
France Télécopie: (33) 42 555-1234

Compétences Spécifiques:

• Une large expérience professionelle dans l'industrie pharmaceutique
• Une formation académique scientifique
• Une perspective internationale

Expériences Professionnelles:

ROBAPHARM, GROUPE PIERRE FABRE 1990 à ce jour
Les Ullis, France
• Déléguée Médicale
  Région Provence-Alpes-Côte d'Azur

BRISTOL MYERS SQUIBB 1989–1990
Paris, France
• Déléguée Médicale
  Région Provence-Alpes-Côte d'Azur

PUBLIMED, GROUPE EXPAND (Prestataire de Service) 1988–1989
Paris, France
• Informateur Médical
• Représentait exclusivement les Laboratoires Jouveinal
  Région Provence-Alpes-Côte d'Azur

PHARMACIE DE L'HOTEL DE VILLE 1984–1988
Aix-en-Provence, France
• Vente en Pharmacie
• Distribution de matériel médical

Formation:

FACULTE DE SCIENCES, SAINT CHARLES 1987 – 1988
Université de Marseille, France
Sciences de la Nature et de la Vie
• DEUG B

FACULTE DE PHARMACIE 1984 – 1987
Université de Montpellier, France

LYCEE PAUL CEZANNE 1983 – 1984
Aix-en-Provence, France
• Baccalauréat D (Sciences)

Langues:

Français: langue maternelle • **Anglais, Italien:** lus et parlés

Séjours à l'étranger:

Royaume Uni, U.S.A, Italie, Brésil, Grèce, Allemagne, Suisse

18 | LETTERHEADS, COVER LETTERS, AND PAPER COLORS

LETTERHEADS

It is <u>so</u> easy to create a letterhead all your own and to make it match your resume. Just copy into a new document the name and address you have already created for your resume. It couldn't be simpler! It makes a very sharp impression when your cover letter and resume match in every respect, from paper color to font to letterhead.

COVER LETTERS

Do <u>not</u> use a generic cover letter with only a "Dear Sir/Madam" for every letter. It is important to personalize each cover letter with the company name and name of a contact person (if possible). The cover letter is the perfect place to mention specific experience that is targeted to the job opening and to bring up where you heard about the position. It is also the best place to state (or restate) your objective. Since you know specifically what job is being offered, you can tailor your objective to suit it.

A good cover letter consists of three parts:

1. The introduction, which mentions the position, where you heard about it, and why you think this company is precisely the place you want to work.

2. The "I'm super-great because" paragraph (or two). Here you summarize why you are absolutely perfect for the position. Really sell yourself. Pick and choose some of your experience and/or education that is specifically related to the company's requirements, or elaborate on qualifications that are not in your resume but apply to this particular job. Entice the reader to find out more about you in your resume. Don't make this section too long or you will quickly lose the reader's interest.

3. The closing should also be short, sweet, and to the point. Let the reader know what you want (an application, an interview, an opportunity to call). If you are planning to call the person on a certain day, you could close by saying, "I will contact you next Wednesday to set up a convenient time to meet." Don't call on a Monday or a Friday. If you are going to wait for the reader to call you, then close with something like: "I look forward to hearing from you soon." And remember to say, "Thank you for your consideration," or something to that effect (but don't be obsequious, please).

Color, like music, creates an atmosphere. Everyone knows that different colors evoke different feelings. Red can make a person feel warm, whereas blue does just the opposite.

Of course, in a resume you wouldn't want to use red! . . . although an artist could probably get away with just about any color. As a general rule, resume papers should be neutral or light in color. After many years in the resume business, I have discovered that brilliant white linen paper is still the most popular, closely followed by a slightly off-white, and then by shades of grey.

Just make sure that the color of the paper you choose is representative of your personality and that it doesn't detract from your message. For instance, a dark paper color makes your resume hard to read.

The type of paper (bond, linen, laid, cover stock, or coated) isn't as important, although it also projects an image. Uncoated paper (bond, linen, laid) makes a classic statement. It feels rich and makes people think of corporate stationery and important documents. Coated stock recalls memories of magazines, brochures, and annual reports. Heavy cover stock and laid paper can't be successfully folded and don't hold the ink from a laser printer very well, so they must be handled gently. All of these factors play a part in your paper choice.

John R. Letterhead

5424 50th Street
Lubbock, Texas 79416
(806) 555-1234

June 10, 1995

Mr. John Q. Smith
Director of Human Resources
Continental Grain Company
123 Park Avenue
New York, New York 10172

Dear Mr. Smith:

I am very interested in the financial analysis position, which you advertised in *The New York Times,* and would like the opportunity to discuss the possibility of working for your company.

I believe my experience in financial analysis, coupled with a strong quantitative and analytical background from my MBA and engineering degrees, make me an excellent candidate. As you will notice in the enclosed resume, I have spent over three years working in various Latin American countries exposing myself to international markets and different cultures. I have also acquired an extensive knowledge of computer systems through my work experience and education.

I look forward to speaking with you soon. Please feel free to contact me if you have any questions or would like to discuss my qualifications further.

Sincerely,

John R. Letterhead

Enclosure

John R. Letterhead

May 14, 1995

Mr. Sam Smith
Director, Logistics
Antarctic Support Associates
123 Inverness Drive
Englewood, Colorado 80112

Dear Mr. Smith:

I returned from McMurdo Station in October and have been corresponding with Tom Jones. I understand that the position of Supervisor, Peninsula Logistics is open, and I am writing to explore the possibility of securing that position.

I have served at Palmer Station as a Materialsperson and at McMurdo as the Senior Materialsperson in the power and water plants. With my 15 years of logistical experience in the military and the experience I have gained since then with Antarctic Support Associates, including my knowledge of all MAPCON applications used at ASA, I believe I am well qualified to excel in the position of Supervisor, Peninsula Logistics. I have a high regard for and interest in the work that is being accomplished in Antarctica by ASA in the support of the National Science Foundation.

Enclosed is a copy of my resume, which provides additional information on my work experience and accomplishments. I would appreciate the opportunity to meet with you to discuss the possibilities of working with ASA on a permanent basis. I will call you next week to arrange a mutually convenient meeting. If you have any questions in the meantime, please feel free to call me.

Sincerely,

John R. Letterhead

Enclosure

JOHN R. LETTERHEAD

12345 West Jefferson Avenue
Phoenix, Arizona 85123
(602) 555-1234

July 21, 1995

Ms. Mary Smith
Nike Employment Center
1 Bowerman Drive
Beaverton, Oregon 97005

Dear Ms. Smith:

The Technical Sales Representative position for Pittsburgh and San Francisco that we discussed today sparked a great deal of interest. This sounds like an exciting opportunity, and I appear to be an excellent match for your requirements.

My qualifications include:

- Master of International Management with an emphasis in Marketing/Finance
  American Graduate School of International Management

- Bachelor of Arts in Political Science/Economics

- Economic Development and Marketing Research Experience

- Retail Sales Experience with The Gap and Footlocker

- Evidence of Interpersonal/Leadership Skills
  - Rugby Club President
  - Fortune Yearbook Business Manager

My extracurricular activities and summer work experiences have enabled me to develop the poise and maturity needed to effectively manage multiple tasks while relating to different levels of management. I believe that these qualifications, along with my drive and enthusiasm, would make me an excellent candidate for your opening.

I would hope to have the opportunity to speak with you about this position. Thank you for your consideration.

Very truly yours,

John R. Letterhead

Enclosure

February 20, 1995

Ms. Judy Smith
Land Use Corporation
Box 1234
Fairfax, Virginia 26651

Dear Ms. Smith:

Please accept a brief summary of my past employment history to serve as application for the position of President of your Florida Project.

I am presently doing land acquisition for various Tampa Bay area builders and developers. I would prefer to work on a steady 3,000 acre site that you own.

I can meet with you at your earliest convenience to discuss my qualifications.

Sincerely,

Paul B. Letterhead

Enclosure

April 16, 1995

Mr. Gene Smith
U.S.-Russian Business Council
1234 Pennsylvania Avenue, N.W.
Washington, D.C. 20006

Dear Mr. Smith:

I am writing to inquire about any openings that might be available within your organization.

I have been extremely interested in East-West trade even before the fall of the Berlin Wall and began my study of the Russian language at the age of 15. In August of last year I completed my graduate degree in International Management with a specialization in international finance. Currently I am working as an intern at The Heritage Foundation in the Foreign Policy Department, Office of Russian Affairs. However, I would like to become more directly involved with stimulating American business in the former Soviet Union, specifically Russia.

I believe very strongly that, with my Russian language skills and graduate business degree, I could be of great use to the Council. I would very much appreciate the opportunity to meet with you to discuss my qualifications and background.

Thanks very much for considering my request and I look forward to hearing from you.

Sincerely,

John D. Letterhead

Enclosure

JOHN LETTERHEAD

June 26, 1995

Ms. Cindy Smith
College Relations Manager
Hallmark Cards, Inc.
P.O. Box 123456
Kansas City, Missouri 64141

Dear Ms. Smith:

It was in my hometown of Bogotá, Colombia, that as a teenager I came into contact with Hallmark for the first time. Even though I was not aware of the vision, effort, and commitment of resources that had gone into the Mother's Day card I had purchased, I was a happy customer. I never thought to wonder about the logistics of how that card had gotten to that small store or why a company more than 3,000 miles away was able to appeal to me, a kid from another country, culture, and language.

Hallmark's aggressive market penetration in more than 100 countries and its striving to provide employees with a supportive and challenging environment to best develop and apply their individual skills demonstrate to me that Hallmark is a company well worth entrusting with my career. In addition, I am impressed and attracted by Hallmark's commitment to supporting the communities in which it operates.

In light of Hallmark's international interest, you may be interested in my background. I started a small business in Colombia, which tested my energy, creativity, and initiative. The business quickly grew to be competitive as a result of innovative marketing and operation strategies. I have since learned to speak English, obtained a Bachelor of Business Administration from a U.S. university, and worked in several countries in varied positions, successfully adapting to both the people and management styles of these countries. Furthermore, in order to be better prepared for today's complex business environment, I am pursuing a Master of International Management degree, which I will complete in December.

It is my hope that my solid academic and cultural backgrounds, business experience, and interest in the international arena will convey to you that I have the qualifications to make a valuable contribution to Hallmark's efforts to remain the worldwide leader of the social expression industry.

I would like to be part of the Hallmark team that once helped me express myself through that card I gave my mother, and to take part in expanding the company to reach even more people all over the world. I would appreciate the opportunity to interview with you during your upcoming visit to Thunderbird, and hope that you will give the enclosed resume favorable consideration. Thank you for your attention.

Sincerely,

John Letterhead

Enclosure

August 1, 1995

Ms. Marilyn Smith
Dallas Partnership
1234 Elm Street, Suite 12
Dallas, Texas 75270

Dear Ms. Smith:

I am writing you at the recommendation of Mr. Bill Smith of the Arizona Economic Council in Phoenix. I developed a very amicable working relationship with Bill and the rest of the AEC staff during the short time I was there. As of September 1, however, I will be establishing permanent residency in the Dallas area and am seeking employment in the field of international marketing/management. Bill believed you would be a good person to talk with about the Dallas business scene and where the best employment opportunities in my field are to be found. Please note my qualifications:

- **Advanced Education – Master of International Management**: Graduated from "Thunderbird" graduate school, devoted exclusively to international business. Performed extensive graduate research and writing projects demonstrating my understanding of management, marketing, and finance on the international level.

- **Unique International Business Skills – Proficient in German**: Earned an undergraduate degree in German. Spent one year living in Freiburg, Germany, while studying German at Albert Ludwigs Universität.

- **Demonstrated Organizational Skills, Technical Competency**: I have a consistent record of achievements and honors. In academics, nonprofit organizations, and employment, I have always taken, or been asked to accept, additional responsibilities, thus reflecting my honest work ethic, skill in organizing work for expeditious completion, and ability to work under pressure.

Enclosed is my resume for your review. Perhaps you may have a suggestion or two of whom to contact or where to look. Aside from my search for employment, I would genuinely enjoy meeting you, as Bill has spoken so highly of you. Since I plan to make Dallas my permanent home, I am interested in developing a relationship with the city and its people for reasons beyond employment. I will call your office next week to see if you may have 5 or 10 minutes to meet with me sometime in the near future.

Sincerely,

John D. Letterhead

Enclosure

JOHN DOE

P.O. Box 1234
Phoenix, Arizona 85123

*Telephone
(602) 555-1234*

May 11, 1992

Human Resource Department
Conservation International
1234 50th Street, N.W.
Washington, D.C. 20036

Dear Recruiter:

I am a graduate student at Thunderbird. In the past week at school, at least five people have approached me to let me know that "the perfect job for me" was advertised in the Career Services Center. As I read over your job description for the Tagua Product Manager, I couldn't help but agree.

Your needs and my skills and experience are a perfect match. In fact, just two weeks ago I met with Coopena, a native Brazilian company operating within the Amazon rain forest to market locally made products in harmony with the environment. "Cause marketing" and international market development are my areas of interest.

My entrepreneurial experience and my education are tailored to your needs. I have run my own business for the past four years. I create and market artwear with ethnic and environmental themes. My marketing is primarily through sales representatives and trade shows, which has resulted in sales to most major department stores (including Nordstroms, Marshall Fields, and Macy's) as well as to more than 500 other accounts. In addition, my cross-cultural and interpersonal skills are conducive to effective teamwork within a multicultural environment.

My education at Thunderbird has included emphasis on marketing and international market development. Often, my studies have centered on environmental issues. I authored an ethics paper on the Exxon Valdez oil spill. Currently, I am conducting an extensive market research project for a company selling food products for emergency aid relief to private voluntary organizations. My language skills include a proficiency in Spanish. In addition, this semester I have continued to work on market development for Tenneco to market used equipment to Third World markets.

It is important to me to believe in what a company does. I plan to apply my skills and interests in assisting such a company achieve its objectives. In addition, I can offer Conservation International the benefit of my creative and innovative thinking.

I look forward to the opportunity to discuss how my skills and education fit into your needs and objectives. Please feel free to call if you have any questions.

Regards,

John Doe

Enclosure

JOHN R. LETTERHEAD

P.O. Box 1234 • Phoenix, Arizona 85123 • (602) 555-1234

April 18, 1995

Mr. Steve Smith
Director of Corporate Human Resources
Circle K Corporation
1234 North Central Avenue
Phoenix, Arizona 85012

Dear Mr. Smith:

Thank you for taking the time to discuss some of the available positions at Circle K Corporation. With this letter, I would like to express my interest in the New Business Development Sales Manager position.

Presently I am the General Manager for a food company that specializes in providing private label products to the natural foods industry. My marketing efforts have been focused on directing the promotion and development of store brands. Specifically, my responsibilities include the coordination of manufacturing, purchasing, distribution, and sale of our entire product line.

Coupled with my experience, I have earned my Master of International Management degree from Thunderbird in Glendale. My concentration was international marketing, and in conjunction with my studies, I directed a market feasibility study that measured new product acceptance levels and encompassed all facets of marketing research.

I am in the Phoenix area periodically and would welcome the opportunity to introduce myself and discuss how I might be an asset to your management team at Circle K Corporation. I will call you later this week to discuss this matter and, if appropriate, to arrange a meeting with you. Thank you for your consideration.

Sincerely,

John R. Letterhead

Enclosure

281

JOHN R. LETTERHEAD

January 31, 1995

Attn: Human Resources
Western Pacific Airlines
123 East Cheyenne Mountain Blvd.
Colorado Springs, Colorado 80906

Dear Sir/Madam:

I have read several newspaper articles about the startup of Western Pacific Airlines here in
Phoenix. I would like to be a part of this exciting opportunity as one of your ramp agents.

As an experienced airline ramp agent, I believe I am qualified to help this new airline grow.
While working for Horizon Air at Sea-Tac International Airport in Seattle, I learned a great
deal about airport and airline operations. It was especially diverse experience since Horizon
is a commuter airline, and I had the opportunity to provide customer service as well as my
technical skills.

I would like to be part of the Western Pacific team and would welcome the opportunity for
an interview to further discuss my qualifications. Please feel free to call me at your convenience. I look forward to hearing from you.

Sincerely,

John R. Letterhead

Enclosure

19 INDEX OF JOB TITLES

How many times have you wished for a line or two to describe something you did in a job long ago or even just yesterday? If you are like me, it happens all the time. Unless you can get your hands on the actual job description for your position, finding the words to tell someone in a few short sentences what your duties were or what you accomplished is one of the hardest parts of writing a resume.

That is why this index is different. Instead of listing only the titles from the objectives of all the resumes in this book, it lists every job that every resume mentions. That means you can turn to a page that has been referenced in the index and find wording somewhere in that resume that applies to one specific job title. Sometimes it will be only one or two lines. Other times the entire resume will be devoted to it. This should assist you in coming up with words to describe the various jobs you have performed in the past. Happy hunting!

A

Abstractor 26
Account Clerk 119
Account Executive 18, 32, 40, 61, 73, 83, 84, 86, 91, 100, 125, 157, 192, 210, 211, 212, 214
Account Executive Assistant 161
Account Executive Specialist 86
Account Management 121, 216
Account Manager 216, 218, 254
Account Representative 121
Account Rotator 125
Account Services Representative 38
Accountant 66, 96, 124, 144, 151
Accounting 151, 179, 220
Accounting Associate 11
Accounting Clerk III 126
Accounting Secretary 126
Accounting Sergeant 12
ACLS Instructor 236
Acquisitions 220
Acting Manager 200
Acting Section Engineer 186

Adjustment Supervisor 200
Administrative Assistant 36, 104, 114, 126, 155, 146, 152, 187, 208
Administrative Assistant Intern 214
Administrative Associate 94
Administrative Clerk 12
Administrative Manager 118, 144
Administrative Support 183
Admission Secretary 126
Adult and Continuing Education 222
Adult Probation 251
Advertising 9, 11, 14, 18, 24, 54, 68, 74, 79, 85, 100, 115, 116, 118, 119, 126, 127, 150, 154, 157, 176, 178, 192, 204, 209, 214, 219, 223, 225, 254
Advertising Associate 204
Advertising Intern 204
Advertising Manager 41, 68
Advertising Sales Representative 210
Advertising Staff 176
Advisory Staff 188
Aerospace 48, 216, 254

Agribusiness Intern 72
Agricultural Marketing 72
Air Force 48, 62, 88, 90, 97, 109, 130, 132, 149, 160, 184, 196, 213, 230
Air Frame License 184, 213
Air Traffic Control Radar Technician 230
Air Traffic Controller 130
Aircraft Armament System Technician 132
Aircraft Crew Chief 48, 184
Aircraft Junior Mechanic 184
Aircraft Maintenance Instructor 48
Aircraft Maintenance Specialist 97, 184, 213
Aircraft Mechanic 213
Aircraft Registration Clerk 17
Airline Customer Service Supervisor 159
Airline Steward 125
Airline Transport Pilot 90
Airport Operations 44
Analyst 178, 216, 224
Animal Handler 128
Animal Keeper 128
Animal Technician 128
Antenna Installation 67
Apprentice to Head Zookeeper 128
Architectural Drafting 194
Area Manager 92
Armament System Technician 132
Army 12, 56, 58, 88, 179, 229
Art History 202
Art Sales 193
Artist 204
Assistant Account Executive 18
Assistant Account Executive Intern 214
Assistant Adjutant 179
Assistant Auditor 103
Assistant Body Shop Manager 123
Assistant Branch Manager 45
Assistant Brand Manager 192
Assistant Business Development Administrator 225
Assistant Controller 96
Assistant Credit Manager 17
Assistant Customer Convenience Manager 200
Assistant Department Manager 101
Assistant Director, Adult Education 223
Assistant Export Coordinator 53
Assistant Golf Pro 197
Assistant Head Nurse 156

Assistant Inventory Manager 103
Assistant Manager 49, 73, 79, 80, 83, 106, 109, 123, 181, 200
Assistant Marketing Manager 28
Assistant Regional Manager 181
Assistant Retail Manager 79
Assistant Sales Manager 51
Assistant Store Manager 111, 187, 195, 208
Assistant Supermarket Manager 112
Assistant to Business Manager 79
Assistant to Director 223
Assistant to Director of Administration 14
Assistant to Europe and Asia Sales Manager 191
Assistant to Marketing Manager 74
Assistant to the Director 55
Assistant to the Program Manager 230
Assistant to the Publicist 204
Assistant to the Vice President of International Finance 22
Assistant to Vice President of Transportation 18
Assistant Treasurer 9
Assistant Vice President 9, 221
Associate Editor 8
Associate Manufacturing Specialist 22
Associate Marketing Coordinator 52
Associate Marketing Manager 85
Associate Pastor 138
Associated Students Legislative Council 190, 206
Atlantic Confidential Disclosure Coordinator 24
Attorney 104, 108
Attorney Service 161
Auditor 66
Au Pair 157
Auto Mechanic 34
Automobile Salesperson 148
Automotive 123
Aviation Operations 130
Aviation Services 184

B
Ballet 227
Ballet Auxiliary 114
Bank Clearance Department Researcher 20, 39

Bank Deputy 150
Bank Officer 45
Bank Teller 45, 190
Banker 40
Banking 9, 23, 26, 30, 42, 45, 74, 80,
    101, 149, 150, 155, 162, 216, 220,
    225
Banking Consultant 177
Banking Intern 24, 177
Banyan Engineer 230
Bar and Grill Owner 92
Barback 19
Bench Technician 67
Benefits 110
Bilingual Education Instructor 160
Bilingual Teacher's Assistant 26
Billing Clerk 17
Biology 15
BLS Instructor 236
Board of Directors 44, 114, 145, 178,
    242
Body Shop Manager 123
Bookkeeper 49, 94, 119, 221
Bookkeeping Assistant 183
Bookseller 41
Bouncer 19
Boy Scouts of America 19
Branch Manager 40, 45
Brand Management 38, 192
Broadcast Traffic Forwarder 18
Broker 27, 33, 70, 116, 182
Budget Control 224
Bulk Scheduling Manager 224
Business Coordinator 18
Business Development 21, 176, 216
Business Development Intern 21
Business Development Manager 191
Business Manager 43, 49, 176
Business Sub-Editor 68
Buyer 57, 82, 89, 126, 154
Buying Analyst 101

C

Cable Communications Plant Operations
    Management 67
Cable Contractor 67
Cable Television 67, 178, 226
Camera Assistant 205

Campus Outdoor Program Trip
    Coordinator 149
Campus Representative 147
Cancer Committee Coordinator 241
Cancer Program Coordinator 240
Cancer Screening/Detection 241
Car Show Entertainer 258
Career Guidance Program Chairman 89
Caregiver 202
Carpentry 68
Case Manager 156
Cast Member 154
Catering 29
Catholic Church 243
Cattle Committee Member 93
Cattle Ranch 44
Certified Public Accountant 66
Chairman, Career Guidance Program 89
Charge Nurse 237
Chartered Financial Consultant 131
Chartered Life Underwriter 131
Cheerleading Sponsor 234
Chemical Specialties 46, 254
Chemotherapy Nurse 241
Chief Technician 67
Chief, Computing Services 230
Child Protective Services 250
Child Sexual Abuse Treatment 114
Chiropractic Assistant 119
Christian Bookseller 41
Church Representative 148
Cinematography Camera Assistant 205
Circuit Board Designer 199
Circulation Assistant 28
Civil Engineering Consulting 46
Classroom Teacher 135, 238
Clerk 7, 12, 112, 119, 126, 183
Client Services Executive 216
Clinic Chemotherapy Nurse 241
Clinical Nurse Specialist 236
Clothing Business 21
Clown 259
Co-Director of Tennis 192
Co-Driver 258
Co-Editor 209
Co-Founder 87, 92
Co-Owner 87
Coast Guard 135, 229

Coffee Service Representative 62
Cold Drink Manager 38
Collaborating Investigator 241
Collections 45, 49, 145
Collections Agent 23
Collections Manager 200
Collections Supervisor 200
College Instructor 238
College of Preceptors Fellow 222
Combat Crew Commander 62
Combat Medic 88
Commercial Banking 45
Commercial Real Estate 36, 70
Communications 47, 67, 216
Communications Director 114
Communications Intern 30
Community Health Nurse 156
Community Service 21, 44
Compensation 110
Computer Aided Drafting 199
Computer Consultant 79
Computer Information Systems 230
Computer Operations 6, 109
Computer System Analyst 109
Computers 47, 216
Conference Liaison 39
Conference Manager 83
Conference Producer 86
Conference Staff 103
Consolidations 220
Construction 116, 118, 186, 198
Construction Subcontractor 54
Construction Technician 64
Consultant 11, 46, 51, 177, 186, 216,
    222, 226, 236, 239, 240, 262
Consulting 147, 186, 206, 208
Consumer Marketing 51
Continuing Education 223
Contract Administration 186
Contract Analysis 43
Contracting 116
Contracts Advisor 186
Contributing Writer 241
Controller 63, 66, 96
Conventions 55
Coordinator 52, 76, 204
Coordinator, Staff Education Services 222
Copy Editor 214

Core Professor 238
Corporate Construction Analyst 178
Corporate Consultant 57, 73
Corporate Consulting Associate 177
Corporate Marketing Consultant 51
Corporate Secretary 44
Cost Accountant 179
Counseling 250
Counselor 94, 160, 180, 238
Counterintelligence Agent 88
Countertrade 36, 121, 161, 177
Country Manager 38
Courier 19
Court Services 251
Courtesy Clerk 97
Crane Operator 136, 229
Credit 49
Credit Analyst 49, 121, 145, 153
Credit Card Fraud Processing 220
Credit Intern 30
Credit Manager 145
Credit Supervisor 121
Credit Union Manager 49
Crew Chief 48, 132, 184
Crisis Intervention 250
Critical Care Nurse 98, 156, 236
Curatorial Intern 202
Currency Future Trading 155
Customer Relations 121
Customer Service 54, 94, 152, 180, 209,
    210, 216, 251
Customer Service Counselor 190
Customer Service Intern 30
Customer Service Manager 40
Customer Service Supervisor 18, 159
Customs Liaison 14
CVICU/ICU Nurse 156

D

Dancer 259
Data Distributions Management System
    188
Data Entry 183
Data Manager/Nurse 241
Day Camp Director 227
DDMS Office Supply System 188
De Nova Setup 220
Delegation Coordinator 146

Dental Assistant 25
Department Coordinator 76
Department Manager 73, 112
Department Store Intern 33
Deputy Editor 68
Designer 194, 199
Designer Apparel Marketing 38
Developer 116
Development Manager 74
Development Training 24
Direct Sales 216
Director 21, 110, 157
Director Human Resources 110
Director of Conference Programming 83
Director of Day Camp 227
Director of Junior Tennis Program 84
Director of Operations 181
Director, Television Station 226
Disc Jockey 19, 68
Disclosure Coordinator 24
Dispatcher 251
Display Coordinator 212
Distribution 38
District Manager 38
District Marketing Analyst 125
District Sales Manager 61, 62
Division Manager 116
Doctor of Education 238
Document Editor 120
Drafting 194, 199
Drawing 199
Driver 258
Dry Grocery Buyer 57
Due Diligence Intern 155

E

Economic Development 72
Editor 8, 68, 120, 209, 214, 242
Education 222
Education Specialist 223
Education Specialist for Nursing 236
Educational Researcher 238
Educator 242
Electro-Mechanical Drafting and Design
    199
Electronics 254
Electronics Advisor 160
Electronics Service 255

Electronics Specialist 160
Eligibility Interviewer 181
Emergency Medical Technician 180, 195
Emergency Room Hostess 89
Emergency Room Nurse 98, 236
Emergency Room Technician 88
Employee Benefits 149
Employee Relations 110
Employment Counselor 126
Engineering 46, 186, 216
Engineman 135
English as a Second Language 176, 223
English Language Instructor 54, 146, 154,
    186
English Teacher 43, 143
Enologist 114
Entertainer 258
Entrepreneur 21, 38, 129, 148, 159, 178,
    198
Environmental Club President 68
Environmental Coordinator 68, 131, 140
Environmental Emergency Response 131,
    140
Environmental Engineering 186
Equal Employment Opportunity 110
Equipment Leasing 43
Equipment Maintenance Superintendent
    34
Equipment Shop Supervisor 34
Equity Associate 192
ESL Instructor 176
Estate Planning 131, 140
Event Management 216
Executive Assistant 70, 120, 147, 176,
    209
Executive Assistant to the General
    Manager 105
Executive Director 83
Executive Producer, Television Station
    226
Executive Trainee 101
Exhibition Coordinator 202
Expeditor 132
Export Consultant 147
Export Coordinator Assistant 53
Export Department Manager 144
Export Intern 7
Export Manager 39

Export Office Intern 69
Export/Sales Administrative Intern 28

F

FAA Aviation Facility Examiner 130
Fabricator 258
Factory Sales/Service Representative 111
Factory Systems Coordinator 22
Family Counseling 250
Family Nurse Practitioner 240
Fellow, College of Preceptors 222
Field Engineer 230
Field Engineer Associate 228
Field Officer 162
Field Representative 64
Field Sales Manager 254
Field Services Officer 113
File Clerk 152
Finance 7, 9, 13, 15, 16, 20, 23, 30, 33,
    36, 39, 42, 52, 58, 68, 76, 79, 80,
    92, 102, 103, 105, 115, 116, 121,
    144–146, 148, 149, 151, 155, 158,
    177, 182, 183, 186, 206
Finance Assistant 191
Finance Desk Assistant 42
Finance Director 145
Finance Intern 151
Financial Analysis and Control Intern 81
Financial Analyst 15, 51, 81
Financial Analyst Intern 23, 151
Financial Consultant 131
Financial Control 129
Financial Manager 115
Financial Sales 40
Financial Services 148
Financial Services Intern 102
Financial Vice President 178
Fine Art Exhibitions 193, 202
Finland 20
Firefighter 64, 136, 180, 195
First Lieutenant 179
Fiscal Management 113
Fixture Designer 194
Flight Attendant 125
Flight Instructor 90
Flightline Expeditor 132
Food and Beverage Supervisor 65
Food Preparer 97

Food Server 180
Foreign Exchange Administrator 162
Foreman 67, 198, 205, 258
Founder 103, 158, 176
    Clothing Business 21
Franchise Owner 118
Freelance Designer 194
Freelance Camera Assistant 205
Freelance Conference Producer 86
Freight Management 224
Front End Manager 53, 112
Front Office Secretary 152
Full-Service Representative 82
Fund-raising 22, 36, 145, 155, 234
Futures 72

G

Gallery Assistant Intern 202
Gallery Installation Manager 193
Gas Station Attendant 97
Gas Station Owner 181
General Construction 116
General Maintenance 55
General Manager 41, 44, 73, 115, 159,
    188
General Office Assistant 35
Geological Assistant 21
Geologist 21
Geophysical Exploration Team 68
Gerontological Nurse 236
Girl Scouts of America 89
Global Operations Analyst 153
Golf Instructor 197
Golf Professional 127, 197
Government Procurement 43
Graduate Assistant 6, 10, 35, 187, 208
Graduate Research Assistant 6, 79
Graduate Teaching Assistant 10
Grants 241
Greenskeeper 197
Grocery 57
Grocery Manager 112
Grounds Maintenance 55
Group Leader 46

H

Hazardous Material Handling 228
Hazardous Materials First Responder 180

Head Fabricator 258
Head Mechanic 258
Head Start 201
Health Care 216, 237, 240
Health Research 106
Heavy Equipment Maintenance 34, 135
Helicopter Pilot 90
Helmsman 64
Hockey Player 70
Home Builder 116
Home Eucharist Minister 243
Home I.V. Therapy Nurse 241
Home Improvement 200
Hospice Case Manager 156
Hospital 222
Hospital Administrator 29
Hospital Auxiliary 89
Hospital Volunteer 89
Host Family Recruiter 143
Hotel Assistant Manager 83
Hotel Management Trainee 105
Hotel Receptionist 176
Housing Manager 112
Housing Services 113
Human Relations 122
Human Resource Development Assistant 24
Human Resources 110, 125
Husbandry 128

I

I.V. Therapy Nurse 241
Ice Hockey Player 70
Import/Export 15, 53, 56, 74, 144, 147, 148, 179, 206
Independent Consultant 186
Industrial Marketing 149
Information Desk Clerk 89
Information Specialist 26
Information Systems Planning 218
Input Clerk 148
Inside Sales Supervisor 255
Inspector 135, 160
Installation Manager 193, 200
Installer Tech 67
Installment Loan 101
Instructor 230, 236, 238
Instructor Supervisor 160

Insurance 76, 149, 216
Insurance Agent 131
Insurance Clerk 126, 201
Insurance Liaison 20, 39
Intelligence Analyst 58
Intensive Care Nurse 98, 156
InterAd 9, 11, 18, 22, 24, 79, 100, 150, 214
Interface 24
Interior Design 194
Intern
    Accounting 103
    Administrative Assistant 214
    Advertising 14, 204
    Agribusiness 72
    Assistant Account Executive 214
    Banking 24, 30, 177
    Business Development 21
    Communications 30
    Counseling 250
    Curatorial 128, 202
    Department Store 33
    Director of Biotechnology 42
    Due Diligence 155
    Executive Assistant 208
    Export 7, 28, 53, 69
    Finance 149, 151
    Financial Analyst 23
    Financial Services 102
    Foreign Policy Department 58
    Gallery Assistant 202
    Import/Export 56
    International Marketing 51, 72, 154, 206
    International Trade 6, 57
    Investment 30, 161
    Legal 101
    Legislative 84, 183
    Licensing 208
    Management 65
    Marketing 6, 18, 20, 35, 38, 39, 101, 102, 143, 154, 157, 161, 204
    Options 81
    Privatization Consultant 155
    Product Management 91
    Psychology 238, 239
    Sales 100, 187, 206, 208
    Sales and Marketing 30

Southeast Asia Programs 176
Trade 100
Traders Assistant 191
Trading 149
Zoo 128
International Delegation Coordinator 146
International Development Manager 74
International In-Flight Service Coordinator 125
International Licensing Coordinator 208
International Marketing Assistant 154
International Marketing Intern 72
International Operations 38, 121
International Relations 222
International Trade Specialist 6, 57, 207
Interpreter 58, 105, 177
   (see also Translator)
Inventory Control 224
Investigator 224
Investment and Financial Analyst 15
Investment Specialist 33
Investments 38, 182
Investments Intern 30

J
Journalism 214
Journeyman 198
Journeyman Clerk 112
Junior Achievement 208
Junior Financial Analyst 151
Juris Doctor 91, 104, 108

K
Key Account Management 38
Kindergarten Manager 89
Kindergarten Primary Teacher 239
Kindergarten Teacher 75

L
Lab Manager 149
Labor Relations 110
Laboratory Supervisor 26
Laborer 92
Landscaping 55, 68
Language Coordinator 47
Language Instructor 26, 79, 135, 147, 176
Language Service 176

Latin America Specialist 192
Law Clerk 91, 104
Law Enforcement 250
Lawyer 108
Lawyer's Aide 101
Lay Eucharist Minister 243
LDS Church Mission 148
Lead Operator 148
Lead Technician 229
League of Women Voters 89
Lease Administrator 43
Leasing 43
Leasing Agent 49
Leasing Representative 70, 145
Lecturer 238
Legal Assistant 102
Legal/Technical Agent 161
Legislative Assistant 36
Legislative Intern 84, 183
Lending Operations 148
Licensing Intern 208
Lighting 259
Livestock Show 93
Load Crew Chief 132
Loan Processing Clerk 7
Loges Coordinator 154
Logistics and Planning Management Trainee 191
Logistics Management 12

M
Machinist 229
Mail Room Supervisor 118, 251
Mainframe Computer Broker 43
Maintenance Contracts Supervisor 145
Maintenance Engineering 228
Maintenance Instructor 48
Maintenance Mechanic 64
Maintenance Specialist, Aircraft 184
Maintenance Technician 228
Maintenance Workshop Supervisor 135
Management Consultant 108, 216
Management Intern 65
Management Trainee 45, 73, 105, 121, 153, 191
Manager 49, 54, 68, 70, 71, 93, 110, 116, 118, 154, 176, 178, 207, 254, 255

Gift Shop 89
Kindergarten 89
Manager of Export Department 144
Managing Director 115
Managing Partner 44
Manufacturing Production 185
Manufacturing Specialist 22
Manufacturing Station Worker 19
Market Analyst 23, 36, 95, 191, 205, 206, 216
Market Development 38
Market Development Manager 149
Market Forecasting 224
Market Research Analyst 106
Market Research Assistant 11
Market Research Consultant 22, 35
Market Research Director 9
Market Researcher 150
Market Strategy Analyst 18
Marketing 6–11, 13, 15, 16, 18, 20–24, 26, 29, 30, 33, 35, 36, 38, 39, 45, 47, 49, 51–53, 55–58, 61, 62, 65, 69, 70, 72, 74, 79, 80, 83–87, 91, 94, 100–106, 108, 111, 115, 116, 118, 120, 121, 125, 126, 131, 143–5, 147, 149, 150, 154, 155, 157, 159, 177, 178, 182, 183, 187, 190, 192, 193, 198, 204–209, 214, 216–219, 224–226, 254, 262
Marketing and Sales Representative 53, 71
Marketing Assistant 28, 52, 84, 146, 210, 211
Marketing Associate 204
Marketing Consultant 21, 100, 161, 262
Marketing Coordinator 16, 43, 85
Marketing Director 18, 122
Marketing Education Support Assistant 24
Marketing Information Services Intern 157
Marketing Intern 6, 18, 20, 35, 39, 101, 102, 154, 157, 204
Marketing Management 226
Marketing Manager 87, 92, 191, 216
Marketing Representative 9, 70, 81, 102, 192
Marketing Research Consultant 35
Marketing Research Director 100
Marketing Sales Assistant 24

Marketing Specialist 10
Marketing Support Representative 216
Marketing Systems Analyst 216
Marketing Trainee 192
Master Control Operator 205
Master Instructor 230
Material Handler 12
Materials Manager 224
Materialsperson 12
Mechanic 64, 97, 184, 213, 258
Mechanic's Helper 34
Mechanical Drawing 199
Media Buying Analyst 101
Medical Service Specialist 88, 196
Medical Technician 196
Medical/Dental Office Management 126
Medical/Radiation Oncology Consultant 240
Membership Coordinator 126
Membership Director 36
Merchandiser 10, 38, 57, 97
Mergers and Acquisitions 220
Micro Computer Information Specialist 216, 218
Military Advisor 160
Mining 21
Minister 138
Mobile Cancer Services Coordinator 241
Modern and Classical Language Instructor 80
Mortgage Broker 116
Motor Actuator Technician 228
MRP Implementation 224
Municipal Facility Worker 55
Muscular Dystrophy Association 180
Music Teacher 234

N

Nanny 157
National Sales Manager 226
Navy 64, 135, 225
Neighborhood Chairman 89
Neighborhood Director 113
Neighborhood Reinvestment 113
Neurological Nurse 98
New Business Development 226
Newspaper 176, 205
Newspaper District Sales Manager 62

Night Manager 112
Nonprofit 21, 146, 154
Nuclear Power Plant Technician 228
Nurse 98, 156, 237, 240
Nursing Assistant 98
Nursing Consultant 237

O

Obstetrical Specialist 88
Off-Road Racing 258
Office Assistant 13, 35
Office Automation Assistant 17
Office Automation Specialist 216
Office Manager 13, 49, 119
Oil and Gas 46, 114
Oncology Education Committee
    Chairman 241
Oncology Nurse 156
Oncology Nurse Specialist 240
Operations 205
Operations Analyst Officer 221
Operations and Polo Manager 15
Operations Assistant 101
Operations Coordinator 221
Operations Director 181
Operations Manager 38, 221, 224
Operations Supervisor 255
Operator 148, 159
Options Intern 81
Optometric Assistant 93
Orientation Leader 204
Outage Management Task Group
    Supervisor 229
Outdoor Program Trip Coordinator 149
Outside Sales Representative 123
Owner 54, 55, 87, 92, 116, 159
    Catering Company 29

P

Painter 198
Paraprofessional Accountant 96
Parent-Teacher Organization 234, 251
Paris Program Coordinator 154
Parish Council 243
Partner 41, 68, 115
Parts Manager 90
Pastor 138
Payment Processor 148

PCB Design 199
Peace Corps 29
Performer 209, 259
Personal Banker 40
Personnel 118, 220
Personnel Coordinator 221
Personnel Vice President 110
Petroleum 46
PGA Golf Professional 197
Pharmaceuticals 56, 74, 106, 182
Photo Promotions 181
Physiology 15
Pilot 56, 90, 130, 179
Pilot in Command 90
Planned Parenthood 250
Plant Operations Manager 67
Platoon Leader 179
Politics 36
Polo Manager 15
Powerplant License 184, 213
Preacher 138
Preceptor 222
Precious Metals Options Intern 81
President 15, 37, 103, 114, 190
Principal 234
Principal Investigator 241
Print Production 118
Print Traffic Assistant 18
Printed Circuit Board Designer 199
Prison Educator 223
Privatization Consultant Intern 155
Probation 250
Probation Field Officer 251
Process Analysis 216
Producer 226
Product Analyst 18
Product Design 47
Product Development 216, 226
Product Engineer 47
Product Line Manager 254
Product Management Intern 91
Product Manager 47, 74
Production Control 224
Production Control Manager 225
Production Control Supervisor 224
Production Manager 8, 195
Production Planner 224
Production Supervisor 8

Production Technician 185
Professional Ice Hockey Player 70
Professor 238
Professor's Assistant 11
Program Administration 222
Program Development 216
Program Director 102, 143, 242
Program Management Specialist 120
Program Manager 113, 230
Program Review Manager 113
Programmer 109
Project Analyst 46
Project Assistant 150
Project Coordinator 120
Project Director 115
Project Engineering 186
Project Financial Manager 144
Project Manager 70, 106, 116, 186, 216
Project Officer for Community Health and
    Sanitation 162
Promotion Manager 41
Promotion Representative: 154
Promotions 38, 143
Property Evaluation 224
Property Management 44, 49, 116
Proprietor 148
Psychiatric Aide 235
Psychological Testing 238
Psychologist 238
Psychology Intern 239
Public Administration 34, 62
Public Relations 119, 143, 147
Public Speaker 238
Publicist 204
Publicity Chairman 89
Pump Technician 228
Purchasing 129, 122, 255
Purchasing Agent 26, 57, 188
Purchasing Assistant 8
Purchasing Coordinator 126
Purchasing Manager 188
Pyrotechnics 259

Q
Quality Control 148, 185
Quality Control Supervisor 160
Quality Control Technician 8
Quality Inspector 148

R
Race Car Fabricator 258
Racing 258
Radiation Oncology Nurse 240
Radiation Technologist 240
Radio Dispatch Operator 251
Radioactive Material Handling 228
Ranger Aide 197
Raw Materials Manager 224
Reactor Coolant Pump Technician 228
Real Estate 36, 126, 224
Real Estate Agent 224
Real Estate Broker 70, 116
Receiving Clerk 152
Receiving Manager 112
Receptionist 152, 176, 183
Reconciliation 220
Reconciliation Intern 81
Refrigeration Shop Mechanic 64
Refueling Lineman 90
Refueling Technician 229
Refugees 162
Refurbishment Technician 228
Regional Manager 226
Regional Manager, South America 87
Regional Sales Manager 226
Registered Insurance Representative 131
Registered Nurse 156, 240
Religious Education Teacher 243
Remarketing 43
Remarketing Analyst 43
Reorder Representative 82
Reporter 68
Research Analyst 68, 147
Research Assistant 6, 7, 9, 11, 28, 68, 80
Research Library Assistant 183
Researcher 104, 120, 238, 241
Reserve Officer 56
Resident Assistant 72
Residential Leasing Representative 104
Resource Nurse 237
Restaurant Manager 15
Retail Manager 41, 112
Retail Sales 23, 41, 82, 84, 111, 200, 216
Retail Sales Associate 154
Retail System Administrator 14
RF Technician 67
Risk Management 76, 84

Robotics 185, 216
Route Driver 64
Route Salesman 62
Rural Sanitation Project 162
Russian/English Interpreter 58

S

Safety 110
Sales 33, 55, 56, 61, 70, 82, 87, 116, 118, 122, 148, 206, 208, 216, 226, 227
Sales and Marketing Manager 86
Sales and Marketing Intern 30
Sales and Service Engineer 46
Sales Assistant 191
Sales Associate 85, 154, 210, 212
Sales Consultant 23
Sales Intern 100, 187, 206, 208
Sales Manager 116, 118, 149, 188, 226
Sales Officer 187, 208
Sales Representative 6, 11, 43, 51, 54, 61, 64, 65, 69–71, 82, 111, 118, 123, 147, 161, 182, 207
Sales Specialist 255
Sales Trainer 40
Sales/Service Representative 10, 211
Salesperson 7, 47, 56, 85, 92, 104, 208, 209
Satellite Field Engineer 230
Scenery Designer 204
Scheduling Manager 224
School Board 234
School Psychologist 238
Scientific Measurements Technician 230
Seaman 64
Seasonal Employee 159
Second Assistant Cameraman 204
Secretary 16, 17, 94, 119, 126, 152, 183, 221
Section Engineer 186
Securities 42, 162
Self-Employed Au Pair 157
Self-Employed Painter 198
Senior Account Manager 254
Senior Accountant 151
Senior Auditor 66
Senior Business Systems Analyst 216
Senior Chemotherapy Nurse 241

Senior Collector 45
Senior Human Resource Position 110
Senior Market Analyst 205
Senior Materialsperson 12
Senior Motor Actuator Technician 228
Senior Product Line Manager 254
Senior Program Manager 83
Senior Reactor Coolant Pump Technician 228
Senior Reactor Maintenance Technician 228
Senior Refrigeration Shop Mechanic 64
Senior Sales Specialist 255
Senior Systems Analyst 216
Senior Technical Sales Representative 254
Service Representative 10, 62, 111
Service Station Attendant 97
Settlement Coordinator 149
Shift Supervisor 229
Shopping Center Leasing 69
Singer 208
Site Supervisor 88, 119
Social Service 181, 250
Social Service Agent 202
Software Engineering and Development 216
Southeast Asia Programs Intern 176
Space Planning 194
Spanish Tutor 35
Special Accounts Correspondent 200
Special Education Instructor 160
Specialty Marketing Consultant 131
Stable Attendant 93
Staff Assistant 36
Staff Auditor 66
Staff Development Coordinator 223
Staff Nurse 98, 156, 237, 240, 241
Staff Researcher 104
Staffing 110
Stage Manager 157
Staging 259
Steward 125
Stock Broker 191
Stock Trading 149
Store Manager 10, 112, 188
Store Planning 194
Stores Clerk 92

Strategic Management 125
Strategic Planning 38, 113, 150, 192, 216, 226
Student Assistant 21, 100
Student Coordinator 204
Student Counselor 238
Student Nurse 98
Student Program Coordinator 80
Student Teacher 75
Student Teacher Supervisor 238
Sub-Editor 68
Subcontractor 198
Substitute Teacher 75, 234
Summer Deputy 150
Sunday School Teacher 138
Supermarket 53
Supermarket Manager 112
Supervisor 109, 120, 145, 185, 228
Supervisor of Accounting 147
Supervisor of Maintenance Contracts 145
Supervisor of Management Accounting 42
Supply Corps Officer 225
Supply Sergeant 12
Supply System Analyst 109
Supply/Demand Manager 224
Surgical Charge Nurse 98
Swimming Instructor 54
Systems and Application Integration 216
Systems Engineering 231

T

Tactical Aircraft Maintenance Specialist 213
Tae Kwon Do Instructor 105
Teacher 75, 135, 160, 201, 232, 234, 238
Teacher's Aide 180
Teaching Assistant 8, 11, 15, 21, 26, 65, 150, 236
Team Manager 50, 258
Technical Adviser 228
Technical Assistant to the Production Manager 105
Technical Instructor 160
Technical Operations Manager 67
Technical Sales Representative 61, 254, 255
Technical Sales Specialist 254
Technical Supervisor 67

Technical Typist 76
Technical Writer 76, 160
Technician 228
    Animal Hospital 128
Teen Advisor 243
Telecommunications 47, 216
Telemarketing 33, 202
Telephone Counselor 160
Telephone Crisis Intervention 251
Television 178, 205
Television Production Planning 226
Television Service 255
Teller 45, 183, 190, 221
Temporary Office Work 183
Tennis 84
Tennis Co-Director 192
Tennis Instructor 54
Tennis Professional 84
Territory Development Manager 149
Territory Manager 61, 82
Territory Sales Manager 149
Theater Director 157
Theater 227
Ticket Brokerage Agency 38
Title Clerk 101
Tour Company Operator/Owner 159
Tour/Transportation Company Manager 159
Trade 6, 15, 20–21, 33, 39, 46, 53, 57, 100, 105, 108, 207
Trade Intern 100
Trade Show 43, 80, 85, 143, 154, 159, 218, 254, 259
Trade Specialist 207
Trader 149
Trader's Assistant 162
Trader's Assistant Intern 191
Training 38, 67, 110, 118, 129, 216, 222
Training Consultant 222
Training Director 53
Training Manager 132
Translator 26, 47, 58, 105, 147, 177, 214
    (see also Interpreter)
Transportation Platoon Leader 179
Travel Agent 239
Travel Consultant 11
Treasurer 15
Trust Operations Administrator 23
Tumor Board Coordinator 241

Tutor 35, 68, 74
Typist 76

U

Underwriter 32, 76, 131
UNICEF Project Officer 162
Unions 110
Unit Clerk Assistant 89
UNV Field Officer 162

V

Vault Clerk 152
Vault Coordinator 152
Veterinary Technician 93, 128
Vice Chairman 21
Vice President 37, 41, 44, 110, 190, 205
Vice President Human Resources 110
Vice President Marketing 155
Videographer 180
Volunteer 94, 242, 251
Volunteer Coordinator 89
Volunteer Counselor 180
Volunteer Telephone Counselor 160

W

Warehouse Manager 188
Water and Sanitation Technician 29
Weapons Maintenance Technician
    132
Welder 136
Winery 114
Writer 76, 160

Y

Youth Pastor 138

Z

Zoo Internship 128
Zoology 128

TITLES THAT GENERATE SUCCESS!

Business Success Series

Twenty titles comprise Barron's innovative series designed to help the business person succeed. All books offer advice and facts on how to master job techniques that generate success. Each book: Paperback, between 86–156 pp., priced individually.

Conducting Better Job Interviews (0-8120-9893-5), $6.95, Canada $8.95
Conquering Stress (0-8120-4837-7), $4.95, Canada $6.50
Creative Problem Solving (0-8120-1461-8), $4.95, Canada $6.50
Delegating Authority (0-8120-4958-6), $4.95, Canada $6.50
How to Negotiate a Bigger Raise (0-8120-4604-8), $4.95, Canada $6.50
Make Presentations with Confidence (0-8120-9892-7), $6.95, Canada $8.95
Maximizing Your Memory Power (0-8120-4799-0), $4.95, Canada $6.50
Motivating People (0-8120-4673-0), $4.95, Canada $6.50
Projecting a Positive Image (0-8120-1455-3), $4.95, Canada $6.50
Running a Meeting That Works (0-8120-9823-4), $6.95, Canada $8.95
Speed Reading (0-8120-1845-1), $4.95, Canada $6.50
Successful Assertiveness (0-7641-0071-8), $6.95, Canada $8.95
Successful Computing for Business (0-7641-0058-0), $6.95, Canada $8.95
Successful Purchasing (0-7641-0057-2), $6.95, Canada $8.95
Successful Team Building (0-7641-0073-4), $6.95, Canada $8.95
Time Management (0-8120-4792-3), $4.95, Canada $6.50
Understanding Business on the Internet (0-7641-0069-6), $6.95, Canada $8.95
Using the Telephone More Effectively (0-8120-4672-2), $4.95, Canada $6.50
Winning With Difficult People (0-8120-4583-1), $4.95, Canada $6.50
Writing Effective Letters and Memos (0-8120-9824-2), $6.95, Canada $8.95

Books may be purchased at your bookstore, or by mail from Barron's. Enclose check or money order for total amount plus sales tax where applicable and 15% for postage and handling (minimum $4.95). New York residents, please add sales tax to total. All books are paperback editions. Prices subject to change without notice.

Barron's Educational Series, Inc.
250 Wireless Boulevard, Hauppauge, NY 11788
In Canada: Georgetown Book Warehouse
34 Armstrong Avenue, Georgetown, Ont. LG7 4R9

(# 53) R 11/96